D0410409

A SHORT HISTORY OF WINE

ROD PHILLIPS

A SHORT
HISTORY
OF WINE

ALLEN LANE
THE PENGUIN PRESS

ALLEN LANE
THE PENGUIN PRESS

Published by the Penguin Group
Penguin Books Ltd, 27 Wrights Lane, London w8 5tz, England
Penguin Putnam Inc., 375 Hudson Street, New York, New York 10014, USA
Penguin Books Australia Ltd, Ringwood, Victoria, Australia
Penguin Books Canada Ltd, 10 Alcorn Avenue, Toronto, Ontario, Canada m4v 3b2
Penguin Books (NZ) Ltd, Private Bag 102902, NSMC, Auckland, New Zealand

Penguin Books Ltd, Registered Offices: Harmondsworth, Middlesex, England

First published 2000
10 9 8 7 6 5 4 3 2 1

Set in 9.25/13.25 pt PostScript Linotype Sabon
Typeset by Rowland Phototypesetting Ltd, Bury St Edmunds, Suffolk
Printed and bound in Great Britain by The Bath Press Ltd, Bath

A CIP catalogue record for this book is available from the British Library

ISBN 0-713-99432-0

CONTENTS

CONTENTS

LIST OF ILLUSTRATIONS

(Photographic acknowledgements are given in parentheses)

LIST OF MAPS

ACKNOWLEDGEMENTS

I started this book somewhat unexpectedly in Australia in 1998, while I held a fellowship in the Department of History at the University of Melbourne and was working on an entirely different project. Wine is as integral to the life of Melbourne as of any other place where I have lived, and Melburnians are amazingly well informed on wine and vineyards. I took advantage of my spare time there to visit many of the nearby wine districts, to drink widely (and, for the most part, wisely), and to enjoy the excellent hospitality of Jimmy Watson's Wine Bar, itself part of Australia's wine heritage. During those pleasant months it was suggested that I might marry my professional engagement in history to my recreational fascination with wine, and this book is the result.

My acknowledgements thus start in Melbourne and with my colleagues and friends in the Department of History: Chips Sowerwine (whose name is distinctly unpromising under the circumstances) and Peter McPhee. They, with Aude Sowerwine and Charlotte Allan, were congenial hosts in 1998, as they had been on my earlier visits to Melbourne. It is always a pleasure to share wine with them, as with other oenophile friends in Melbourne, like Jim Hammerton and John Cashmere.

As I worked on this book I have asked many colleagues for information and advice. Some have answered specific questions, others have provided data, and yet others have read parts of the manuscript. Patrick McGovern of the University of Pennsylvania Museum of Anthropology and Archeology generously shared his vast expertise on ancient wine. Scott Haine gave me excellent advice on the eighteenth and nineteenth centuries, Kolleen Guy shared her work on champagne, Ian Tyrrell brought his expertise on the United States to bear on several chapters, and Trevor Hodge of Carleton University gave me very useful advice on the classical period. Others who provided specific information were Sonya Lipsett-Rivera, Carman Bickerton, Geoffrey Giles, Peter McPhee, Larry Black, José C. Curto, Valmai Hankel, Rebecca Adell and Kim Munholland. Ruth Pritchard read over some of the manuscript with her usual skill. I remain responsible for the final product, of course, not least because I did not always follow the advice I received.

The notes and bibliography make clear the debt I owe to the many others who have laboured in this particular vineyard before me. There have been few general histories of wine, and this is the first attempt to cover so many themes over such a long period and wide geographical area. It could not have been written without the more recent ground-breaking work of scholars like Tim Unwin and Thomas Pinney, and of prolific and engaging wine writers like Hugh Johnson and Jancis Robinson.

My general knowledge of wine has been deepened by the hospitality of wine-makers in many parts of the world. They are too many and their influence too diffuse to mention them by name, but I would like to mention my great pleasure at spending some time with Jean-Michel Guillon in Gevrey-Chambertin as I was doing research in Burgundy. Jean and Janie Bart offered their usual superb hospitality a few kilometres north in Marsannay-la-Côte, and I would also like to note the recurrent pleasure of meeting up with Jim Farr and with Bob Schwartz and Marietta Clement in Dijon.

In Ottawa my interest in wine has been stimulated and sustained by the instructors and students in the excellent wine courses coordinated by Vic Harradine at Algonquin College and by the camaraderie of my colleagues in the National Capital Sommelier Guild. Climatically inhospitable to the vine, Ottawa offers more and more to wine-lovers, thanks in large part to the professionalism of the staff at the local stores of the Liquor Control Board of Ontario. They are an excellent example of how effective and responsive to consumers a state-run liquor system can be.

Last, and far from least, I wish to raise my glass to the group of friends who meet regularly at one another's homes for blind tastings. Most recently the group has consisted of Ruth Pritchard, Carter Elwood, Jill St. Germain, Sonya Lipsett-Rivera, Sergio Rivera Ayala, Ted Cohen, James Miller, Franz Szabo and Catherine Szabo. Our gatherings are that perfect blend of serious attention to wine with the sheer, simple enjoyment of drinking wine in good company.

As this book approached completion and went into production, I was delighted to work with a number of excellent people at Penguin Books. My editor, Simon Winder, was enthusiastic about the project from the moment he and I first discussed it, and the final text was improved by his suggestions. Ellah Allfrey coordinated production with great skill and an astonishing reservoir of good humour, while Richard Duguid brought to the copy-editing his own enthusiasm for wine. Cecilia Mackay found excellent alternatives when illustrations I had wanted proved unavailable.

Like the acknowledgements of any work that has been far longer in the making than it seems, these words of thanks and recognition are scarcely adequate. I hope the final product justifies the support and assistance of everyone who, knowingly or otherwise, contributed to it.

NOTE ON USAGE

Wines named after regions or districts are given a lower-case initial. Thus a wine from Bordeaux is called a bordeaux and one from Chianti is called a chianti.

Temperatures are expressed in degrees Celsius. Other measurements, like volumes of wine, vary according to the context. A comparative guide to the size of wine measurements is given on pages 334–5.

INTRODUCTION

In October 1999, plans for a state visit to France by the president of
Iran were abandoned because of a dispute over wine at a state dinner.
Invoking Muslim law, the president declared that not only could he not
drink wine, but he could not even sit at a table where wine was served.
For their part, the French authorities declared that such a dinner without
wine – French wine, of course – was unthinkable. The dinner was
cancelled and, because protocol demands that a state visit must include
a state banquet, the visit itself had to be downgraded from 'state visit'
to 'official visit'.

This disagreement raised hardly a ripple in the often turbulent waters
of diplomacy, but it drew attention to the history of wine. Indeed, the
incident made sense only when read in light of the divergent meanings
that different cultures have, over time, given to wine. On the Iranian
side, it reflected the ban on alcohol imposed by Muhammad in the early
seventh century, when he saw that wine not only made his followers
happy and sociable but also, when it was consumed in excess, made
them violent and destructive. He decreed that the faithful might be able
to drink wine in paradise, but that they were to abstain from it on earth.

The French position, that wine was indispensable at a state dinner,
expressed a quite different historical tradition that portrays wine in an
overwhelmingly positive light. Here wine is not a danger but a benefit,
a beverage that for thousands of years has facilitated social relationships
and the making of alliances, and that has been consumed on every
important occasion. The French refusal to make an exception to this
tradition also reflected the particular relationship that for centuries
has existed between France and wine. The government of another
country might have been willing to serve water or fruit juice in order to

accommodate the Iranian president's religious sensitivities. But for the French, wine has come to be an expression of national identity. Fine French reds and whites on the banquet table represent the nation as surely as its red, white and blue flag.

While history is unlikely to make much of 'The 1999 Franco-Iranian Wine Incident', it does remind us that wine is perhaps the most historically charged and culturally symbolic of the foods and beverages with which we regularly have contact. It is true that everything we eat and drink has a past, as shown by recent histories of bread and breakfast cereals and of beer and coffee. But no other element in the western diet has a history that is as rich and complex as wine, and this book sets out to describe it.

In some respects the history of wine seems reasonably straightforward. At the economic level, for example, wine has long been important in many regions, some of which are leading wine-producers today. Wine makes substantial contributions to the economies and exports of countries like France, Italy, Spain and Portugal, and it is the mainstay of some regions like Bordeaux and Burgundy, the Douro, and Jerez. Wine is an increasingly important export for Australia, Chile and several east European countries.

The geographical distribution of wine production today is the result of a complex history that has seen wine regions flourish and decline according to circumstances that are both natural and social. But as this book shows, it is often difficult to differentiate the natural from the human factors in the long-term history of wine. Environmental conditions are obviously important in so far as vines produce grapes suitable for wine only in certain parts of the world, but in the past wine was made commercially in regions from where it has either completely or virtually disappeared. It is not that the climate in these localities has changed dramatically, but that social, cultural and economic conditions have altered. For example, tastes in wine have evolved, and many wines that were readily drunk two or three hundred years ago are no longer acceptable. Some regions have failed under the onslaught of wines produced more cheaply elsewhere.

On the other hand, wine is now made in regions that until recently would have been ranked very low on the list of likely locations. Commercial vineyards flourish in almost every state of the USA, in the eastern regions of Canada, and in the southernmost parts of New Zealand. Many of these localities benefit from the presence of microclimates that distinguish them from their surrounding region but, even so, human intervention has been important to their success. Viticultural and wine-making techniques have overcome many of the obstacles presented by the environment: grapes are cloned to improve their resistance to cold and disease, canopy management practices enhance the ripening potential of the fruit, and in many sun-deficient regions sugar is added to wine to increase alcohol levels.

Such techniques can go only so far to counteract the climatic conditions of a specific locality, and the extent of viticulture remains heavily influenced by climate and soil conditions. Even if vines could be coaxed to grow in desert or arctic regions, there would be no financial point to it. Still, the promising potential of a region for viticulture does not necessarily mean that wine will be made commercially there for, in the most basic sense, production depends on a market. That in turn means that wine must be sufficiently valued, for its nutrient or other qualities, before consumers will pay the price of its production, transportation and sale. Over time these 'other qualities' have included religious properties attributed to wine, its social cachet and its medicinal value.

Production also depends on the ability of producers to get their wine to markets, and historically obstacles have included tariff barriers and transportation problems. For a century and a half, from 1703 to 1860, the French were discouraged from exporting to the lucrative English market by preferential tariffs on Portuguese wine. As for simply moving wine, the cost and sheer difficulty of shipping heavy and fragile barrels that too often began to leak when transported on carts along rough roads was a deterrent to the opening up of some regions to viticulture. On the other hand, wine production in both California and Languedoc was boosted in the later 1800s when railroads provided relatively rapid and secure access to major urban markets in their respective countries.

Clearly, the journey that wine made from the vine to the glass (or the kylix or the mug or whatever was used to drink from) has always been one in which humans and the environment have collaborated, and part of the history of wine is the story of that relationship. Yet if wine-makers like to think of their wine as representing the harmony of their skills with the best fruits of nature, they are expressing the optimism that is probably necessary for their trade, for vine-growers and wine-makers have battled nature – in the form of freezing winters, volcanoes, floods, droughts, pests and diseases – as much as they have fought the economic and other obstacles that humans put in their way.

This tension between nature and society is a constant feature of the history of wine, and it begins with the substance itself, the fermented juice of grapes. One Australian wine-maker has described wine in disarmingly ingenuous terms:

> It's simple really. You start with rich fertile soil.
> Into this you plant vine cuttings of noble pedigree.
> Nature adds water and sunlight. The vines bear fruit.
> The fruit is picked, crushed, fermented and aged.
> And then you drink it.[1]

And indeed, the process of making wine can be described just that baldly, for this concise description covers the main stages of viticulture (the cultivation of vines) and viniculture (the making of wine). It also neatly expresses the fundamental fact that wine is a joint venture on the part of nature and humans.

At the most elementary level, wine is the result of a natural process of fermentation. The chemical elements of wine are all contained within or on the surface of a grape, and to this extent each grape is its own little winery. The pulp or flesh contains water, sugar and pectin, and the skins provide tannins and yeast as well as the pigments that give red and rosé wines their colour. All that is necessary to turn grapes into wine is to crush the berries so that the yeasts come into contact with the sugar in the juice, and to keep the juice at a temperature that allows fermentation to occur. During that process the sugar is converted to alcohol and carbon dioxide, and the juice becomes the beverage we call wine. But grapes do not ferment spontaneously, and human intervention is needed to crush them and to control the temperature. Afterwards, the wine must be protected from the air by being stored in barrels, tanks or bottles to prevent it from turning to vinegar.

In its simplest form, then, wine-making demands little more of humans than providing the conditions that allow fermentation to take place. This is what all wine-makers do, whether they are North American city-dwellers who make wine from concentrated juice in their kitchens, southern Europeans who produce wine for their own use from their small vineyards, wine-makers employed by corporations that produce millions of litres of wine for the world market, or those who make a few thousand cases of world-famous wines from small estates in regions like Burgundy and Bordeaux.

The earliest stone-age wine-makers might well have picked wild grapes, crushed them, let the juice and grape residue ferment in an indentation in a rock, then drunk it before it turned sour. But rarely has the human contribution to wine-making been that limited, and over time the range of human intervention in wine-production has expanded steadily. Grapes were cultivated and the most suitable varieties were selected and bred. Fermentation was measured and controlled, and steps were taken – before, during and after the wine was made – to achieve specific tastes. In other words, humans gradually shifted their role in wine-making from simply facilitating a natural process to shaping the process to achieve a specific and planned result.

More human activity goes into making the wine we drink today than at any other time in the history of wine, and the bottle of wine we buy is the final result of scores of decisions. Many affect viticulture: where to plant the vines; which varieties of vine to grow; how far apart rows should be spaced; how vines should be trained and pruned; whether to irrigate and fertilize them; whether to thin the leaves and the bunches; and when and how to pick the grapes – by machine or hand, by day or night, by bunch or individual berries. In short, growing grapes for wine is a complex process by which the vigneron not only tries to optimize the result of a particular variety in a specific location, but also tries to achieve a level of yield, sugar, concentration and other properties that satisfy legal requirements and the aesthetic and other demands of the market for which the wine is destined.

Decisions continue throughout the vinification process: how to extract the juice from the grapes; how to ferment it; whether to ferment it with the grape skins or without them; when to stop the fermentation; whether to leave the wine on its lees (the dead yeast cells); whether to adjust sugars or acids; whether to blend different varieties and in what proportion; whether to use preservatives or other additives; whether to filter the wine; whether to age it in barrel, tank or bottle; when to release the wine to consumers.

Both viticulture and viniculture have their histories, for both have evolved over millennia under the influences of necessity, experience, tradition and scientific research. Vines were allowed to grow up trees before training them on trellises became common. At different periods, crushing grapes by foot gave way almost everywhere to manual presses and then machines, harvesting by hand was replaced in many areas in many regions by machinery, and methods of increasing alcohol content have ranged from drying grapes in the sun to adding sugar to grape juice or brandy to wine.

While it is true that the essential flavour of a wine comes from the grape variety or varieties from which it is made, and that in turn is greatly influenced by the soil in which the vines grow, it is also indisputable that many dimensions of the appearance, aroma and taste of a wine result from decisions taken during vinification. Over the centuries the taste of wine has been changed and enhanced by myriad substances, ranging from herbs and spices to honey, from brandy to lead, from tree resin to the flavours extracted from the oak used in modern barrel-ageing.

It is a commonplace among wine-makers that wine is made in the vineyard, which is to say that the essential quality of any wine comes from the grapes from which it is made. At one level that point is so obvious as to be not worth making. But if the argument is that wine is a product of nature and that humans do little more than act as stewards of a natural process, it is clearly misleading. Fermentation is indeed a natural process, but so is the leavening of flour when it comes into contact with yeast and water in warm conditions. Humans make wine as surely as they make bread, and when they sit down to a glass of one and a loaf of the other, they are confronted by two products that are products of society more than of nature. It might not be very romantic, but it is historically more accurate.

This history of wine is, though, about more than growing grapes and making wine. The very production of wine for the past thousands of years raises the immediate question: why make wine at all? The simple answer is that there is a market for it, but that only raises the question of why people drink wine, why they drink the wines they do and in the quantities they do, not only on a daily basis but in particular circumstances and on specific occasions. The emergence of markets, the development of the wine trade, and changing patterns of consumption of wine are other facets of its history.

The market for wine, without which there would be no production, has sometimes reflected the religious values attributed to it. From the earliest times wine has been intimately bound up with religious ritual, and drinking it has often been considered a means of attaining a level of spirituality that brings humans closer to their gods. A potent symbol, wine has represented the blood of deities in religions as diverse as those of ancient Egypt and Christianity. In stark contrast, other religions, notably Islam and a number of Christian denominations founded in the nineteenth century, have banned the consumption of wine and other alcoholic drinks.

On a more secular level, the simple taste of wine and its effects have proved attractive in many cultures. Its effects include not only the psychotropic feelings of well-being and its ability to foster social relationships by reducing inhibitions, but also its consequences for health. For centuries wine was regarded by doctors as a healthy beverage, and even if some of the claims made on its behalf in the past are more than a little dubious, there is no doubt that it was often a safer option than the water that was available. For much of the twentieth century, claims that wine was healthy were muted, but more recent studies have pointed to the role of wine in reducing the risks of certain diseases.

The opposite arguments are also part of the history. It was recognized that frequent, excessive drinking was harmful to the drinker personally and affected society more generally. Attitudes have included tolerance of moderate wine-drinking, opposition to any drinking, and the prohibitionist position that the production and consumption of wine (and all alcohol) should be banned entirely. Regulations on trade and retail sale have almost always aimed to control the consumption of wine, but it is remarkable that no policies, including Prohibition in the United States, ever banned the production and sale of wine completely.

Not all wines have been created equal, and there have historically been different markets for different wines. The Egyptians recognized some wines as better than others and set out some of the parameters of connoisseurship that have evolved in the last three thousand years. The distinction between mass-produced wines for the many and quality wines for the few was as much a reality of ancient Greece and the Middle Ages as it is today. Wine, then, has long been a marker of social distinctions, including class and gender and sometimes other qualities such as age and religion.

The market for wine could be expanded by the ready availability of supplies, but historically it has often been defined by cultural and social criteria. In some cultures, like ancient Egypt, the consumption of wine was confined to the elites, while beer was the drink of the masses. Even where wine was consumed at all social levels, distinctions took the form of the quality and price of the wine and the context of its consumption. Men of the ancient Greek upper classes drank sweet wine from ornate cups at highly ritualized occasions, while the poor consumed thin, acidic wine from crude pottery mugs. Even inebriation has been perceived through the prism of class. Drunkenness on the part of the wealthy might be excused or even admired (by them) as harmless, but intoxicated workers or the poor only proved to the better-off that their social inferiors were brutish and potentially dangerous.

Wine has long been attributed other values, too. Drinking wine helped to bond individuals and groups by facilitating conversation and easing social interaction. One aspect of wine's association with sociability is its link to romance, sensuality and sex, a link that long predated the development of sparkling wine, the quintessential accompaniment to romance in modern western society. Women have historically been expected to drink less, because men have long feared that excessive drinking released women's inhibitions and made them more likely to be sexually promiscuous. When women did drink wine, they have often consumed different kinds. Red wine has frequently been thought masculine, leaving women to drink whites, and when male tastes turned to drier table wines, women continued to prefer sweeter varieties.

Wine, in short, has a place in many kinds of history. It is integral to the histories of agriculture, industry, commerce and state regulation, and it is prominent in the histories of medicine, religion, gender, culture and the senses. This book places wine in the broad sweep of these histories in Europe and the lands colonized by Europeans in the Americas, Africa and Australasia. Within this broad scope it is impossible to devote equal space to all regions, and in some cases it might be argued that some wine-producing countries have been given short shrift. But within the confines of a short book – or at least, one that could have been many times longer – I have tried to describe the outlines of a rich and complex history and to give it depth and flavour. Giving equal weight to all regions would have made the book more comprehensive in some ways. It would also have made it thematically more limited and generally more superficial, and it would have seemed more like a catalogue of places and people, of varietals and vineyards, than a coherent history.

A Short History of Wine sets out not only to describe but also to explain the story of wine as a product, a commodity and an icon. Wine, we shall see, has rarely been thought of and written on in neutral terms, for in its very essence it is marked by dualities. The tension implicit in the debate as to whether wine is a product of nature or society underlies its more general history as one of paradoxes. Wine is consumed by the destitute and homeless and by the powerful and wealthy. Wine can be bought very inexpensively or at fabulous prices that only the very rich can afford. Wine has been called a gift of God and the work of Satan. It is a sign of civility and sophistication and a threat to social order. It is part of a healthy diet and it kills. It is this very complexity that makes the history of wine so compelling.

ONE

ON THE TRAIL OF THE EARLIEST WINES

From the Fertile Crescent to Egypt

The origins of wine are as cloudy as the first vintages must have been. We will never know who first allowed grape juice to ferment to the point that it became wine, just as we will never know who ground grain and baked it to produce the first loaf of bread. But the impossibility of tracing the very first batch of wine ever made has not deterred archaeologists and historians from searching for the earliest evidence, a quest that has taken them back more than 7,000 years. There is, of course, no possibility that 7,000-year-old wine could have survived in liquid form. What was not consumed at the time would have evaporated long ago. The most we can expect to find now is earthenware jars or other vessels bearing evidence that they might have held wine: the remains of grapes – seeds, stalks and empty skins – or stains and residues from wine. Evidence of this kind has been found in pottery jars at a number of sites in the Middle East dating from the neolithic period (Late Stone Age), which lasted from about 8500 to 4000 BC.

Even then, seeds and other residue of grapes are not in themselves evidence of wine. Jars were used to store both dry and liquid goods, and jars with grape remains could have originally contained fresh grapes, raisins or even unfermented grape juice. But it is likely that grapes or grape juice stored in jars would ferment and become wine, especially in the warm temperatures of that part of the world. More important, we also know from literary and pictorial sources from later periods that wine *was* fermented and stored in jars and that skins, seeds or other grape residue was often left in it, rather than being filtered or strained out.

The most persuasive evidence of early wine has been obtained by a combination of chemical analysis and archaeological inferences.[1] At a number of neolithic sites in the Zagros mountains, in what is now western Iran, archaeologists have located jars that have reddish and yellowish deposits on their interior walls. Analysis of these deposits has shown them to be rich in tartaric acid and calcium tartrate. These are good indicators that they are the remains of a grape product that evaporated thousands of years ago, because grapes are rare among fruits in that they accumulate tartaric acid. Although it is still not direct, unassailable evidence of wine, the presence of a liquid grape product in a jar leads us to assume that wine must have been made, for, as suggested above, at room temperature in that region any grape juice kept in a container for more than a short time would have fermented into wine. It is not clear why some of the deposits were red and others yellow, but it is possible that they are the remains of different kinds of wine.

The earliest of these neolithic finds were six nine-litre jars embedded in the floor of a mud brick building, dating from 5400–5000 BC, in the community of Hajji Firuz Tepe in the northern region of the Zagros mountains.[2] These vessels contained not only the residues appropriate to grape juice but also bore deposits of resin. Resin from the terebinth tree that grew wild in the region was widely used as a preservative in ancient wine because it has the ability to kill certain bacteria, and tree resin (generally pine) is still used in Greek retsina wine.

Beyond the fact that wine existed in Hajji Firuz seven thousand years ago, we know little about its derivation or consumption. The community is in a region where vines grew wild in ancient times (and still do), but it is not clear whether the wine was produced from wild or cultivated grapes. The volume of wine that could have been kept in these vessels – a total of fifty-four litres – suggests that wine was made on a fairly large scale. Consumption, however, could have been gradual and extended over the year following the harvest: not only was the wine preserved by resin but clay stoppers about the same size as the jars' mouths were located close by, suggesting that the wine might have been protected effectively from the air.

Further evidence of ancient wine comes from Godin Tepe, a trading post and administrative and military centre also in the Zagros mountains, but much further south than Hajji Firuz. There, archaeologists discovered thirty- and sixty-litre earthenware jars dating from 3500–3000 BC, just after the neolithic period. The deposits in these jars not only contained tartaric acid but they lay in a line along one side of the interior of the jars from the base to the shoulder. This suggests that the vessels were lying on their sides when they contained the liquid and that the deposits remained when the liquid evaporated. These jars also had clay stoppers, which reinforces this impression; the vessels might have been stored like bottles in modern wine cellars to protect the wine from oxygen, which would turn it into vinegar. Other discoveries at Godin Tepe included a large basin that might have been used for treading grapes and a funnel that could have been used for straining grape juice before or after fermentation.[3]

Future discoveries might well push the date of the earliest known wine back even further or, more likely, broaden the known geographical range of early viniculture. Even so, we will never know who first made wine or the circumstances under which it was made. This has not deterred scholars from speculating about possible scenarios. One suggests that as pre-neolithic humans foraged for food, they gathered wild grapes into an animal hide or crude wooden container and that some of the berries at the bottom ruptured and exuded their juice. 'As the grapes are gradually eaten over the next day or two, this juice will ferment . . . Reaching the bottom of the "barrel", our imagined caveman or woman will sample the concoction and be pleasantly surprised by the aromatic and slightly intoxicating beverage. Additional intentional squeezings and tastings might well ensue.'[4]

A variation on this, proposed by two prominent American wine experts, places the discovery of wine in the neolithic period somewhere in the region that is now northern Iran. There, they suggest, 'some early housewife probably left crushed grapes in a jar and found, a few days later, that an alcoholic beverage had been formed.'[5] The bizarre image of a neolithic housewife apart, such scenarios could be correct in two essential respects: that the first wine was made unintentionally, and that human involvement was initially limited to picking the grapes and leaving them in conditions where they could ferment spontaneously. It is noteworthy that wine is generally said to have been *discovered*, unlike beer and bread which are usually thought of as having been *invented*.

Serendipity was the tenor of one ancient account of the discovery of wine. This story refers to the Persian King Jamsheed, a monarch who was so fond of fresh grapes that he stored them in jars so that he would have supplies out of season. When Jamsheed found one lot no longer sweet because, unknown to him, the grapes had fermented, he thought they had become poisonous and labelled the jar thus. But, the story goes, a woman from the royal harem, suffering from headaches so severe that she wanted to die, drank some of this 'poison' so as to put an end to her suffering. She was promptly overwhelmed by the alcohol and fell into a deep sleep. When the woman woke she was surprised to find that her headache was gone (and we must assume she was also surprised to be alive). She told the king of the magical cure, and he set about making more wine.[6]

Despite the consensus of traditions, myths and scholarly speculation that wine was first made accidentally, it is also quite possible that the first vintage was produced intentionally. Ancient Middle Eastern societies fermented many kinds of produce to make alcoholic beverages: grains, honey and fruits such as dates and pomegranates. It is quite likely that the first alcoholic beverage was made from fermented honey, and there is no reason why the same process should not have been applied deliberately to wild grapes long before vines were systematically cultivated.[7] An argument can be made that the production of wine should have preceded beer because wine is easier to make: all that is necessary to ferment grape juice is to crush the grapes and expose the sugars in the flesh to the wild yeasts on the skin, whereas it is necessary to add yeast when making beer from grain.[8]

However wine was first discovered, humans had to have access to grapes when they turned to making it deliberately, and this limits the geographical origins of wine to those parts of the world where vines grew wild. Wild vines that produce grapes capable of making wine (the species *vitis vinifera sylvestris*, or 'wine-bearing vines of the forest') flourished in many parts of the Northern Hemisphere, notably in Eurasia, North America and Asia. Some did grow in the forests, where they trailed along the ground or twisted up the trunks and along the branches of trees, while other varieties thrived along river banks or on rocks. Wild grapes still grow in many parts of Europe and western Asia, not only in the broad region where the earliest evidence of wine has been found but also in parts of Greece, Italy, France, Spain and Algeria.[9]

Early nomadic humans of the paleolithic period, which preceded the neolithic era, would have eaten the grapes from these vines. Grapes, either fresh or dried as raisins, are a good source of calories, minerals, vitamins and other nutrients, and raisins are durable and easily portable. But if early societies also used grapes for wine they could have enjoyed the beverage for only a very brief period each year. Grapes ripen sufficiently to be used for wine (that is, they accumulate enough sugar to be converted to alcohol) in late summer or early autumn, and the juice ferments quickly – in three or four days – in the warm weather. It would have been necessary for pre-neolithic people to consume the wine quickly, because in the absence of airtight containers it would have turned to vinegar soon afterwards. Thus if wine were consumed before the neolithic period – and there is no direct evidence that it was – it could have been only for a very short period each year. The fleeting appearance of this young wine might well have been eagerly anticipated each autumn, making it a sort of paleolithic beaujolais nouveau.

But although its transience and scarcity might have endowed wine with a particular cachet, it also prevented wine from entering diets in a meaningful way before the neolithic period. It was only then that the preconditions were met that enabled wine to be made and consumed on a regular, year-round basis. Because it takes vines two or more years to produce fruit, compared to the few months it takes cereal crops like barley to reach maturity from seed, grape vines could have been cultivated only by a settled society, not by a nomadic one. Beyond that, growing vines that produced regular and plentiful crops of grapes was labour-intensive and demanded year-round care.

The two vitally important elements in the development of systematic wine production were the beginning of vine cultivation and the invention of a means of conserving wine for months or even years.

Wine could, of course, be made from wild grapes, and undoubtedly the earliest wines were. Humans probably began to cultivate vines in order to satisfy a desire for wine that they had already acquired and because cultivating vines enabled them to select those grapes that they found were best suited for it. It is likely that larger and sweeter grapes with a higher ratio of juice to skin and seeds were preferred over those that were smaller, more acidic and less juicy. Over time the selection of these vines led to the emergence of specifically domesticated varieties of wine grapes.

Cultivating vines was further complicated by the fact that wild vines are mostly dioecious: separate plants have single-sex flowers, and they will not fruit unless they are pollinated by insects. Cultivated vines are hermaphroditic, which is to say that their flowers combine both male and female characteristics on the same vine, allowing pollination by the wind. Efficient wine cultivation that limited the role of chance thus meant identifying and breeding stock from suitable vines.

The long-term result was the species commonly known as *vitis vinifera* (meaning 'a vine of wine-bearing grapes'), which is used for most of the wine made in the modern world. The most familiar varieties like cabernet sauvignon, chardonnay, pinot noir, riesling, sauvignon blanc and syrah (shiraz) are all examples of *vitis vinifera*. Native North American varieties such as concord and scuppernong, and hybrids such as müller-thurgau and baco noir, are not.

However, in many parts of the world where vines grew wild, people simply did not cultivate them, and nor did they use wild grapes to make wine. There is no evidence that the grapes that grew wild throughout much of Europe were used for wine until the Greeks and Romans introduced viticulture and wine. Similarly, in the Americas some native populations made alcoholic drinks from maize and other plants, but it was not until settlement by Europeans that there were known attempts to make wine from the grapes that grew wild. Those attempts failed, which at least raises the possibility that native peoples in many parts of the world could have also tried and given up without their experiments having been recorded.

Archaeological and botanical evidence, in the form of vine pollen and grape seeds, strongly suggests that vines were first cultivated in the Middle East before 4000 BC, possibly as long as two thousand years earlier. The seeds of what seem to be cultivated grapes (which differ in shape from the seeds of the wild variety) dating from about 6000 BC have been found in Georgia, and there is similar evidence from other locations for the period 6000–4000 BC.[10] Vines could only have been first cultivated in the neolithic period, when humans began to farm animals as well as hunt wild animals and started to cultivate crops for subsistence in addition to gathering the berries, fruit and other plants that grew wild. The desire to cultivate crops, including vines for wine, was a powerful incentive towards settled society. Indeed, if wine were sufficiently highly valued, it could be seen as one of the motivations for the development of settled societies (and, by extension, civilization) rather than a product of it.

Wine was integral to new diets and culinary processes that emerged during the neolithic period. It was at this time that staples such as bread and beer began to be produced, and that humans began to process foods by heating, soaking, fermenting and seasoning them. When it was part of the diet, wine must have conferred real health benefits, for both wine and tree resin were soon recognized as having important medicinal properties. It has even been suggested that societies that consumed wine were likely to be healthier than those that did not, so that wine-drinking peoples had a better chance of surviving over the long term.

Not only were neolithic societies the first to be able to cultivate vines and thus have more certain access to grapes, but around 6000 BC they also developed the ideal means of conserving wine: pottery vessels. The malleability of clay enabled people to fashion vessels with narrow necks that could be more effectively stoppered with an airtight seal than the wide mouth of a bowl. The firing process created an impermeable material that effectively protected wine from the air that would turn it to vinegar. Stone and wood were far less versatile and useful, and although animal skins could be used to hold wine, they had a limited life compared to pottery jars that could be re-used indefinitely.

Although grapes grew wild in many parts of western Asia and Europe, the earliest evidence of wine-making comes from a fairly restricted region in the Fertile Crescent: the slopes of the Caucasus mountains between the Black and the Caspian seas, the Taurus mountains of eastern Turkey, and the northern section of the Zagros mountains of western Iran. In terms of modern political boundaries, this is the region where Iran, Georgia and Turkey converge on Armenia and Azerbaijan. It is possible that humans were cultivating vines here as early as 6000 BC and, as we have seen, the earliest physical evidence of wine production comes from this region in about 5000 BC, although as yet it is not known whether that wine was made from wild or cultivated grapes. The region that produced the first signs of wine has for some years been politically troubled, and many sites with potential for throwing light on the earliest history of wine have yet to be excavated. There is no clear evidence yet whether wine-making began at one single location and spread out from there, or whether it began more or less simultaneously at a number of locations.

The notion that the origin of wine production can be traced to a single location is sometimes called the 'Noah hypothesis', after the account of Noah and wine in the first book of the Old Testament. There the intriguing suggestion is made that viticulture and wine production began on Mount Ararat, where Noah's Ark finally came to rest after the waters of the Great Flood receded. As the Bible describes the genesis of wine, Noah was the first viticulturalist and wine-maker: 'Noah, a tiller of the soil, was the first to plant the vine. He drank some of the wine, and while he was drunk, he uncovered himself inside his tent.'[11] There is a compelling element to this story, because Mount Ararat is located near the Taurus mountains of eastern Turkey, where vines grew wild and where wine was certainly made in ancient times. Vines are today cultivated at the foot of Mount Ararat. Some religious commentators, anxious to reconcile the virtuous Noah saved by God with the man who drank himself insensible and stripped off his clothes, have suggested that he became drunk because, having no previous experience or familiarity with wine, he was not aware of its intoxicating effects. This interpretation tends to reinforce the notion that Noah had not planted vines before the Flood.

The notion of a Great Flood, a cataclysmic event that is recounted not only in the Bible but in texts such as the Sumerian *Epic of Gilgamesh*, has led two American scientists to suggest a scenario that might explain some aspects of the early history of wine.[12] Investigations have shown that until about 5600 BC the area now covered by the Black Sea was a fresh-water lake, with a much smaller surface area than today's. The fertile land around this lake, which was essentially a large oasis in a mostly arid region, supported a substantial population that was diverse in cultures and languages.

This fresh-water lake had a much lower elevation than the Mediterranean Sea and was separated from it (technically from the Sea of Marmara, an arm of the Aegean Sea) by a thin strip of land about twenty miles wide. In about 5600 BC, however, the Mediterranean burst through this natural dam and created what are now the Bosphorus straits. In a short time the fresh-water lake was swamped by the inrush of salt water.

As the surface of the new sea rose to the level of the Mediterranean, and the Black Sea was formed, the area around the original lake was drowned in what could only have been perceived by the displaced inhabitants as a great flood.

Those who survived the inundation, it is suggested, migrated in all directions as they fanned out from the new sea. Those who had lived on the northern and western edges of the lake migrated to Europe and Ukraine, while those on the south went to Anatolia and beyond. They took with them the memories of the inundation, which was translated into accounts of the flood in many traditions. They also took with them knowledge of wine. It is argued that this diaspora of different peoples from a single region explains why the word for wine is so similar in so many languages: *vino* in Russian and Italic, *Wein* in Germanic, *wino* in Kartvelian, *wijana* in Anatolian, *wajnu* in proto-Semitic, and *woi-no* in Indo-European.[13]

If this scenario does not explain why wine was not subsequently made in regions of Europe by migrants who settled where grapes grew wild, it might yet account for what appears to be the more or less simultaneous production of wine in the mountainous areas of the Fertile Crescent around 5000 BC. From there it seems that knowledge of wine production spread south, both through the Zagros mountains and down the eastern edge of the Mediterranean Sea. The evidence of wine in jars found at Godin Tepe about 3000 BC suggests not only that wine-making knowledge was transferred there but also that domesticated vines were used, because there is no evidence that vines grew wild that far south. These were the first steps in the long journey through time and across land and seas, as vines travelled from a small region in the Middle East to many parts of the globe.

We do not have enough evidence to enable us to plot the precise chronology and sequence in which the knowledge and techniques of viticulture and viniculture spread from the Caucasus, Taurus and northern Zagros mountain regions to other parts of the Middle East and beyond. We do, however, have some records of viticulture, wine production and wine-consumption in certain locations at specific times. They provide us with vital coordinates for a map of the route that wine took, even if the paths between the known coordinates and the time it took wine to

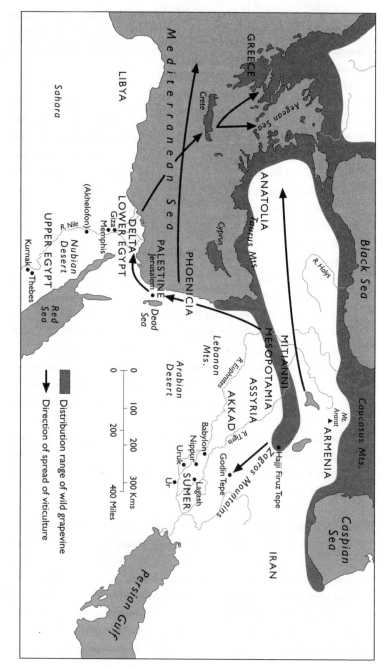

The spread of viticulture in the Middle East, 5000–1000 BC

Distribution range of wild grapevine

Direction of spread of viticulture

travel them must remain matters for speculation. The detectives who solve the mysteries of this period – archaeologists, historians, botanists, linguists, chemists – are constantly filling in gaps, but it is likely that many sections of the route that wine followed have been irretrievably lost.

Before we discuss the itinerary of viticulture in more detail, we should note that although the geographical *distribution* of vines and wine-making was the result of both the environment and human decisions, the geographical *limits* of vine cultivation were largely dictated by climate. Even though the climate several millennia ago was in some respects different from today's (for example, it was probably wetter around 3000 BC, thus allowing cultivation in areas that were too dry at other times), the ecological limits to viticulture were broadly similar to those with which we are familiar today. In the Northern Hemisphere grapes suitable for wine grow successfully for the most part only in a narrow band between the 30° and 50° latitudes. In those regions there is generally sufficient sunshine and warmth in the spring and summer months to produce grapes that have a high enough sugar content to produce wine-strength alcohol during fermentation. *Vitis vinifera* grapes accumulate sugar until it accounts for about a third of their volume.

Of course, we must bear in mind that both wine and tastes have changed dramatically over time. Early wine was probably less alcoholic than modern vintages, so that grapes with less sugar – wild grapes have about half the sugar content of the cultivated varieties – could have been used to make wine that was quite acceptable to contemporaries. What was considered perfectly palatable seven thousand years ago might well be thought of as utterly undrinkable today. Ancient wine was, in any case, often flavoured with herbs, honey and other additives. Moreover, wild vines often survive in colder climates than cultivated varieties, and they grow and bear fruit outside the climatic range of *vinifera* vines. For a number of reasons, therefore, ancient viticulture for wine was not necessarily constrained by the same climatic and soil requirements that we now generally accept as suitable for vines.

But climate and soil established only the geographical limits for viticulture and thereby a region's *potential* for producing wine-grapes. The *actual* cultivation of grapes and production of wine were human activities that reflected social, economic and cultural decisions, and these were determined in their turn by the economic and social value attributed to wine. The spread of viticulture, wine production and consumption throughout the Mediterranean and much of southern and western Europe in the long period between its known origins around 5000 BC and the collapse of the Roman Empire by 500 AD was driven by four broad factors.

First, knowledge and practices of viticulture and viniculture were part of the transfer of information and technology among cultures as they came into contact with one another. Travellers to regions where grapes were cultivated probably returned with root stock along with information on growing grapes and making wine. Producing wine successfully for the first time almost certainly meant importing (or abducting by military conquest) skilled workers, especially horticulturalists and wine-makers. Societies would have introduced viticulture only after having been exposed to wine as an imported commodity to the extent that they developed a demand for a local source. In regions where climate or other conditions ruled out local viticulture, a trade in wine must have developed so that wine would be readily available from elsewhere.

Viticulture and wine-production also accompanied colonization by wine-producing societies. The Greeks, for example, intensified and extended the existing viticultural activities when they colonized Egypt from 300 BC, and they introduced wine-making to southern Italy. The Romans in turn promoted vines and wine in regions of their empire that are now major wine producers. France, Germany and Hungary are among the European countries that can trace the origins of their wine industries back to Roman times.

The second major impetus to the spread of wine was the fact that it became endowed with powerful cultural meanings, both religious and secular. In almost all ancient cultures wine was associated in some manner with specific deities and became an integral element in religious rituals. Offering wine to gods was common in Mesopotamia, Egypt, Greece and Rome, and gods came to be associated with the vine and with wine. Wine became a powerful symbol of fundamental concepts such as death and rebirth, and it represented the blood of specific deities in religions as diverse as those of ancient Egypt and Christianity.

At a secular level, the scarcity and cost of wine contributed to making it a luxury drink in many societies. It was consumed almost exclusively by the wealthy and powerful elites, for whom it was a potent symbol of status. In the cultures of Mesopotamia and Egypt only the elites drank wine: the masses drank beer. Even in Greece and Rome, where wine was consumed far more widely, class distinctions were conspicuously marked not only by differences in the quality and price of wine but also by the occasions and manner in which it was consumed.

The third motor driving the spread of wine throughout the Mediterranean and Europe was the position it quickly developed as a profitable agricultural product and an important commercial commodity. Where it was a luxury, wine was traded in limited quantities, but it none the less became vital to a number of regional economies. For several centuries it was the object of a vast commerce throughout the Mediterranean and Europe, not to mention parts of Africa and Asia. In specific localities, many of them in Italy, Spain and France, wine-making became vital to long-term economic development and prosperity.

The fourth but by no means least important factor was the emergence of markets that represented wine cultures. Simply put, there was a growing demand for wine as it became integral not only to religious occasions but also, and more importantly in terms of quantity, to secular life. In the ancient period wine consumption spread socially over time: only the elites in Mesopotamia and Egypt drank wine, but two or three millennia later it was consumed among all social classes in imperial Rome. Steadily increasing wine production and the massive wine trade that developed are only the most obvious evidence of the growing market for wine at this time.

These four general factors, all of which are discussed more fully in this chapter and the next, explain how and why wine-production and consumption spread geographically and socially throughout the ancient world. In some cases one was more important than the others, but almost everywhere all four were closely interrelated. Of course, the long-term investment in cultivating vines and producing wine, not to mention the costs of transportation, paid off only because consumers were willing to pay for them. The price of wine and the return to producers was in turn based not only on the costs of production, transportation and sale, or on the intrinsic nutritional value of fermented grape juice: it also reflected the social and cultural values that were attributed to wine generally and, sometimes, to specific wines.

*

There is little information on the cultivation of grapes and the production and consumption of wine in those regions of the Fertile Crescent believed to have been the first to produce wine. It is quite possible that wine was widely consumed there, even by ordinary people who made wine for their own consumption. By about 2000 BC a veritable cottage industry in wine-making might have developed in Anatolia and the Zagros mountains. Wine is not difficult to make, and there seem to have been no legal restrictions on cultivating vines and using the grapes for wine.[14]

Even so, the wealthy in these areas consumed wine in ways that distinguished their status. In Godin Tepe, in the southern Zagros range, wine might well have been consumed by the general populace, but it appears to have been traded as a luxury commodity. Wine jars were found in close proximity to other luxury items such as stone beads and artifacts made of copper and bronze. Other wine jars in this community were located in what appears to have been an upper-class residence: its floor was finely plastered and objects found there included a marble bowl and a necklace of black and white beads.[15] In Mari, in northwest Mesopotamia, wine was a regular part of the upper-class diet by 1700 BC. It was exchanged as presents between kings and was a standard item in diplomacy, being mentioned when rulers received foreign visitors or ambassadors. Over time, however, and no doubt as supplies of wine became more plentiful, the social range of its consumption expanded and soldiers began to receive wine as part of their basic rations.[16]

Outside wine-producing regions, however, wine was a luxury product well beyond the means of ordinary folk. Some records of wine-consumption come from southern Mesopotamia, home to several early civilizations based on cities like Ur, Lagash, Sumer and Babylon but a region inhospitable to the vine. Not only was the climate too warm, but the water table in the alluvial plain was too close to the surface for vines, which do best in well-drained soil. It is possible that vines were grown in gardens attached to temples in the southernmost cities of Ur and Lagash, where they might have been planted on the better-drained levees, but it is not clear whether wine was produced from them.

A number of contemporary authorities wrote that wine was not made from the grapes in the southern areas of Mesopotamia, and it is possible that rather than being fermented, grape juice was instead heated slowly and reduced to a syrup that was used as a sweetening agent. According to one scholar, Babylon was a Mesopotamian Bavaria: a society that drank beer. Barley-based beer was cheaper to produce and tasted better than any wine that could be made locally.[17] Imported wine was consumed by the Mesopotamian upper classes and used in religious ceremonies. No doubt part of the social cachet of wine stemmed from its religious associations. Wine is mentioned in texts written on clay tablets from Ur that date to about 2750 BC, while a drinking song from Ur roughly 750 years later provides a list of the implements needed for making both wine and beer. Some seals show banquet scenes, with members of the royal family and their entourage drinking two beverages. One, probably beer, was drunk from large jars through tubes or straws, while the second, which is thought to be wine, was sipped from cups.

Most of the wine consumed in southern Mesopotamia was shipped by river and over land from the mountainous regions to the north and east. Mesopotamia was thus the destination of the earliest known wine trade. It must have been a limited commerce, because wine was an expensive luxury, and the distances between the Mesopotamian cities and many of its sources of wine, especially those to the north, were considerable. The Caucasus and Taurus ranges lay a thousand miles away, but goods could be brought down the Euphrates and Tigris rivers. Many of the vineyards in the Zagros mountains lay hundreds of miles away in a direct line, and it would have been necessary to transport wine over the mountains to the Mesopotamian plain.

The wine trade might well have been difficult and limited, but it might also have been very profitable. A letter dated about 1750 BC from a merchant of Babylon named Belânu, displays a note of urgency perhaps born of concern at missing out on the profits wine could represent. In the letter Belânu complained bitterly to his agent about the absence of wine in a consignment of goods that had been sent down the Euphrates. 'The boats have arrived here at the end of their journey at Sippar [a shipping centre fifty kilometres north of Babylon],' he wrote, 'but why have you not bought and sent me some good wine? Send me some and bring it to me in person within ten days!'[18]

Belânu was a merchant who appreciated either wine or its profits, for he pressed his agent in another letter: 'A boat loaded with wine has arrived at Sippar. Buy me ten sicles worth and tomorrow bring it and join me in Babylon.' This transaction might have involved two or three hundred litres of wine, a considerable quantity for a dealer in a luxury product at that time.[19]

The Mesopotamian wine trade remained viable for thousands of years. In the fifth century BC, more than a millennium after Belânu was harassing his agents and selling wine to his Babylonian clients, the Greek historian Herodotus described the trade in wine from Armenia to Babylon. Boats, he wrote, were built in Armenia, filled with straw, loaded with wine in casks, and then floated downstream to Babylon, where the wine was sold. The boats were broken up, because it was impossible for them to return back to Armenia against the current.[20] The retail price of wine must have been considerable once it included the cost of building a disposable barge for each delivery.

Quantities of wine were limited, however, and the costs of transportation alone raised the price of wine well above that of the beer made from grain and the other alcoholic beverages made from grain and dates and other fruit that could be grown locally. An indication of the social level of Mesopotamian wine-drinkers is that by about 2340 BC the ruler of Lagash had established a wine cellar, 'into which wine is brought in great vases from the mountains'.[21] The continuing preponderance of beer in Mesopotamia is indicated by the fact that there was no word for 'wine cellar', and the term used in this inscription normally meant a 'reserve of beer'. Wine was sometimes referred to as 'beer of the mountain' because of the association of viticulture with the mountainous regions from which wine was imported. Basic daily fare was described as 'bread and beer'.

As viticulture expanded through the Middle East, wine remained a pleasure largely restricted to the wealthy and the powerful. A relief from Nineveh in the seventh century BC shows King Assurbanipal reclining and his queen seated under a trellis of vines and drinking what was probably wine made from grapes.[22] Paintings and engravings from this period are more likely to depict the activities of the elite than of the masses, but there is no evidence to suggest that wine was drunk by ordinary people.

Exceptions were sometimes made for people of lesser rank, however, when they were associated with the elites. In Nimrud a ration of wine was provided to all 6,000 members of the royal household, whether they were members of the royal family or unskilled workers. The basic male ration was about 1.8 litres for ten men each day (a little more than a modern glass of wine per man), while skilled workers got about twice that amount. Members of the household with higher status appear to have had more generous rations, but it is impossible to be precise about them. The queen and her retinue received 54 litres a day, but it is not known among how many people this quite substantial quantity was shared.[23] Rations of this magnitude imply the consumption of substantial volumes of wine on an annual basis.

The region that included Anatolia and the Fertile Crescent remained important for wine-production long after the cultivation of vines extended to other parts of the Middle East. By the third millennium BC, wine was being made along the eastern fringe of the Mediterranean, and both Syria and Palestine were exporting wine to Egypt. The eastern Mediterranean wine trade took off more generally around 1000 BC with the rise of Phoenician seapower based in the port cities of present-day Lebanon. Phoenician wine was exported not only to Egypt but also much further afield. The Phoenicians planted vines on the island of Ibiza and probably also introduced viticulture to Spain and Portugal, although it is also possible that viticulture developed in Spain quite independently of outside influences.[24]

Egypt followed a pattern that was common to other Middle Eastern regions where vines did not grow wild. Wine was first imported (in this case from the eastern Mediterranean regions such as Palestine and Syria) and once a market had been established, vines were planted and domestic wine-production began. Dramatic evidence of Egypt's wine imports before this time exists in the form of hundreds of wine jars that were found in the burial chamber of one of the first Egyptian kings, probably known as Scorpion I, who lived about 3150 BC.[25] Many of the jars contain the same kinds of wine and tree-resin deposits as were found in vessels excavated in the Zagros mountains of western Iran. The wine jars excavated at Godin Tepe are almost contemporaneous with those found in Scorpion's tomb at Abydos in the Middle Nile region.

The clay from which the Abydos jars were made bears no resemblance to the clay along the banks of the Nile, however, and best matches the material used for jars made in the southern Levant: the region now occupied by Israel, the Palestinian uplands and the Jordan Valley. We do not know how extensive the trade in wine at the end of the fourth millennium was, but the volume of wine buried with Scorpion I was impressive: if all the wine jars interred with his body were full, he would have had 4,500 litres of wine to consume in his afterlife.

It was in Egypt that a major wine culture developed and left the earliest comprehensive records of wine-making and patterns of wine-consumption. As was the case elsewhere in the ancient world, in Egypt beer was the most common alcoholic drink, and date-wine was also produced. The period 3000–2500 BC, however, produced pictorial evidence of wine-production in Egypt, about the same date as similar evidence from Mesopotamia. The main grape-growing region in Egypt was the most fertile area, the Nile Delta, where the high temperatures that would otherwise have ruled out viticulture were cooled by the Mediterranean. Upper Egypt (in the south) did not have this benefit, although there were some scattered vineyards even there. Some oases also became important locations for vineyards, and for a time many owed their prosperity to wine. In about 1000 BC a census listed some 513 vineyards owned by temples throughout the country. The amount of land under viticulture was expanded by the Greeks when they colonized Egypt from about 300 BC, although this did not mean that Egyptians had greater supplies. The increasing Greek population, with wine central to its culture, consumed most of the additional wine.

Egypt's vines were cultivated by kings, priests and great officials, only rarely in specialized vineyards and more often in walled gardens where they grew among other plants and trees. One private vineyard, belonging to Metjen, a high official of Saqqara about 2550 BC, was described in this way: a domain '200 cubits long and 200 cubits wide . . . very plentiful trees and vines were set out, a great quantity of wine was made there'.[26] This was a sizable estate of about two and a half acres, although we do not know what proportion of it was occupied by vines.

Within the larger gardens, vines were generally found at the centre, possibly so that they would be sheltered from wind by the taller trees that surrounded them. Vines were often irrigated and wells were formed of mud to retain water at the base of the trunks. Pigeon droppings were often used as fertilizer. In some vineyards vines were allowed to form a natural canopy supported by poles, while in others they were trained along trellises, a technique that provided the basis for the hieroglyph for wine: grapes hanging off a supported trellis with the root of the vine in a well.

More detailed information on viticulture in Egypt comes from the later period of Greek colonization, when viticulture covered a larger area. Wine was no longer made in limited quantities for consumption only by the elite, but was provided for a wider market of consumers, most of them Greek. Viticulture had the status of an important commercial enterprise, and by that time, too, some of the ancient Egyptian practices had undoubtedly been modified by Greek settlers. Even so, wine-makers still had to contend with Egypt's difficult climatic conditions.

Records relating to the vineyards of Appianus, a prominent citizen and councillor of Alexandria until his death in 260 AD, show that by this time viticulture was being carried out on a quite different scale from the time of the pharaohs. The Appianus estate consisted of twenty vineyards, with a total of 20 hectares in production at any time, producing a respectable 50,000 litres of wine a year. The vineyards were closely planted in vines – tying vines to trellises in three of the vineyards alone required 58,800 reeds – and Appianus threatened his workers with severe punishment if they left any land uncultivated without a good reason.[27]

The fundamental techniques of ancient Egyptian wine-making were common to the ancient world as a whole, although there were regional variations and some changes in detail over time. Grapes, almost always depicted as blackish-blue in colour, were picked by hand (rather than the bunches being cut) and taken in baskets to be crushed. Juice was extracted from the grapes in two or three processes, each of which produced must (juice ready for fermentation) of different quality. The most pure was produced as the grapes at the bottom of the vat were crushed by the weight of the fruit above. This run-off juice, a very small proportion of the total extraction, was sometimes used to make a very sweet and syrupy white wine that was only slightly fermented.

This preliminary juice extraction does not appear to have been employed in ancient Egypt, however. There, as elsewhere, most of the juice (about two thirds of it) was obtained by treading the grapes in a vat or other container. Egyptian wall paintings show men (usually between four and six of them) holding straps hanging from overhead poles in order to keep their balance while treading the slippery grapes in large vats made of wood, baked clay or stone finished with plaster.[28] Sometimes the treaders worked to a cadence set by singers or musicians. One song, to Rennutet, goddess of the harvest, went: 'May she remain with us in this work . . . May our lord drink it [the wine] as one who is repeatedly favoured by his king.'[29]

The juice produced by treading ran off or was drawn off into jars. Because the juice is almost always depicted in paintings as being a variety of red or a dark colour, it is possible that it included some grape skins or (less probably) that it was allowed partially to ferment in the vat so that it gained colour from skin contact before being transferred to jars. Treading alone does not transfer much colour from the skins to the juice. It is possible, too, that the dark colour of the must in these depictions was an artistic device that reflected the final colour of the wine, not the colour of the must as it was poured from the vats. One of the problems with Egyptian portrayals of wine-making is that they convey no sense of the time that elapsed between the different stages of the process.

The pulp, skins, seeds and stems that remained in the vat after the juice obtained by treading had been removed were then pressed in a variety of ways so as to extract as much of the residual juice as possible. In Egypt the remains of the grapes were placed in a sack attached to two poles that were twisted so as to squeeze out the remaining liquid.

Even if some fermentation had taken place in the vats where the grapes were pressed, it was completed in the large clay jars into which the must was transferred. After the jars had been filled they were closed with pottery lids and then sealed with a large lump of Nile clay, usually shaped in a conical form and roughly smoothed, that extended to the shoulder of the jar. Small holes were made or hollow reeds inserted to allow for the escape of carbon dioxide during fermentation, but they were later closed up to prevent the wine being spoiled by contact with air. A clay seal fixed on the cap provided information that might include the vineyard from which the wine came, the name of the wine-maker, and the year of the vintage. These were the forerunners of wine labels. Little is known of the way the jars were stored, although one picture shows them being stacked side by side, each leaning on its neighbour.[30]

We cannot recover the qualities of Egyptian wine in terms of colour, aroma, taste or body. Most were reds and a few were whites, but the degree of sweetness must remain unknown to us, and in any case wine was often flavoured with herbs and spices before being consumed. What was siphoned from the jars for consumption can frequently have been little more than a wine base for what was, in effect, an ancient form of liqueur. One thing we can say with some certainty is that Egyptian wines had limited ageing potential. Grapes were picked and crushed in August, and the slow treading and pressing, followed by the rapid fermentation that wine must have gone through in Egypt's hot summer temperatures, would almost certainly have made for an unstable wine. The jars in which the wine was fermented and then stored would have been somewhat porous unless they were coated with resin or oil, and wine would therefore have been gradually exposed to air. It is likely that most wine was consumed within a year of production and that it would have soured within three or four years.[31]

Again, the records of the Appianus estate, although from a much later date (the third century AD), might enlighten us about the quality of Egyptian wine. Most of the produce from that estate appears to have been white that was blended from more than one grape varietal, an attempt to emulate the sweet whites that were so highly prized in Greece at that time. It was judged by sweetness and to a lesser extent by age: some wines were described as 'readier' or 'more aged'. Even so, most wine was consumed within a year of the vintage, because the summer heat and poor sealing methods meant that wine quickly turned to vinegar or began to smell bad. For example, many of the jars of wine made in August 245 were 'off' by February 247, eighteen months later. The wine-producer's response to this problem was clear: sell the wine as soon as possible after it was made, and let the buyer deal with the problem of conservation and take the risk of being stuck with spoiled wine.[32]

Not only was wine largely confined to the upper ranks in ancient Egypt – kings, nobles and priests – but the vineyards themselves were exclusively owned by them. Wine-production was therefore limited and the price of wine was high, about five times that of beer. It was consumed by kings and nobles in the royal courts, by wealthy private individuals, and by priests attached to temples that produced wine and received more as part of their income. It also played a role in religious rituals, whether being poured as a libation to the gods or being left with the dead for consumption in the afterlife.

Many caches of wine jars have been discovered in the cellars of royal palaces and in tombs. One of the most interesting collections of Egyptian wine – though by no means the largest – was discovered in 1922 in the tomb of King Tutankhamon. This boy-king came to the throne in about 1348 BC at the age of ten, and when he died nine years later (at the legal drinking age in many modern societies) three dozen jars holding wine were buried with him. Twenty-six of the jars bear seals that identified the estate, year of vintage and name of the wine-maker. The most common vintages in the collection were those of the fourth, fifth and ninth years of Tutankhamon's reign (1345, 1344 and 1340 BC): jars for those years accounted for twenty-three of the twenty-six jars with seals. One read: 'Year 4. Sweet wine of the House-of-Aton – Life, Prosperity, Health! – of the Western River. Chief vintner Aperershop.'[33]

It has been suggested that only goods of exceptional quality would have been left in such a tomb, so that these wines must have been among the best available.[34] But we do not know Tutankhamon's (or his steward's) cellaring principles, and it is possible that these wines were what was left after the better wine had been consumed. It is noteworthy that the oldest wine in the collection dated back only five years, an indication of the limited lasting qualities of Egyptian wine.

The seals on the jars give tantalizing but frustrating hints of the quality of the wine. Only four were labelled 'sweet', which might mean that most were not, and one was described as 'wine of good quality', which might also tell us something about the rest. It is possible that some estates, the *premiers crus* of ancient Egypt, were so highly regarded that it was unnecessary to record that the wine was excellent, and that quality was specified only when wines came from vineyards that were not reputed for their excellence. But even in Egypt, where wine-drinking was largely limited to a select few, Tutankhamon's wines cannot be thought of as representative of wine more generally. The seals on jars found in other locations describe their contents in varying ways: 'good wine', 'very good wine', and even wine 'for merry-making', perhaps indicating a poor vintage best suited for quaffing. Jars with seals reading 'wine for taxes' and 'wine for offerings' might also have contained wine of mediocre quality.

Although it was frequently used in religious observances in ancient Egypt, wine also served quite secular functions. Wall paintings that depict banquet scenes show wine being served in considerable quantities to both men and women. When large amounts were needed, wine was brought to banquets in the big earthenware jars in which it had been fermented and cellared. Some banquet scenes show participants drinking wine directly from the jars through tubes or straws. More often, however, wine was brought to the feasts in smaller containers like decanters, from which servants siphoned or poured it through strainers into drinking vessels. These were either bowls or cups, but by the 18th Dynasty they included stemmed goblets made of glass or alabaster.[35] The process of straining or siphoning suggests that even if wine had been racked (that is, drawn off its sediment) at some point during fermentation, there remained enough grape residue to make the wine aesthetically unpleasing or unpleasant to drink.

Most Egyptian banquet scenes show convivial guests drinking and chatting, but painters did not shy away from revealing the less attractive consequences of the availability of apparently endless supplies of wine. Drunken revellers, men and women alike, are sometimes shown vomiting, sometimes depicted being carried away unconscious by servants. Some guests might well have come to these occasions in order to get drunk. In a banquet scene from one tomb a woman says: 'Give me eighteen cups of wine ... don't you see I want to get drunk! My insides are as dry as straw!'[36] There is a tendency for women to be disproportionately depicted as excessive drinkers, being sick or suffering other effects of intoxication. Other Egyptian banquet scenes link wine-drinking with love and sex, themes that would become even more common and explicit in Greece. Women at one Egyptian festivity are shown wearing transparent garments and holding lotus leaves and mandrake fruits, both symbols of love. Servant girls, all but naked, are shown pouring the drinks.

Since ancient times there have been both positive and negative attitudes towards the consumption of wine. Social commentators have pointed to the benefits of wine in facilitating social interaction, while warning about the dangers that drunkenness posed to social order. Medical commentators have praised wine as beneficial, but warned that excessive drinking was not only hazardous to health but even potentially fatal. These positions were not necessarily contradictory, for it is quite consistent to recommend moderate consumption of wine while warning against excess. Even so, social critics and medical authorities have historically had difficulty defining a generally acceptable position that balanced the extremes.

Attitudes toward wine-consumption in Egypt were as diverse as in other cultures and at other times. Drinking was seen as a natural pleasure to be enjoyed by the wealthy on a daily basis and particularly on holidays and during festivals. A scene from the tomb of Nakhet shows a girl offering wine to her parents during the Valley Festival with the words: 'To your health! Drink this good wine, celebrate a festive day with what your Lord has given you.'[37] Modest drinking was approved of, and even drunkenness was referred to positively in some contexts. There were warnings, however, about the effects of over-indulgence. One sage, Ani, commented of the drunk person: 'When you speak, nonsense comes out of your mouth; if you fall down and your limb breaks, no one will give you help.'[38] Another sage advised: 'Do not get drunk, lest you go mad.' If there was some recognition that being drunk could be enjoyable, there was also disapproval of those who disgraced themselves by being drunk in public. This distinction, between what was acceptable in public and what was permissible in private, was echoed in many cultures.

Concern about the effects of unrestrained drinking has meant that from the earliest times there have been attempts to regulate the production, sale and consumption of wine. One of the first recorded attempts was the Code of Hammurabi, an early set of laws issued about 1750 BC by one of the most important Babylonian kings. A number of the laws regulated aspects of the retail wine trade, notably establishments variously described as wine-shops and taverns. In either case it is clear that both beer and wine could be bought there, and Hammurabi's code expressed concern about them. Tavern-keepers, apparently always women, were required to report to the authorities any meeting that took place on their premises that might be a political or criminal conspiracy. Women in religious orders were forbidden, on pain of being burned, to set up wine-shops. Tavern-keepers found guilty of watering down drinks were to be sentenced (appropriately, it might be argued) to be drowned.[39] It is possible that the concern about religious women setting up wine-shops reflected a desire to retain wine's association with religion or to prevent the public sale of wine designated for religious rituals.

Parallel to warnings about the harmful effects of wine have run ideas of its health-giving properties. It was a medium for other medicinal substances, such as herbs and spices, and was attributed curative properties in its own right. In Egypt, wine was prescribed to increase the appetite, purge the body of worms, regulate the flow of urine, treat asthma, and to act as an enema. When used for such purposes it was often mixed with *kyphi*, a concoction of gums, resin, herbs, spices and even the hair of asses, animal dung and bird droppings. We can detect here early evidence of the pharmacological tradition that medicines must taste unpleasant in order to be effective. There was a rationale behind this, namely a belief that many physical ailments resulted from evil residing in the body, and that one way of evicting the unwelcome tenant was to ingest unpleasant substances so as to make the body uninhabitable. Wine was also applied externally as a salve and to bring down swelling, and it was applied to bandages to treat wounds.

A balm for the body, wine was also succour for the soul, for it quickly took on religious associations. The beginnings of a culture of wine, in which the fermented juice of grapes was given varied social, cultural and economic values, are as much a mystery as the origins of wine itself. Why did the inhabitants of a particular area of the world begin to cultivate vines and produce wine when other populations that also had access to wild grapes did not? One explanation is that wine came to be associated with a particular set of religious beliefs and that as these beliefs spread, so did wine, first for religious purposes and later for secular enjoyment. Although we should not over-emphasize the role of religion in the geographical expansion of the wine-conscious world, it is notable that in many Western cultures wine has often been associated with similar religious concepts.[40]

One of the most common associations of wine is with the mystery of death and rebirth, a mystery that came to be represented by the vine itself. Vines appear to die in the winter as their leaves fall and trunks dry, and the 'rebirth' of a vine in the spring is particularly dramatic. In many Egyptian funerary scenes, grape-vines symbolize resurrection. Even so, many other plants follow the same cycle, and there is no obvious reason why vines should have been endowed with exceptional significance. Perhaps some importance was attached to the fact that the fruit of the vine, in the form of wine or dried grapes, survives the apparent death of the parent vine. There was also a more mundane link between wine and fertility: wine was recognized as having the ability to relax social convention and control and to facilitate social interaction, including sexual relationships. The link between wine and sex, a connection both celebrated and deplored for millennia, relates back to the association of wine with fertility.[41]

Even more likely as an explanation of the unique religious status that wine achieved is the effect of fermentation. The juice of the grape undergoes a marvellous transformation, accompanied by bubbling and the production of heat; ordinary, if pleasant-tasting, juice becomes a substance capable of intoxicating anyone who drinks it. That very psychotropic effect was a mystery, even a wonder, that provoked much social, medical and religious inquiry and concern. Many ancient commentators saw intoxication in some contexts as a form of 'otherworldliness', a breaking of the earthly bonds of reason and self-control, enabling the inebriated person to approach closer to the gods. Yet it is not clear why inebriation from beer, date-wine, or any other alcoholic drink should not have been attributed the same association. Perhaps the answer is simply that wine made from grapes was more alcoholic than the other beverages and brought its consumers close to the gods more rapidly.

Wine became an element in many of the religions of the ancient world. It was commonly used in libations, the pouring of a liquid (beer, oil, honey and water were also used) in the name of a particular god, generally while a prayer was said. Libations can be seen as an exchange between mortals and a divinity, as wine was given in return for the gifts that the god conferred. Wine was also used in other religious rituals. In Mesopotamia it was present on the tables of food and drink offered to the gods. In Egypt, wines from five different regions, perhaps the best available, came to be prescribed as essential provisions for the afterlife,[42] and the planting of vines might well have become a religious obligation. Addressing the great god Amon-Re, Ramses III pointed out his contributions in that sphere: 'I made for thee wine-gardens on the Southern Oasis, and Northern Oasis likewise without number; others in the South with numerous lists . . .' He claimed to have presented 59,588 jars of wine to the god.[43] Finally, wine and the vine were prominent as symbols in many religions. Although other alcoholic beverages, especially beer, could also be found performing symbolic roles, wine came to occupy a privileged position. As we shall see, with the ascendancy of Christianity in Europe, wine pushed its rivals almost entirely out of the religious picture.

Just as women were frequently associated with the discovery of wine, so many of the early deities linked to wine were women. One was Gestin, the Sumerian goddess of the vine. In the Syrian religion, Danel, a demi-god, was assisted by his daughter in cultivating vines. Later in Egypt, where male gods dominated viticulture and wine, we find the snake-goddess Renen-utet, present at the vintage.[44] Over time, however, men replaced women as the deities associated with wine. Osiris, the Egyptian god of nature and god of death and rebirth, was also god of the vine. It was Osiris who presided over the festival celebrating the flooding of the Nile, the annual event that was vital for the survival of agriculture in much of Egypt.

It has been suggested that wine was all the more appropriate as a symbol of rebirth because when the Nile flooded each year it was a reddish colour resonant of wine, owing to the ferrous alluvium that was washed into the river by one of its tributaries. But we should bear in mind, in this respect as in cases where wine symbolized blood, that a small proportion of the wine produced in the ancient world was white, not red.

Wine had yet other religious connotations in Egypt. Some texts depict wine as the perspiration of Re, the sun god. Others refer to it as the eye of the god Horus, with red wine representing the right eye, white wine the left. Wine was often associated with blood, a connotation reinforced by the frequent portrayal of Shesmu, the god of the wine-press, as a slaughterer. Blood was also a link between wine and the goddess Hathor, who, the story went, was enraged when she was brought to Egypt from Nubia by Re. Hathor was eventually appeased by music, dancing and wine, and annual offerings were made to her at the Festival of Drunkenness. Wine in this case was seen as symbolic of the blood of Hathor's enemies.

The religious significance of wine was a common feature of the cultures of the pre-classical ancient world, but it straddled many changes. Four thousand years separated the known origins of wine in the Fertile Crescent and the establishment of an elite wine culture in Egypt. Although we do not know much about viniculture before it reached Egypt, where it was recorded in details by artists and bureaucrats, we can see that by 2000 BC wine-makers were already wrestling with problems of quality and conservation. They were, of course, making wine in difficult climatic conditions, and it was not until wine was made in the more temperate areas of Mediterranean Europe that many of the problems were resolved.

During that time viticulture spread beyond the regions where grapes grew wild, but there is no evidence that, outside wine-producing areas where it might have become a subsistence product, wine was anything but a luxury commodity. Undoubtedly there were climatic and environmental limits to expanding production, but social values also militated against the development of a large-scale wine industry at this time. The upper classes of ancient Egypt were not alone in their self-conscious adoption of wine as a beverage to be consumed only by the gods and by great men and women. In this respect the passage of wine from Egypt to ancient Greece represented more than a voyage across water and through time: it was a passage from one culture where wine was monopolized by the few to one where it was embraced by the many.

TWO

DEMOCRATIC DRINKING

Wine in Ancient Greece and Rome

As early as 2500 BC, commercial and cultural links between Egypt and Crete began to include trade in wine. A pottery jar discovered on Crete and dating from about 2200 BC contains grape seeds, stalks and skins, and if this was the residue of wine it had probably been imported. In time, however, grapes were cultivated and wine was made on the island itself. A wine press found at Palaikastro dates from the Mycenaean period (1600–1100 BC), as do references to wine in clay tablets describing agricultural products controlled by the royal palaces on Crete.[1] From Crete, wine production spread to other islands of the Aegean. Even more important, the Mycenaean rulers of Crete might have been responsible for transferring viticulture and wine-making to mainland Greece, although it is possible that wine was being made there earlier.[2] Whatever the precise mechanism and timing, this was to prove a critical stage in the history of wine, for the Greeks accelerated its geographical and social expansion throughout and beyond the western Mediterranean region.

In the first centuries of Greek viticulture it is likely that grapes were grown alongside other crops, especially olives, but gradually exclusive vineyards developed. Initially vineyards were concentrated close to the main population centres such as Athens, Sparta, Thebes and Argos, which were also the principal markets for wine. By the sixth or fifth centuries BC, however, increasing demand for wine encouraged the establishment of wineries further afield, notably on the more distant Greek islands. The wines of some of these, such as Thasos, Lesbos and Chios, became particularly valued for their quality.

Vineyards were almost always planted near water, because sea or river transportation was far less costly than over land. Some were extensive properties, like a 30-hectare estate on Thasos that employed large

The spread of viticulture to Europe up to c. 100 AD

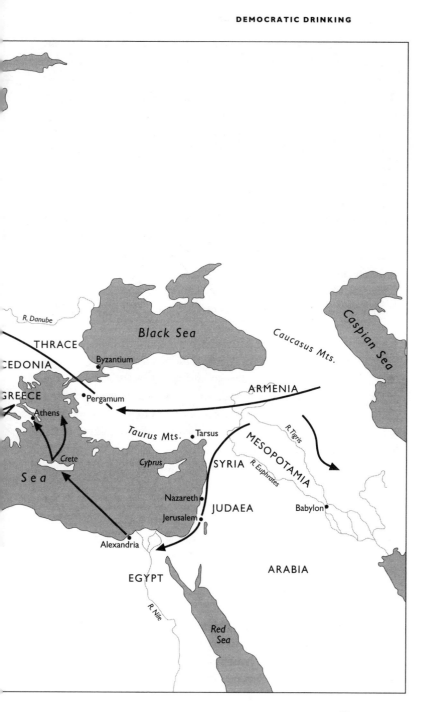

numbers of slaves and other workers, both male and female. The cultivation of vines demanded more specialized skills than growing olives
or grain. Vine-dressers, responsible for the vital pruning operations,
developed into a profession and many of them worked on contract in a
number of vineyards.

The Greeks combined innovation with what we might think of as
already traditional viticulture practices. For example, they largely abandoned the widespread method of growing vines up trees in favour of
training them along trellises and stakes, making the grapes more accessible for harvesting. But in order to ward off the damaging effects of rain
or drying winds on the flowers, less scientific approaches might be
employed: one ritual required two men to tear a white cock in half and,
each taking a piece of the unfortunate fowl, run around the vines in
opposite directions. The two halves of the cock were buried at the point
where the two men met.[3]

By the third century BC a true wine industry had developed in Greece.
It was during the period of Greek dominance of the region that viticulture
came into its own and that grapes became, with olives and grain, one
of the three main products of Mediterranean agriculture. The Greeks
not only entrenched wine consumption within their society in a way no
other culture had, but they extended it by trade to many other parts of
Europe. By the fifth century BC Greek wine was to be found in various
parts of France (such as the upper Saône valley and Jura), Egypt, around
the Black Sea, and in the Danube region. Not only did the Greeks export
their own wine, but they also expanded viticulture in some colonized
areas and introduced wine-making to others. As we have seen, wine had
been produced in limited quantities in Egypt since about 3000 BC, but
when the Greeks began to dominate the region from 300 BC they planted
numerous new vineyards and expanded wine production considerably.

When they came to Sicily, the Italian mainland and southern France,
however, the Greeks encountered wineless societies, and they introduced
domesticated vines and wine-making. The Roman historian Justin
ranked viticulture along with urban life and constitutional government
as one of the benefits of civilization that the Greek settlers of Massalia
(the region around present-day Marseilles) conferred on the indigenous
inhabitants of the area.[4] It is also possible that the Greeks introduced
viticulture to Spain and Portugal in the eighth century BC, although

other theories suggest that the sponsors were the Phoenicians and that viticulture was established in Spain independently of outside influences.

The viticultural colonization of the southernmost parts of Italy was so successful that the Greeks called the region *Oenotria*, or 'the land of trained [or staked] vines'. So important was wine in the region that in one southern Italian site, dating back to the fourth and third centuries BC, grape-vine remains make up a full 30 per cent of vegetation recovered by archaeologists.[5] The Greeks did not colonize northern Italy, where the Etruscans already had a tradition of viticulture and wine-production. The origins of the Etruscans are a matter of debate, but they appear to have come from the eastern Mediterranean or Asia Minor, where wine-making had long been known. By the time the Greeks were planting vineyards in the south of Italy the Etruscans were already making wine and exporting it across the Alps as far as Burgundy.

The Greek wine trade, whether in the form of rural producers supplying urban markets or Greek producers exporting long-distance, was undoubtedly profitable. Its extent is demonstrated by the remains of thousands of pottery amphoras that are found scattered throughout Europe. Until the first century AD, when they were largely replaced by wooden barrels, amphoras were the most common vessels for fermenting, ageing, storing and transporting wine, as well for shipping oil, olives and even dry goods. Ungainly looking but oddly attractive objects, amphoras came in a variety of shapes and sizes, each typical of a region or individual producer. Most held between 25 and 30 litres. They had pointed bases, bodies that broadened at the top, and two handles. Their design enabled them to be carried at both ends because a full amphora was too heavy for one person to carry. Even an empty one was a challenge, for it weighed as much as the wine many of them held.

Their shape made them easy to move for, like the barrels that later replaced them, amphoras could be pivoted, although unlike barrels they were carried rather than rolled. The pointed base made upright storage difficult, and in wine cellars they generally leaned against one another, like so many drunks with bellies full of wine. When it was necessary to stand an amphora on its end, supports made of pottery, wood or basketry were used, and when transported by ship they were planted in a wooden framework or a bed of sand.

Most wine was transported by sea, but maritime commerce was a high-risk venture and hundreds of thousands of amphoras lie at the bottom of the seas across which the Greeks traded. These are cargoes of wine lost when ships sank during storms or were blown on to rocks. There are particularly heavy concentrations of shipwrecks containing wine amphoras along the southern coast of France. One which has been excavated by marine archaeologists was carrying an astonishing 10,000 amphoras that would have contained as much as 300,000 litres of wine, the equivalent of some 400,000 standard bottles. It is estimated that ten million litres of wine were shipped to Gaul each year through Massalia, the Greeks' main gateway to Gaul.[6]

Evidence of the penetration of Gaul by Greek wine also lies underground, in the hundreds of thousands of amphoras found buried on land. There are pockets of them in such disparate areas as Toulouse in south-western France and at Châlon-sur-Saône in the east. It is thought that there are hundreds of thousands of amphoras in the bed of the river Saône alone, representing between five and ten million litres of wine. A particularly striking manifestation of the social impact of the Greek wine trade is treasure discovered near Châtillon-sur-Seine in the subterranean burial chamber of a Celtic princess of the Vix lineage. The Vix treasure included not only jewellery, statues and other luxury objects, but a massive Greek *krater*, a receptacle used for mixing wine and water. Ornately decorated, almost two metres in height and holding more than a thousand litres, this krater was clearly more decorative than functional. Most kraters hold a few litres of wine and water. But together with other Greek wine paraphernalia, such as pitchers and cups, that were also found in the tomb, the Vix krater points to the status of wine in the high society of Celtic Gaul.[7]

If that were the case on the fringes of Greek influence, it was even more so towards the centre. By the time a new empire, the Roman, began to dominate southern Italy in the fourth and third centuries BC, wine production had already been well-established there under Greek sponsorship. The Etruscan wine industry in the north was, as we have seen, even older. The first Latin work on viticulture, Cato's *De Agri Cultura* (*c.* 200 BC) suggests that grape-growing was no longer a subsistence activity but had already become a profitable commercial enterprise. The rapid growth of Rome's population, from about 100,000 in 300 BC to over a million at the beginning of the Christian era, was accompanied by an equally rapid growth of demand for wine, particularly cheap wine that the masses could afford. It is estimated that Rome absorbed some 1.8 million hectolitres of wine a year at this time, almost half a litre a day for every man, woman and child in the city.[8]

The significance of this Roman market was thrown into sharp relief in 79 AD, when the eruption of Mount Vesuvius buried the important wine-shipping port of Pompeii in ash and devastated its vine-rich hinterland. Two vintages were lost and Rome suffered immediate shortages of wine and, we can assume, a commensurate rise in prices. Almost immediately there was a rush to plant vineyards – to replace those lost and to cash in on the higher prices – with the result that a few years later overproduction produced a glut of wine.

Claiming that too much arable land was being turned to viticulture, Emperor Domitian in 92 AD forbade the planting of any more vines in Italy and ordered the grubbing up of half the vines in Rome's overseas provinces. The purpose of the edict might have been to protect Rome from a shortfall in grain, but it might equally well have been designed to protect growers in Italy from outside competition. It must have been a sense of irony that led the French authorities to name part of the A9 autoroute, which runs through completely vine-covered plains near France's Mediterranean coast, after Domitian. If they were thumbing their noses at him from the safety of almost two thousand years, their forebears were more forthright, for Domitian's order prohibiting planting was not widely observed, and it was eventually repealed in 280 AD.

It was in the Roman period, in the last centuries BC and the first few hundred years of the Christian era, that viticulture and wine-making first attracted a coherent body of writing. By far the most comprehensive account was given by the Spaniard Columella who, in about 65 AD, set out the principles of viticulture with astonishingly confident precision. He recommended methods of staking and density of planting (far more dense than in modern vineyards), and stressed the importance of selecting appropriate locations for different kinds of wine. Columella also costed viticulture in great detail, calculating how many stakes a worker could make in a day, how many workers were required, and even how much it would cost to feed slaves employed in the labour-intensive industry.

Although Columella's assumptions and calculations have been questioned by modern scholars, his work and that of other Roman writers attests to the seriousness with which viticulture was approached. Columella himself was evidently concerned about the quality of wine as much as quantity, and he advised against replacing trusted varietals, such as the aminean grape, with new and exotic vines just because they gave a higher yield.[9]

This is not to say that there was any consensus among Roman viticultural writers on the best techniques and practices. There was disagreement over how many vine-dressers were needed for a vineyard of a certain size and whether vines should be trained on trellises or grown up trees. Cato called for vines to be trained up trees as high as possible so as to expose the grapes to the maximum amount of sunshine, and to the same end he called for leaves to be stripped once the grapes had begun to ripen. Cato also alluded to the importance of soil preparation for the finished wine. To make a laxative wine (wine was often classified by its medical properties) he suggested treating the roots of the vines with black hellebore, old manure and old ashes.[10]

There was also a wide-ranging discussion of the viability of vineyards as an investment. They could, of course, turn immense profits, but harvests were vulnerable to weather and profits could be affected by prices. Abundant harvests could produce a glut of wine and depress prices, while poor harvests were simply unprofitable. In short, viticulture was a high-risk investment of money and land. Cato reckoned that good-quality grape-vines were the most profitable crop for a moderate-sized agricultural property, far ahead of the olive trees which he ranked fourth in the return they provided a proprietor. On the other hand, Varro, another commentator on vines and wine, wrote that 'there are some who consider that a vineyard eats up the money that is spent on it'.[11]

The attraction of potentially high profits from wine was as powerful then as it would so often prove to be, and as demand rose, so did production. Small peasant proprietors making wine for their own consumption with some surplus for market could not possibly satisfy Rome's needs, and the period saw the growth of large-scale vineyards in the region around Rome, most of them relying on slaves for their labour force. Even so, millions of litres of wine were imported to the capital of the empire each year from Greece and other parts of the eastern Mediterranean.

The Romans, whose domestic wine industry originated in Greek plantings, in turn extended viticulture and wine production to those parts of Europe that they dominated. By the first centuries of the Christian period, wine was being produced throughout the Roman Empire wherever climatic and other environmental conditions permitted. The Greeks had introduced wine to their main French colony Massalia (Massilia to the Romans), but it was under Roman dominance that the wine trade and production – especially production – spread throughout Gaul. Even then, much of the trade remained in the hands of Greek merchants. The Romans perceived the Gauls as having a thirst for wine that was as keen as that of traders for profit. In the middle of the first century AD, Diodorus commented: 'The natural greed of many Italian merchants exploits the passion of the Gauls for wine. On boats that follow the navigable rivers or on carts that roll across the plains, they transport their wine which brings them unbelievable profits, going so far as to trade one amphora for one slave, so that the buyer gives up his servant to pay for drink.'[12]

Viticulture was first intensively practised in Gaul in the large province of Narbonensis, a region (with its centre in present-day Narbonne) that covered much of Provence and Languedoc. From there viticulture extended to the Bordeaux region, where vines were first reported in the first century AD. By the early third century vines were planted in Burgundy, and within a few decades vineyards had been established as far north as Alsace. In short, some of the greatest European wine regions were initially planted by Romans. The Romans pushed viticulture as far as Britain, where the climatic conditions were far from ideal for growing wine grapes. There appears to have been a vigorous but short-lived English wine industry that included the manufacture of amphoras.[13] The growth of these provincial wine industries did nothing to help the trade in Italian wine, which went into decline from the first century AD.

At this very time there was a shift in technology as amphoras, the large earthenware jars used for centuries to transport wine and other products, were replaced by other containers. Roman exporters began to ship wine in wooden barrels, the vessels overwhelmingly used for transporting wine until glass bottles began to be widely employed in the twentieth century. Quite why amphoras were abandoned is not clear, but one result is that evidence of the wine trade is much more difficult to find. Amphoras survive thousands of years of burial underground or at sea, but wooden barrels rot and disintegrate without trace.

If shipping methods changed, the basic processes of wine production that had been established in the Middle East persisted in Greece and Rome and, for that matter, in Europe and other parts of the world until quite recent times.

Although treading remained the only way to crush grapes, methods of secondary juice extraction varied. On Crete grapes were pressed under boards weighted with rocks, a technique also used to extract oil from olives. More sophisticated presses, widely used in Greece and Rome, employed heavy beams that were pressed on the grapes by a windlass or screw mechanism. Presses of this kind were too expensive for small producers, of course, and they were found only in the larger, commercial wineries.

It is unclear if the juice obtained from treading was blended with the pressed juice or whether they were fermented separately. The juice obtained by each process had different qualities that were passed on to the wine. Wine produced from the small quantity of juice that ran off before any treading kept longer than most and was often used for medicinal purposes.[14] Wine made from juice obtained by treading (most of the wine) was generally of a high quality and stable, and might last years under favourable conditions. But wines made from pressed juice, which was exposed to more impurities, had a much shorter life. The blending of juices would have lowered the overall quality, stability and longevity of the vintage.

For the most part wine was fermented in sealed amphoras. Small holes permitted carbon dioxide to escape during fermentation, but after the process was complete they were blocked up. The wine was not always racked or filtered, and when it was not it was siphoned or run through a sieve as it was poured out to be consumed. Some Greek wine was fermented in skins (often goat skins), which were carefully filled to allow room for the gases produced during fermentation. The biblical warning against keeping new wines in old skins was essentially a caution that old skins, being less supple than new, might crack and leak under the pressure if used to ferment wine.

Although Egyptian wine-makers appear to have crushed the grapes immediately after picking, many of their Cretan, Greek and Roman counterparts might have added an intermediary stage in order to increase the sugar content of their grapes. The aim was to produce wine that was sweeter, had more alcohol, and was longer-lasting. One technique, leaving the picked grapes to dry in the sun for a week or more, was described in the eighth century BC by Hesiod, but it is not clear whether the aim in this particular case was to dry grapes as raisins or to prepare them for sweet wine:

> . . . when Orion and the Dog Star move
> Into the mid-sky, and Arcturus sees
> The rosy-fingered Dawn, then Perses pluck
> The clustered grapes, and bring your harvest home.
> Expose them to the sun ten days and nights
> Then shadow them for five, and on the sixth
> Pour into jars glad Dionysus' gift.[15]

On Crete the stalks of bunches of grapes were sometimes twisted but left on the vine where, deprived of sap, the grapes would shrivel as their sugar content rose. In Rome, Cato recommended drying grapes in the sun for two to three days, while Virgil advised a different means to the same end of increasing sugar content: leaving grapes on the vine until they were exposed to frost. The products of Virgil's method were the forerunners of modern late-harvest wines.

No one method seems to have been followed to the letter in any two localities. The Greek island of Thasos produced a distinctive red-black coloured wine said to have had an aroma of apples. The grapes were dried in the sun for five days and on the sixth day were plunged into a mixture of boiled grape juice and salt water. They were then pressed, the juice was fermented and, after the wine was racked, a further amount of boiled must was added. This product seems to have satisfied all manner of aesthetic and medicinal needs. Not only was it highly prized as a premium wine in the Greek world, but it was also said to be good for insomnia, to be a successful abortifacient, and, when mixed with vinegar, to be very good for the eyes.

It is likely that most of the wine produced in the ancient world was red, although many of the most highly praised wines were white. When they were portrayed, grapes were almost always black, and grape juice and wine are shown as red or generically dark. Homer's description of the Aegean Sea as being 'wine-dark' is evocative, and descriptions of specific wines generally refer to shades of redness. Some Greek authors mention the production of white (or, more accurately, greenish) wine in Egypt, and it is possible that it was produced there as a result of Greek influence. Many of the most valued wines of Greece and Rome were sweet whites, but they were made in small quantities.

Actual grape juice is always light-coloured, no matter what the colour of the skin or flesh of the grape, and red wine is given its colour in the fermentation process, when the red or black grape skins remain in the fermentation container, in contact with the juice. It is the duration of this contact that largely determines the colour of the finished wine. White wine, on the other hand, is generally fermented without skin contact, and thus retains the off-white colour of the original juice. In most ancient viniculture the juice was not filtered to exclude the residue of the grapes during fermentation, although it might have been racked afterwards. Cato recommended that during the thirty days of fermentation the insides of wine jars should be regularly scraped with brooms made of elm twigs to stop the dregs sticking to the sides. This process was the equivalent of bâtonnage and other methods of ensuring that the lees stay in contact with the must during fermentation. Depending on the grapes used, it should have ensured a darker and more tannic wine. The jars were then sealed until spring, when the wine was racked off into clean amphoras for ageing.

Finally, we should note that 'wine' referred to a number of products in ancient Greece and Rome. It meant not only fermented grape-juice but any of a number of beverages having wine as their base. Cato provided several recipes for 'Greek', 'Coan' (that is, from Cos) and other wines, including this one which he described as suitable 'for the hands to drink through the winter':

Pour into a jar ten quadrantals of must, two quadrantals of sharp vinegar, two quadrantals of boiled must, fifty quadrantals of fresh water. Stir with a stick thrice a day for five consecutive days. Then add sixty-four sextarii of old sea-water, cover the jar, and seal ten days later. This wine will last you until the summer solstice; whatever is left over will be a very sharp and excellent vinegar.[16]

Other recipes involved various additives and processes. In addition to grape-products such as boiled must and old wine, others such as salt, flour, pitch, marble-dust, herbs and spices were all added, in varying quantities and combinations, to provide taste and aroma. In southern Gaul, herbs like thyme and lavender were grown among the vines in the expectation that they would communicate their aromas and flavours to their fruit. In other cases the herbs and spices were steeped in the wine just prior to its being consumed.

Cato and others recommended heating must in copper or lead boilers. The latter was particularly valued because it added sweetness to wine, and even though Vitruvius warned about the harmful effects of lead, it was used in vessels and in glazing for another two thousand years before serious attempts were made to ban its use in wine-making. It is clear that in the ancient world 'wine' was the product of a vast range of decisions that involved greater or lesser degrees of human manipulation of the fundamental processes of vinifying the juice of the vine.

Throughout much of the ancient world before 1000 BC, wine had been a special drink. In many regions cost alone ruled out wine as a rival to the relatively inexpensive grain-based beers that were already widely consumed when wine arrived on the scene. But although there were places where wine might have been produced in larger volumes and at lower costs, the religious and other cultural associations it quickly developed made its exclusivity attractive to the ruling classes. Even where wine was consumed at all social levels, as in ancient Greece, social distinctions were marked by the quality of wine and the contexts in which it was consumed. Distinctions of both sorts have persisted into the present.

It is important to remember that alcoholic drinks were part of the everyday diet of the ancient world, as they have remained in many parts of Europe ever since. Fermented grains, in the form of beer, contributed valuable calories and nutrients, and wine also provided calories and a range of other beneficial properties. But although wine was a useful part of the daily diet, it was not merely an alternative to beer. What made wine more than just another kind of fermented beverage were the cultural properties that were rapidly attributed to it. Wine became integrated into a series of religious and cultural practices and beliefs, and was drawn into debates bearing on the most fundamental aspects of human existence: fertility, life, social relationships, sex, death and the afterlife.

As wine spread throughout the ancient world greater proportions of the population consumed it on a regular basis. Cato proposed that even slaves in chains should have about ten amphoras of wine a year each, about five litres a week. Wine was provided for slaves not for their enjoyment, however, but because it was believed to give them strength. The wine ration of a sick slave, one who could not work and who did not need strength, was reduced by half.

To some extent the social broadening of wine consumption was a result of the spread of viticulture to climatically more favourable regions. Much of the Middle East, eastern Mediterranean and Egypt were quite marginal for viticulture, whereas Greece and Italy provided conditions in which cultivated grapes flourished. In Greece and Italy viticulture and wine-making became a major commercial industry for the first time and wine was produced in quantities that could supply a large market and at prices the mass of the population could afford.

But that is only part of the explanation for what looks like a democratization of wine over time. The expansion of viticulture was not an unconscious process, with vineyards being planted more and more widely simply because conditions were favourable. Increased production was the result of decisions to make wine available to all social groups, for had wine been perceived as a luxury product to be kept in the hands of a few, production could and would have been restricted. Wine production could, after all, have been increased in regions of limited production, as the example of Egypt shows: the Greeks planted more vineyards there when they began to dominate Egypt under the Ptolemiacs. Before that time wine in Egypt had distinct religious connotations and was a sensitive marker of social distinctions, both important considerations in decisions (conscious or otherwise) to limit the supply of wine.

The difference between cultures that restricted wine to their elites and those that did not can largely be explained in economic terms. In Greece, wine was recognized as a profitable area of agriculture and it made economic sense to expand the market. This meant not only developing export markets, as the Greeks did throughout the Mediterranean and beyond, but broadening the domestic market as well. There were, however, limits to economic rationalism for, as we shall see, in both Greece and Rome there was resistance to the idea that some social groups, notably women, should drink. We must also bear in mind that wines were no more equal than individuals in ancient society. Social distinctions were reflected in the wines that were consumed. It scarcely needs pointing out that the well-off drank more expensive and better quality vintages while the masses made do with inferior wine. There were also differences in the circumstances in which wine was consumed and the cultural value attributed to it. All these considerations alert us to the fact that as much as ancient societies reveal to us in words and images about their wine, wine can equally well tell us a great deal about them.

It seems only right that the Greeks, who gave us the word democracy, should have allowed somewhat wider participation in the consumption of wine than any society that preceded them. Wine was consumed at all levels of Greek society, from the most wealthy and powerful to workers and slaves. This equality of wine was suggested by Euripides when he wrote that Dionysus, the Greek god of wine, had given 'the simple gift of wine, the gladness of the grape' to 'rich and poor' alike.[17]

But like individuals in political democracy, some wine-consumers in Greece were more equal than others. The poor very likely drank inferior wine on a daily basis, often what was later known in France as *piquette*, a thin, low-alcohol and frequently bitter solution made by fermenting water added to the skins, stalks and seeds that were left after the final pressing. In contrast, the upper ranks of Greek society drank wine that was sweet, fuller-bodied, more stable and considerably more expensive. The extremes of Greek wine were almost completely different beverages, although both were wine in a limited technical sense.

In Greece, wine was consumed on public occasions, privately at home, and in taverns. Wine-drinking by men of the upper social ranks was institutionalized in the symposium (from the Greek word *symposion*, meaning 'drinking together'), a formalized occasion that took place in private dwellings after the main evening meal. A dozen men, and sometimes twice that number, all wearing garlands on their heads, reclined on couches, drank wine and conversed. They were attended by young boys and entertained by female dancers and musicians. Symposia were idealized as occasions for high-minded discussion of all manner of subjects, but they were sometimes nothing more than boisterous drinking parties where entertainment was more important than conversation and where the drinkers had sex with prostitutes, each other, or the serving boys. These activities were popular themes for decorators of Greek pottery, especially the vessels used at symposia for mixing, serving and drinking wine.

The ideal symposium was a relatively sober affair, not so much despite the centrality of wine but because of it. Symposia began and ended with prayers and libations of wine. In Greece wine was generally not consumed straight but was diluted with water (often sea-water), and one of the first tasks of the host of a symposium, who was known as the symposiarch, was to specify the ratio of water to wine for the group. As a rule wine was poured into water because it was believed to produce a less intoxicating beverage than that produced by pouring water into wine. The two were mixed in a central krater from which boys served the participants. Wine was drunk from a shallow bowl called a *kylix*.

There was no standard strength for the wine, but water-to-wine ratios of 3:1, 5:3 and 3:2 appear to have been common. Given that wine made from dried grapes had a relatively high alcoholic content (perhaps as high as 16 per cent), dilution along these lines would have produced a drink with between five and ten per cent alcohol. Most would have been at the lower end of that range. Even if they had a substantial meal first and then paced their drinking, the participants in a symposium must certainly have become somewhat intoxicated after several hours' drinking and conversation. Depictions of symposia on Greek vases and wine cups sometimes show participants keeling over, holding on to one another for balance, and vomiting.

The centrality of wine in symposia is further shown by the games the participants sometimes played. Some involved inflated wineskins, and in one game a skin was smeared with grease and players had to balance on it. In another game, called *kottabos*, players threw small quantities of wine or wine dregs from their bowls at a bronze disc balanced on top of a pole. The aim was to knock the disc off so that it fell and struck a larger disc fixed halfway down the pole, making it ring like a bell. Sometimes a small saucer was floated in a bowl of water and the wine had to be aimed so as to fill the saucer and sink it.[18] Such games that involved throwing wine away reinforce the sense that the symposium was in part an occasion of conspicuous consumption.

By its very nature the symposium was restricted to the well-off, and by convention it was restricted to males. Those women who were present at symposia were there as accessories, as musicians, servers or prostitutes, and sometimes to tend men who had drunk so much they were ill. Women of the same class as the men who gathered in symposia also drank wine, but there are many suggestions in literature that men did not approve of women drinking wine. A number of Greek writers, all male, alleged that, whereas men diluted wine, women tended to drink it straight, and with predictably unfortunate consequences. Whether or not this is true, it placed women on the same level as barbarians, for the Greeks deplored as uncivilized anyone who did not drink wine in the manner that they themselves did.

Women were often portrayed as drunk in Greek comedies, and drunkenness was seen as the standard female vice. Moreover, the male view that women become dangerously immoral when drunk, a persistent theme in Western culture, was starkly expressed in ancient Greece. It was women who were first attracted to the wine god Dionysus, just as women were prominent in the Bacchic cults in Rome. A further indication of the gendered culture of wine in Greece is evident in an eighth-century BC cemetery in Athens. The graves of men and women were differentiated by the pottery vessels that marked them: men's graves were marked by a krater, while women's were marked by a tall jar appropriate for the storage of foodstuffs.[19]

Wine was even more widely consumed in Rome than in Greece. Archaeologists have discovered large numbers of bars in such cities as Ostia, Pompeii and Herculaneum. Some two hundred bars have been excavated in Pompeii, the major wine-shipping port of Italy where many people involved in the wine industry gathered. The eighty-yard-long block of one street must have been a particularly lively place, for it was the location for no fewer than eight bars.[20]

In the higher social levels the Romans developed their own version of the Greek *symposion*, the *convivium*, an occasion for fellowship in which wine-drinking was central. A formalized occasion like the symposium, the convivium also differed from it in several respects. Food was consumed with the wine, and women sometimes participated as drinkers. Even so, the presence of women was a much debated issue and it was denounced by some writers who argued that married women who drank wine lost their sense of discretion and were more likely to commit adultery. As Juvenal put it, 'When she is drunk, what matters to the Goddess of Love? She cannot tell her groin from her head.'[21]

No matter how socially widespread drinking was in any ancient society, distinctions were carefully made on the basis of class and gender. Rome was the most wine-positive culture of them all, but even in that centre of oenological enlightenment there remained anxieties about the relationship of women to wine. The writings and art of the classical world have told us more about the wine and drinking cultures of the elites than the masses. Yet the vast trade that developed to supply Rome with wine makes it clear that wine was consumed by an increasing proportion of the population, and it seems that consumption rose significantly during the second century BC.

One of the factors involved in this could have been a shift in the Roman diet. The basic foods in the Mediterranean were cereals, the most important in Rome being emmer, a hulled wheat. For centuries most Romans consumed these grains in the form of a gruel or porridge known as *puls*, which was essentially the national dish of Rome. It is thought that there were problems using emmer for bread because the toasting process needed to make the hulls brittle enough to be removed destroyed the gluten-forming proteins that would have allowed emmer flour to rise when leavened. Whether or not that is so, bread made a relatively late appearance as a commonly consumed food in Rome. It might well have been made in homes, but the first bakeries were set up between 171 and 168 BC.[22] The shift from a wet to a dry food as the staple of the Roman diet must go some way to explaining the increased popularity of wine, for it is necessary to wash bread down with a liquid in a way that is not so with a bowl of porridge. From the end of the second century AD, bread and wine were paired in the Roman diet.[23]

At about the same time, the Roman prohibition on women drinking wine seems to have fallen into disuse, and this adds weight to the notion that wine-drinking was linked to a shift in the general diet. Women had been banned from any association with wine, including the pouring of libations for religious purposes, and various laws had allowed a woman caught drinking wine to be put to death or divorced; the last divorce on this ground was granted in 194 BC. There were signs that some men clung to the former prohibition – when the emperor Augustus exiled his daughter to an island he also forbade her access to wine – but they were more the exception than the rule. Women seem to have rallied to their new freedom, a trend that gave Roman moralists many opportunities to deplore the effects of alcohol on society.

When we talk about the expansion of wine-drinking to all classes of Roman society, however, it is important to recognize that the wine was not always what it appeared to be. The wine that Cato provided for his slaves, for example, was a mixture of which must (freshly pressed grape-juice) constituted only about a fifth. Moreover, free labourers in Roman society were unlikely to have been able to afford wine as a normal part of their diet. Instead, there were several wine-based beverages available. One of these was *posca*, which was a mixture of water and sour wine. A careful distinction was made between sour wine and vinegar, for although both were wine that had been attacked by acetobacters, sour wine had not reached the final stage of becoming vinegar and it retained some of the taste qualities of wine. It was less sharp and acidic than vinegar, but it was far lower in alcohol than wine and therefore lacked the ability to intoxicate. This, as well as cost, was an important consideration underlying the supply of posca, rather than wine, to soldiers in the Roman armies. In the Justinian Code, for example, it was posca that was part of the military rations, and it is probable that soldiers received about a litre of it a day.[24]

Soldiers did receive wine when they were sick or wounded, but then it was provided as a medicine, not as a beverage. Soldiers were also able to purchase wine, and it is reported that when Metellus arrived in Africa in 109 BC he found an army that had pillaged the locality so as to get slaves and livestock to exchange for wine. In 38 BC Herod provided wine – as well as oil, grain and cattle – to Roman soldiers besieging Jerusalem after they threatened to mutiny because of the lack of supplies.[25] As we shall see in later chapters, it became military practice to provide wine and other alcoholic beverages to armies because they were safer than water supplies. This was especially so at sieges, when drinking water could easily be contaminated by dead and decaying bodies and by human and animal waste.

The other beverage that was commonly consumed in Rome was *lora*, made from soaking in water the solid residue that remained after all the juice had been squeezed from grapes to make wine. Lora was often provided to slaves in the period after the harvest. Cato reported supplying it to his slaves for the three months after the grapes had been picked, and Varro gave it to his agricultural workers during the winter. In both cases, however, wine was provided for most months of the year.

The means by which lora and posca were made tell us that they tasted entirely different from the wines more widely distributed in Roman Europe and especially from those consumed by the well-to-do. Yet the precise taste of any ancient wine is lost to us: even if an undamaged and sealed amphora full of wine should be discovered, the wine would have broken down long ago. But descriptions of the process of vinification make it clear that if we could sample an ancient wine as it was consumed at the time it would certainly taste quite different from almost all the wines familiar to us today. Moreover, it is by no means always clear what we should consider as 'wine' in the ancient world. Should we try to describe the character of the wine that was stored in the jars and amphoras where it was fermented and conserved, or should we attempt to reconstruct the taste of this wine after it had been diluted with fresh water or sea-water and had various other substances like herbs, spices and honey added to it?

Before we try to answer these questions, it is important to remind ourselves that although wine as it is presented to us today in a bottle has all the appearance of being a natural product, perhaps gently guided one way or another by its maker, wine is also the end result of a series of careful decisions and calculations. This process extends from the planting of vines to the circumstances in which the wine is consumed. Decisions along the way concern grape type, location, irrigation, pruning, crop yield, time of harvesting, method of fermentation, blending, additives, preservatives, barrel-ageing, and time of release for sale. Increasingly, wine-makers try to influence the taste of the wine even after it has left their hands by recommending cellaring periods for better wines and, for many popular wines, a food that will enhance the taste for which the maker aimed. As later chapters will show, wine cultures sometimes lean towards sweeter wines, sometimes towards drier. Wine-makers can influence trends but they also follow them and customize their wines to the prevailing taste of the market.

The wine-makers of Greece and Rome attempted to make wines that suited the sweet preferences of their clients. They maximized the sugar content in their grapes by drying them before fermentation, and afterwards they sweetened wine even more by adding boiled must and honey. One recipe called for almost as much honey as wine to be blended together. The result must have been viscous in its texture, but with that amount of honey the taste would very much have depended on the type of blossoms and flowers from which the bees had gathered pollen. Even though words like 'sweet' and 'light' are relative, and we have no reliable points of comparison, a mixture that was half honey and half wine would undoubtedly have occupied the sweet end of the spectrum.

The addition of salt-water to wine before drinking cut the sweetness to some extent by increasing acidity. As Pliny put it, sea-water was used 'to enliven a wine's sweetness',[26] which we might understand as concentrating the sweetness and perhaps promoting a wine's fruitiness, but removing the sickly sweet edge that ingredients like honey might have imparted. The wines purchased by the masses and provided for slaves were probably not as sweet as those loved by the upper classes. Cato's recipe for wine suitable for workers (above) would have produced a thin, low-alcohol and pale wine, and bulk-produced wines must generally have been thinner and less alcoholic. Herbs and spices that were added must have enhanced the taste, and they must also have helped to conceal evidence that a wine was deteriorating.

Some Greek and Roman wines also picked up flavours from the pitch and resin that was sometimes used to coat the insides of earthenware jars to ensure that they were impermeable. Resin was not only a reasonably effective preservative but it also gave a flavour that was considered pleasant (or at least it concealed unpleasant ones). Even when it was not used to seal earthenware it was sometimes included in the fermenting wine for these other purposes. This practice was recommended by Pliny, but Columella advised against using resin in good-quality wine. Resin is still used in some Greek wine, known as retsina, to give a characteristic taste.

Sweetness was also added by the use of lead. Some recipes recommended boiling must in vessels made of lead, while others specified the addition of lead compounds to wine. The lead-based glazes would also have contaminated wines that they held. Lead not only sweetened but also preserved wine by killing the bacteria that could break it down.

Lead also poisoned many of those who drank the wine, of course, although outbreaks of lead poisoning in the ancient world appear to have been localized.

It is very difficult to reconstruct tastes from the descriptions given in historical sources. Words are often inadequate as a means of conveying sensations among contemporaries and they are even less successful in communicating them across millennia. For the most part, Greeks and Romans who commented on specific wines tended to locate them on the two spectrums of sweetness and strength. Wines were more or less sweet and more or less strong, and on the whole classical connoisseurs liked strong, sweet vintages. We can assume that the point of reference for sweetness was honey, and indeed some wines were described as being 'honey-sweet'. Other than sweetness and strength, commentators noted, with pleasure or otherwise, the flavours imparted by additives, such as herbs and salt-water, and other substances the wine was exposed to, including resin and pitch. Overall, however, the vocabulary of ancient wine-tasting was very limited. Many of the aromas that appear in the vocabulary of wine-tasters and on modern aroma wheels (like chocolate, pineapple, diesel and tobacco) were simply unknown to the connoisseurs of the ancient world.

Classical wine commentators were none the less aware of aroma and colour. Depth of colour was appreciated, and we can assume that an association was made between the depth of a wine's colour and its strength. Relatively few ancient writers mentioned aroma or bouquet, but it was a recognized quality. Cato provided a recipe for imparting a 'sweet aroma' to wine: add to the fermenting jar a tile that had first been smeared with pitch and covered with warm ashes, aromatic herbs, rush and 'the palm that the perfumers keep'.[27] Aroma was perhaps more important as indicating that a wine had gone off, and Cato also provided a recipe for removing a bad odour from wine.

One of the limitations on our ability to imagine the taste of ancient wine is that we do not know which varieties of grapes were used. Greek and Roman writers sometimes referred to specific grapes, but there is no way of matching them with modern varieties. Pliny, for example, wrote that one Egyptian wine was a blend of the Thasian grape, the soot-grape and the pine-tree grape,[28] but, as informative as this might have been to his contemporary readers, it is little help to us. Our ignorance of the character of many classical grape types is a real obstacle to understanding the qualities of wine in this period.

Greek and Roman wine-drinkers themselves were aware of variations in taste and they translated them into taste preferences. A number of scholars produced lists of wines with commentaries on each one. Perhaps the likes of Pliny the Elder were the Robert Parkers of the ancient world, awarding Caecuban wine XCVI marks and Falernian wine XC marks out of C, guiding drinkers toward certain vintages, and perhaps contributing to the development of taste preferences. Perhaps they, too, had the effect of driving up the prices of some wines by stimulating demand for them. There was also some recognition that there was a correlation between the quality of wines and their age, although it is not clear whether this was an appreciation that wine improved as it aged or that only good wine had the ability to age. Age is, of course, relative, and Romans would not have expected wines to age for decades, as we expect of varietals like cabernet sauvignon and blends like bordeaux. When Ulpian asked the question, 'What is old wine?' he answered that it is any wine that derived from the previous year.[29] This effectively meant that a wine had survived the summer heat, and we would expect it to have done that because it was high in alcohol, acid or tannins. Athenaeus gave the optimum age of the best wines as lying between five and twenty-five years, but the upper range seems optimistic for the period. Even so, aged quality wines commanded higher prices than new ordinary vintages. An edict of the emperor Diocletian in 301 AD set the price of ordinary wine at eight deniers a setier, and old wine at between sixteen and twenty-four deniers a setier.[30]

In the rankings that have come down to us, wines were classified by broad region, rather than more precisely by locality, individual proprietor or wine-maker, or year. The refinement of ranking wines from individual properties and smaller localities was largely a seventeenth- and eighteenth-century development. In Greece, Mareotic wine from Egypt was widely praised, despite the suggestion by Horace that Cleopatra had become crazed under its influence. Athenaeus thought that Taeniotic wine, produced southwest of Alexandria, was even better than Mareotic; it was pale, pleasant, aromatic and slightly astringent, with an oily quality that dissolved when gradually diluted with water. Pliny praised the wine of Sebennys in the central Nile Delta.

There was clearly a hierarchy of Greek wines, and some regions jealously guarded their reputation. The rulers of the island of Thasos, off the coast of Thrace in the north of the Aegean Sea, set down in the fifth century BC regulations designed to ensure the quality of the wine which was then widely reputed to be the second best Greek wine (after those of Chios). Thasian wines were described as heavy and sweet. They had a high alcoholic content (possibly as high as 18 per cent) as a result of a vinification process that included drying grapes in the sun and boiling the must. The regulations, unparalleled elsewhere, governed the sale and transportation of Thasian wine. It was to be sold only in containers of a specified size (Thasos was also a major producer of amphoras), and it could not be watered down before sale. Consumers were expected to dilute it to their own taste. Moreover, Thasian ships were forbidden to carry non-Thasian wine, a measure designed either to limit competition or to minimize confusion in consumers' minds as to the origin of the wine they bought.[31]

It is possible that all these regulations were a reaction to competition. Although Thasian wine was highly prized, its reputation declined in the fourth and third centuries as wines from places like Rhodes, Cos, Lesbos and Skiathos rose in prominence. By the second century BC, Thasos was starting to decline as a wine-producer, and within four centuries its wine industry had effectively disappeared. The rise and fall of the wines of Thasos clearly show not only the existence of a market concerned for quality, but also shifts in taste. The wine-producing regions of Greece must have fought for their market share as keenly as regional and national producers do today.

As in Greece, so in Rome there was a ranking of wines that linked quality to region. Initially Romans preferred Greek wines, but eventually they began to appreciate wines made on their own peninsula, particularly those from Latium and Campania, the coastal regions to the south of Rome. Strabo, writing at about the time of Christ, provided a wide-ranging assessment of wines from Turkey in the east to Portugal in the west, but he drew on the accounts of others as well as on his own experience. Among the wines Strabo praised were those from Turkey and the Aegean islands (especially Cos, Chios and Lesbos), but he was less kind to those from Liguria (mixed with pitch) and Libya (too much salt-water). Most of the wines he praised were from southern Italy.[32]

One of the Italian wines ranked high on Strabo's list was a legendary wine that hailed from the Falernum vineyard on the border of Latium and Campania. There are references to the exquisite character of the wine and to the spectacular Falernian vintage of 121 BC, known as Opimian, after Opimius, who was consul in that year. Opimian wine was clearly a byword among Roman connoisseurs. In his *Satyricon*, Petronius has a banquet host bring out wine bottles labelled 'Falernian. Consul Opimius. One hundred years old.' Clearly Petronius expected his audience to understand the reference. In the bar of Hedonus, one of Pompeii's many taverns, the wine list posted on the wall offered wine for one *as* (a unit of currency), the best wine for two *as*, and Falernum for four *as*.[33] In a system where there were no controls on production, merchandizing and labelling, expensive wine fraudulently described as Falernian must often have passed down gullible Roman throats.

In the first century of the Christian era, Pliny the Elder provided Romans with a veritable catalogue of wines from various parts of their Empire in his *Natural History*.[34] His list included ninety-one varieties of wine, fifty kinds of quality wine and thirty-eight varieties of foreign wines, as well as a range of other salted, sweet and artificial wines. Pliny's list is notable for its comments on particular varietals, a shift from the usual emphasis on provenance. He preferred the varieties of the aminean vine, followed by nomentian and apiana, all of which he described as being indigenous to Italy. But Pliny also ranked wines by their region of production, both in Italy and elsewhere.

It is notable that when wines were ranked according to quality and taste, reds and whites were compared to one another without distinction. Although most wine in the ancient world was red, simply because skins remained in the fermentation vats, many of the wines most prized by Romans were sweet whites. They were usually aged two or three years and allowed to maderize, that is, to oxidize in warmer temperatures than wine was normally conserved at. This was often achieved by storing the wine in lofts above hearths. The process gave the wines a darker colour, and the famous Falernian wines were described as amber or brown when they had matured. As for taste, Pliny described wines as coming in three varieties: dry, sweet and light.

Even so, taste was not everything in ancient wine-judging, for some of the scholars who drew up tasting lists of the best wines were doctors who assessed wines as much for their purported medicinal properties as for the pleasure they gave the senses. Athenaeus, although not a doctor, followed the tradition by describing Mareotic wine, a white produced near Alexandria, as: 'excellent, white, pleasant, fragrant, easily assimilated, thin, not likely to go to the head, and diuretic'.[35] It is not easy to imagine modern tasting notes or the back labels on wine bottles recommending a wine for its diuretic or laxative properties. As for the quality of 'not going to the head', it might mean that the wine in question was low either in tannins (which contain histamines) or in alcohol. The perceived positive aspects of wine in relation to health are explored further below.

Greek literature abounded as much with commentaries on the social benefits of wine as with warnings on its harmfulness when consumed excessively. One argument often made was that drinking wine in a symposium led men to be more transparent and truthful, and there were as many ways as writers of expressing the oenophile's aphorism 'in vino veritas' ('in wine there is truth'). The early Hellenistic writer Philochorus put it this way: 'People who are drinking wine reveal not only their inner being but also everything else, observing no restriction of speech.'[36] For Aeschylus, 'Bronze reflects the appearance; wine is the mirror of the soul.'[37] In the symposium men were expected to be truthful and frank and to talk without dissembling or taking account of tactical considerations and opportunism. It was an occasion of mutual respect and acceptance of ideas and opinions, and wine was the medium through which this was achieved.[38]

Greek writers praised their civilized symposiums as the epitome of civility, as occasions where men exercised self-control and drank just enough to enliven conversation. Like sexual comportment, behaviour with respect to alcohol has long been a way of suggesting morality or immorality among different nations, genders, social classes, religions and political groups. Wine, portrayed as a more 'civilized' form of alcohol than beer or spirits, has often been a specific reference in these discourses, whether they took place in the ancient world or the nineteenth and twentieth centuries.

The Greeks certainly used wine and drinking customs as a measure of civilization: consuming wine in the Greek manner – diluted, in company, and only to the point of modest inebriation (the way Greeks liked to see themselves) – were marks of civility. Drinking beer, consuming wine without mixing it with water, and drinking any alcohol excessively, were signs of incivility at best, undiluted barbarity at worst. Needless to say, this meant that the inebriation of well-off men at symposia had to be distinguished from crass drunkenness by ordinary folk. The former might be a necessary implication of a civilized and finely regulated occasion, while the latter demonstrated nothing more than deplorable inability to hold liquor.

Whole peoples believed to abuse alcohol – like Thracians, Scythians and Macedonians – could thus be written off as uncivilized, and prominent individuals could be portrayed as accurately representative of their people. The Macedonian leaders Alexander the Great and his father, Philip II, both accurately reputed to have been heavy drinkers, made excellent targets. Philip was likened to a sponge and was said to be drunk every day, including the days he led his troops into battle. It did not help that Philip was said to have forced Greek captives to labour, chained, in his vineyards.[39] For his part, Alexander was prone to bouts of drinking that rendered him unpredictable, violent and homicidal.[40] Justin reported that Alexander 'often left a banquet stained with the blood of his companions', and that he had killed his friend Clitus in a drunken quarrel.[41]

Greek writers frequently couched their discussion of drinking in terms of the dilution of wine: how much was harmful depended upon the strength of the wine. Euenus put it this way: 'The best measure of Bacchus is that which is neither great nor very little, for he is the cause of either grief or madness. He likes to be mixed as a fourth with three Nymphs, and then he is readiest for the marriage-chamber, too. But if he blow strong, he turns his back on love, and plunges us into sleep, the neighbour of death.' This is a recommendation for diluting one part of wine in three of water, a mixture said to be most conducive to love-making. Stronger than that and wine makes the drinker too tired for sexual activity.[42] Other Greek writers followed a similar line of argument. One suggested that finishing the first krater of wine was healthy for the participants at a symposium, drinking the second made them fit for making love, drinking the third put them to sleep, while the fourth so relaxed inhibitions that it opened the way to unspecified immoral behaviour.

The potentially harmful effects of excessive drinking were the subject of much Greek writing. Homer had Elpenor, one of the companions of Ulysses, get drunk and fall from a roof with fatal consequences. To reinforce the point he had Polyxenos, who was portrayed as habitually drunk, slip and die on a wet road after a bout of heavy drinking. In the fifth century BC Plato set out guidelines for correct behaviour with respect to wine. No wine should be consumed by anyone under the age of eighteen, and people in their twenties should drink moderately and avoid drunkenness. Individuals in their forties could drink as much as they wanted 'in order to relieve the desiccation of old age'.[43] Anyone whose professional performance would be impaired by drinking wine – soldiers, helmsmen and judges were examples that Plato gave – should stick to water. Slaves should not attempt to match their master's drinking, for to do so implied arrogance. Finally, couples wishing to have children should abstain from alcohol during the night they planned to conceive.[44] This might be sound advice, at least for the male involved, but it deviated from the more common association of wine with sexual activity and fertility.

Although Plato generally condemned drunkenness because it produced an anti-rational state, in his *Laws* he suggested that there might be benefits in older people drinking to the point of intoxication. Drunkenness, he argued, was a means by which the old could recapture their youthful spontaneity. When their inhibitions were relaxed they would dance and sing. More to Plato's point, however, was that the return to a kind of childishness rendered the old more open to learning. Drunkenness might be a means to make the old, who were otherwise resistant to changing their ways of thinking and acting, more susceptible to becoming more virtuous.[45]

Plato's advice was more cautious than that of many of his compatriots, but it was nowhere near as restrictive as the regulations applied in Sparta under the governance of Lycurgus. Abstinence from alcohol was only one unpleasant element in the regime of muscular masculinity for which Sparta has become the byword. From time to time *helots*, the serf under-class of Sparta, were given undiluted wine in sufficient quantities to get them roaring drunk, after which they were paraded into the city and encouraged to sing obscene songs and perform indecent dances. The purpose of this was to give Spartan youth a horrifying graphic impression of the adverse effects of alcohol on personal and social behaviour. Yet Sparta and other societies and religions that over time have prohibited alcohol represent a minority extreme position on wine and alcohol. Total abstention from alcohol has often been derided. Demosthenes was much criticized and ridiculed by his political opponents for giving up wine in favour of water.

The widespread consumption of wine in Rome speaks of a positive attitude towards wine rather than a merely tolerant one. Moderate quantities of wine, mixed with water of course, were widely viewed by Roman social and medical commentators as beneficial. There were, of course, warnings as to the personal and social consequences of over-indulgence, and there was particular opposition to wine-drinking by women. One Roman myth made a hero of a certain Egnatius Mecenius, who was supposed to have beaten his wife to death with a stick for having drunk some wine. This deed earned him the praise of Romulus, one of the founders of Rome.[46] Another story concerned a woman who was condemned to death by starvation by her family because she opened the purse containing the keys to the wine cellar.[47] True or not, such accounts convey unambiguous opposition to the principle of women drinking wine.

Consuming wine in these cases might have been fatal, but wine was not the actual cause of death. Romans were warned, however, that wine could lead to many ailments and problems, and even death. Lucretius for one argued that wine's fury disturbed the soul, weakened the body and provoked quarrels, while Seneca wrote that wine revealed and magnified defects in the character of the drinker. Pliny the Elder, while praising quality wines, warned that many of the truths spoken under the influence of wine were better unspoken.

For evidence that excessive drinking was frowned upon in Rome, we need only look at the way that allegations of it were frequently used to discredit political opponents. Cicero in particular was fond of labelling his rivals drunkards. He alleged that Mark Antony, his main enemy, led a dissolute life at home and started drinking early each morning. To illustrate the general point, Cicero constantly reminded people of the occasion when, supposedly as a result of drinking to excess, Mark Antony had vomited in the senate. What gave allegations of riotous drunkenness resonance in Rome was that such behaviour was associated with uncivilized peoples such as the Gauls and, especially, those living beyond the Mediterranean world. Some of those peoples, called Barbarians by the Romans, would later invade the Empire, and it would be alleged that their immorality included a tendency towards drunkenness. For the Romans, as for the Greeks, wine and the social forms of its consumption were criteria of morality and civilization.

Besides being a marker of culture, wine was also attributed therapeutic and health-giving properties. The modern debates on the role of wine in promoting health and causing disease began in the ancient world. On the one hand wine was widely described as part of a healthy lifestyle, a substance that promoted physical and emotional well-being. More cynically, perhaps, wine was portrayed as staving off unhappiness by acting as a more or less effective anaesthetic against the troubles the world inflicted on people. Using wine to cope with depression and grief is not a strategy that would attract a lot of support from modern doctors and therapists, but Euripides has a character express the view that Dionysus had done immense good 'by inventing liquid wine as his gift to man':

> . . . For filled with that good gift
> suffering mankind forgets its grief; from it
> comes sleep; with it the oblivion of the troubles
> of the day. There is no other medicine for misery.[48]

Yet throughout the ancient world wine, alone or in conjunction with other substances, was believed to have curative properties, particularly for gastric and urological problems. The apostle Paul, for example, advised Timothy: 'You should give up drinking only water and have a little wine for the sake of your digestion and the frequent bouts of illness that you have.'[49] Cato wrote that the flowers of certain plants (such as juniper and myrtle) soaked in wine were effective against such ailments as snake-bite, constipation, gout, indigestion and diarrhoea.[50] He set out recipes for specific wines to treat a number of such ailments. For laxative purposes hellebore should be added to wine as well as to the roots of the vine; to aid in the retention of urine, old wine and juniper should be boiled in a lead vessel; for 'gripes, loose bowels, for tapeworms and stomach-worms, if troublesome', strong wine should be mixed with acidic pomegranates. Wine could also be used for diagnostic purposes. In Sparta wine was prohibited as a drink, as we have seen, but it was used to detect epilepsy: newborn children were dipped into undiluted wine and it was believed that those having epilepsy would go into convulsions.

Hippocrates, whose writings are the basis of the western medical tradition, commented extensively on the relationship of various types of wine and digestion. He noted that 'wine is hot and dry, and it is something purgative from its original substance'. Among different wines Hippocrates noted that 'dark and harsh wines are more dry, and they pass well neither by stool nor by urine, nor by spittle'. Rather more productive were 'soft dark wines . . . they are flatulent and pass better by stool', and 'harsh white wines . . . [that] pass better by urine than by stool'.[51] The relationship between wine and digestion became a principle of Western medicine, as did the notion that wine was 'hot'. This was important in those ages, extending to within the last couple of centuries, when the body was understood as containing hot and cold elements that needed to be treated appropriately. Wine benefited not only ailing humans but also animals. It was included in preparations for sick oxen and to prevent sheep getting scabies. Wine was, in short, an essential item in the medical and veterinary dispensary of the ancient world as much as an indispensable element of its secular and religious cultures.

Yet if wine could calm troubled spirits it also had the potential for harming the body. Among the wine-related ailments enumerated by Seneca and Pliny were memory loss, identity confusion, narcissistic self-indulgence, anti-social behaviour, impaired speech and vision, a distended stomach, halitosis, quivering, vertigo, insomnia and sudden death.[52] Nor was substantial wine consumption thought to be part of a good diet for an athlete. In the second century Epictetus noted that successful Olympic competitors avoided desserts and cold water and drank wine only sparingly, rather than when they felt like it. Philostratos noted that athletes who drink too much wine 'have an excessive paunch . . . [and] too much drinking is discovered by a fast pulse'.[53]

Finally, wine was endowed with important religious associations in the classical world. It was in Greece that the most enduring connotations of this sort emerged, with the spread of the cult of Dionysus or, as he was known later in Rome, Bacchus. According to some accounts,

Dionysus was the son of the god Zeus and the mortal Semele. Zeus was tricked into burning Semele while Dionysus was still in her womb, but Zeus rescued him and implanted him in his own thigh until he was born. Later Dionysus was expelled from his home on Crete and fled to Egypt, and it was there he learned the art of viniculture with which he became identified. The story parallels the probable transfer of viticultural techniques and viniculture from Egypt to Crete.

In Rome, Bacchus was widely celebrated and a cult centred on him had emerged in central and southern Italy by the third century BC, but it is not clear how strong his actual following was. Members of the cult, most of whom were women, held festivals (called Bacchanalia) that were often portrayed by outsiders as sexual orgies punctuated by animal sacrifices. In 186 BC the Roman senate banned the cult, an act often attributed to a moral position against the activities said to take place at Bacchanalia. The probable reason for the ban, however, was the senate's perception that the cult of Bacchus was a form of protest against the Roman authorities. The structure of Bacchic cells, with their oaths of loyalty, their hierarchical structure, their funding and property, cut across officially accepted patterns of family and political authority. It was very likely this, more than any supposed drunkenness, orgiastic rituals or criminal activities, that provoked the ban.[54]

Within the wine-friendly Roman Empire existed ethnic and other groups in whose religions wine played distinct roles. One was the Jews, for whom the vine was so prominent among God's creations that it came to represent the land of Israel. In the Torah wine is portrayed as one of the first agricultural products in the era after the Great Flood. The book of Genesis relates that after his Ark had come to rest on Mount Ararat, Noah set about cultivating the land. He planted vineyards, made wine, and drank sufficient quantities that he took off his clothes and lay naked in his tent.[55] Grapes were also prominent in accounts of the Jewish migration from slavery in Egypt to Israel. Moses sent men to reconnoitre the land of Canaan, and they returned after four days with a cluster of grapes so big that it had to be carried on a pole between two men, as well as some figs and pomegranates. When they returned they reported to Moses that the land was flowing with milk and honey, and that 'this is its produce'.[56] The vine is mentioned in the Bible more than any other plant, and it represents the gifts God promised humans. Whenever prophets threaten that God will punish his people, they cite the vine and wine as benefits that will be withheld or destroyed: 'you will . . . press the grape but never drink wine from it,'[57] and 'wail, you vinedressers . . . the vine has withered.'[58]

But although Jews saw wine as God-given, they portrayed it negatively when it was abused. In some cases it was linked to illicit sex, as in the case of Lot. After Lot's wife was turned to a pillar of salt, his daughters plied their father with wine so that he would sleep with them, and in due course they became pregnant. Yet other biblical passages are critical of wine for its effects on behaviour: 'wine is reckless, strong drink quarrelsome; unwise is he whom it seduces,'[59] and 'these, too, are reeling with wine, staggering from strong drink. Priest and prophet are reeling from strong drink, they are muddled with wine.'[60] The prophet Hosea includes in God's complaints against Israel the allegation that 'wine, new wine, addles the wits.'[61]

There were Jewish sects that were opposed to any consumption of wine, including the Rechabites, who adopted nomadic practices in emulation of the first Jewish tribes. A nomadic existence ruled out the possibility of cultivating grapes, needless to say, but the Rechabites went further and prohibited their followers from consuming wine at all. Such sects were, however, exceptions to the generally tolerant and positive attitudes of Jews towards wine. The Jewish tradition carried over to the Christian religion, and a rich stream of wine runs through the New Testament. The vine and grapes are the most common plants and fruit referred to, and there is evidence of a more tolerant attitude towards wine than in the Old Testament, perhaps a reflection of Greek influence. Although the Bible contains many warnings about the secular and spiritual consequences of excessive drinking, it was only much later that schools of Christian thought called for total abstinence from wine and other forms of alcohol.

The first miracle that Christ performed involved wine – the turning of water into wine at the wedding at Cana. When the wine ran out Christ's mother hinted that he might do something about it, and after some hesitation Christ ordered servants to fill six jars with water. When they drew some off to take it to their master, they discovered that it had turned to wine. This was not just ordinary wine, but apparently of high quality, for the steward praised the bridegroom, saying, 'People generally serve the best wine first, and keep the cheaper sort till the guests have had plenty to drink; but you have kept the best wine till now.'[62] Not only does this story highlight the place of wine in festivities, but it speaks to the contemporary practice of serving the best wine first, when it can be appreciated by fresh palates.

Christ himself is not depicted drinking wine, but his words at the Last Supper imply that he had drunk wine even though he was on that occasion abstaining: 'I tell you solemnly, I shall not drink any more wine until the day I drink new wine in the kingdom of God.'[63] It has been suggested that Christ did drink wine in the hours before his death, for the Roman soldiers offered him what was variously described as vinegar and 'wine mixed with gall' as he hung on the cross, perhaps an anaesthetic proffered as a humanitarian gesture. It is likely that what the soldiers had to offer was not wine but posca, the mixture of water and sour wine that was part of Roman military rations.

Wine became integral to Christian theology, ritual and tradition. In the Eucharist wine came to represent the blood of Christ, just as it had represented blood in earlier religions: 'This is my blood, the blood of the covenant, which is to be poured out for many.'[64] There were many similarities between the representations of Bacchus and Christ. Both were born of a god and a mortal woman. By the time of Christ, Bacchus had become a saviour figure having the power to grant life after death. Christ's miracle of turning water to wine echoed one of the feasts that was distinctive of Bacchus. For the Greeks, drinking wine was drinking the god, a belief echoed in the Christian Eucharist.

The adoption and adaptation of symbols and stories of Bacchus by Christians testifies to the continuing importance of the wine god in the early Christian period. From some perspectives, Christ became a new wine god, and in the first Christian centuries there is ample evidence of confusion among pagans and Christians alike. A fifth-century mosaic from Cyprus shows a child, his head lit by a halo, sitting on a lap and surrounded by worshippers. At first glance it is a classic example of the 'Adoration of the Magi', the Christ-child on Mary's lap. The infant portrayed in the mosaic, however, is Dionysus, sitting in the lap of Eros.

The Christian Church became a stalwart of wine and an important sponsor of viticulture and wine-making. Even if their role was not as critical as often thought, monasteries were important centres for wine-production in the Middle Ages. In parts of Germany during the early Christian period, beer was banned and wine-drinking was seen as a sign of conversion. There is a clear religious echo here of the secular Greek and Roman notion that pagans and barbarians drink beer but civilized (or pious) peoples drink wine. In some cases, however, Christians rallied too enthusiastically to wine, and this too was associated with pagans. In the fifth century Saint Jerome described a drunk Christian woman as behaving like a pagan, while Salvien, a priest of Marseilles, accused some Christians of drinking like unbelievers.[65]

Wine, then, occupied a place in many dimensions of the ancient and classical world: religious, dietary, medical, cultural, social and economic. These cultures, ranging from Mesopotamia and Egypt to Greece and Rome, were like a series of vast fermentation vats in each of which the juice of the grape comes into contact with a different combination of political and social structures, religious beliefs and economic imperatives. In each case, the result was a different wine, one that bore unique cultural qualities. The ancient world thus established the principle that would flow through the later history of wine: that in its fullest sense wine is not only the product of a natural process, or of the winemaker's skill. It is also a construction of the society in which it is produced and consumed. The Roman aphorism *in vino veritas* might equally well be rendered *in vino societas*.

THREE

WERE THE 'DARK AGES' THE DRY AGES?

Europe 500–1000 AD

By the first centuries of the Christian era, wine-production had spread throughout much of Europe, from Crete in the south to England in the north, and from Portugal in the west to Poland in the east. Wine had also achieved a significant cultural position. It was privileged in Christian doctrine and ritual, and the adoption of Christianity as the state religion of the Roman Empire served to put the status of wine on an even firmer basis. This religious association clearly had some impact on secular attitudes towards wine, but we should not overstate its religious associations as the driving force behind the expansion of wine and its popularity. It symbolized the blood of Christ, but it was also a profitable commercial product, and that alone must go a long way to explaining the extension of vineyards and wine-production.

Moreover, if wine had spiritual connotations that gave it a particular cultural status, it was also pleasant to drink, gave its consumers a sense of well-being, and made for convivial social occasions, and those qualities were evidently attractive to many of its consumers. Modern wine-drinkers will recognize these sentiments, and the explanations of the enduring popularity of wine through the Middle Ages and beyond might be just that banal: that wine was enjoyable on many levels. In many areas where it was produced, wine began to replace beer as an important part of the daily diet.

The collapse of the western half of the Roman Empire under the impact of Germanic invasions seemed to threaten the status that wine had attained. The impact of the Germanic tribes on wine production and consumption in Europe has often been distorted, however, largely because of the prejudiced records left to us by the Romans whose empire they effectively destroyed. The Roman ruling classes (like the Greeks before them) were terrible wine snobs. Not only did they set themselves off from their social inferiors by the types of wine they drank and the circumstances in which they drank it, but they judged foreigners harshly because of their preferred alcoholic drinks and their alleged drinking habits. The general rules applied by the Greek and Roman upper classes were that peoples were uncivilized if they did not drink wine, if they drank wine but did so straight instead of diluting it with water, or if they drank excessive amounts of whatever it was they did drink. Various groups were labelled uncivilized for these reasons: the Greeks identified Scythians, Macedonians and Thracians, while the Romans pointed to the Germanic tribes that lived in the farthest reaches of the Empire and beyond its borders.*

In the eighteenth century Edward Gibbon, the great historian of the decline and fall of the Roman Empire, re-stated the Roman prejudices. He described the ancient Germans as 'immoderately addicted' to 'strong beer, a liquor extracted with very little art from wheat or barley, and *corrupted* . . . into a certain semblance of wine'. The resulting concoction was 'sufficient for the gross purposes of German debauchery'. Oddly, however, Gibbon credited these crude Germans with an almost instinctive attraction to fine wine: 'those who tasted the rich wines of Italy, and afterwards Gaul, sighed for that one delicious species of intoxication.' Here, indeed, lay one of the reasons for the barbarian invasions of western Europe for, according to Gibbon, the Germans would rather obtain what they wanted – in this case, wine – by force than by honest work: 'The intemperate thirst of strong liquors often urged the barbarians into the provinces on which art or nature had bestowed those much envied presents.'[1]

The invasion of the western Empire by these tribes from the fifth century thus seemed to herald bad news for wine. The barbarians lusted for wine yet lacked the discipline and patience that was needed to produce it. Would western Europe's new unruly rulers ruin the vineyards so painstakingly established by the civilized Romans? Would they adopt

---

* The German 'barbarians' seem, in turn, to have been beer snobs. When they first encountered wine they were profoundly suspicious of it. According to Caesar, they initially resisted the importation of wine into their territories out of fear that men who drank it would become effeminate.

a laissez-faire attitude towards them? Or would they – contrary to expectations – promote the expansion of wine?

It is difficult to describe the impact of the Germanic tribes on wine production, largely because records on viticulture in this period are very patchy. If there were adverse effects, however, it was unlikely to have been the direct result of wilful neglect or deliberate damage to vineyards. If the most negative portrayal of Germanic drinking habits were accurate (perhaps *especially* if it were accurate), we should surely have expected the new arrivals to have promoted wine production rather than reduce it. Indeed, during the turmoil and sporadic invasions of Germanic tribes between the third and fifth centuries, viticulture in Europe not only flourished but continued to spread. It was in this period that vineyards were consolidated in many regions: along the Mosel near Trier, for example, and in the valleys of the Seine, Yonne and Loire rivers.[2] Yet the kinds of evidence we would like to have in order to confirm the vibrancy of wine production and trade are too often missing. The replacement of amphoras by wooden barrels in the first century might have had advantages for shippers, but it was a real disservice to historians.

But the evidence, as sparse as it is, leads us to believe that there were continuities and even some regional growth in viticulture during the centuries that the various tribes vied for control of Europe. For one thing, the barbarians seem to have supported wine production. Visigothic law codes, for example, set out severe punishments for anyone found guilty of damaging vineyards. In Portugal the Gothic king Ordono (who ruled from 850) granted vineyards near Coimbra to a monastic order.[3] Such examples suggest that the rulers who replaced the Romans took care to protect vineyards and that rather than the monasteries protecting wine production from the barbarians, the barbarians actually increased the Church's holdings.

In Saxon England there were many signs of a positive view of wine, but unambiguous evidence of vineyards is rare and the best evidence of English vineyards derives from the late eleventh century, when many vineyards were planted by the conquering Normans. Earlier, in the eighth century, Bede referred to vineyards in some parts of England, but his reliability is open to question: he also insisted that there were vineyards in Ireland, a region where there almost certainly were none at all. An apparent indication that vines were cultivated in England during the

Early Middle Ages lies in the laws issued by King Alfred in the ninth century. One of these laws seems to specify that anyone who damaged a vineyard had to pay full compensation, and the point has sometimes been made that such a law would hardly have been issued had there been no vineyards to damage. The reference to vineyards is not part of Alfred's laws, however, but comes from the preamble, which quotes from the Bible in order to reinforce the principle of compensation.[4]

Evidence of English vineyards is more secure in the tenth century. Alfred's great-grandson, King Eadwig, granted vineyards in Somerset to the monks of Glastonbury Abbey in 956, and King Edgar gave a vineyard and its vine-growers to Abingdon Abbey.[5] The fact that there were any vineyards at all at least opens the possibility that there were more that were unrecorded, and it certainly weakens the argument that vineyards were absent from England because of its climate. Moreover, if it is true that vineyards had been planted in England in Roman times, there is no reason to think they disappeared between then and the Norman Conquest. Not only is there strong evidence of the continuity and expansion of viticulture in continental Europe in this period, but the climate was probably warmer and drier and thus conducive to vine-growing in regions as far north as England.

In addition, the Saxons seem to have held wine in good esteem. *Aelfric's Colloquy*, a seventh-century Anglo-Saxon text, echoed many classical attitudes: 'wine is not the drink for children or the foolish, but for the older and wiser.' Contemporary recipes included wine, and Saxons prepared chicken stewed in wine for invalids, as well as apples and other fruit marinated or stewed in wine. Wine was also among the provisions left for the dead to feast on.[6]

The Vikings, whose reputation for plundering is among the worst, also seem to have had positive attitudes towards wine. In the northern Frankish river settlements they developed permanent commercial interests that offset their better-known hit-and-run economic activities. In addition to consuming much of the produce themselves, they participated in the northern Frankish wine trade, controlling the traffic down the rivers to ports from where wine was shipped to destinations like England.[7] In the Carolingian Empire that dominated western Europe from the late eighth century, wine was the drink of the upper classes and great men boasted of the quality of their wine. Powerful rulers in the German provinces tried to acquire land in the Paris basin and the Rhône valley, where grapes grew well.[8]

All the evidence suggests that if there were negative effects on wine production in the period following the collapse of the Roman Empire they were not the result of deliberate policies on the part of Europe's new rulers. Rather, they were the product of the shock waves felt throughout Europe as the political unity of the Empire was replaced by many smaller political units and as existing patterns of commerce were disrupted. At the very heart of the Empire, the city of Rome went into rapid decline, and it is likely that its demand for wine decreased apace, depriving many wine-producing regions in Italy of a major market. Bordeaux, where viticulture was introduced by the Romans during the first century AD, is a striking example of the instability many wine-producing regions in western Europe experienced. In the fifth century alone it was invaded successfully by Goths, Vandals, Visigoths and Franks. The Gascons arrived from Spain in the seventh century (giving the region from the Pyrenees to the mouth of the Gironde river the name 'Gascony') and the Carolingian Franks took the area in the eighth century.

The disruption of commercial links does not mean that the European wine industry entered a period of crisis in the five hundred years after the collapse of the Roman Empire. It might have stagnated or even ebbed in those regions particularly affected by war, but overall it seems to have continued to flourish in most areas where it was established by the time the Empire began to crumble. In some localities – like Burgundy, where forests were cut down to make way for vineyards – land area devoted to viticulture increased, and vines were planted for the first time in parts of central and eastern Europe. By the ninth century, with the emergence of a more stable political entity in the form of the Carolingian Empire, security and long-distance trade links were re-established and the wine industry rebounded. Its recovery was further stimulated by a burst of population growth from about 1000 AD.

The Church, through its vineyard-owning bishops and monasteries, played a vital role in both the maintenance and spread of viticulture during these times of turmoil, but it would be wrong to think that the Church was alone in this.[9] The image of pious and diligent monks carefully protecting and husbanding their vines contrasts nicely with that of barbarians from the east running around drunk, ripping out vines, or lying in intoxicated stupors and letting vineyards decay by neglect. It contributes to the notion that the period after the collapse of the Roman Empire could fittingly be called the 'Dark Ages', but it is a gross oversimplification.

None the less, the Church did have a particular interest in seeing that vineyards flourished. The clergy required a constant, if modest, supply of wine for communion, and they could best guarantee that supply by producing wine themselves. This might simply have been impractical in many cases, for viticulture is labour-intensive work and many church missions would have lacked the resources to cultivate a vineyard large enough to make wine in viable quantities. Many of the ecclesiastical vineyards we do know about were very small. They might have produced enough wine for communion and for the clergy's own consumption but there would have been no surplus for the market.

Some religious orders prescribed wine on a daily basis. In Benedictine monasteries each monk was permitted a daily ration of wine if they could not abstain from wine entirely. This was a pragmatic concession to reality, for St Benedict noted that, 'wine is no drink for monks; but, since nowadays monks cannot be persuaded of this, let us at least agree upon this, that we drink temperately and not to satiety.'[10] In practice this meant '. . . we believe that a hermina [about half a pint] of wine a day is sufficient for each. But those upon whom God bestows the gift of abstinence, they should know that they have a special reward.' In recognition of the medicinal value of wine, a sick monk was to be allowed a greater ration at the discretion of the prior. (This contrasts with the Roman practice of reducing a sick slave's wine ration because he was not working.) The Benedictine rule added that when circumstances did not permit the full ration or, even worse, no wine at all was available, the monks should not complain.

A number of monastic vineyards were substantial. In 814 the abbey of St-Germain-des-Prés near Paris owned a total of 20,000 hectares of cultivable land, 300–400 hectares of which were planted with vines. These vineyards were not one single estate but were scattered among scores of small holdings throughout the countryside, none of them too far from the rivers Seine or Marne. Fewer than half the vineyards were cultivated directly by the monks themselves, and most were leased to tenants who paid their rents and other tax obligations in wine. The yield of the abbey's vineyards was between 30 and 40 hectolitres of wine per hectare, providing the abbey each year with about 640,000 litres of wine for use at masses, for consumption by the monks, or for sale. Equally significant, the tenants who grew the vines retained almost 700,000 litres for their own use or for sale, a volume that speaks loudly for considerable peasant consumption or the existence of a wine market or, more likely, both.[11]

The church sponsored the growth of vineyards in several regions that are now in Germany, Austria and Switzerland. The number of wine-producing villages in the area of Fulda, north of Frankfurt, rose from 40 to nearly 400 between the seventh and ninth centuries, and vineyards multiplied in the Rhine district and Alsace. One reason for the church's interest in sponsoring and encouraging viticulture by peasants was that the church collected a tithe from all parishioners. In principle the tithe was a tenth (though in practice it was less), levied on each peasant's annual production, and it was paid in kind (that is, in the produce on which it was levied, rather than in money). Quite clearly, a tax paid in barrels of wine was much more easily convertible to cash than a payment in many other kinds of crop.

Beyond obtaining wine as taxation, the Church benefited from gifts of wine. In the sixth century Gregory of Tours cited a pious widow who brought a measure of wine every day to her church. In the eleventh century, just after our immediate period, Robert, Earl of Leicester, gave the cathedral in Evreux (France) three muids of wine (about 800 litres) a year for the celebration of mass. The wine came from his own vines.[12]

Individual bishops owned vineyards in their own right. In the sixth century, Felix, bishop of Nantes, had vineyards in the nearby Loire region, and other bishops are reported to have been so devoted to the emerging science of viticulture, or perhaps to the consumption of its product, that they moved to locations more suitable for grape cultivation.[13] Gregory of Langres (later Saint Gregory) moved to Dijon, where he would be close to the vineyards of Burgundy, and the bishop of Tongres moved to Liège, while the bishop of Saint-Quentin moved his residence to Noyon on the River Oise, a region considered favourable to grape-growing. For his part, Archbishop Siegfried of Mainz was urged by his peasants to let them cultivate cereal on wasteland on a hill near Rudesheim, but he insisted the land should be used only for grape production.[14] One church council, the Council of Aachen, decreed in 816 that every cathedral should have a college of canons who lived under monastic rule, and that among their obligations was the duty to plant a vineyard.

The religious motivation to have vineyards attached to churches and monasteries is clear enough, but the size of the vineyards went well beyond the immediate ritual needs of the Church. Not only were religious orders large landowners in their own right and vineyards profitable enterprises, but they had many social functions that demanded supplies of wine. Travellers, who frequently stopped and rested at monasteries, expected to be fed and provided with wine, and the heads of religious houses often hosted banquets at which wine was served. Wine was needed, too, for the daily consumption of the monks and nuns. But for several reasons, the proportion of ecclesiastical wine that was used for communion, the purpose most often associated with the Church, was very small.

First, early medieval Christians rarely took communion and many even failed to do so the three times a year that religious authorities often suggested was an acceptable minimum. If every parishioner who turned up to communion took a sip from the chalice, the volume required would still have been negligible. Second, during this period the church began to restrict communion wine to the celebrating priest, with the laity receiving only bread. This practice did not reflect a shortage of wine, but was the Church's response to a heretical doctrine stating that both bread and wine were absolutely necessary for salvation. The Church decreed that the whole Christ was present in *either* bread *or* wine, and, partly because of the difficulties of transporting and distributing wine to the farthest reaches of Christendom, it became a rule that the laity would receive only bread. The priest would drink consecrated wine on behalf of the community. This rule was elaborated by church councils from the eleventh century onward, and communion wine was not restored to the Catholic laity for nearly a millennium, in the 1960s.

It is possible that in many cases the prohibition on the laity receiving wine might have been circumvented by the priest's giving them unconsecrated wine, while reserving the consecrated wine for himself. But in strictly religious terms, the Church's requirements for wine were minuscule even though wine retained its high status and symbolism in Christian ritual and doctrine. The great bulk of wine used by the Church was consumed by clerics in contexts that had little or nothing to do with religion. Bishops and the higher-ranking members of religious houses probably drank wine every day, and ordinary monks might have done so when their monastery had a vineyard. Where vineyards were less common and wine was more expensive, monks drank ale and received wine only on special occasions such as feast-days.

Yet many vineyards had no relation to the church at all, being owned by nobles and princes who produced for their own consumption and for the market. Wine was an obligatory offering to distinguished guests, and a banquet without wine was as unthinkable then as it is now. The problem with describing and quantifying the vineyards that were not owned by the Church is that many records of land cultivated by secular proprietors have been lost. The records of monasteries have generally survived better because religious orders had long, continuous histories and because monks were not only highly literate but they valued and conserved the written word.

In fact, much of our knowledge of the extent of secular ownership comes from the bequest of vineyards to churches and monasteries in wills. In the sixth or seventh centuries, for example, Ementrud, a Paris aristocrat, left property including vineyards to members of her entourage and to several Paris churches. She also bequeathed a small vineyard to her slave, whom she emancipated.[15] On its foundation near Heidelberg in 764, the monastery of St Nazarius of Lauresham was given vineyards by two landowners and in the next century accumulated many more. By 864 it had received more than a hundred vineyards at nearby Dienheim alone.[16] The Church thus owned an increasing proportion of land under viticulture; even so, many vineyards remained in secular hands, passing down through families from generation to generation.

Although it is impossible to specify the respective proportion of vineyards owned by the Church and secular proprietors in western Europe during the centuries following the collapse of the Roman Empire, it is evident that proprietorship was broadly spread. Of the forty-two properties clearly identified as vineyards in the Domesday Book, the agricultural census of England in the late eleventh century, only twelve were in monastic hands. This was probably a smaller fraction than in continental Europe, because it is likely that many of the English vineyards were planted by Norman lords in the two decades between their invasion of England and the taking of the Domesday census. Even so, it suggests that a considerable proportion of vineyards elsewhere in Europe might have been owned by proprietors who were not associated with the Church. The absence of good records from the early Middle Ages must leave us with many uncertainties, but the fact that the Church and monastic records have survived better than others should not lead us to believe that the clergy owned virtually all the vineyards or saved viticulture from the barbarian hordes.

In some respects, monasteries and bishoprics had advantages that were not shared by secular vine-owners. They enjoyed greater continuity of cultivation because their properties were not threatened by subdivision through inheritance: laws relating to inheritance varied from place to place, but in many areas landowners had to leave their property to more than one heir, forcing the division of land into small, and often uneconomical, plots. Moreover, although monks are often thought of as unworldly and devoted to prayer most of each day, they were in fact intensely involved in the material and natural world around them. They studied agricultural techniques and it is likely that they adopted scientific methods of viticulture and experimented with grapes, as they did with other produce. They learned to clarify red wines with egg-whites and white wines with isinglass (fish-bladder).

Moreover, monks put the by-products of viticulture and wine to myriad uses. Poor or spoiled wine was used as vinegar, and grapes not used for wine were eaten or turned into verjuice for pickling ham and cheeses. Grape seeds were used for flavourings or as a source of oil for making soap. Finally, the leaves and excess wood of the vines were used, respectively, for autumn cattle feed and for fuel.[17]

There is no doubt that the Church was the main force behind the spread of viticulture in many regions in this period. As Christianity spread through Europe, priests sponsored the planting of vineyards wherever viticulture was viable in order to ensure local supplies of wine. This was particularly significant in the regions that were far from established viticulture. Wine in this period was so unstable that it neither lasted long before going sour nor took well to transportation over long distances. An example of wine accompanying religion was the planting of vineyards in Poland in the early Middle Ages, as the number of communities named 'Winnica' attests.[18] There is positive evidence, too, that from the sixth century onwards new vineyards were planted in the western provinces of Germany. Within three centuries, eighty-three villages in the Palatinate were producing wine, as were twenty-three in Baden and eighteen in Württemberg. In some regions, like the Main Valley and Freising, viticulture was introduced by Christian missionaries.[19] In some regions, however, factors other than the Church influenced the introduction or extension of viticulture. It is possible that the Magyars who invaded northern Hungary at the end of the ninth century had learned to cultivate vines and make wine from their contact with the Caucasus.[20]

The eastern region of the former Roman Empire, known as the Byzantine Empire, was not subjected to the same problems as the west. Agriculture there – viticulture included – prospered while the west was affected by political and economic turmoil. Although there might have been some loss of vineyards in Judaea, viticulture flourished in the eastern Mediterranean region as it had done in the ancient period. Greece and its islands continued to be prominent wine-producers, and from the fourth century Greece and Turkey began to produce a sweet wine from muscat grapes. It was known as 'Romania' wine in northern Europe because of its origin in the Roman Empire. With the development of monasticism and pilgrimages in the Holy Land, vineyards were established in areas of the Negev, in the south of present-day Israel.

Throughout the Byzantine Empire, as in western Europe, vineyards were owned by both ecclesiastical and lay proprietors, although the tendency for secular owners to bequeath vineyards to monasteries (as in western Europe) meant that ecclesiastical ownership steadily increased. Monastic rules generally provided for wine not only with supper but with the morning meal as well. Some orders allocated two mugs of wine for each monk daily. There were attempts by heretical groups in the east to have wine banned, but all were rejected by the church fathers such as Basil the Great. Wine, along with bread, was a staple of the region's diet. Penances often included mandatory abstinence from wine, which would have been a real hardship, one that deprived the penitent not so much of an enjoyable beverage as of a basic food.

The wines of the Aegean, so often prized by ancient Greek connoisseurs, continued to be prominent in this period. Classified by Byzantine writers according to their colour (white, yellow, red, black), their body (thick or thin), and by taste, they comprised a wide range of styles. They were consumed by themselves and also used for cooking and medicinal purposes. One additional use for wine, a military one this time, also emerged: linen fabric, soaked in wine and salt and then dried, developed a hardness that enabled it to be used as a replacement for armour. Now soldiers could use wine both inside and out to fortify themselves for battle.

Viticulture, wine-production and the wine-trade were undoubtedly disrupted by the instability into which much of Europe was thrown by the collapse of the western half of the Roman Empire. It began to rebound, however, with the emergence of the Carolingian Empire in the late eighth century. The first emperor, Charlemagne, actively encouraged wine production. He is said to have ordered the planting of the first vines in the Rhine district and to have given a part of the famous hill of Corton, in Burgundy, to the Abbey of Saulieu. (The wines from this estate are known as Corton-Charlemagne.) In the new calendar he drew up to replace the Roman version, Charlemagne designated October as Windume-Manoth – the month of vintage. Carolingian ordinances also regulated wine-making to ensure proper levels of hygiene, and one went so far as to insist that grapes should only be pressed, not crushed by foot. It is unlikely that this had much impact on techniques of wine production, for treading grapes by foot continued for centuries afterwards.

The Carolingian period was undoubtedly beneficial to one of France's wine regions in particular: Champagne. Many of the region's great abbeys, including that of Epernay, were founded in the seventh century, and vineyards were soon planted on their domains. Within two centuries the vines of Champagne were extensive enough for distinctions to be made between specific districts. What undoubtedly gave Champagne wines a boost was the coronation of Charlemagne's son Louis in Reims in 816. The high-born guests at the coronation would have had ample opportunity to sample the local wines. As Reims became the traditional place for the coronation of French kings, the wines of Champagne gained an aura of royalty, an image intensified much later when champagne came to refer to the distinctive sparkling wine made in the region.

Intentionally or otherwise, the Carolingians adopted policies that promoted viticulture and wine production. We should note, however, that Charlemagne himself is reported to have been a moderate drinker – he rarely drank more than three cups of wine with dinner – and he prescribed harsh penalties for drunkenness. In the end, however, it was less Charlemagne's specific policies concerning wine that led to the recovery of wine-production and trade than the political stability that he imposed on Europe after centuries of territorial conflict.

Perhaps the best argument for the persistence of viticulture and wine-making in western Europe after the collapse of the Roman Empire is the evidence of continued and widespread wine consumption. Drinking alcohol (beer as well as wine) was integral to Germanic culture, and the most important social decisions – electing leaders, deciding matters of war, peace and marriage – were made during banquets and other occasions of communal drinking. Drinking was also a ritual that bonded men together, and the consumption of large quantities of alcohol was seen as an act of manliness. In southern France, the bishop of Arles, who had strong views on drinking, noted with dismay that drunks not only ridiculed those who did not drink to excess but also expressed doubts about their masculinity.

Bouts of heavy drinking were far from uncommon, and the historical record suggests that drunkenness was a cultural trait. If the weight of documentary evidence is any guide, the Anglo-Saxon inhabitants of England were the worst offenders of all: there are more references to intoxication there than to the rest of Europe combined.[21] Yet there is no reason to think that populations of continental Europe drank notably less. As far as Merovingian Gaul is concerned, there are many records of public drunkenness that depict drinkers stumbling through the streets vomiting and, when they retained enough physical control and co-ordination, engaging in acts of violence. Drinking cups, many with traces of ale or wine, have been recovered from graves throughout France and southern Germany, indicative of a culture of drinking. Some of the cups bear inscriptions such as: 'I'm thirsty', 'Fill it up, boss, pour it', and 'Rejoice, I'm full of joy'.

As for the Carolingian period, one historian has described it as 'an age obsessed with wine'.[22] Bilingual Latin–Germanic conversation manuals generally began with the apparently vital phrase 'Give me a drink,' and taverns were intrinsic to patterns of rural and urban sociability. For religious or more banal reasons the clergy appear to have been particularly devoted to wine. Whenever the Carolingian empire was threatened by invasions by the Normans, fleeing monks were said to have often tried to take their wine supplies with them. When in 845 the monks of the religious house at St Germain returned after their community had been attacked by Normans, they thanked God not only for their deliverance but also for the survival of their wine cellar, which meant that they would have enough wine to last until the following harvest.[23]

As the Christian church extended its sway over the populations of Europe, it not only promoted viticulture but also had to confront the reality that many of the faithful – clergy and lay men and women alike – drank too deeply and too often. As a rich theme in the Bible and an element integral to church ritual, wine had to be approached positively, and questions of abuse and drunkenness were difficult to resolve. Although many church authorities condemned the excessive use of wine, there remained a sense that alcoholic intoxication was a physical and emotional state related to spiritual ecstasy. A number of Church fathers developed the notion of 'sober intoxication' to express a state of spiritual bliss achieved without the help of wine, and perhaps this might have prompted the less godly to use wine as a short-cut.

For the most part, however, the Church opposed heavy drinking and drunkenness and it was an issue discussed repeatedly, not only by individual church leaders but also by church councils. It was seen as problematic from social, moral and spiritual angles. The sixth-century bishop of Arles, Caesarius, condemned drunkenness on three grounds: it led to violent and immoral behaviour, it wasted money that could have gone to charity, and it was sacrilegious. The records of Caesarius's time vividly illustrated his complaints, for descriptions of violent, immoral and impious behaviour related to wine were legion. Eberulf, the treasurer of King Childebert II (570–95), 'flung a priest on a bench, beat him with his fists and belaboured him with blows, simply because he had refused to give Eberulf wine when he was obviously drunk'. There were complaints that people refused alms to the poor, telling them to 'Go, go on, God will give it to you,' while they themselves consumed large quantities of expensive wine. As for sacrilege, drinkers toasted the angels and the saints with the same wine that rendered them drunk and immoral.

The clergy were no better in this respect than lay persons. Bishop Cautinus of Tours was reported to be 'often so completely fuddled with wine that it would take four men to carry him from the table'. The bishop of Soissons, for his part, was said to have been 'out of his mind ... for nearly four years, through drinking to excess', such that he had to be locked behind bars whenever there was a royal visit to the city.[24] Gregory of Tours complained that monks spent more of their time in taverns drinking than in their cells praying. In 847 the Council of Prelates decreed that any person in religious orders who habitually drank to the point of drunkenness should do forty days' penance – which in this case meant abstaining from fat, beer and wine.

Drinking and drunkenness were also treated in penitentials, contemporary manuals for priests that listed the kinds of penance Christians should perform when they had committed sins. In general the penalties imposed on clerics, of whom greater self-discipline was expected, were greater than on lay drunks, and high-ranking clergy were expected to perform greater penances than mere monks and parish priests. An early-eighth-century penitential attributed to the Venerable Bede set out the penance for drinking to the point when it 'changes the state of the mind and [when] the tongue babbles and the eyes are wild and there is dizziness and distention of the stomach and pain follows'. These symptoms sound like punishment enough, but further penance was demanded: the offender was to consume no wine or meat (the wine would surely be easily given up for the first days after such inebriation) for three days if he was a layman, seven days if a priest, two weeks if a monk, three weeks if a deacon, four weeks if a presbyter, and five weeks if he was a bishop.[25]

Another penitential, this one from the monastery of Silos in Spain, made further distinctions. A cleric who got drunk was to do penance for twenty days, but if he vomited as a result he did forty days, and if he compounded the offence by vomiting up the Eucharist, the penance was extended to sixty days. The penance for a lay person in these circumstances was less severe, and set at ten, twenty and forty days respectively.[26]

The simple presence of drunkenness in these penitentials should not necessarily be understood as indicating that drunkenness was widespread in early medieval Europe. What is clear is that in many parts of Europe, particularly in regions where wine was produced or easily accessible, it was an integral part of the diet and, even more so, of occasions of sociability and celebration. It seems that the Barbarian invasions did not cut too deeply into wine production. Indeed, it is easy to make the argument that, from the seventh century, the future of viticulture and the cultural status of wine were subject to a much more serious threat: the rise of Islam.

Muhammad prohibited the production and consumption of alcohol, and observance of this rule implied the end of brewing and wine-making wherever Islam became the dominant faith. By the early eighth century, Islamic armies had conquered not only most of the Middle East but also North Africa along the Mediterranean coast, Spain, Portugal and even, for a short time, parts of south-western France. A religion committed to rooting out alcohol was thus established in those regions where wine had first flourished, as well as in areas (like Spain and Portugal) where viticulture had developed later but in which wine had become economically and culturally important.

Underlying the Islamic prohibition of the consumption of wine lay the polarity between the genial, social feelings alcohol can inspire and the antisocial violence it can provoke. The Qur'an contains several references to wine, both positive and negative. Wine is described as an intoxicant and a wholesome food, but one reference in particular was understood as a prohibition on wine: 'Believers, wine and games of chance, idols and divining arrows are abominations devised by Satan. Avoid them so that you may prosper. Satan seeks to stir up enmity and hatred among you by means of wine and gambling and to keep you from the remembrance of Allah and from your prayers.'[27] This verse is thought to have been a response to conflicts that had arisen within the early Muslim community.

On one occasion, visiting a friend's house where a wedding was in progress, Muhammad saw the good effects of wine on the guests. They were happy and convivial and they embraced one another, and as he left Muhammad blessed wine for having this effect. But, when he returned the next day, he found carnage and bloodshed, the result of brawls that had erupted when the guests had drunk yet more wine. Muhammad changed his blessing on wine to a curse and forbade his followers ever to drink it. The problem was not wine itself, however, but its abuse, and Muhammad's vision of paradise, where abuse would not occur, included 'rivers of delectable wine'.

Muhammad appears to have ruled out wine-production by limiting the kinds of vessels in which fruit juice could be made or stored. Gourds, glazed wine jars, earthenware vessels coated with pitch, and hollowed out trunks of palm trees, were forbidden, and only containers made from skins were permitted. This would not have prevented fermentation, however, for it is known that wine was sometimes made in skins in ancient Greece. Indeed, there is some suggestion that Muhammad's wives made a slightly fermented drink for him in these leather containers: 'we used to prepare *nabidh* [date wine] . . . in a skin; we took a handful of dates or a handful of raisins, cast it into the skin and poured water upon it. The *nabidh* we prepared in this way in the morning was drunk by him in the evening, and when we prepared it in the evening he drank it the next morning.' The beverage consumed in this way would have been in the process of fermentation and low in alcohol. Whether or not it was wine is a matter of definition.

The actual effect of Muslim conquest on viticulture and wine-production was more mixed than the Prophet's prohibition might lead us to expect. Recent experience with attempts to ban the drinking of alcohol in societies where it is entrenched suggest that the Muslim leaders must have faced considerable resistance to the new rules. Only the most determined efforts, combined with the adoption of the new faith, could have curtailed production and brought about a dramatic change in drinking habits. Within decades of the birth of the new faith the Arab poet Abu Jilda al-Yaskuri wrote of repentance of the old ways:

> I was once made rich by a choice wine,
> [I was] noble, one of the illustrious men of Yaskur.
> That [was] a Time whose pleasures have passed –
> I have exchanged this now for a lasting respectability.[28]

The prohibition on alcohol was, however, enforced differently in various parts of the Islamic empire. It was very likely more rigorous in regions closest to the geographical origins of the faith, although in the early phase of Islam wine was available. The vineyards nearest to Mecca were about a thousand miles away, but wine from Syria and other sources was imported by Christian and Jewish merchants. It was consumed in taverns and also in the court of the caliph of Baghdad.

In the more distant regions conquered by Muslims, rulers tended to take an increasingly tolerant attitude toward local traditions. In Spain, Portugal, Sicily, Sardinia and Crete, for example, a number of policies co-existed. Some Muslim rulers made wine-production illegal but in practice permitted it to continue and went so far as to give it recognition by taxing it. Arabic sources suggest that vineyards were widespread in southern Spain, especially in Andalusia, and in the region of Coimbra in Portugal. Islamic horticulture was so advanced that the number of varieties of grapes increased and some Muslim texts on agriculture included instructions on taking care of fermentation vats.

In Spain, an intriguing interpretation by Muslim legal commentators of the prohibition of alcohol allowed it to be drunk there. It was argued that the beverage referred to in the Qur'an was wine made from grapes and that wine made from dates was thereby excluded from the prohibition. But, the argument went, if date-wine was allowed, so was grape-wine as long as it was no more intoxicating than date-wine.[29] Such reasoning was not universally accepted by Muslim scholars, of course. It failed to answer the objection that even if drinking did not lead to drunkenness and immorality, it certainly distracted the pious from thinking about God. Although there was a debate among Muslim jurists about the meaning of wine and its prohibition, there was universal agreement that drunkenness was forbidden.

The possibility of drinking appears to have been embraced enthusiastically by Muslims in Spain, although it is thought that wine consumption was lower among them than among Christians.[30] Muslims drank at occasions reminiscent of the Greek symposia discussed in the previous chapter. Men would gather after the evening meal and drink wine, diluted with water, while relaxing on cushions. Wine was poured by serving boys, and the participants talked, recited poetry and were entertained by female singers and dancers. They were expected to spend the night drinking, talking and dozing, then waking and drinking again. The same sort of wine-drinking occasions were common among Jews in Muslim Spain, and they gave rise to a particular genre of poetry that flourished between the tenth and twelfth centuries. Some of it celebrated the ability of wine to banish cares and bring joy to the drinker. Other poems celebrated wine itself and commented on its appearance, age and aroma.[31]

Despite the tolerance extended in some regions, a number of individual rulers were set on a more strict application of Islamic law in Spain. In the tenth century, for example, the caliph Ozman ordered the destruction of two thirds of the vineyards of Valencia. Presumably the remaining vineyards were to produce grapes to be eaten fresh or as raisins. Yet whatever setbacks Spanish wine producers suffered, they rebounded quickly from the twelfth century after Christian rule was ultimately restored to the entire Iberian peninsula. The many new contracts for vineyards that were entered into in Aragon between 1150 and 1180 can only mean that wine was being exported, and by the middle of the thirteenth century Spain was shipping large quantities of wine to England.

Even at the heart of the Islamic empire, however, it is likely that wine was still produced. The Muslim prohibition was on wine, not on grapes, and vineyards were still extensively cultivated to provide fruit to be eaten fresh or dried. Although vineyards for wine production might well have been ripped up, it was possible to make a poor, perhaps rather sweet and certainly unstable, wine from table grapes, and wine was produced here and there in defiance of the law.

The rule of abstinence created some cultural problems. Wine had been an important theme in classical Arabic poetry, where it was associated with love and sex. Wine persisted as a theme even after the coming of Islam, but literary strategies were employed to accommodate the new faith. One early-ninth-century poet, Abu Nuwas, seemed to defy the rule in some of his works: 'You have made me fear God, your Lord . . . If you will not drink with me for fear of [God's] punishment then I will drink alone.'[32] Later, a group of twelfth- and thirteenth-century Persian poets, of whom Omar Khayyam is probably the best known, made wine and love prominent themes. Khayyam's *Ruba'iyat* is a long work in praise of wine that includes sentiments such as, 'I cannot live without the sparkling vintage/Cannot bear the body's burden without wine.' More to the point, he implied that illegal drinking and relationships were common:

They say lovers and drunkards go to hell,
A controversial dictum not easy to accept:
If the lover and drunkard are for hell,
Tomorrow Paradise will be empty.[33]

It is possible, but unlikely, that wine remained no more than a cultural memory that was invoked in these poems. It is more likely that wine and other alcohol (such as date and raisin wine) were illicitly produced and consumed, although the surviving culture of wine drinking must have been a pale shadow of pre-Islamic times. While it is difficult to know the exact effects of Islam on wine, we can be certain that viticulture was geared for table grapes, that what wine was produced was inferior and made in dramatically smaller quantities, and that the culture of wine, especially in the Middle East and North Africa, virtually disappeared.

The early Middle Ages, from the fall of the Roman Empire until about the end of the first Christian millennium, thus saw wine exposed to a number of threats. In Europe itself, as in the Middle East, north Africa and Iberia, the danger was posed by external forces that were in one case believed to be culturally disdainful of wine and in the other case theologically opposed to it. But the Barbarians adopted policies that were generally benevolent when they were not positive towards wine, and Islam did not eradicate wine-production from the regions it conquered. The upheavals of the period might well have disrupted production and trade, but in Europe at least, wine remained culturally important and well placed for the resurgence of the later Middle Ages.

FOUR

WINE RESURGENT

The Middle Ages, 1000–1500

By the year 1000, vines were being cultivated throughout Europe, even in regions where the climate meant that yields were low, harvests unreliable and the wine of poor quality. We should not be too surprised to find wine being made in such regions: it was stretching the limits of the environment to cultivate vines in places like Flanders and England a thousand years ago, but wine is commercially produced – if in small quantities – in both places today. On the other hand, wine was made in some regions from which it has now disappeared, such as Normandy in northern France. In the following five hundred years, however, the geography of viticulture began to change in response to the development of new and important markets that accompanied a burst of population growth and a widening connoisseurship. It was in this period that several major French wine regions, including Bordeaux, Beaune and the Rhône valley, emerged, each in response to specific but different market demands. In many respects, the later Middle Ages laid the foundations of the modern European wine industry.

The second millennium of the Christian era opened with a wine mystery. In his westward voyage from Greenland about 1000 AD, Leif Ericsson encountered land he called Vinland (Wineland) because of the grapes that grew prolifically there. The area was probably on the northern coast of Newfoundland, a location now too cold for vines but one that might conceivably have supported wild vines a thousand years ago. According to the saga telling the story of Leif's voyage, the grapes were identified by a German member of the party who 'was born where there is no lack of either grapes or vines'. Later accounts of Vinland, in the eleventh century, had it that the area was so named 'from the circumstance that vines grow there of their own accord, and produce the most excellent wine'.[1]

Vinland remains an enigma. It is wholly unlikely that the explorers encountered wine, and perhaps Vinland is no more than an optimistic appellation that expressed the hope that the grapes might be put to that purpose. But if there were grapes but no wine in the area, why was it not called Vinberland (Grapeland)? The latest hypothesis is that Leif Ericsson and his companions got it entirely wrong, and that the 'grapes' they found were wild cranberries.[2] If this is true and cranberries were fermented, the resulting beverage would have been the precursor of the berry-based wines now made in Newfoundland.

Whether or not grapes were grown in Newfoundland around the year 1000, there is no doubt that the new millennium ushered in a period of sustained growth in viticulture and wine production in many parts of Europe. In the tenth and eleventh centuries, French landowners cleared forests and drained marshes in order to extend the land under viticulture, and many large landowners converted poor arable land to grape production. Spanish viticulture surged forward as the Muslim power ebbed from the Iberian peninsula. A similar expansion took place in Germany in the eleventh and twelfth centuries, in regions of the Rhineland, then in Swabia, Franconia and Thuringia.[3] Further east, vineyards had by the early 1300s spread to the eastern frontier of Hungary, as a result of deforestation. One of the areas that came under viticulture at this time was the Tokay region, which gives its name to the famous sweet wine produced there from the seventeenth century.[4]

Vineyards increased in England, too. The Domesday Book listed forty-two vineyards in the late eleventh century, but two hundred years later, when English vine-growers finally surrendered to competition from abroad, more than 1,300 vineyards were grubbed up to make way for other crops. Nor was Italy an exception to the general pattern of expansion, and a sense of the wine-boom there was captured by Michelangiolo Tanaglia:

> Now is the time, in my opinion,
> on the open hills, to never tire,
> of planting vines, of the best kind,
> or of attending the plant of Bacchus . . . [5]

This increase in land under viticulture throughout much of Europe was due to a sudden growth in demand for wine. The period 1000 to 1300 witnessed a significant rise in the population of the continent, which probably doubled from about 40 to 80 million. Coupled with this was a burst of urbanization, particularly in northern Italy (Venice, Milan, Florence, Genoa) and Flanders (Ghent, Bruges, Brussels), while the populations of cities like London and Paris also grew rapidly.

With urban growth and the expansion of trade emerged a wealthy middle and merchant class which, added to the existing church and aristocratic elites, made up a formidable market for luxury goods. Wine was one such commodity as it became entrenched as part of a wealthy lifestyle. The question was how these markets, many of them in regions not particularly favourable to viticulture, were to be supplied. Wine drinkers in the northern Italian cities could be supplied by vineyards in Italy itself – from the south and from the expanding industry in central and northern Italy, particularly in Tuscany. Similarly, the growing cities of Spain, especially Seville and Barcelona, were provisioned from local and regional vineyards, increasingly so after the expulsion of the Muslims and the revival of wine-production. Much of the product of the wine-producing regions of Germany, mainly located on the Rhine, Main and Mosel rivers, was transported downstream to Cologne and Frankfurt, but it also found markets further afield in Flanders, England, France, and in the Baltic area.

Providing wine to the northern European markets was more problematic, because they were located in regions where yields from vines were low and the finished product was probably less and less acceptable to what were very probably the increasingly demanding palates of bourgeois consumers. Parisians were perhaps the most fortunate, for they could be supplied by wine produced in their own region. By 1000, vineyards were well established in localities close to the rivers Seine, Marne and Yonne, and the fact that these wines were made only a short distance by water from Paris kept the costs of transportation down.

The expanding English and Flemish markets, as well as those further east in the Baltic area, were too large to be supplied by local wine-producers, and they had to rely on long-distance wine imports. The major source was the western regions of France, but initially they traded with the area to the north of the Gironde river. There in the twelfth century the new port of la Rochelle was constructed, initially as a point of export for the salt that was left by the evaporation of sea water in nearby lagoons. Salt was in high demand as the principal means of preserving foods, especially fish and meat. La Rochelle's population grew as people flocked to new employment opportunities in the salt industry, shipping and other trades, and they quickly planted vineyards in the port's hinterland. This was effectively the beginning of the Charente wine region, whose vineyards today are almost solely devoted to the production of wine for distilling into brandy, including cognac.

The Bordeaux region emerged as a major player in the international wine trade only in the thirteenth century, and then directly as a result of a series of dynastic upheavals. In 1152 Eleanor of Aquitaine (which included Gascony – and thus Bordeaux – as well as Poitou) married Henry, Duke of Normandy and Count of Anjou. Two years later he became Henry II of England, so that England, Normandy and Aquitaine were ruled by the same crown. It was an unstable arrangement, however, marked by family conflict on a grand military scale as Eleanor tried to recover control of Aquitaine. Eventually her son Richard (the Lion Heart) restored the duchy to her, but she favoured la Rochelle over Bordeaux, ignoring the persistent complaints of Bordeaux's wine-growers that their quality Gascon wines were being denied recognition by punitive taxes. It was not until Eleanor's youngest son, John, became king of England that Bordeaux was able to emerge from the shadow of la Rochelle, and even then dynastic considerations were uppermost. In 1203 John agreed that in exchange for Bordeaux providing ships and other support for his war against the king of France, the taxes on Gascon wine would be lowered.

La Rochelle and Poitou vigorously protested against the arrangement that now gave Bordeaux a commercial edge, and in 1204 John granted them the privileges he had extended to Bordeaux. In principle the wine regions of western France were now in a position to compete equally for the important English market. But once again dynastic events proved critical. As a reward for resisting the attack of the king of Castile, John placed an order for Bordeaux wine, a conspicuous and valuable sign of support for the region's exporters. Even more important, however, was the capitulation of la Rochelle to the king of France in 1224. Bordeaux's main competition had left the field.

During the rest of the thirteenth century Gascon wine became the staple of the English market. In 1243 alone, Henry III bought 1,445 casks of French wine, probably Gascon, for £2,310 2s. 8d. If these casks were the standard English tun of just over 250 gallons, then Henry's purchase amounted to more than 350,000 gallons, about 1,655,000 litres. Almost a thousand casks were top quality wine, while the rest was mediocre or poor quality.[6] Even these substantial royal purchases represented only a fraction of total English imports, but their political significance gave the order extra weight.

It was not until this English market for French wine developed that the region around Bordeaux became intensively planted with vines. In the first decades of the century one of the main sources of wine was the area immediately around the city itself, for vineyards spread out in a fan-like pattern from the city's limits. Other important wine districts were to the south in present-day Graves, and the area between the Garonne and Dordogne rivers, known as Entre-Deux-Mers ('between two seas') because it was between these two bodies of water. Of the modern Bordeaux region, the Médoc had scarcely any vines.

The most important sources of Gascon wines, however, lay much further inland, up the valleys of the Garonne, Tarn and Lot rivers and in what was known as the 'high country'. From locations as distant as Gaillac and Cahors (both of which still produce notable and distinctive wines) barrels were shipped to Bordeaux for export as Gascon wine. It is from about this time that the lighter-coloured wines of the region closer to the coast became known as *clairet* (later claret), to distinguish them from the darker reds produced in the high country and Spain that were shipped from Bordeaux.

As viticulture was intensified in the region immediately surrounding Bordeaux, the wine-makers there adopted restrictive policies to protect their own products – this even though the policies were aimed at wines that had been indispensable in enabling Bordeaux to establish itself as the heart of a massive commerce in wine. Under the new regulations, high-country wines could not be brought into Bordeaux for shipping before a fixed date (set between mid November and Christmas). This meant that wines from the regions closest to Bordeaux had no competition early in the year, and in general it was not until those wines had sold that the high-country wines came on to the Bordeaux market.

The Gascon wine trade, which was to become so important, started modestly at first.[7] By the mid thirteenth century, Bordeaux was supplying three quarters of the wine ordered by the English royal household. In 1282, Edward I bought 600 barrels to supply his armies fighting the Welsh. The vital contribution of the high-country wines is demonstrated by the more reliable though still incomplete figures on exports that are available from the 1300s. In 1305–6, for example, they accounted for between 59 and 78 per cent of all wine exports from Bordeaux, while in 1335–6 they accounted for between 63 and 82 per cent.[8] Scotland also imported substantial amounts of claret, either directly from Bordeaux or from the English market. In one year in the late 1200s King Alexander III had to pledge all his revenues from the port of Berwick to guarantee payment of the £2,197 he owed a Bordeaux merchant. The amount of wine involved might have been 400 hundred hogsheads, about 115,000 litres.[9]

The opening up of the English market to Gascon wine stimulated a boom in viticulture, and before long vines were being cultivated throughout the wine region now known generally as Bordeaux. But the development of the region during the fourteenth and fifteenth centuries was anything but smooth. Like other wine-growing areas, Bordeaux was sensitive to changes in the market, which often reflected political, economic and social instability. The Black Death, the devastating plague epidemic that broke out in the late 1340s and killed between a quarter and a third of Europe's population, disrupted production, markets and trade. Bordeaux suffered an additional scourge because it was the site of military conflict. In the 1450s French armies entered the region and did terrible damage to the vineyards. Throughout these upheavals, the Bordeaux merchants applied themselves to the task of exporting the region's wine. Although precise figures are not available, it is clear that England was a major market for this wine – well over three quarters of it at the end of the fourteenth century. The rest of Bordeaux's exports were distributed among Spain, Flanders, Germany and other parts of France.

Every year in October, only weeks after the annual vintage, fleets comprising hundreds of ships carrying the young French wine set sail from Bordeaux. Smaller convoys departed from Nantes and la Rochelle. The voyage to England took a week or more, depending on the weather and political conditions. The wine that remained in Bordeaux's ware-houses after December was racked into fresh barrels and shipped during the spring. Known as *reck* (there are several alternative spellings), these wines were considered inferior and sold for a lower price. Reck, having experienced a longer maturation, might have appealed more to the modern palate, but medieval English tastes preferred younger Gascon wines that might have been reminiscent, in colour and body, of modern beaujolais nouveau.

English wine-makers were soon casualties of the success of French exporters. Notwithstanding the glowing recommendation of William of Malmesbury for the vintage produced in Gloucestershire, it is unlikely that much English wine was of a quality that could compete with the flood of Gascon wine that began to enter the English market. With better and less expensive French wine available, consumers turned their backs on the domestic industry, and by the middle of the thirteenth century it was in steady and permanent decline. It was not long before the great majority of commercial vineyards in England, an estimated 1,300 of them, were ripped up and the land put to alternative use.

The Bordeaux wine trade reached its height in the early 1300s. In the three years 1305–6, 1306–7 and 1308–9, exports from all Gascon ports averaged 98,000 barrels annually, almost 900 million litres. Production was always dependent on weather, of course, and exports of the 1310 vintage fell to 51,000 barrels because of a poor harvest. Changes in the political climate could be even more harmful, because they tended to be longer-lasting. Exports fell in 1324 when war broke out between England and France and again in the 1330s with the outbreak of the Hundred Years War.[10]

By the first half of the fourteenth century Bordeaux's exports had stabilized at about 10,000–15,000 barrels of wine a year. From the 1450s, however, the incorporation of Bordeaux into the kingdom of France reduced exports to England. Although tempted to prohibit the export of wine to an enemy, French kings recognized the importance of the wine trade to Bordeaux's economy. Instead of banning the trade they simply placed a tax on wine as it left Bordeaux. This policy enabled the trade to continue (although at a much reduced scale), provided revenue for the French royal treasury, and increased the price of Bordeaux wine in England. That price had always fluctuated according to supply, but by the end of the fifteenth century it was selling at over eight pence a gallon, two or three times the price during the heydays of the Gascon wine trade in the early 1300s.

Bordeaux was by no means England's only French supplier of wine: imports still arrived from Anjou and other parts of France. But the durability – or rather lack of it – of French wine in general meant that other suppliers were needed. The wine was expected to last a year at most, so that by the summer following each vintage what was left of the imported wine was not only scarce but often turning sour. Consumers were faced with buying wine that was declining in quality at prices that were rising because of falling supplies. When the new vintage began to arrive in October, what was left of the previous year was sold off at cut-rate prices or simply poured away. There remained, however, a critical period in late summer when the quality of one vintage had peaked and the next had not yet arrived.

Into the breach stepped the wine-makers and merchants of the Mediterranean, whose wine was altogether sweeter and more robust, alcoholic and, above all, durable than the French. Often given the generic name malmsey or malvasia (from a town in Greece that exported large quantities of wine from its region), these wines came from a variety of sources. Candia provided much-prized sweet wines made from muscat grapes; Corfu provided romania, a sweet wine of a lower quality; and Tuscany provided vernaccia (known as vernage in England), named after a grape varietal but probably used at this time as a generic term for a range of wines made in central and northern Italy.

The voyage from Italy to England through the Straits of Gibraltar and the Bay of Biscay was sometimes accomplished by sailing ships, sometimes by galleys with merchants themselves at the oars. The trip was long – as long as five months and never less than one – and it could be hazardous. More than one ship lost its cargo to pirates en route. But the profits from transporting wine and other luxury goods, like silk and spices, and returning with cargoes of wool for Italian textile mills made it worthwhile.

It was the timing of their arrival in England that was also important. Vessels carrying the more stable wines from Greece, the Mediterranean islands, Italy and Spain generally arrived in English and other northern European ports in July and August, just as consumers there were beginning to face the prospect of drinking deteriorating French wine. It was not that the Mediterranean wines were simply substitutes for the French. Everything about them – their depth of colour, level of alcohol (which could be up to 16 or 17 per cent, almost twice that of Gascon wines) and sweetness – appealed to the contemporary palate. But they were also more expensive, and not all wine-drinkers could have availed themselves of the Mediterranean vintages. The wholesale cost was up to twice that of Gascon wine, and only three of London's taverns in the fourteenth century were licensed to sell it retail.

Mediterranean wine, together with wines from other parts of Europe, also penetrated markets in eastern Europe and the Baltic area. This wine route, dominated by merchants from Venice and Genoa, had as its principal hub the Polish city of Cracow. The location of a royal court and home to a wealthy merchant elite, it was a market for wine in its own right. Equally important, though, were its location at the junction of a number of trade routes and the commercial privileges it enjoyed, both of which made Cracow an ideal transshipment point for wine destined to other parts of eastern and northern Europe.[11] Wine converged on Cracow from several directions, notably from Hungary and Moldavia, although smaller quantities arrived from Greece and Italy – even a little from western Europe. The routes taken were often tortuous and involved a lot more overland travel than was desirable in an age when water transportation was much less expensive.

By the early 1300s three major long-distance commercial networks in wine can be identified, each drawing on significant wine-producing regions. The Mediterranean wine trade moved wine from producers to markets within the Mediterranean area itself, but also by sea to England and northern Europe and by river and land to Poland and the Baltic. German wines were exported down the Rhine to northern Germany, Scandinavia and Baltic areas, as well as to England in small quantities. Finally, wines from the west of France found their major external markets in England and Flanders, with lesser outlets in Spain and eastern Europe.

Each wine region also supplied its own local and regional markets but, as one might expect, wine tended to flow from regions that produced to regions that did not. In other words, there was probably relatively little wine from one wine-producing region on sale in another wine-producing region. Transportation and taxes so raised the retail price of wine that only the very wealthy were likely to spend the extra on imported wine if a good alternative were produced locally. There was a small commerce in highly reputed wine, but it rested on the limited demand by connoisseurs for specific wines from specific localities.

There was a broad continuity in the ownership or cultivation of vineyards from the early to the later Middle Ages. While many were in the hands of the Church and monastic orders, others were owned by secular proprietors. Throughout Europe, peasants played an important role in wine production, frequently as tenants cultivating vines on a sharecropping basis. The important role of secular wine-producers is suggested by the fact that many monastic vineyards did not produce wine for the market. For example, despite the importance of the Abbey of Cîteaux in Burgundy, which attracted scores of vineyards in bequests and gifts,[12] most of the houses belonging to the Cistercian order in southern France showed little interest in expanding production beyond their own requirements. Given that many vineyards owned by the Church were not commercial, wine production and trade could not have reached the scale it did in the Middle Ages had there not been important participation by secular wine-producers.

It is pointless even to attempt to calculate the proportion of vineyards in ecclesiastical and secular ownership in the later Middle Ages. It was a period when the land under viticulture expanded rapidly, and it was also marked by the transfer of many vineyards to the Church, specifically to religious houses. Monasteries benefited immensely from the Crusades, because many of the knights who participated, fearing death while out of Europe, gave land to the Church for prayers to be said for their souls. Almost every house in the important Cistercian order received at least one vineyard in the course of the twelfth century. In 1157, for example, one Cistercian monastery received three arpents (about four acres) of vines from a widow, Regina, and her six sons so that the monks would pray for the soul of her husband and their father.[13]

The widow's gift was particularly appropriate, not simply because of the long association between monasteries and viticulture but because the Cistercian monks developed an especially strong link with wine. Established in the early twelfth century as a more rigorous branch of

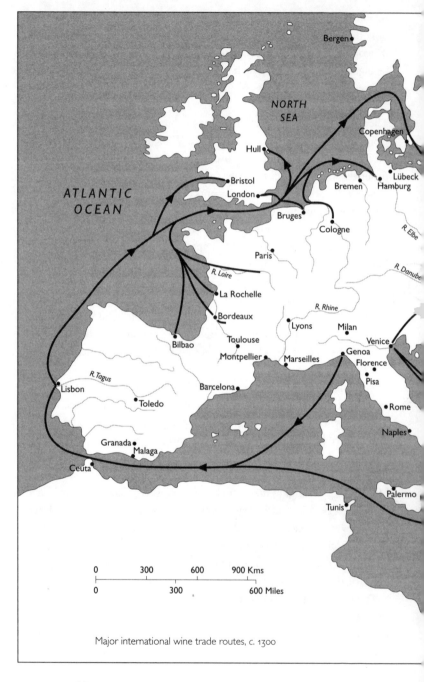

Major international wine trade routes, c. 1300

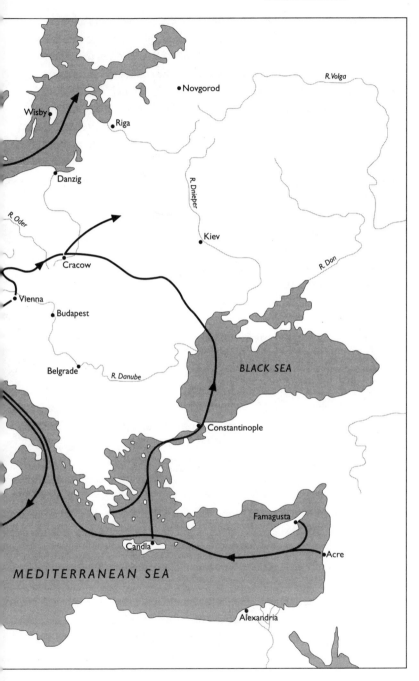

the Benedictine order, the Cistercians took their name from their abbey at Cîteaux. The rule of Saint Benedict recommended a ration of wine a day for monks who could not abstain. This appeared to include almost all of them, but that alone does not explain the conscientious approach that the Cistercians adopted toward viticulture and wine-making. Rather, it was a reflection of their commitment to seek perfection in whatever they undertook and to treat God's creations, in this case the vine and wine, with the respect they deserved.

Starting with a single vineyard in Burgundy, the abbey of Cîteaux extended its holdings right along the Côte d'Or, including vines in localities that were to become famed as the source of exceptional wines: Beaune, Pommard, Vosne, Nuits and Corton. Between 1100 and 1336, the abbey of Cîteaux purchased or received as gifts dozens of small vineyards in the community of Vougeot. By 1336 the combined vineyards totalled 50 hectares, which at that time was the largest single parcel of land in Burgundy given over to viticulture. When a stone wall was built around the vineyard it became known as the Clos de Vougeot, later the name of one of Burgundy's most renowned wines.

It was not that the Cistercians acquired vineyards that made great wines but that they started to make reputed wines from the vines that came into their possession. The monks' devotion to their work took the form of systematic research into the relationship between soil and climatic conditions, vine cultivation, and the wine that resulted. They experimented with soil preparation, training, pruning and grafting, as well as the process of making the wine. They contributed to viniculture the notion of *cru* (growth) and the idea that certain sections of a vineyard produced wines that had definable qualities and tastes, distinctive characteristics that remained fairly constant from one vintage to another. So reputable did the Cistercians' wine become that the order was granted not only land but also extensive privileges. In 1171, for instance, Pope Alexander III exempted them from paying the tithe (a church tax) on their vines, and nine years later threatened to excommunicate anyone who challenged the exemption. Also in 1171, King Louis VII of France freed the Cistercians from paying any of the duties that would normally be levied on the transportation and sale of their produce.[14]

With such encouragement the Cistercian order expanded rapidly – it had four hundred abbeys within fifty years of being founded – and it practised viticulture wherever its houses were established. One of the most noteworthy was founded at Kloster Eberbach in the Rhine district. This was an example of Burgundian or perhaps oenological imperialism, for the founding monks came from Burgundy and brought vines with them. It did not take long for them to realize that these vines did not produce the red wine that had been so successful in Burgundy, and they replanted with vines that made a white. By the end of the Middle Ages the abbey's vineyards, including the Steinberg holding, covered almost 700 acres, making them the largest anywhere in Europe. Not surprisingly, Kloster Eberbach was a major commercial producer. It owned a small fleet of ships that ferried its wine down the Rhine to Cologne.

The innovations of the Cistercians are that much more remarkable because, for the most part, the Middle Ages witnessed few major developments in viticulture or wine-making. In this respect wine-production was little different from the rest of agriculture and food-processing. Paintings and other images of viticulture in the period suggest that vines continued to be trained in the variety of ways they always had been. Some were trained on trellises, others on poles, yet others high up trees. Caring for the vines and making wine followed traditional labour-intensive methods that often demanded skills that were honed over years of experience.

The demands of the viticultural year are set out in the eleventh-century charter of the Abbey of Muri, southwest of Zurich. It described the essential activities like loosening the soil around the base of the vines so that rainwater would soak in deeper, fertilizing the vines with manure, pruning, tying up the shoots, loosening the soil again before midsummer, and removing leaves that shaded the grape clusters from the sun.[15] Once picked, grapes were crushed initially by foot and then pressed, although those destined for better-quality white wine were probably processed first. Wine-presses, particularly of the screw-type, became larger as the volume of grapes involved increased. Small proprietors, including peasants, could not afford their own presses and instead used those of their lords or wealthier neighbours, usually for payment in wine. Once the juice had been extracted, it was transferred to wooden barrels for fermentation and later transportation. Barrels were generally made of oak and their size varied according to region.

*

Overall the production of wine increased in the medieval period, but political instability and war ensured that the growth was neither continuous nor smooth. Production was also affected when the population of Europe declined by as much as a third between 1348 and 1400, when the bubonic plague called the Black Death was at its most virulent. Big towns and cities that had seen their populations increase dramatically for two or three centuries witnessed them decline in a few years, while in vast areas of the countryside communities were devastated as many inhabitants fled and many of those who remained died. Simultaneously, the market for wine fell sharply, and the labour-intensive vineyards experienced a shortage of skilled workers.

Throughout the oscillations in production, the general growth of wine-drinking and the wine trade in the Middle Ages was accompanied by increasing concern to protect regional reputations. By the late fourteenth century Burgundy was already becoming known for wines produced from pinot noir grapes, but viticulture there, as elsewhere, was hard hit by plague and warfare. Vineyards were often neglected, soil was allowed to erode, and there were shortages of the skilled labour needed to cultivate the vines and make wine.

It is possible that these conditions underlay the decision taken by a number of proprietors in Burgundy to increase their holdings of gamay vines, a variety known to have been used in the region as early as the 1360s. Although gamay (the grape now used to make beaujolais) made a wine that was widely considered to be inferior to that made from pinot noir, it possessed (as it still does) certain clear advantages: gamay vines were easier to cultivate than the notoriously sensitive pinot noir; the gamay grapes ripened more quickly, so that they were at risk from frost or other climatic adversity for a shorter time; and they had a much higher yield – gamay yield was between two and four times that of pinot noir vines in the fourteenth century.

The decision by some proprietors in Burgundy to increase gamay stocks, understandable in the circumstances, provoked reactions not only from rival producers who clung to pinot noir but also from the Duke of Burgundy.[16] Philip the Bold declared in July 1395 that the gamay was 'a very bad' plant that was repugnant to law and custom. Burgundy's wine trade was sagging under the impact of the Black Death, which reduced demand, but Philip attributed the decline to the gamay-based wines, which he alleged were naturally bitter. According to the Duke, merchants were adding hot water to the wine to sweeten it, but after the effects had worn off the wine reverted to type and became 'quite foul'. The duke ordered all gamay vines to be cut down within a month – that is, before the next vintage would be ripe – and the vines ripped out by the following Easter. Whatever the political reasons for this draconian order and its observance by growers, the effect was to protect the pinot noir as the representative grape of red wine from Burgundy. None the less, gamay retains a presence there: apart from being the beaujolais grape, it is used with pinot noir to make the wine known as passetousgrains.

Although wine continued to be made throughout the medieval period virtually wherever grapes could be grown, it was in the later Middle Ages that regions of viticultural speciality became more clearly defined. The Loire and Rhine valleys, Bordeaux, Burgundy, Tuscany and Alsace, for example, witnessed a rapid growth in wine-production. Other localities, particularly where climate made viticulture marginal or where access to markets was difficult, grew more slowly, stagnated or even declined.

Expanding markets were clearly fundamental to any growth in production, but environment and access defined the regions that could successfully supply them. Areas where climate and soil ensured vine-owners a regular high yield won out over those where yields were low and harvests unreliable and whose wine was therefore likely to be more expensive. Similarly, producers who could transport their wine to large markets easily by water were more competitive than those who supplied local consumers or were not located on the major water routes. The regions that prospered enjoyed the best combinations of environment and access to substantial markets, giving their wines a good balance of quality and price.

The main regions of France that prospered in this period were the area centred on Bordeaux, which benefited from trade with England; Auxerre in lower Burgundy (now the Chablis region), whose wines were known in this period as burgundy and found their principal market in Paris; and Beaune, further to the south in what is now the Burgundy wine region. In contrast, the southern vineyards of the Rhône valley and Languedoc, despite their favourable growing conditions, were unable to benefit from increasing demand. They were located too far from the major centres of consumption, and those producers who tried to export their wine to the east found the passage blocked by their Burgundian competitors.[17]

It was in this period, between the thirteenth and fifteenth centuries, that the wines of Beaune shot from obscurity to being regarded as the greatest wines of France. This was an exceptional case of quality overcoming the obstacles of geography, for although the region around Beaune was ideal for grape cultivation, the town was not located on any major waterway. To reach the large Paris market, wine had to be moved by land from Beaune to the river Yonne before being shipped on barges to the capital, a route that added considerably to the end-cost of the wine. Once they recognized the wine's quality, however, Parisian consumers were willing to pay the price, even though it was further inflated by a higher tax than those imposed on other French wines. The Paris authorities applied to wine from Beaune a levy more than twice that imposed on wine from Auxerre and four times that on wine from around the capital.

There was virtual unanimity among wine connoisseurs that beaune (which was not considered burgundy until the fifteenth century) was the best available. Its reputation was enhanced by its popularity among the rich, famous and powerful. From the 1300s it was ordered for the tables of successive French kings. In 1564, in the face of an impending visit to Dijon by Charles IX, the mayor declined to present the king with some of the reputable wine that was made in the locality, as we might expect a modern civic leader to do. Instead, he set up a special commission to go to Beaune to buy 'the most exquisite wine that can be found to be presented to the king upon his arrival'.[18] Beaune's wines also became favourites of the papal court when it took up residence in Avignon.

Like Beaune's, the vineyards of Tuscany expanded from the twelfth to fourteenth centuries. Their immediate markets lay in the rapidly growing Italian cities like Genoa, Naples, Milan, Venice and Florence. By the early 1300s the population of Florence had reached 90,000 (from a mere 6,000 three hundred years earlier), and each inhabitant drank, according to one contemporary calculation, an average of a gallon of wine a week. Florence might thus have provided a market for a third or more of the 7.9 million gallons (300,000 hectolitres) the city imported annually in the first half of the fourteenth century. The remainder was shipped on by Florentine merchants to markets elsewhere. To be sure, not all this wine was produced in Tuscany, but the scale of consumption and commerce involving Florence alone conveys a sense of the significance of the Italian wine industry in the later Middle Ages. Among the smaller Tuscan regions that participated in the burgeoning wine industry was Chianti, and in 1398 a white wine bearing that area's name was mentioned in a document for the first time.

Other European regions prospered because of specific local conditions. In the early fourteenth century the split within the Roman Church known as the Great Schism produced two popes. One remained in Rome and the other established himself in Avignon, in the southern Rhône region of France. This created a new demand for wine in the Rhône valley, not so much because of sacramental requirements as because the establishment of the alternative papal residence was accompanied by a huge bureaucracy of prelates and officials, all of whom drank wine. Such was the devotion of many members of the pope's retinue to it that they resisted returning to Rome for fear of being unable to get supplies of Beaune wine there.[19]

The papal court also required different (and less expensive) wine, a need that stimulated the expansion of vineyards in the Rhône valley, and they were later known and famed as Châteauneuf-du-Pape ('the new castle of the pope'). There is some question whether it was the first or second of the Avignon popes who ordered the planting of a vineyard next to the papal summer palace to the north of the city, but at the time little importance seems to have been attached to the wine's pontifical connections and it was known simply as wine of Avignon (vin d'Avignon).

Avignon makes an excellent case study of the way a market could stimulate production in a particular locality, and the growth in production between 1000 and 1500 speaks loudly to a generalized increase in demand. This does not mean that everyone turned equally to wine, for beer remained the most common alcoholic drink in most of medieval Europe. Among wine-drinkers, too, there were immense variations in consumption according to region, class and gender. We would expect wine to have been consumed more in wine-producing regions, where it was less expensive because its price did not include the costs of transportation. Wine might have been consumed daily at some social levels, less often at others, while the poorer members of society might have tasted wine only on special occasions such as festivals, if at all. We must also make allowances for different grades of wine. Small-scale producers frequently drank piquette, the thin wine made by adding water to the grape pulp left over after pressing, so that they could sell the maximum amount of wine on the market, and most of what they sold was relatively inexpensive and at best mediocre in quality. But the burgeoning urban, middle-class society demanded more and more luxury consumer goods of all kinds, including fine foods and wines.

The small French community of Montaillou, in the foothills of the Pyrenees, gives us some sense of wine-drinking in a region without vineyards. In the fourteenth century Montaillou had a population of between 200 and 250, large enough to support a wine-seller who made rounds of the houses selling wine that had been brought in by mule from Tarascon and Pamiers. Yet wine was not part of the daily diet. Shepherds might include sour wine in their daily fare, along with milk, but the community's inhabitants generally drank wine only on special occasions, such as weddings, and around the fire at night. According to a popular belief current in the community, the dead also enjoyed a nocturnal glass of wine: at night the dead were said to go from house to house, lighting fires in the hearths, drinking the best wine and sometimes emptying barrels in the wealthiest houses. According to one version of this belief, even when the wine was thus consumed, the level of wine in the barrels did not fall.[20]

As for the situation in a wine-producing area, documents from Lorraine, in eastern France, are revealing of consumption in the fourteenth and fifteenth centuries.[21] Although it is no longer an important producer of wine, having been eclipsed by its southern neighbour Alsace, Lorraine did produce significant quantities of wine in the Middle Ages, and its inhabitants seem to have been loyal consumers of the local product as well as importers of wine from elsewhere. Wine was consumed in households as grand as those belonging to the Duke of Lorraine and as poor as those of peasants who produced wine for their own use. Between these extremes lay nobles, high-office holders in the Church, and the bourgeois and artisans of Lorraine's towns, all of whom bought wine.

Purchases show that the household of the Duke of Lorraine consumed about 7,000 litres of wine a month (234 litres a day). There is no way of knowing for sure how many people shared this wine, although it was clearly more than the duke and his wife. Nor does this monthly average take feast days and banquets into account, when more wine was drunk than on ordinary days. When the dukes travelled they seem generally to have taken enough wine to allow each person in their retinue between one and three litres a day. The dukes' kitchens also used startling quantities of wine in the preparation of sauces for fish and meat: in 1481, some 468 litres were designated 'for cooking his lordship's fish'.

English rulers also helped boost demand for wine. In 1243 Henry III alone spent more than £2,300 on 1,445 casks of wine, about 350,000 gallons. Some of it was of a low standard, but more than two thirds of the purchase was top-quality wine that sold for almost £2 a barrel. When Henry's daughter Margaret married Alexander III of Scotland in 1251, the guests consumed 25,500 gallons of wine. It seems like a lot, but the quantity is brought into perspective when we consider that it was to accompany the 1,300 deer, 7,000 hens, 170 boars, 60,000 herrings and 68,500 loaves of bread the wedding party and guests went through. Edward II's coronation in 1307 was lubricated by a thousand barrels of wine – a quarter of a million gallons.[22]

Lower down the social scale, consumption was more moderate. Domestic accounts show that the household of Dame Alice de Bryene, of Acton Hall in Suffolk, took care of 262 gallons of red wine and 105 gallons of white in 1419. A century later the Earl of Northumberland's household consumed 1,600 gallons of wine in one year, a substantial quantity but still far less than the 27,500 gallons of ale the earl's family and staff drank in the same period. Yet even here, extraordinary occasions might call for extraordinary measures – of wine. The installation of the Archbishop of York in 1464 was celebrated by the consumption of a hundred casks of wine, about 25,000 gallons.[23]

Some people – women and men alike – received wine as part of their wages and pensions. Records show gifts of wine to religious orders for their consumption: in 1499 the nursing sisters of Nancy were given 1,874 litres of wine, while in 1502 the Minor Brothers received a gift of 2,342 litres of red wine 'to assist them to live'. In religious houses in England the dignitaries might have consumed wine regularly, but ordinary monks were more likely to subsist on ale. Yet they could be provided with wine on special occasions, like the monks of the Abbey of Ramsey who were given half a gallon of wine on festival days in 1284.[24]

Wine was included in annuities provided by the dukes of Lorraine to reward men and women who had served them in capacities as varied as valets, trumpeters, falconers and midwives. During 1406 the six men responsible for guarding the Château de Custines were supplied with just over two litres a day – more than was desirable, one might think, for men whose job was to keep a sharp lookout for intruders. (English soldiers seem to have received about half this ration.) Artisans employed in the duke's residences – masons, carpenters and cartwrights among them – received wine and other foodstuffs as part of their wages. Elsewhere, when the belfry of the church of Bonlieu-en-Forez was being built, the labourers were provided with eggs, meat, rye bread, beans for soup – and 'plenty of wine'.[25]

Although wine was enjoyed at all levels of society in medieval Lorraine, it is very unlikely that wine seriously challenged beer as the drink of mass consumption. If that were so in a region, like Lorraine, that produced wine, it was even more so where consumers relied on imports. In fourteenth-century England ale cost a penny for two gallons in the city and about half that in the country, while the price of Gascon or Spanish wine was about six pence a gallon, making wine twelve to twenty-four times the price of ale.[26]

None the less, wine was regularly supplied to soldiers as part of their provisions, and special care was taken to ensure that wine rations were received during military campaigns. The Bayeux Tapestry, depicting the Norman conquest of England in 1066, features a cart loaded with a cask of wine and military weapons making the crossing of the English Channel. In 1470 when an army led by the Duke of Lorraine was laying siege to Châtel-sur-Moselle, ninety-one barrels of wine (about 43,000 litres) were delivered.

We might cynically suggest that these supplies were designed at best to boost the soldiers' fighting spirits, at worst to render them oblivious to the dangers they faced. But it is clear that wine was a normal part of the soldier's diet and was treated as a basic commodity, like, for example, bread. Undoubtedly, too, wine protected the health of soldiers. Water supplies were frequently contaminated, and we can imagine that water at siege sites was especially so. Adding wine to water (another way of looking at diluting wine) was a means of killing some of the harmful bacteria and staving off sickness within armies. It is known, for example, that the microbes that carry typhoid die off when immersed in wine.[27] Support for this notion might lie in the fact that it was not only French soldiers, many of whom might have consumed wine on a daily basis, who received wine rations. English soldiers, who would have drunk beer, also received wine while on active service. In 1316, for example, Edward II of England ordered 4,000 barrels of wine for his army in action in Scotland. If these supplies helped the English, the Scots appear to have got their revenge two centuries later: in 1543 they captured the sixteen ships carrying Henry VIII's annual wine requirements.[28]

By the later Middle Ages, wine drinkers who could afford to were becoming increasingly discriminating and aware of the source of better-quality wines. English consumers gave high marks to the body and light red colour of the Gascon wine that was imported in such large quantities, and price variations reflected preferences for wines from some areas over others within Gascony itself. The sweeter wines of the Mediterranean region were also popular, but they were more expensive. Italy witnessed a similar development of connoisseurship during the twelfth and thirteenth centuries, when many new grape varieties were introduced. It is likely that the number of Italian vineyards increased, and those around Florence were not only extended further away from the city walls, but some might even have been planted within the walls: one Florentine church is named S. Jacopo Tra le Vigne (Saint James among the Vines).[29] Wine made from the traditional varieties ('Latin wine') was considered good enough for the masses, but those with more refined palates sought newer types and wines imported from Greece, Crete and elsewhere. The late-thirteenth-century poet Cecco Angiolieri put it this way:

> And I want only Greek and Vernaccia,
> For Latin wine is more distasteful
> Than my woman, when she nags me.[30]

The associations of wine with religion, power and wealth that persisted through the medieval period are expressed in a fictitious 'Battle of the

Wines' – a forerunner of international wine competitions – that was the subject of two poems written in the thirteenth and fourteenth centuries.[31] Each gave an account of a wine-tasting organized by King Philip Augustus of France, who nominated an English priest to judge the wines. The tasting was more than just an aesthetic occasion: the priest donned his stole as he tasted the wines so that he could 'excommunicate' any that he found unacceptable.

The 'Battle of the Wines' might give us a good indication of the wines thought superior early in the thirteenth century. In the earlier of the two versions, most of the wines tasted were French and the vast majority were from the north of France. Of the seventy mentioned by name, only two were from the Bordeaux region, six from Anjou-Poitou, two from Burgundy and four from Languedoc. A handful were from outside France, including Alsace, Mosel, Cyprus and Spain. It is notable that almost all the wines described in it were white, even the representative from Beaune.

The entry from Cyprus was judged the best overall and received a fitting tribute:

> The king crowned the wines judged good
> To each with a title he honoured
> A pope he made of the Cypriot wine
> For like a star in the heavens it shone[32]

Other wines received lesser titles. The second-best was named a cardinal, after which the titles shifted from ecclesiastical to secular: there were three kings, three counts and finally a dozen peers. In all, twenty of the seventy wines were honoured in this way, but eight wines, all from the north of France, were 'excommunicated'. Here, perhaps, was an indication of the way French viticulture was going over the long term, for in time (especially during the nineteenth century) vineyards in many parts of northern France became less and less viable and were ripped out.

As production became more important to specific regions and consumption spread, wine became increasingly subject to regulations. Some were designed to control the quality of wine at the point of production, some tried to prevent adulteration by merchants or retailers. Guilds imposed regulations on aspects of the wine trade as they did on scores of activities and other products in the Middle Ages. All were signs that a veritable wine industry was emerging.

In many parts of continental Europe, including France, agriculture generally was subject to communal controls, and vineyards were no exception. To take the example of the vineyards around Dijon, in France's Burgundy region, the grape harvest was jointly regulated by the city council and representatives of the wine-growers. They set the dates at which pruning could begin, when the vines could be tied up, and when the harvest could begin (the *ban de vendange*). They also protected the vineyards from animals and insects, sometimes by leading a religious procession through the town invoking God's intercession against infestations. At times of war the city council raised a militia to protect the vineyards or the workers during the harvest.[33]

It was in this period, too, that the Vintners' Company, the guild of wine merchants, emerged as a powerful commercial force in London. Although it did not receive its royal charter until 1437, organized vintners were by the early thirteenth century effectively regulating the city's important wine trades, both wholesale and retail. They were also a social force to be reckoned with, for more than a third of the city's aldermen were vintners, as was the mayor who represented London at the signing of Magna Carta in 1215.[34]

The most important issue, the price of wine, was fixed by the crown each year for different regions of England according to the quantities available, but the vintners were consulted. They had more direct power in other matters. Imported wine arriving in London could be unloaded only at a fixed location on the River Thames and then only by master wine-drawers. It could be moved – to special warehouses – only by a wine-drawer and twelve associates, and it could not be sold until each barrel was measured. Wine could be bought wholesale (by taverns and merchants) directly from shippers, but retail sales were the monopoly of the vintners' guild.[35]

The scale of the wine trade understandably attracted the fiscal interest of Europe's chronically needy rulers, and the English crown was only one of many that levied taxes on wine. As early as 1000 the Saxon king Ethelred II imposed a toll to be paid 'by the men of Rouen who come with wine', but with the expansion of the wine trade two hundred years later more exacting levies were set. English wine-shippers were struck with 'prisage', which gave the monarch (through an official called the 'king's butler') the right to two barrels from every shipment of wine of more than twenty-one barrels, and one barrel from smaller shipments. In the 1340s more than a hundred ships were levied prisage each year, garnering the crown more than 200 casks (180,000 litres) of wine annually.[36]

Foreign shippers were not subject to prisage, but from 1302 they had to pay 'butlerage', a tax of two shillings per cask. That sum was more or less equivalent to prisage when it was first set, but it became less and less significant as prices of wine rose. English shippers complained for centuries before prisage was replaced in the late sixteenth century by a monetary tax. A further levy, 'tunnage', was sometimes paid by all shippers. A tax imposed on each tun (barrel) of wine, tunnage was granted by parliament to the monarch for limited periods to meet extraordinary financial needs.

England was by no means the only state to tax wine, and levies were imposed on imports and sales throughout Europe. Duties were imposed on wine as it crossed provincial boundaries in France and municipalities large and small levied duties on wine brought into their markets: Paris taxed wine as it passed through the gates in the city walls, and the town of Romans in Dauphiné raised more from duties on wine than from duties on general merchandise crossing the bridge into the community. In Poland the administration of Cracow taxed the wine traded by the town's merchants. In the Byzantine Empire owners of taverns were subjected to the *kapeliatikon*, a tax levied by the emperor but sometimes delegated to a landowner to impose on any taverns on his land. Some exemptions were granted, such as that to the monks of Mount Athos in 1408. They were allowed to sell their wine free of the *kapeliatikon* as long as they did not interfere with one another's business.[37] In Flanders, the town of Bruges frequently derived most of its municipal revenues from excises on wine imports, most of which came from France. In 1335, 65 per cent of revenues were obtained this way, and even though the proportion fell to about 45 per cent in the 1420s, it is clear that the appetite for wine among the 35,000 inhabitants of Bruges largely funded the city's operations.[38]

Taxation had no purpose but to raise money for the various levels of

European governments, but many of the guild and communal restrictions on the production and transportation of wine were designed to ensure quality. Further attempts were made to regulate the sale of wine so that the health and financial interests of consumers were protected. The English authorities were as concerned about the adulteration of wine as they were of other food and drink. The quality of wine varied greatly, but much of it was light and unstable, and this, added to the fact that it was stored in barrels, meant that wine deteriorated quickly, often within a year. Unscrupulous merchants were tempted to mix bad wine with good rather than pour their investments away, the sort of practice that Geoffrey Chaucer, writing in the late 1300s, had the Pardoner warn of in *The Canterbury Tales*:

> Keep clear of wine, I tell you, white or red,
> Especially Spanish wines which they provide
> And have on sale in Fish Street and Cheapside.
> That wine mysteriously finds its way
> To mix itself with others – shall we say
> Spontaneously? – that grow in neighbouring regions.[39]

Various regulations were imposed in England to prevent such practices or at least to make them more difficult. Tavern-keepers were permitted to sell red wine or white wine but not both, and in 1353 they were forbidden to stock sweet wine with any other type. As a further precaution, cellars were required to be visible so that customers could see their wine being drawn from its barrel. Such regulations could easily be circumvented, of course, and some tavern-owners hung curtains over the doors of cellars so that they could carry out their blending activities in private. John Penrose, a tavern-keeper found guilty of adulterating wine, was not only sentenced to drink some of his own concoction and throw away the rest, but was also banned from selling wine for five years.[40] In 1456, when it was discovered that the Lombard wine merchants had adulterated their sweet wine, the Lord Mayor of London ordered 150 barrels to be staved in. The result was that 'liquor running forth, passed through the cittie like a stream of rainwater in the sight of all the people, from whence there issued a most loathsome savour'.[41] Other dishonest vintners tried to disguise wine that had gone bad by adding pitch, wax, gum, powdered bay and other ingredients. The fact that substances like turnsole, a purple dye, were added to some wines, suggests that colour was important to wine consumers as a guide to quality; that is, the deeper the red, the better the wine. Yet although such additives might have restored some body and colour to 'broken' wine, it is unlikely that they did anything to improve the taste. Regulations were introduced in London in 1419 specifically to stop the 'counter-feiting' of romeney, a Greek wine similar but inferior to malmsey, by adding illicit substances to Spanish or French wine. William Horold, a barrel-maker, was promptly convicted under this law for adding gum and powdered bay to his 'old and feeble Spanish wine'.[42]

Given the methods of storing wine in the Middle Ages, deterioration was an ever-present risk, but not all corrupted wine was thrown out. Some was given to the poor (their appreciation of this charitable gesture is not recorded), and in England some of the king's old wine was sold off. Perhaps there was some social cachet attached to drinking wine that had been in the royal cellar, even if it did taste awful. For his part, the cost-conscious Earl of Northumberland had all his 'brokyn' wine made into vinegar, while yet others looked for ways to make theirs drinkable again.

Some suggestions for restoring wine that had gone off were included in *Le Ménagier de Paris*, a work written in the late fourteenth century, possibly by a knight in the service of the Duke of Berry, to advise his young wife on such diverse but useful matters as obedience to her husband, hiring servants, training dogs, ridding hawks of lice and prepar-ing food and drink. According to this guide, a wife should have the steward check the household's wine every week and take urgent steps when any had gone bad. One method, applicable only in winter, was to set the barrel on trestles in the courtyard so that it caught the frost. Another, to treat wine gone sour, was to put a basket of black grapes into the barrel through the bunghole. If wine smelt bad, bags of elder wood and powdered cardamom should be placed in the barrel. Muddy wine could be clarified by hanging in it bags containing the hot whites and shells (but not the yolks) of a dozen eggs that had been boiled then fried. Alternatively, one could heat a big new pot over a fire until it was well baked, then shatter it and put the pieces into the wine. Redness could be removed from white wine by adding holly leaves to the barrel. Bitterness could be neutralized by adding hot boiled corn or, if for some reason that failed, a basketful of sand that had been well washed in water from the Seine.[43]

Some of these remedies might have worked. Egg whites, for example, can be used to clarify wine. As for many of the rest, their effectiveness is anybody's guess, but there is no reason to think that they worked. If the recommendations were faithfully followed, a barrel of thoroughly bad wine would have been full of eggs, corn, leaves, various herbs and broken crockery. And the wine would still be bad. Perhaps the most viable among these suggestions was to expose the wine to frost: that would at least chill it to the point where offensive tastes would be less noticeable.

The problem of wine going off or being adulterated was significantly reduced only with the introduction of bottles in the seventeenth century, but it was not until the 1900s that wine-makers began to bottle their own wine on a significant scale. Until then, regulatory bodies like the Vintners' Company in London, which carried out regular inspections of taverns, did their best to control the conditions under which wine was stored and sold. Yet these were far from the only spheres of regulation in England. Others included the standardization of serving size in taverns; wine could not be served in the small cups from which it was drunk but had to be drawn into vessels whose volume was certified to be true by the sheriff. Even the size of private cellars was restricted when Edward VI banned commoners with incomes or property under a certain level from keeping more than ten gallons of wine in their houses for private consumption.[44]

Other regulations concerned consumption more directly: drunkenness, particularly in public, was an offence in legal codes throughout Europe. We have no idea of the frequency of alcoholic intoxication, but it was clearly a recognized phenomenon. It could hardly have been otherwise in a culture where wine and beer were widely consumed.*

'The Pardoner's Tale' in Chaucer's *Canterbury Tales* includes a long section on the perils of excessive wine-drinking, even when the wine had

---

* Indeed, drinking was positively promoted by criers employed by the city and paid for by tavern-keepers. Each morning the criers would visit taverns to find out what was available, and then went through the street carrying a bowl of the wine (which could be sampled) which they beat with a stick.[45]

not been adulterated. Wine, said the Pardoner, was linked to all manner of immorality:

> Witness the Bible, which is most express
> That lust is bred of wine and drunkenness.
>   Look how the drunken and unnatural Lot
> Lay with his daughters, though he knew it not;
> He was too drunk to know what he was doing . . .
>   But seriously, my lords, attention, pray!
> All the most notable acts, I dare to say,
> And victories in the Old Testament,
> Won under God who is omnipotent,
> Were won in abstinence, were won in prayer.
> Look in the Bible, you will find it there.[46]

The Pardoner might just as well have preached to his clerical colleagues. The Church had its own rules of discipline applicable to members of the clergy, and although they were not so extreme as to require abstinence, they did demand moderation. Many priests and monks fell short of these expectations, however, as ecclesiastical records amply reveal. On one mid-thirteenth-century visit to parts of northern France officials found many priests in breach of rules concerning alcohol: the priest of St Rémy was notorious for drunkenness and for frequenting a local tavern, where he had been beaten up on several occasions; the priest of Gilemerville had occasionally lost his clothes in taverns (presumably by gambling, possibly under more dubious circumstances); the priest of Pierrepont was a drunkard; the priest of Grandcourt was notorious for his excessive drinking; and the priest of Panliu was infamous for drinking and compounded this offence by selling wine and getting his parishioners drunk.[47]

Urban taverns and inns, which of course sold other alcoholic beverages besides wine, became objects of official concern because of the drunken disorder that often emanated from them. They are often portrayed as places where excessive drinking mingled with gambling and sexual immorality – associations that anti-alcohol activists would take up in the nineteenth century. Medieval taverns were indeed often the locations of brawls, but quite possibly no more so than market places, where sober merchants and customers frequently came to blows over transactions and prices. Some municipalities tried to limit drinking hours in taverns, but they were generally unsuccessful, for example the royal decree of 1350 that required Paris innkeepers not to allow drinkers in after the bells of Notre Dame cathedral had rung out the curfew hour.

Some tavern incidents were notable, like the one that broke out in 1229 near the church of St Marceau in Paris. A group of theological students, apparently in oenological training for their vocation, drank deeply and then quarrelled with the proprietor about the cost of the wine they had consumed. A fight ensued, but the innkeeper, assisted by other tavern owners who came to his help, beat the students off. The students returned the next day, however, with their own reinforcements, and did immense damage. The authorities intervened and dealt with the students, but the incident soured relations between the university and the community for some time.[48]

Alongside the alarm frequently expressed about the personal and social effects of excessive drinking, medieval medical writers continued to praise the health-giving properties of wine. They drew heavily on Greek, Roman and Arabic traditions, which, as we have seen, used wine to treat a wide range of illnesses and other medical problems. In accordance with the recommendations of Hippocrates and Galen, wine was frequently used as an antiseptic to dress wounds, as well as to reduce fever and to treat many gastro-intestinal disorders. Wine was also popular because, since it contained alcohol, other substances could be dissolved in it, and it was the preferred base of many herbal medicines. Herbs mixed with wine were prescribed for cataracts, styes and general swellings and pains in the eyes.[49] Wine containing the berries of the gladden plant was recommended to women suffering sore breasts.

One of the most prominent advocates of the curative and health-giving properties of wine was Henri de Mondeville, a fourteenth-century French surgeon.[50] Like other medical writers, he stressed the benefits of wine for the blood in particular, but, reflecting the growth of connoisseurship, he insisted that only good wine would do the job. It had to be the best one could find, rosé or white, light, with a good aroma and pleasant taste, and it should certainly not be one of the poor French wines like those from Auxerre or Montpellier. Good wine, Mondeville wrote, is the most effective food for generating blood, for it enters the bloodstream directly, where it is itself transformed into blood. (Mondeville stressed the similar appearance of wine and blood, even though he recommended white and light red wines.) He broke with accepted medical opinion and prescribed wine for injured patients, writing that the issue was not whether a patient should have wine but how much a patient should have.

The physical benefits of wine-drinking were visible to Mondeville's discerning eye. Along with wine he recommended the drinking of milk, and noted that each of these liquids had its parallel in the human body: wine resembled blood, milk resembled other bodily fluids like phlegm and maternal milk. Each presented itself in the skin, for that of a wine-drinker tended to be reddish while that of a milk-drinker was pale. A proper balance of wine and milk in the diet (though they should never be drunk together) would make for an ideal complexion, pale with rosy cheeks.

In some cases wine might have been used in an attempt to make very bitter or unpleasant concoctions more palatable, but, in general, medieval doctors seem to have cared little for their patients' aesthetic sensibilities. Indeed, many seem to have appreciated the classical view that because many illnesses and diseases were the work of a devil or demon that had taken control of the afflicted body, it was desirable to administer medicines so revolting that no evil spirit would want to share the body with them. This theory ignored the possibility that a patient faced with the ingestion or application of such appalling substances as bird droppings, dog brains and goat urine, whether or not they were mixed with wine, might lose the will to live.

It was recognized, however, that whatever properties wine might possess as a curative, it could also be responsible for illness. The influential work *On the Properties of Things*, written by the Franciscan monk Bartholomeus Anglicus in the mid thirteenth century, acknowledged that excessive consumption of wine was a common reason for headaches.[51]

Such warnings about the potentially harmful effects of wine-drinking clearly went as unheeded in the Middle Ages as at any other time. In the first 500 years of the second Christian millennium, wine consolidated its position in the diet of a significant portion of the European population. As the secular attraction of wine spread, its religious associations also deepened as the Church, the single most important institution of the medieval world, stressed the link between wine and the divine. Many images on the theme of 'Christ in the wine press' depicted the crucifix as an integral part of the press's beam, and showed the blood from Christ's hands and feet mingling with the must. So intimate was the connection of wine to the dominant religious doctrines that they became almost impossible to separate. As a daily or special beverage, a religious icon, and as the object of an industry and growing commerce, wine emerged from the Middle Ages on as secure a basis as it had ever known.

FIVE

NEW WINES, NEW SKILLS

The Revolution in Alcohol, 1500–1700

The production of wine in Europe expanded from 1500 to 1700. Population, and therefore the market for all goods including wine, increased during the sixteenth century as Europe finally recovered from the demographic disaster of the Black Death. Even though there was little population growth in the seventeenth century, there were many more inhabitants in Europe in 1700 than there had been two hundred years earlier. Wine producers were able to meet growing demand thanks in part to a warming tendency in the early sixteenth-century climate that enabled grapes to be cultivated in parts of Europe where they had previously been marginal. Throughout the whole of Europe, in fact, more and more land came under viticulture, and the sixteenth century was generally a good period for wine. But the following hundred years were different. Not only did temperatures cool, but war devastated many central European vineyards and shifting political alliances played havoc with the wine trade in important regions such as Bordeaux.

One of the success stories of the time was Spain's wine industry, for the sixteenth century saw Spanish viticulture make great leaps forward. In part the reason was that from 1519 Spain became, by dynastic marriage, part of the Habsburg Empire. This gave it an affiliation with the Netherlands, and the Spanish exploited the opportunity by exporting wine there, both for consumption and re-export. By the mid 1500s Antwerp had become a major wine-exporting centre, shipping Iberian wine to other parts of northern Europe.

Spanish viticulture was also stimulated by a growth in domestic demand. The expansion of the royal court and its bureaucracy probably stimulated a small wine boom in itself, but there was also a general increase in urban demand. This was met by an expansion of viticulture in Castile, particularly in the region southwest of Valladolid where the royal court was established until 1606. Evidence of the growing importance of wines from this region is a series of laws issued by Philip II in 1597 to control the quality and sale of wine. They forbade the mixing of red and white and the use of harmful additives. The laws also restricted the period in which wine could be imported from the countryside to Valladolid (by the last day of February following the year of vintage) and required the producers of wine made in the town to obtain a licence. These laws had two principal purposes: to ensure quality for the consumers in the royal court and to prevent the production of cheap, poor-quality wine which, it was thought, was causing widespread drunkenness.[1]

A third factor in the expansion of Spanish wine production, and by no means the least significant, was the growing popularity of Spanish wine in the important English market. The Spanish were quick to benefit from the English loss of Gascony to France in 1453 and the resulting decline in French exports. English wine-consumers developed a taste for the sweeter wines of southern Europe the Mediterranean over the drier French product, and one in particular became fashionable: Spanish 'sack'. The derivation of the name, sometimes written 'seck', is often thought to have been from the Spanish word for 'dry' (seco). That explanation makes no sense, however, because this wine, the forerunner of sherry, was in fact sweet. An alternative, but unconvincing, suggestion is that 'sack' comes from the Spanish word sacar, to draw out, implying that the wine was intended for export.[2]

Wherever the origins of its name, sack was a best-selling wine in England from the late sixteenth century on, and its name has been immortalized in the words put in Falstaff's mouth by William Shakespeare. Falstaff, Henry IV's drinking comrade in his youth, waxes rhapsodic about 'sherris-sack' (that is, sack from the region of Jerez, the home of sherry) and attributes some of the best qualities of the prince (whom he calls Harry) to his extensive consumption of the wine. Sherry, says Falstaff, drives out foolishness and dullness and quickens the intellect and the wit. It warms the blood and makes the coward brave. If Henry has such fine qualities, they are due to both his lineage and to a healthy appetite for sherry:

Hereof comes it that Prince Harry is valiant; for the cold blood he did naturally inherit from his father he hath like lean, sterile and bare land manured, husbanded, and tilled, with excellent endeavour of drinking good and good store of fertile sherris, that he is become very hot and valiant. If I had a thousand sons, the first principle I would teach them should be to forswear thin potations and to addict themselves to sack.[3]

The combined effects of growing domestic and export markets, accompanied by a price inflation fuelled by silver from its American colonies, led to a rapid increase in the price of Spanish wine. In Andalusia prices rose nearly eight-fold between 1511 and 1559, a much higher rate of increase than for grain and olives, the other principal products. One result was that farmers rushed to plant new vineyards so as to cash in on the wine boom. The mania became so widespread that from 1579 the Cortes began petitioning the emperor to restrict the planting of new vineyards because too much land was being converted to viticulture.[4]

Spain was spared one of the great historical transformations of this period. The Protestant Reformation, the challenge to the Roman church by reformers like Martin Luther and John Calvin, saw the creation of new churches in many parts of Europe. Protestantism was, however, a cool-climate religion. For the most part it took root in northern Europe (Scotland, Scandinavia, the Netherlands, northern Germany, Switzerland and England), where viticulture was marginal if it existed at all. The main exceptions were the implantation of Protestantism in some of the north German wine regions and the popularity of Protestantism in southwest France in an arc that included wine areas in Bordeaux and parts of Languedoc.

For the most part, however, the wholesale confiscation of monastic lands that took place when Catholic religious orders were dissolved by Protestant rulers (as in England and Switzerland) had relatively little effect on the ownership of vineyards. Even so, the breakdown of a common European religious order into states with divergent religions had implications for the subsequent history of wine.

In one respect, Protestants promoted the demand for wine. Although they differed from Catholics on the meaning of the Eucharist, they stressed that Christians should take communion frequently, not merely once a year as Catholics generally did. Moreover, Protestants insisted that the laity should receive both bread and wine, not only the bread, as in Catholic communion. Calvin, whose theology was influential in Switzerland, the Netherlands and Scotland, and later among Puritans in England and America, wrote that by depriving the laity of wine the Church had 'stolen or snatched [it] from the greater part of God's people ... [and] given a special property to a few shaven and anointed men.'[5] It could be that the faithful were only too happy to follow the new teachings. At the first Presbyterian communion in Scotland the congregation was provided with so much wine that it was worth bringing it in a barrel. The volume of wine consumed in communions of this period suggests that 'people didn't take a little sip of wine ... they took a big mouthful, and refreshed themselves, as it were ...'[6]

Calvinists and other Protestants have earned a reputation for being puritanical in matters of sex, drinking and recreations like the theatre, dancing and gambling. As far as alcohol is concerned, though, their main concern was not to prohibit drinking but to prevent excessive consumption. This was a position not so different from the Catholic church which, as we have seen, consistently stressed the sinfulness and social dangers of persistently excessive drinking and drunkenness, not of drinking in itself. Thus we should not expect the Reformation to have a significant impact on wine, especially given that its appeal was for the most part in regions that were not centres of wine-production.

From the Reformation onwards, however, there were quite marked differences in the various churches' relationship to wine and other forms of alcohol. As we shall see in a later chapter, the nineteenth-century temperance and alcohol abolitionist movements attracted very little support from the Catholic church, while evangelical Protestant faiths were enthusiastic advocates. That the temperance movement would have very little support in France and other wine-producing states is perhaps not surprising; considerable proportions of their populations depended on wine for their livelihoods and it was a part of the daily diet. But even in minor wine-producing countries, like the United States and Canada, the Catholic church had a very low profile in the nineteenth-century anti-alcohol movements. Could it be that there was a connection between Catholicism and wine that was absent from Protestantism? Was the sixteenth-century Reformation for the most part unsuccessful in wine-producing regions because of factors associated with wine? It might be going too far to suggest that devotion to wine warded off the appeal of Protestantism, but there are suggestions that wine was implicated in the religious struggles of the period.

One notable example was Dijon, the largest town in the Burgundy wine region. In the sixteenth century, vineyards extended right to the walls of the city and the wine-growers tended to live in the city, rather than outside among their estates. They were, moreover, a considerable part of the city's population, accounting for between a fifth and a quarter of households in the 1500s. Not only were they numerous, but they were quite well-off and politically active, and what is notable about their political activity is that it was geared to supporting rigorous Catholicism over the newly arrived Protestantism. In the 1561 mayoral elections in Dijon, for example, 93 per cent of wine-growers supported a fervent Catholic candidate, and he won the election thanks to their support: 58 per cent of his votes were cast by wine-growers.[7]

This does not seem to have been an isolated case. Wine-grower support for the traditional church against Protestant encroachment seems to have been general throughout France. Wine-growers were conspicuous by their absence from Protestant movements in communities as widely dispersed as Rouen, Amiens and Troyes in the north, and Béziers, Montpellier, Toulouse and Bordeaux in the south and west. Dijon is a case from the east. This is not to say that wine-producers never rallied to Protestantism, for we know that many of the Huguenots (French Protestants) who fled religious persecution in this and later periods helped establish viticulture in North America and South Africa. But they were probably a small minority.

Assuming wine-growers did not see Protestantism as any more hostile to wine than Catholicism, and therefore not a threat to their economic well-being, why did most of them resist the new religion? In part it was perhaps because the Catholic religion was a much more communal faith that stressed the community of believers rather than, as in Protestantism, each individual forging his or her own personal relationship with God. Community was a strong value among wine-growers. Even the Catholic church's restriction of wine to the priest at communion was viewed as a more communal act – the priest drinking wine on behalf of the community – than the Protestant practice of each communicant taking an individual sip from the chalice.

In addition, wine-growers might well have had a sense of special responsibilities because they worked with the vines and made the wine that were such rich themes throughout the Bible. Wine-makers in Dijon referred to the words of Christ: 'I am the true vine, and my Father is the wine-maker . . . I am the vine, and you the branches. He who dwells in me, as I dwell in him, bears much fruit; for apart from me you can do nothing.'[8] These were powerful images that gave wine-makers a special status among the faithful, perhaps making them much more likely than many of their fellow citizens to be doctrinally conservative.

Equally powerful was the sense that God favoured or punished wine-makers according to their virtue. A late-sixteenth-century anonymous work from Burgundy, the *Monologue of the Worthy Wine-Maker*, noted that, 'It is when our vines are frozen in winter or hailed upon in summer, or when by some other means we harvest very little wine, that God has means enough to punish our past sins.' On the other hand, 'God protects the noble wine-grower.' God helped rid the vines of drought, lice and insects, and it was proper that the wine-growers of Dijon repaid this by ridding the city of Protestants. They frequently referred to Protestants as insects or vermin attacking the holy church as if they were the insects and vermin with which wine-growers had to contend in their vineyards.[9]

Perhaps Dijon's wine-makers also sensed a threat from the Calvinists active in Burgundy, which is not far from the border with Switzerland. When in the first half of the sixteenth century Calvin first began to proselytize in Geneva, he placed French-language Bibles in the city's taverns, a sort of forerunner of the distribution of Bibles in hotels by the Gideon Society. Calvin's act had all the appearance of toleration of drinking, as did his permission for a priest (who might himself abstain) to provide wine 'for the weaker brethren, and those who without it cannot attain bodily health'.[10] Later Calvinist ordinances forbade not only carousing but even one person treating another to a drink. This smacked not only of a mean attitude towards alcohol, but it also flew in the face of widely accepted notions of sociability and community. For Calvin, it seems, wine was to be consumed in very small quantities and as part of the diet or as a medicine, not for pleasure.

If we take the writings of Protestants at face value, however, their position on wine was little different from that of the Catholics. Protestants approved of drinking as long as it was in moderation, and they also recognized that it could have medical benefits. At the same time wine was regarded with suspicion because of its ability to inebriate and relax, both of which were thought to incline men and women towards immoral thought and behaviour. This was a cultural belief that cut across religious lines. Protestants were rigorous opponents of excessive drinking and drunkenness, and they insisted that the Church of Rome had been lax in enforcing discipline in this area as in others. They were particularly critical of the Catholic clergy, whom they condemned as lazy, wine-sodden fornicators.

The Protestant clergy were forbidden to drink excessively, and strict laws were drawn up against drunkenness on the part of anybody. Calvin's 1547 regulations for the supervision of churches in rural areas specified that, 'There is to be no treating of one another to drinks, under penalty of three sous.' In cases of drunkenness, a first offence was punished by a fine of three sous, a second by a fine of five sous, and a third by a fine of ten sous and imprisonment.[11] Nor were these mere threats. In the Dutch Calvinist community of Emden in the second half of the sixteenth century, convictions for drunkenness made up more than a quarter of all breaches of social order. Men arraigned for the offence outnumbered women by five to one.[12]

Despite Protestant allegations, Catholic writers frequently condemned excess, both in eating and drinking, as responsible for harm to the body, the soul and society. Wine, they argued, sent smoke and vapours to the brain that brutalized the spirit. Some clerical commentators invoked the example of Lot, while others condemned wine as provoking sensual pleasure and all the other passions, including anger. In the early seventeenth century the Franciscan Benedict considered it a mortal sin for a man to give himself to excess such that he could not pay his debts or feed his family; in such a case the confessor was to ask if he had impoverished his family by his drinking.[13]

But the cure for drunkenness, even persistent drunkenness (the concept of alcoholism had not yet been invented) called for temperance, not complete abstinence. Proverbs captured the prevailing sense that wine should be consumed in moderate quantities. 'Eat bread as long as it lasts, but drink wine moderately,' advised one. Drunkenness threatened the natural order and could create conflict in a community: 'Whoever surrenders to too much wine retains little wisdom.' Many proverbs revealed a particular anxiety about the mixing of women and wine: 'A drunk woman is not the mistress of her body,' and, 'Gambling, women and wine make a man laugh while he is being ruined.'

Apart from court cases where men and women were charged with being drunk, evidence of excessive consumption of wine tends to be anecdotal. Engravings of peasant festivities in sixteenth- and seventeenth-century Germany generally show at least one guest turning round on the bench to vomit away from the table. Echoing Roman allegations about the drinking habits of the Germanic tribes, one visitor to Montpellier in 1556 noted that all the 'boozers' in town were German, and that they were to be found snoring under barrels.[14]

Wine was not the only alcohol implicated in the discussion of excessive drinking, for ale was even more widely consumed. It was the alcoholic beverage of longest standing and was drunk at all social levels throughout Europe. It could be made almost everywhere because its main ingredient, grain, was the staple of the contemporary diet and was cultivated anywhere it could be coaxed to grow. In regions where apples grew well, cider was also drunk, albeit mainly by the poorer members of society. By 1500 these areas included Normandy and Brittany in France and southwest England (especially Devon), all regions that remain centres of cider-making today.

Wine began to have a significant impact on the consumption of beer during the later Middle Ages. By 1500, wine was still confined to the better-off in many regions, particularly in northern Europe, far from the grape-growing areas. But it was socially widespread in wine-producing areas and in cities sufficiently close to vineyards that it could be imported cheaply. Paris, which drew primarily on vineyards along the rivers Seine, Marne and Yonne, is an example.

During the seventeenth century, however, beer made a comeback in some regions. Many German vineyards were ruined during the Thirty Years War in the first half of the century and by Louis XIV's wars in the second. These disasters, compounded by several poor grape harvests in the later seventeenth century, drove many Germans back to beer.

There were also innovations in brewing during the seventeenth century that increased the popularity of beer. Hops became more widely used and more aromatic beers were made. It is significant that in 1662 the municipal authorities of Bordeaux forbade the brewing of beer in the city because of the threat it represented to sales of the wine on which much of Bordeaux's prosperity depended.[15]

But beer was not the main threat to wine in this period: the real competition came from distilled alcohol, particularly in the form of brandy. The process of distilling was well known, but it was largely restricted (in many places by law) to apothecaries and doctors who used distilled wine, known as *aqua vitae*, or 'water of life', as a medicine. In early sixteenth-century France, however, vinegar-makers were permitted to distil wine, and in 1537 the privilege was extended to victuallers.

The distilling industry began slowly at first, not least because the stills were expensive to construct, but before long it emerged as a major sector of alcohol production. The impetus was the market provided by The Netherlands, which began to import brandy both for domestic consumption and for re-export to other parts of northern Europe. Dutch merchants also purchased immense volumes of brandy for their merchant fleet, then the world's largest. Added to casks, brandy tended to slow down the souring of water supplies during voyages in hot climates, and consumed directly by seamen it was a useful resource in cold regions. So important was the Dutch role in the development of brandy that the word itself comes from the Dutch *brandewijn* meaning 'burnt wine'.

Brandy had several commercial advantages over wine. First, distilling wine increases the amount of alcohol. It took about five or six units of wine to make one of brandy, but brandy had up to eight times the alcohol content of wine by volume. In short, grapes produced more alcohol as distilled wine than as ordinary wine. There were also immense advantages in terms of transportation because the costs of shipping brandy were much lower, per unit of alcohol, than shipping wine. For consumers, brandy provided a different but palpable benefit: an immediate feeling of warmth that wine and beer lacked. It was perhaps this quality that explains the popularity of brandy and other distilled spirits in the colder northern markets.

The savings on transporting brandy rather than wine could only be realized, however, if brandy was manufactured before being shipped. To this end, Dutch entrepreneurs were instrumental in setting up distilleries in those regions of France on which they had come to rely for wine, notably Bordeaux and the Loire Valley. When Bordeaux began to make higher-quality red and sweeter white wines, the Dutch turned to the Charente region to the north of Bordeaux. Not only was this an area of poor-quality wine, but it was well furnished with forests and, therefore, the wood needed to fuel the brandy stills. The Dutch encouraged the cultivation of grapes specifically for distilling, instead of relying on wine that was available because it had not been sold owing to its quality or because of a glut on the wine market.

In Charente the first still was set up in 1624 and the next year brandy was being shipped from la Rochelle, which quickly became the main export centre for the region. By 1640 brandy was being taxed, a sure sign of its growing significance. By the 1660s Charente, which includes the area of Cognac that later gave its name to a brandy of distinction, was the centre of a massive distilling industry. Dutch merchants were the foremost shippers, taking brandy (along with wool and salt) to England and to ports in the North Sea and Baltic such as Danzig, Riga and Königsberg.

With the Dutch at the heart of the brandy trade, the beverage became popular throughout northern Europe. Brandy was quickly adopted as the alcohol of choice on merchant and naval ships, for it occupied less space and travelled far better than wine. It is thought that the taste for brandy quickly spread to the terrestrial populations of ports as seamen drank it in taverns while on shore. Varying qualities and prices permitted brandy to become popular throughout many social levels in The Netherlands, England and other countries.

So quickly did the demand for brandy grow that wine-makers in other parts of France and Europe began to distil their own poor-quality wine. In Languedoc and elsewhere, producers distilled wine that was so poor that it would otherwise have been sold as vinegar within six months of grape harvest. Brandy became a common drink in Languedoc from the 1660s onwards, and the port of Sète, established in 1670, became a major export point for the region's distilled alcohol. In 1699 some 10,000 hectolitres of alcohol passed through Sète.[16]

Brandy was also the base for a number of new drinks produced by the addition of ingredients that could easily be dissolved in the alcohol. In the sixteenth century a monk at the Benedictine Abbey of Fécamp in Normandy made a cocktail of brandy, honey and herbs, which he called Benedictine. Early in the seventeenth century an infusion of what was said to be more than a hundred herbs in brandy was created by Carthusian monks in Paris. Their concoction was given the name Chartreuse. These were only two of what would become thousands of liqueurs, representing various combinations of herbs, spices and other ingredients infused into distilled wine.

As if this were not enough, even more forms of alcohol came on to the market once the principles of distilling became widely known and practised. Wine was not the only substance that could be distilled, and, from the seventeenth century especially, grain was distilled to make beverages that included whisky, vodka and gin. For the first time, regions in northern and eastern Europe, where vines do not grow easily or at all, were able to produce their own alcohol with a strength greater than that of beer. Being made from grain, these beverages were often inexpensive, although the production of alcohol during poor harvests used grain that might better have been consumed as bread. This was a turning-point in the history of alcohol, if not of wine, especially in the Nordic regions and Russia.

Distilled alcohol was also to become particularly important in Europe's colonies, as we shall see in the next chapter. In the Spanish territories in South America, especially in Peru, a major brandy industry developed during the seventeenth and eighteenth centuries. In the English colonies of the Caribbean, sugar cane was distilled into rum. This beverage not only became popular in the English colonies of North America, where attempts to make wine failed consistently until the nineteenth century, but it also sold well in England and The Netherlands and became the staple alcohol of the Royal Navy.

The advent of inexpensive spirits, especially brandy, appears to have increased alcohol consumption throughout Europe. In 1675 about 4,000 tuns of French brandy (about 4,500,000 litres) were exported to England, and in 1689 twice that amount.[17] In terms of pure alcohol, then, brandy quickly gave wine a run for its money. Over time, other spirits also gained in popularity. In the eighteenth century, gin became so widely consumed in England that it was regarded as a real threat to the social order, just as rum, whisky and vodka have been in other places in more recent times.

The Dutch role in the alcohol trade expanded during the first half of the seventeenth century when it became Europe's commercial powerhouse, and Dutch merchants involved themselves in virtually all forms of commerce. The Netherlands established colonies in North America, the West Indies, South Africa, Ceylon and the East Indies, and by 1650 its merchant fleet numbered ten thousand. Not for nothing were the Dutch called 'the waggoners of the seas', as they plied the world's maritime highways. Much of Europe's important and lucrative wine trade fell under their control. Dutch merchants shipped vast quantities of wine from French and Spanish wine regions to Rotterdam, which replaced Antwerp as the pre-eminent wine port after the Dutch won their independence, and from there re-exported most of it to other north European ports along the coasts of the North Sea and the Baltic.

But the Dutch were not just mere conveyors of wine from one port to another. Just as they were active in promoting the French distilling industry, they also began to participate in viticulture and wine-making in many regions, of which Bordeaux was one of the most important. It can be said that during the seventeenth century, a period of critical change in much of France's wine industry, the Dutch were in control. Not only did they dominate shipping and many European markets, but by doing so they were able to influence production, quality and even the types of wine that were produced. One of the skills the Dutch brought to Europe was land reclamation, a practice they had honed as they reclaimed much of their own country from the North Sea. In Bordeaux Dutch technicians drained land along the banks of the major rivers, and were influential in planting vineyards in what is known as 'palus' (marshland), the reclaimed alluvial land that was before long recognized as being excellent for viticulture.

Dutch and northern European tastes in wine differed from that of Bordeaux's traditional English customers. Whereas the English had preferred light-red clarets, the Dutch opted for whites that were sweet and reds that were deep-coloured and full-bodied. By the middle of the seventeenth century the Dutch had become such important customers that Bordeaux's vine-owners were planting to suit them. Many growers switched from red wine to white, frequently replanting with muscat vines, so as to fill the Dutch order-books for sweet whites. Among the districts that switched was Sauternes, identified by the Dutch as a locality where the harvest could be delayed well into the autumn so as to maximize the sugar content of the grapes. It was in this period of Dutch hegemony, specifically in the 1660s, that Sauternes began to produce the sweet white wine for which it became famous. As for the stronger reds, it was discovered that they could be produced from the reclaimed alluvial lands, and the result was the beginning of significant viticulture in the Graves and Médoc districts of Bordeaux.

Dutch preferences were clear in the prices they paid for different wines. In the scale of prices for 1647, merchants paid between 95 and 105 livres for a 900-litre barrel for the red wines of the palus and between 84 and 100 livres for sweet whites, including those from Sauternes. Other whites commanded lower prices (Entre-Deux-Mers, for instance, fetched between 60 and 75 livres a barrel), while reds that would within a century become recognized as premium wines earned their producers relatively modest returns. Wines from Graves and Médoc were priced at between 78 and 100 livres and Saint-Emilion from 60 to 78 livres.[18]

The Dutch not only constituted the market for much of Bordeaux's wine production and extended the land available for vines, they also helped improve the durability of the wine. This was sometimes achieved by adding alcohol to the wine, but more importantly the Dutch transferred to France the technique, already used in the Rhineland, of burning sulphur in barrels before filling them with wine. This had the effect of stabilizing wine, especially the sweet whites, and preventing them from completing their fermentation (and thus losing more of their residual sugar) while they were being shipped. On the negative side, it was necessary to keep these wines in the barrel longer before releasing the wine for sale, to allow the odours from the sulphur to dissipate.

But despite the evident benefits that Dutch merchants and technical expertise brought to the Bordeaux wine industry, there was growing resentment in the English and French governments at the Dutch commercial success. The Dutch had implanted themselves so thoroughly in Bordeaux's wine economy that hundreds of Dutch families had become naturalized citizens of the city, not least so that they could benefit from the trading privileges that accompanied citizenship. There were persistent complaints from French commentators that wine was being made to order for foreigners and concerns in some regions about the effects on wood supplies caused by cutting down trees to fuel the brandy stills.

The activities of the Dutch merchants and entrepreneurs were soon limited, but not because the authorities were worried that French wine-making was being corrupted by profits. Rather, the French and English governments saw Dutch commercial power as a threat, and both began to adopt policies to protect their own merchant fleets. In England a series of Navigation Acts was passed to make it difficult for goods to be imported to England in any but English ships. For their part the French embarked on a rapid building programme to create a merchant fleet that could compete with the Dutch. In the 1660s Colbert, Louis XIV's finance minister, imposed punitive tariffs on foreign merchants, an act that harmed Bordeaux's wine exports and led to open conflict between Bordeaux and the royal government.

Undaunted, Dutch merchants began to look further afield for wine supplies, and they located them in Spain. The vineyards of Jerez, the home of sherry, along with Malaga and Alicante, began to supply substantial quantities of wine for Dutch shippers and also to England. By 1675 some 17,000 barrels of Spanish wine (about 2,400,000 litres) entered England, an impressive quantity compared to the 34,000 barrels of French wine that were the staple English import that year.

Politics, national and international, played havoc with the wine trade in the final decades of the seventeenth century. In 1679 the English parliament completely banned French wines, in order to prevent Charles II from receiving tariffs which were contributing the income that enabled him to govern without asking parliament for funds. The English turned to Portugal for wine supplies. Portugal had been a small exporter to England, its wine in 1678 accounting for a mere 427 tuns, compared to more than 15,000 tuns of French wine. In 1679, however, just over a thousand tuns of Portuguese wine were imported, and in the years 1682, 1683 and 1685 they averaged an incredible (literally so) 14,000 tuns a year – some 16 million litres.[19] These figures were scarcely believable at the time and are no more so now, and it is assumed that much of the 'Portuguese' wine was in fact French wine that was shipped via Portugal or reached England in other ways (such as in Portuguese barrels) that disguised its true origins.

In 1685 the English lifted the ban on French wine, and in 1687 some 15,500 tuns were imported, the largest amount ever from France in a single year before the twentieth century. (It is important to bear in mind that the population of England at the end of the seventeenth century was only about 4½ million, compared to 36 million two centuries later.) But any relief England's wine-drinkers might have felt as the flood of claret engulfed them was short-lived. The ban on French wine was reinstated after the 'Glorious Revolution' of 1688, which saw the anti-French William of Orange crowned king of England and a new alliance thus forged between England and The Netherlands. At last in 1697 a treaty was signed between England and France. It allowed the importation of French wines to England but subjected them to a tariff twice that applied to Spanish and Portuguese wines.

Although the wine regions of western France were buffeted by the political squalls of the seventeenth century, those in other parts of Europe fared worse. Many suffered from the Thirty Years War (1618–48), which devastated parts of central Europe. Vineyards were typically grown right up to walls of cities, and invading armies ripped out vines so as to put pressure on towns under siege. Not only were vineyards affected, but equipment including presses, barrels and barges were destroyed and many skilled vineyard workers were dispersed or lost their lives.

Vineyards that were not destroyed by armies as they made their way across hostile countryside suffered decades of neglect during the drawn-out conflict that raged across central Europe. Some 1300 hectares of land around Ammerschwihr, in Alsace, were under viticulture before the war, but only 200 hectares after it. Land suitable for vines lost its value to the point that at Riquewihr, where notable rieslings are now produced, three quarters of an arpent of vines was exchanged for one horse. The slow recovery of Alsatian viticulture was also due to the loss of markets. Even though Lorraine, Germany and Switzerland reopened trade in 1648, their populations had been ruined. The Netherlands was closed as a market from 1672 when the Dutch Wars broke out, and Alsace lost its markets in England and Scandinavia.[20] On the more positive side, over the longer term the devastation of Alsace's vineyards allowed for widespread replanting with what turned out to be productive and profitable riesling vines.

Throughout much of Europe, the end of the seventeenth century was problematic for wine producers in other regions, too. Not only had the century been tumultuous in political and military terms, but for several years during the 1690s grape harvests were nothing less than disastrous. In Bordeaux four terrible vintages followed in succession between 1692 and 1695, to the point that the region had to import wine from Languedoc.

It is not surprising, in light of the problems faced by German vineyards and trade bans imposed on their French counterparts, that Spanish and Portuguese wines began to dominate the important English wine market. Within this broad category we should note the high status accorded to wines from the Canary Islands (which are discussed in the next chapter). By the end of the seventeenth century the rich Canary wines were prized above all others; in the 1690s a gallon of Canary wine sold for eight shillings, compared to six shillings and eight pence for sherry, six shillings for Tuscan wine, and only four shillings and eight pence for port. But the problem with Canary wine, which led eventually to its decline, was an imbalance of trade. There were simply not enough goods that England could export to the Canary Islands to pay for the volumes of wine that were available. The woollen textiles that were English merchants' common currency had little commercial value in the warm climate of these islands off the African coast.[21]

The increased production of wine in Europe from 1500 could be supported only by an expansion of the wine market, and for the most part that meant an expansion of the European market itself. Spain had the possibility of exporting wine to its Central and South American colonies, but the potential was never realized. Despite persistent attempts by Spanish wine-makers to limit it, a major wine industry developed in colonies such as Peru and Chile, which enabled Latin America to become largely self-reliant for wine supplies. The English colonists in North America were less fortunate, and they did constitute a new outlet for French and other European wines. But it was a small market because most English settlers drank ale and later rum and whiskey.

For the most part, then, we must look to an expansion of the European demand for wine. Wine generally strengthened its position in the European diet in the Early Modern period, but this does not mean that large amounts were consumed per person. By the middle of the sixteenth century the inhabitants of the Spanish city of Valladolid, a city surrounded by vineyards, were consuming about a hundred litres of wine a year, a modest two modern bottles a week for every man, woman and child.[22] Assuming that children drank no wine, or a statistically insignificant volume, and that women consumed less than men, it is likely that the city's adult males had access to almost a bottle a day. The growth of the market for wine thus lay more in the increase in the European population and the fact that an increasing proportion of it was consuming wine on a regular basis, not just on special occasions. Wine had become part of the daily diet in much of Europe, especially in wine areas where it was inexpensive. It is likely to have been more widely consumed in cities than in rural areas and, ironically, it seems that many small wine-makers drank little of their own produce. The economics of wine-growing dictated that peasants had to sell all the wine they could in order to purchase the essentials – notably grain – that they did not produce because they practised viticulture.

The social spread of wine is suggested by the way it began to appear in proverbs, which were frequently expressions of common attitudes towards everyday experiences. French proverbs current in the sixteenth century revealed a number of attitudes.[23] Red wine was favoured over white, and Greek wine retained its reputation, as in the saying 'Of all the wine, the Greek is divine.' The association of wine and royalty placed wine at the top of the hierarchy of drinks, water at the bottom: 'Drink wine like a king, water like a bull.' Wine made for happiness: 'Water makes you cry, wine makes you sing.' It was best drunk in company: 'Wine without a friend is like life without a witness.'

So integral was wine to the diet that it was often supplied as part of the regular wages paid to workers. Domestic servants were supplied a ration of *vin des domestiques* as an integral element of their food. Independent workers were less likely to drink wine, not least because wine had to be purchased in large quantities; the law in France forbade the sale of wine wholesale in less than 68-litre quantities (a quarter of a *muid*).[24] Some workers received a wine ration to help them through the conditions they had to endure. Fishermen from Brittany and Normandy who made the long voyage to catch cod off the coast of Canada took with them a ration of one and a half barriques of wine or cider (about 240 litres) each. They sometimes watered white wine down to make 'breuvage'.[25]

Those who were not provided wine by their employers and who could not afford to buy it in bulk had several alternatives for obtaining small quantities. In France until 1759 the owners of vineyards who lived in cities were permitted to sell wine at their door – as long as the purchaser did not step inside and create the possibility of consuming it on the spot. Taverns were also an option, but in France the law prohibited tavern-keepers from selling to anyone who lived in the town; taverns were exclusively for travellers. This restriction, which dated back to the Middle Ages, was renewed by the Parlement of Paris in 1579, and this suggests that it might have been widely ignored. It continued to be flouted, and the availability of taverns as outlets for wine can only have reinforced the spread of wine consumption.

A striking example of the provision of wine to workers is the Arsenal of the Republic of Venice, a massive shipyard and munitions factory that employed some 2,500 skilled and unskilled workers in the sixteenth and seventeenth centuries, making it the largest concentrated workforce anywhere in Europe in this period. The biggest single outlay in the Arsenal's budget was wood (for ship construction), followed by wine. Far more was spent on wine than on pitch, rope, iron or canvas.[26]

Each worker in the Arsenal received, on average, more than two litres of diluted wine a day. To organize this was a major effort, with around 6,000 litres of wine being taken around in buckets to workers scattered over the sixty acres that the Arsenal covered. Moreover, wine was not considered a discretionary item in the budget. Whenever the supply of wine was threatened, the Arsenal managers went to all lengths necessary to ensure that there was no interruption to supplies, because the Arsenal workers 'cannot get along without it'. This is a striking reminder that the principles of keeping alcohol and work separate, and of discouraging drinking on the job or during breaks, are relatively recent.

Three bottles of wine a day, even of diluted wine, seems quite substantial, especially when it does not include whatever the workers might have consumed when they were not at work. Given the size of the Arsenal workforce, it was a significant burden on the Venetian state. Each year more than 2 per cent of the Republic's annual expenditure was spent on the half million litres of wine consumed by the workers of the Arsenal. Moreover, these workers appear to have increased their consumption steadily over time. In the 1550s daily consumption of diluted wine was about 2.5 litres per worker, but by 1615 this had risen to 3.2 litres and in the 1630s to nearly 5 litres. By 1696, the wine ration accounted for more than 10 per cent of the total labour costs of the Arsenal.

The wine provided daily to workers was generally mixed with water in the ratio of 1:2. To permit this degree of dilution, wines had to be reasonably full-bodied, which meant using wines from southern Italy, Spain or some of the Mediterranean islands. Such wines had an alcohol content above 12 per cent, so that dilution produced a beverage of about 4 per cent alcohol, lower than most modern beer.

Free wine seems to have been supplied to many workers who served the Republic, from cattle butchers to sailors and oarsmen, but the Arsenal workers appear to have been especially favoured. In addition to the normal daily rations of diluted wine, another two litres – but of undiluted wine now – were provided to each member of the construction team when a ship was launched. Arsenal managers were given bonuses in wine that were worth up to a third of their basic salary, their allocations ranging from 450 to 1,800 litres of wine a year.

Rising per capita consumption of wine in the Arsenal in the 1640s provoked an inquiry that uncovered various irregularities. Suppliers were providing weaker northern wine but charging the higher rates applicable to more robust southern vintages, passing off spoiled wine as drinkable, and diluting wine to the point that 'one could say it was mere tinted water'.[27] The main reason for rising costs and apparently increasing consumption, however, was that the free wine attracted hordes of unauthorized consumers. Anyone visiting the Arsenal on official business felt free to help themselves to the wine, and men and women would pass themselves off as friends, relatives or servants of Arsenal employees so that they could get on to the premises and avail themselves of the complimentary alcohol.

If the Arsenal's management wanted to restrain wine consumption, it was its own worst enemy, for in the 1630s it actually constructed a wine fountain. Wine flowed from bronze tubes, and all that workers – or anyone else, evidently – had to do was to fill up their containers from it. One visitor from France reported that wine from the fountain 'is not of the best', but another from England, apparently less discriminating, gave his opinion that it was 'pretty good too, but that it is a little mingled with Water'.[28] The Arsenal and its fountain of wine might not have been typical of wine consumption in this period, but it speaks loudly of the way wine was thought of as an integral part of the European diet, not only to be consumed with meals but as a source of sustenance during the working day.

Nor was the Arsenal the only dockyard to serve alcohol to its employees. In the eighteenth century the Royal Navy provided rum (in the form of punch) to land-based workers as well as to sailors. The practice was noted by a pair of French spies, who wrote that it was easy to get access to British shipyards: 'One needs to know the language with facility, not show any curiosity, and wait for the hour when punch is served.'[29]

Wine coursing through fountains which exposed it to air cannot have retained its character for long. It is hardly surprising that fountains do not figure in the debates on how best to conserve wines. Throughout this period and beyond, barrels remained the containers in which wine was shipped and stored, and when wine was purchased in taverns it was drawn directly from the barrel into a cup or pitcher. Although glass wine bottles had been made since Roman times, it was only in the early sixteenth century that they gained popularity for the temporary storage of wine and for its presentation at the tables of the well-to-do.

Initially the walls of glass bottles were thin, the glass was light in weight and cloudy, and the bottles generally had square bases. In the 1630s, however, a new type of bottle was developed in England, largely the result of a shift from wood-fired to much hotter coal-fired furnaces. The new bottle, the direct ancestor of the modern wine bottle, was much heavier and stronger and had thicker walls. The glass was dark-coloured – olive green, brown or even black – and the bottles tended to have globe-shaped bodies and a long tapering neck with a collar that was used for tying down the stopper. These new bottles, like the old, varied in size because each was blown individually, though most were probably of a similar volume – a lungful of air. Larger bottles were also made, some having up to thirty times the volume of an ordinary bottle.[30] Bottles could be blown to order, and a round seal, made in the same glass as the bottle, was often attached to display the name (or, in the case of the nobility, the heraldic device) of the owner.

Not only were the new bottles more durable than the old but they were also cheaper. Instead of costing six or eight pence each, as the older style did, the newer bottles could be purchased in the late seventeenth century for five shillings a dozen with the customized owner's seal incorporated, or three shillings and six pence without. The unit price of generic new bottles was thus half that of the old. It is not surprising that the new vessels, known as 'English bottles', became immensely popular as status symbols among England's wine-drinking elite. In 1684 some 3,000 dozen bottles were shipped from factories in Newcastle alone.[31]

During the last decades of the seventeenth century and until the 1720s, British wine bottles became shorter and more squat, until they took on an onion-shape: a short compressed globe-shaped body with a stubby neck. Thereafter bottles began to lose their rounded profile, and the sides became flatter, a tendency that continued when it was discovered that wine was best preserved in bottles lying on their sides. Bottles with curved bodies did not lie down easily, and they were especially precarious when bottles were stored row on row. By the middle of the eighteenth century, cylindrical, straight-sided bottles were being produced.

But the development of bottles suitable for storing wine did not quickly lead to the selling of wine in them. Some wine merchants began to do so, but because there was no uniformity in the size of bottles (a process to standardize size was patented only in 1821) there were enormous possibilities for customers to be sold short. In 1636 a law was passed in Britain to prohibit the sale of wine in the bottle. The law was not changed until 1860, and until then customers had to purchase wine in regulated measures and have it poured into bottles. Samuel Pepys, whose wine experiences are described below, noted in his diary his pleasure at going to The Mitre tavern to watch as his wine was poured into his new crested bottles.

The second innovation that made possible the storage of wine in bottles was the discovery that cork could be used as an effective barrier against air entering bottles. Cork, assisted by pitch, had been used to seal amphoras in ancient Greece, but it was not used again until the seventeenth century. Until then, stoppers for containers were made of leather, wood and textiles, but none of these materials alone was airtight, although combinations such as wooden stoppers with a layer of textile between wood and neck were somewhat more effective. With the development of glass wine bottles, glass stoppers were sometimes used, but because of the varying shapes and sizes of bottles each stopper had to be made to fit an individual bottle for it to be effective against air.

The development of cork stoppers was an important step in wine conservation because of the flexibility of cork and its tendency to expand when wet to provide a virtually airtight seal. At first the effectiveness of corks was not fully recognized because they were not completely inserted into the neck of the bottle. To have done so would have made it impossible to get the cork out. The invention of the corkscrew (initially called a 'bottlescrew') solved this final problem.

Cork had one disadvantage, however, and that was the problem of supply. The trees whose bark is processed to make corks grow in limited climatic conditions and are concentrated in Spain and Portugal, although other less important locations are scattered throughout the Mediterranean. This meant that a country wishing to bottle wine had to maintain trading relations with Spain or Portugal. The Methuen Treaty of 1703 that regulated trade between Portugal and England not only ensured a supply of port to English consumers from the eighteenth century onwards, but also guaranteed English wine merchants access to the corks they needed.

The development of bottles and corks made possible the development of two entirely different styles of wine in the seventeenth century: sparkling wine and port. Apart from these new styles, both requiring specific vinicultural processes, other wines distinctive for their provenance or varietal came on to the market. Along with the spread of distilling, these wines reinforce the image of the Early Modern period as a turning point in the history of alcohol.

Sparkling wine, of which champagne is the best-known example, is made by holding carbon dioxide in the fermentation vessel (bottle or vat) rather than letting it escape through an airlock. The gas is eventually dissolved in the wine, but when the container is opened the carbon dioxide emerges from the wine in the form of small bubbles. The invention of sparkling wine is frequently attributed to Dom Pierre Pérignon, a wine-maker at the abbey of Hautvillers near Epernay in Champagne during the seventeenth century.[32] As the story is often told, Dom Pérignon developed bubbles in wine by accident, and, on drinking some of his unplanned vintage, exclaimed, 'I am drinking the stars!' In fact Dom Pérignon, whose link with champagne has often been romanticized, put much of his vinicultural effort into trying to eliminate the bubbles in the wine made at his abbey.

Like most advances in viticulture and wine-making, however, the development of sparkling wine was a long process. It seems to have occurred in Champagne, which was already in the seventeenth century known for its slightly pink but quite still wines made from pinot noir grapes. They were so highly thought of that they were served at the court of Louis XIV. The bubbles in the wine for which champagne eventually became famous occurred because of the low winter temperatures that temporarily halted the process of fermentation before it was complete. The yeasts remained dormant during the winter, but they became active again when temperatures rose during the following spring, and fermentation began once again. Wine that had already been transferred to glass containers developed immense pressure, often enough to burst them. The invention and use of stronger bottles alleviated this problem, although it was a long time before they could be relied upon not to burst.

In a still-wine culture the bubbles might well have been considered a flaw that needed correcting, rather than an exciting innovation. But as the history of champagne makes clear, it was quickly regarded as a marvel. The first appreciative clientele was not French, however, but English, thanks to the Marquis de St-Evremond, who took bottles of it to London when he was banished from France. He was fortunate in being able to do so, for as many as half of the new type of strong bottles failed to withstand the pressure of the second fermentation.

The rarity of sparkling wine made it both desirable and expensive, and it soon became a sign of a luxurious and wealthy lifestyle in both England and France. Samuel Pepys noted in his diary that in March 1679 he travelled through Hyde Park in his carriage, 'the first time this year, taking two bottles of champagne in my way'. Jolting the bottles in a horse-drawn carriage with steel-rimmed wheels was probably not the best way to ensure the survival of the wine, but Pepys makes no mention of disaster.

At about the same time, another new but very different wine was making its debut. Like champagne, the original success of port was a combination of vinicultural factors and market considerations, although in the case of port politics also played a role: it was because of one of the periodic English bans on French wine that merchants turned to Portugal, a country with which England had a long history of trade. By the 1660s England was importing from the northern Minho region of Portugal red wines that were considered inferior to claret but an acceptable alternative when the claret supply ran low.

English trade in Portuguese wine rose in the last two decades of the seventeenth century. During two periods (1679–83 and 1689–93), French wine was banned from England, and in 1693 a heavy tariff was placed on it. Searching for sources of additional supplies of Portuguese wine, English merchants penetrated the upper reaches of the Douro river, where the warmer climate produced a red wine that was far darker and heavier than those produced along the lower Douro, closer to the coast and to Oporto at the mouth of the river. These wines became known as *porto* or port-wine, although their taste and appearance led to their being called 'blackstrap' for a time in London.

What is distinctive about port is that it is fortified by the addition of brandy. In the seventeenth century brandy was often added to barrels of wine just before they were shipped in order to stabilize the wine. Needless to say, this added to their strength and consumer appeal, but in genuine port the brandy is added during the process of fermentation, not after it is complete. The difference is that brandy added before fermentation is complete stops the fermentation and leaves the wine much sweeter than it would be had more sugar been fermented out. At the same time, the addition of the brandy more than makes up for the alcohol not produced when fermentation is interrupted. Credit for developing this process is generally given to an abbot of a monastery at Lamego, a village in the mountains above the Douro. It is thought that English wine merchants came upon his wine, the true forerunner of port as we know it, in 1678.

In addition to champagne and port, which involved particular processes of vinification that made them, in effect, different sorts of wine from mainstream table wines, distinctive wine-types began to emerge in other parts of Europe. One was tokay, the sweet wine of the Tokaj-Hegyalja region in northeast Hungary. Towards the end of the sixteenth century wine-producers in this area are said to have begun blending their wine with the juice of grapes that had been left late on the vine and had thereby accumulated higher levels of sugar. In the seventeenth century, however, sweetness was obtained in another way, by leaving grapes on the vine until they were attacked by botrytis (noble rot). It is said that the effects of botrytis (*aszú* in Hungarian) were discovered by accident in the seventeenth century when one harvest was delayed because of fear of imminent attack by Turkish armies. Some of the botrytized grapes were crushed separately and added to the must of grapes that had not been affected. The wine that resulted was much admired and eventually became popular in royal courts as varied as the French, Prussian and Russian, a sign of status that ensured commercial success.

Being a blend of wine and the juice of botrytis-affected grapes, tokay was not a new wine in the sense that champagne and port were. We must remember that in this period it was common, even normal, for wines to be blended and added to, not so frequently by producers as by merchants, whose primary concerns were that the wine should survive transportation in the best possible shape and that its taste and appearance should be matched closely to the preferences of the markets for which it was destined. If that meant adding stronger Spanish wine to lighter claret to give it body, or adding elderberries to light red wine to deepen its colour, then that was done.

In this same period, however, there were also trends that seem more familiar to modern wine-drinkers, notably a concern in some areas to pay attention to grape varieties such as the riesling. This variety was first mentioned in the sixteenth century as growing in the Mosel and Rhine regions. What gave riesling its initial impetus was the destruction of many vineyards during the Thirty Years War. From the 1650s the vine-growers of Alsace (which had been annexed to France as a result of the war) and the Rhine region began to replant. Looking for a vine that would produce large amounts of wine quickly, they soon opted for riesling, a vine that is not only hardy and prolific, but also has the advantage of ripening late but yet producing a sweet wine. This meant that rieslings would meet the increasing demand for sweet white wines – the same demand that led to the popularity of tokay and the sweet whites of Bordeaux, including sauternes.

In many vineyards vines that had produced red wines were replaced by riesling. By 1695, the abbey of St Maximin at Trier had planted 100,000 vines, mostly riesling. Even more impressive was the planting, early in the eighteenth century, of a million riesling vines on the estates of the Benedictine monastery of Johannisberg on the Rhine.

Red wine held its own against sweet whites, but there was increasing demand for the fuller-bodied vintages rather than the light claret-type wines that for centuries had been the staple of the French–English wine trade. This was the context for the development of Bordeaux wines that were closer in style to what we know under that name. The expansion of vineyards in Graves and Médoc, in particular, responded to changes in taste and in turn established new benchmarks of both style and quality. Such developments in wine, along with the appearance of distinctive types like champagne and port, ensured that wine retained the loyalty of a limited but wealthy segment of English and other European societies, despite the competition from spirits.

During the seventeenth century a more systematic sense of wine connoisseurship developed. It was very likely related to the possibility of keeping wine in bottles, which reduced the chances of deterioration. Increasing appreciation of wine was also due to a heightened awareness of the distinctions among wines, not only between wines of different regions but also among wines of the same region. Until the seventeenth century, wine drinkers referred to wines as coming from broad regions rather than from specific localities within those regions. For the most part, clarets were clarets, Rhine wines were Rhine wines, and burgundies were burgundies. If Beaune was singled out, it was because Beaune was considered a region in its own right, separate from Burgundy. Not only was there little sense of differences between localities; there was no awareness that individual producers might be distinguished from one another.

It is hardly surprising that wines were not identified on narrower bases. Right through this period, and long after it for that matter, the wines that reached consumers were blended with little regard to grape varietal or the provenance of the wines. The wines on the English market, whether sold retail in taverns or wholesale by the cask, were not necessarily the wines produced by individual wineries, but the blends created by merchants. One producer's light wine might be mixed with another's full-bodied, some brandy might be added to raise the alcohol level and give it some durability, other ingredients might be included according to the merchant's recipe. Whatever the process, and even if a merchant shipped a barrel of wine without altering it, no customer had (or expected to have) confidence that the wine purchased represented a particular vineyard or estate.

Growers began to pay more attention to grape varieties in the eighteenth century, but it was in the seventeenth that the notion of distinctive wines from specific estates began to gain some currency. To a large extent the credit for this can be attributed to one Arnaud de Pontac, the head of a powerful family in Bordeaux. The Pontac family had carefully increased its status for generations, and by 1660 Arnaud de Pontac was a noble and the president of the prestigious parlement (the royal court) of Bordeaux. Among the family's interests were vineyards, notably one in what is now the Graves region, where in the sixteenth century Arnaud de Pontac's grandfather had built a château called Haut-Brion. By the mid seventeenth century the Haut-Brion vineyards covered some 38 hectares.

There is little to suggest that de Pontac innovated in wine-making, although his wealth would have enabled him to improve his wine by, for example, selecting the best grapes and rejecting the rest, or by using new barrels instead of re-using barrels over and over again. Rather than change his viticultural and vinifying techniques, however, de Pontac innovated in the marketing strategies he adopted. To the wine made from grapes grown in his vineyard in Graves he gave the name Haut-Brion, and to the rest of the wine he made he simply gave his family name, Pontac. De Pontac thus created a premium wine that appealed to the status-conscious London wine market. Samuel Pepys, whose commitment to wine is described below, was not the only connoisseur to remark on the quality of 'Ho Brian'. The implication of scarcity – there was plenty of wine available, but only a limited supply of Pontac and even less of Haut-Brion – meant that these designated wines could be priced considerably higher than other wines. A bottle of Haut-Brion began to sell for more than three times the price of other good red wines.

Arnaud de Pontac's brilliant notion was perfectly timed. With the restoration of the monarchy in England in 1660, there was a relaxation of the more strict moral codes that had prevailed during the Puritan republic, and alcohol probably became more widely available and consumed. Not only that, but the launch of Haut-Brion and Pontac, both fuller-bodied red wines, coincided with the palling of English taste for the lighter clarets. Haut-Brion and Pontac wines were enthusiastically received by London society, and in 1666 de Pontac opened an expensive restaurant in the city. Called 'Pontac's Head', it sold Haut-Brion and Pontac with meals. The restaurant quickly established a clientele of contemporary celebrities and remained in business for more than a century, evidence of the willingness of London's elite to pay for premium wine.

A number of signs strongly suggest a growing interest in wine in England and elsewhere during the 1600s. British travellers in Europe commented frequently and for the most part positively on food and wine to be found in locations like Italy. Many of these travellers were on the Grand Tour, designed to give well-off Englishmen an appreciation of the history and culture of Europe. Some were more attracted by the other diversions offered in foreign places, and a number cited wine in their published accounts of their travels. John Raymond commented of Albano that the town 'deserves seeing, if not for the Antiquity, yet for the good wine; one of the best sorts in Italy': Richard Lassel's guide to the gardens, streams and fountains of Caparola noted: 'Having walked these gardens about, youl [sic] deserve after so much water, a little wine, which will not be wanting to you from the rare *cellar* lyeing under the great Terrasse before the house, and perchance youl think the *wineworks* here as fine as the *waterworks*.' In case travel was thought to broaden the mind, we might note that the quality of the wine was not necessarily considered by English visitors to reflect positively on the Italian people themselves. Clearly appreciating terroir but not the wine-makers' contribution, Richard Fleckno noted of Rome in 1654, 'good meat there is, delicious wine, and excellent fruit . . . but that is the Climat's virtue, and none of theirs.'[33]

Whether they were abroad or at home, wealthy Englishmen

commented on wine increasingly from the second half of the seventeenth century. John Evelyn, for example, noted wines and vineyards as he travelled through France and Italy and recorded many of his drinking experiences when he returned to England.[34]

An extended account of one wine-drinking career is provided by Samuel Pepys (1633–1703), a high-ranking official in the English navy, who in the 1660s kept a detailed diary of his private life. Pepys might not have been a connoisseur, but he loved wine. He occasionally worried about his consumption patterns and swore to abstain, but he never successfully kept these promises he made to himself. Pepys drank a wide variety of wines in various contexts and seems never to have one he did not like. Commonly he drank claret, the French wine most popular among English wine-drinkers, but he also admired Spanish reds as well as whites from Spain and Germany. Pepys's diary also records various wine-based drinks, including Hippocras and 'burnt wine' (not brandy but mulled wine, sweetened with sugar and flavoured with spices).[35]

Pepys was one of the first to mention the Haut-Brion wine that Arnaud de Pontac launched on to the London market in the 1660s, and Pepys's comment suggested that its qualities were already evident: '. . . to the Royall Oak Tavern . . . and here drank a sort of French wine, called Ho Brian, that had a good and most particular taste I never met with.'[36] But he was no wine snob, and his appreciation also extended to English wines. On one occasion Pepys visited Lady Batten, 'and there we dined and had very good red wine of my Lady's own making in England'. On another occasion Pepys was among the guests to whom Sir William Batten served some of his previous year's wine, grown at Walthamstowe, 'than which the whole company said they never drank better foreign wine in their lives.'[37] It is understandable that Sir William's guests would be complimentary to his face, but Pepys was usually frank in the opinions he committed to his diary, and his appreciation of this English wine seems to have been genuine enough. In addition to the vineyard at Walthamstowe, Pepys mentioned others at Hatfield (Hertfordshire) and Greenwich.

Although much of Pepys's wine-drinking was done at home or in others' houses, he was also a frequent visitor to taverns. There are many references to 'Rhenish wine houses', which specialized in Rhine wine.

Pepys also mentions food and wine combinations, including 'a pint or two of [Rhine] wine and a dish of anchovies'.

Pepys also allows us a glimpse of the private cellar belonging to Thomas Povy, a senior government official. Pepys was very impressed by the cellar, 'where upon several shelves there stood bottles of all sorts of wine, new and old, with labells pasted upon each bottle, and in order and plenty as I never saw books in a bookseller's shop'. On a return visit six months later Pepys noted that the cellar included a well to keep the bottles cool.[38] He also listed the contents of his own cellar: 'I have two tierces of Claret, two quarter casks of Canary, and a smaller vessel of Sack; a vessel of Tent [Spanish red], another of Malaga, and another of white wine, all in my wine cellar together.'

Pepys was impressed that he had risen to such a status that he himself could afford to keep a wine cellar, 'which, I believe, none of my friends of my name now alive ever had of his owne at one time'.[39] The vagueness of the description does not allow us to estimate the volume of this cellar with any precision, but it was certainly more than 150 gallons, or the equivalent of more than 750 standard bottles of wine. It is notable that while Thomas Povy's wine was stored in bottles, which were still an innovation, at this time Pepys's was still kept in large, traditional wooden containers.

Whether or not Pepys actually bought all this wine or acquired it in other ways is open to question. In 1679 an anonymous leaflet accused him and his assistant in the navy office, both of whom had become wealthy, of corruption by accepting bribes. Specifically it called on them to

refund those chests of Greek wines and chests of Saracusa wines . . . and quarter casks of old Malaga and butts of sherry . . . and jars of Tent . . . and chests of Florence wine . . . and hogsheads of claret, white wines and champagnes, and dozens of cider . . . all of which were received from Sea-Captains, Consuls, Lieutenants, Masters, Boatswains, Gunners, Carpenters and Pursers, or from their wives or sons or daughters.[40]

The preoccupation with wine that these allegations suggest sometimes bothered Pepys himself, and his diary is littered with vows to abstain from wine. In 1661 he wrote, 'I have newly take a solemn oath about abstaining from plays and wine,' and the following year, '. . . did promise to drink no more wine but one glass a meal till Whitsuntide next upon any score.' Occasionally Pepys congratulated himself on keeping his word (which permitted him to drink ale and spirits), although he exempted mulled wine from its scope. He attributed his new-found inner peace and improved prosperity to his abstinence. The catalogue of vows taken and broken ended in 1667, and they are not mentioned in the last two and half years of diary entries. Perhaps Pepys simply gave up and allowed his fondness for wine to win over whatever beliefs he had that it was bad for him. Overall, Pepys's diaries provide a rare insight into the place of wine not only among the upper levels of English society, but in the mind of one of its members.

Associated with wine-drinking as an aesthetic experience were changes in the style of wine glasses. Until the seventeenth century wine was frequently drunk from cups and other vessels made of silver, pottery, wood or leather. English inventories of the late 1500s show very few drinking glasses of any sort, but they appear more and more commonly in the early 1600s. It is possible that various papal bans on the use of glass chalices for communion wine might have been adopted in the secular context, too. Interestingly, glass drinking vessels started to become increasing popular for wine within decades of the Reformation, which dramatically undercut the influence of the papacy.

It is more likely, however, that the spread of glass vessels had more to do with developments in technology than with religious politics. Venice was the early centre of glass-making, and Venetian glass was highly prized by European elites. More common glassware was manufactured in other parts of Europe, and developments in English glass-making in the seventeenth century made England a major source of glass products. Early wine glasses were priced well beyond the reach of ordinary people, but those who could afford wine were able to stretch to a few.

Prices declined as production techniques evolved. Small English-made glasses for wine cost four shillings a dozen in 1621, but by 1635 the price had fallen nearly a third to two shillings and sixpence. Wine glasses made from crystal were more desirable and more expensive. The price of English-made crystal glasses fell steadily in the early seventeenth century, from about sixteen shillings a dozen in 1621 to five or six shillings a dozen twenty years later. At that price they were a little less expensive than crystal glasses imported from Venice, which sold for seven or eight shillings a dozen.[41] Glass styles varied immensely but already by the early 1600s they had the stem that became characteristic of wine glasses. Few, however, had the bowl shape that traps aromas.

Finally let us note growing awareness that the temperature of wine affects its taste. In the sixteenth century, in France at least, wine was often warmed before being drunk. Francis I's doctor Bruyerin Champier noted that this practice was common to all social classes and seasons. 'Some put their cups or bottles near the fire,' he wrote, 'others warm the water with which the wine is diluted; some toss toasted bread into their drink; certain others heat up iron blades, and the elegant and wealthy gold blades, which they dip in their cups, while the poor plunge therein burning sticks from the fire.'[42] While Champier did not approve of warming wine, he was firm in his disapproval of drinking wine straight from a cool cellar. The temperature of such wine damaged the throat, chest, lungs, stomach and intestines, corrupted the liver and brought on incurable illnesses, even a rapid death. He advised anyone with a cool cellar to bring the wine out a few hours before drinking it so that it was warmed in the external air. (No distinction was made between red and white.) Here was early advice to bring wine to room temperature, although that in itself varies widely by location and season.

Yet to show that a consensus was far off, a few decades later another doctor advised just the opposite. Laurent Jaubert wrote that it was necessary, particularly for a young person with hot blood, to correct the warmth of the atmosphere with a cool drink. If no cool cellar were available, the wine could be cooled in a fountain or a stream. Jaubert's advice reflected a shift in medical thinking from maintaining the temperaments of the body to correcting them.[43] The custom of drinking wine chilled in the summer became widespread in France during the sixteenth century, and eventually the French adopted Spanish and Italian practice and cooled their wine with snow and ice.

The relative warmth of wine and the body was a preoccupation of many writers. The sixteenth-century Italian medical writer Baldassare Pisanelli recommended wine in the diet of old people because 'the progressive decline of their natural heat requires a supplementary source of warmth to overcome the coldness that accompanies old age.'[44] The heating properties of wine in already warm bodies was worrisome, however, because it could bring the emotions and passions to boiling point. Pisanelli discouraged giving wine to children, in whom it 'adds to more fire on slender kindling, and it disturbs their minds'. Likewise, young people 'have a warm and fervent nature', and when they drink wine they 'run the risk of becoming powerfully impassioned in the spirit, and in the body furiously excited'.[45]

These concerns about the hot properties of wine endured. In 1753 the American preacher Jonathan Edwards wrote to his sick daughter and proposed a number of remedies for her illness. They included a dead rattlesnake (he apologized for having been able to procure only one) and ginseng. With regard to the ginseng (not the rattlesnake) Edwards wrote: 'Try steeping it in wine, in good Madeira or claret; or if these wines are too harsh, then in some good white wine . . . And for a cordial take some spices steeped in some generous wine that suits your taste, and stomach.' But, Edwards added as a postscript, he and his wife feared that 'the heat of 'em might raise a fever', so he suggested diluting the wine with water 'to abate the heat of it'.[46] It seems clear that aesthetic or sensory notions about the appropriate serving temperature of wine were intimately related to a persistent medical notion that the intrinsic 'heat' of wine was independent of its physical temperature.

Within medical writing, wine maintained its strong position as a source of nutrition and a basic medicine during the early modern period. A number of medical writers began to make increasingly stark distinctions between kinds of wine, not only in terms of the respective properties of sweet and dry or red and white, but of the classes of people that would benefit from them. They drew upon the biological theories of the ancient world and also upon beliefs that people of different social classes or occupations had different biological characteristics. Olivier de Serres wrote in 1605 that 'good, full-bodied [gros] red and black wines' were 'appropriate for working people . . . and greatly sought after by them as much as white and claret wines are by people of leisure'.[47] (The difference between red and black wines here was between medium-coloured and very dark reds.)

This was not simply a matter of taste, as Jean Liebault, a French doctor, explained a few years later. 'Red wine nourishes more than white or claret and it is more suitable for those who work hard; because work and vigorous exercise neutralize any of the disadvantages that red wine has.' As for black wine, 'it is best for vignerons and farmers; because once digested by the activity of the stomach and work, it gives more solid and plentiful nourishment and makes the man stronger in his work.'[48]

Liebault linked social class and wine type even more closely. Even if these full-bodied earthy wines (black wine was called 'blood of the earth' in ancient times) had the effect of weighing on drinkers and making their blood 'thick, melancholic and slow-flowing', there was no cause for concern: peasants were reputed to be earthy, crude, thick and slow anyway. But the same wine would have terrible effects on nobles, bourgeois and the clergy, whose work required them to be lively and spiritual. Such men would suffer obstructions of the liver and spleen, lost appetite and rawness in the stomach. There was a medical consensus that light red or white wines were more suitable for the better-off consumers, because such beverages passed easily from the stomach to the liver, producing rich blood and rejuvenating the heart and the brain.

Medical ideas of the health properties of wine entered popular consciousness and were expressed in proverbs.[49] Some expressed the good effects of wine throughout the year: 'In summer when it's hot and in winter when it's cold, wine gives you energy.' Wine was excellent for the digestion: 'If you don't drink wine after raw vegetables you risk being ill.' Many proverbs reflected contemporary concern about pears, which were reputed to be very difficult to digest. One saying advised, 'After pear, drink wine,' while a Breton proverb direly predicted that 'If pears are not followed by wine, they will be followed by the priest.' Pears were regarded not only as hard to digest but also essentially feminine. As such they needed to be balanced by masculine wine.

It is suggestive of the significance of wine in the French diet by this period that in times of great hardship alternatives to wine were suggested. One doctor suggested that 'in place of wine, because it is expensive for the poor, one should drink beer, cider, perry . . .' Elsewhere it was suggested that bodies weakened by famine should not be subjected to the harshness of beer and that a weak solution of wine was beneficial. Some doctors recommended using piquette as the basis of gruels that included nuts, herbs or spinach as other ingredients.[50]

Wine was so central to the diet of the sick that when in 1670 Louis

XIV founded Les Invalides, the famous military hospital, he exempted it from paying taxes on the first 200 muids (about 55,000 litres) of wine each year.[51] Wine was regularly distributed to the patients, and such was the level of consumption that the exemption was progressively raised, until by 1705 it was set at 3,000 muids, or some 800,000 litres. Officers were given a ration of one and a quarter litres of wine a day, a quarter litre being brought to their rooms each morning and a half litre being served at lunch and dinner. Non-commissioned officers and ordinary soldiers had a smaller ration, half at each meal. Rations were doubled at the evening meal on certain festivals (like Mardi Gras). Wine was also dispensed to employees of the hospital, and some was used in cooking. In February 1710, when there were an average 2,500 resident military, Les Invalides went through 460,000 litres of wine. Wine appears to have been intrinsic to the care of military patients in a way that it was not for civilians in hospital. When some soldiers were sent from Les Invalides for a two-month thermal treatment, special provision was made for them to have wine because there was none in the hospital at which they would stay.

In addition to their rations, some pensioners who were residents of Les Invalides drank wine in local bars, and there are ample records of drunkenness leading to violence, blasphemy and offences against public morality. Officers found drunk were arrested and deprived of wine for eight days. Soldiers who had been convicted eight times were sent to prison for a year. Deprivation of wine was clearly a major punishment and it was also the penalty for writing obscenities on the walls, throwing refuse, urine or water out of the hospital windows, not respecting the rules regarding cleanness and having a fire or a candle lit at night after the beating of the retreat.

Over time the panegyrics on the benefits of wine were challenged by medical writers who drew attention to the harmful effects of alcohol. One of the earliest criticisms of wine as a health-giver was published in the late sixteenth century by a partisan of another fermented beverage who was tired of the privileged position attributed to wine in medical writing. Julien le Paulmier, author of a number of medical works, was clearly a loyal inhabitant of Normandy, a province where vines had been cultivated unsuccessfully but which became famous for its apple cider and later for the apple-based spirit calvados. A pall had been cast over the cider industry by the allegation that leprosy, which was widespread in Normandy, was caused by drinking cider.

Le Paulmier set out to correct the bad press that cider had received and to show that it was superior to wine in every respect. Describing wine as one might a dangerous drug that should be carefully controlled by professionals, he noted that it possessed excellent qualities but that it could be dangerous if not used with judgement and discretion. It could cause 'an infinity of illnesses and indispositions' because patients do not know what sort of wine to drink, how much to dilute it, and how to suit it to the climate, season and individual needs.[52]

The point of the treatise was not simply to highlight the problems with wine but to show the superiority of cider which, le Paulmier insisted, had all the qualities attributed to wine but none of the disadvantages. Cider was good for the digestion and the blood. It was warm but moderately so: the best and strongest cider rarely exceeded the first level of warmth while the strongest wines reached the top of the third level. Le Paulmier's ultimate claim for cider was an immodest one: 'A man who drinks cider lives longer than a man who drinks wine.'

This was a voice in the wilderness of Normandy, where vines grew so poorly that attempts to cultivate them were eventually abandoned. Elsewhere the consensus remained strong that wine was not only a healthy beverage, but that it was also enjoyable to drink. The emergence of fine wines, like Arnaud de Pontac's Haut-Brion, and of growing awareness of the characteristics that were imparted by specific grapes, localities and producers, led in the early modern period to a more stark divergence between the mass of wine consumers, for whom wine was part of the diet, and connoisseurs, for whom it was also an aesthetic experience. In the following centuries connoisseurship would play an increasingly important role.

SIX

WINE IN NEW WORLDS

The Americas, Africa and Australia, 1500–1800

The 1500s saw the beginning of European exploration and political expansion into the far reaches of the globe. Earlier explorers had travelled eastward into Russia, China and India, but now they began to look west for a route that would take them more directly to Asia. Thus began a new age in the history of the world and a new stage in the history of wine. Grapes grew wild in some of the lands that Europeans encountered but, as far as is known, none of the indigenous populations had used them for wine. Wine was one of the commodities that the Europeans brought with them, and in time they established vineyards in their new territories. New World wine, as non-European wine is generally known, experienced many different histories before reaching the point where it is widely considered (especially in the New World itself) the equal of its Old World counterpart.

The discovery and colonization by Spain and Portugal of the islands scattered across the Atlantic hundreds of miles off the coast of Africa was a slow process. The Canary Islands were conquered by Spain and vineyards quickly established there. Canary wines found a strong export market by the late sixteenth century, and the main wine island of the group, Tenerife, already by then relied on wine exports for its prosperity. At that time the main markets were the Spanish and Portuguese colonies in the Americas, but during the seventeenth century England became by far the single biggest customer for Canary wines. The wines that found particular favour in England were the sweeter whites made from malvasia grapes. James Howell commented that Canary wines 'are accounted the richest, the most firm, the best-bodied and lastingst [sic]', all outstanding qualities when everyday wines were thin, unstable and had to be consumed young.

The volume of Canary wine imported to England rose steadily during the seventeenth century. In the 1620s an average of 2,483 pipes (about 1,250,000 litres) were imported each year, but that rose to 5,522 in the 1660s and 6,700 (nearly 3.5 million litres) in the 1680s. The figure for the 1680s represents the importation of the equivalent of more than 3 million bottles of wine a year. It was certainly an exaggeration for James Howell to write that whereas Canary wine used to be consumed in small measures and only by the wealthy, 'now they go down everyone's throat both young and old, like milk'.[1] But there was certainly a lot more of the wine on the market by the end of the century.

The boom period for Canary wine exports to England died at the turn of the century. Trade between the Canaries and England was permanently unbalanced, for the English simply could not sell there the textiles that were their main export. Canary wine was expensive and merchants experienced chronic cash-flow problems, and in the 1690s Canary wine was gradually displaced by the sweet wines imported in increasing volumes from Portugal and Spain. Although Canary wines continued to find a market in England well into the eighteenth century, it was only in small quantities, and the islands' vineyards experienced a steady decline.

The other major Atlantic island brought under viticulture was Madeira, settled by the Portuguese in 1420. At that time Madeira was uninhabited, but it was heavily wooded and was named for the Portuguese word for 'wood'. The island was promptly planted with sugar cane and vines, including the malmsey variety, which were brought from Crete in the hope of replicating the famous Cretan wine that was increasingly difficult to obtain. Both these exotic crops thrived. By 1500 Madeira was the world's largest producer of sugar, although it was subsequently outstripped by Latin American plantations. The vines also flourished, and by the end of the sixteenth century wine was more profitable than the sugar crop.

What drove Madeira's wine production was the island's location, which made it ideal as a port of call for ships travelling from England to the English colonies in North America and the Caribbean. Most of the island's wine was quite conventional table wine of the time – light and not very durable – and was not the fortified kind that is now known as madeira. That wine, or an early version of it, was made from the malmsey vines and fermented separately. Experience showed that not only did it have durability but it even benefited from being exposed to the tropical heat. The oxidation (also known as maderization as a result of the practice on Madeira) darkened the wine to a deep brown and, instead of turning it sour, gave it more depth and smoothness. By the late seventeenth century Madeira's wine industry was booming. In seventeen days of December 1697 alone, eleven ships took on a total of about 100,000 gallons of Madeira wine for shipment to Boston and various Caribbean islands.

The Canary Islands and Madeira were important acquisitions, in strategic as well as oenological terms, but the major territorial conquests of the Spanish and Portuguese were in Latin America. Spanish armies defeated the Aztecs in Mexico in the 1520s, and within a mere twenty years had conquered and begun to colonize the western regions of South America, those areas now known as Bolivia, Colombia, Peru and Chile. Wine, as a central part of the Spanish culture from which the colonizers were drawn, was integral to settlement. Barrels of wine were prominent among military supplies, and wine was an important part of the trade that developed between Spain and its American colonies. More significant, however, was the development of viticulture within the colonies themselves. Grapes did grow wild in Latin America, but there is no evidence that the indigenous populations used them to make wine, although they did make alcoholic drinks from fruit and cereals. Some settlers drank *pulque*, a fermented drink made from the agave, that Indians provided. Others tried making wine from the indigenous grapes, but they were quickly judged unsuitable, and imported European vines were planted. Wine production began within years of the arrival of the conquistadores, and as Spanish settlement spread south, so did viticulture.

The rapidity with which vineyards were planted is nothing short of amazing. After being established in Mexico in the early 1520s, vines were planted in Peru in the early 1530s, and in Bolivia and Colombia in the later years of the same decade. Vineyards reached Chile by the early 1540s, and Argentina, on the other side of the Andes, by 1557.[2] In short, vineyards were established throughout most of Latin America in a forty-year period. Moreover, the skill with which the missionaries and others identified suitable areas for viticulture is shown by the fact

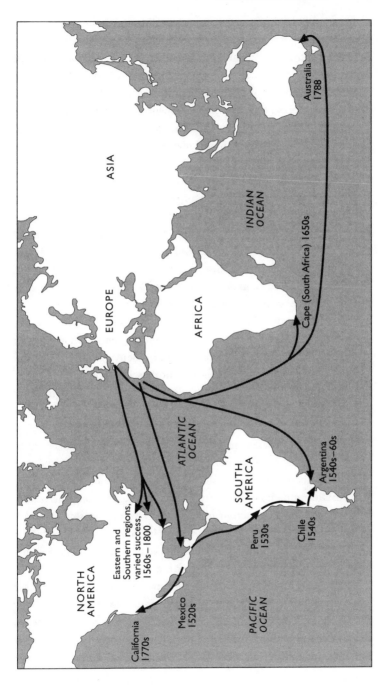

The spread of New World viticulture, 1500–1800

NORTH
AMERICA

California
1770s

Mexico 1520s

Eastern and
Southern regions,
varied success,
1560s–1800

ATLANTIC
OCEAN

EUROPE

ASIA

AFRICA

INDIAN
OCEAN

Australia
1788

Cape (South Africa) 1650s

Argentina
1540s–60s

Chile
1540s

Peru 1530s

SOUTH
AMERICA

PACIFIC
OCEAN

that most of those planted in the sixteenth century remain centres of wine production today. The vineyards of Mendoza, the heart of Argentina's modern wine industry, were already planted by the end of the 1560s.

Settlers were not only encouraged but positively required to engage in viticulture. In 1524 Cortes, the commander of New Spain (as Mexico was called), issued an ordinance that settlers in the area of what was to become Mexico City were to plant vines. Spaniards had been given land, and Indians to work it, and Cortes required the landowners to plant a thousand vines of the best quality for every hundred Indians they had.[3] The same official encouragement of, if not insistence on, local wine production was evident in other regions colonized by the Spanish. In a 1567 visit to southern Peru a Spanish official called for the planting of 1000 to 1500 more vines in an existing vineyard near Lake Titicaca.[4]

The ordinance relating to Mexico is thought to have had little effect and viticulture failed in many areas of Mexico. Part of the reason was that the climate was unsuitable for vines: even though it was more temperate in Mexico than in Spain, frosts followed quickly on warm periods and damaged the young shoots. In addition, the incentive to make wine in Mexico was soon undermined by the availability of plentiful supplies from other areas of Latin America, especially Peru.

This is not to say that no Mexican wine was made, for a small industry survived. One Mexican winery, at Parras de la Fuente, not far from the border with Texas, has had a continuous existence since 1597, when King Philip II issued a land grant to one Don Lorenzo Garcia to establish a winery. Parras de la Fuente means 'grapevines of the fountain', a reference to the fact that in this locality the underground streams of the Sierra Madre mountains gush from the surface, irrigating the nearby land and providing conditions in which vines were flourishing (though not used for wine) when Spaniards arrived in the sixteenth century. The wine produced in what is claimed to be the first official winery in the New World is still made from the native grape varietal.[5]

Why was there such urgency to establish vineyards in the Americas? It has often been assumed that the prime reason was that the Catholic Church, established wherever there was a Spanish presence, needed supplies of communion wine. It is true that vineyards were planted at Catholic missions throughout Latin America as European conquest advanced. So tight was the connection that the variety of vine used became known as mission. (It was brought from Spain and might be related to the monica varietal.) Even so, the Church's requirements for sacramental wine were small and could easily have been satisfied by regular imports from Spain. The Church in Latin America certainly did not need the millions of litres of wine that were soon being produced annually by its own vineyards and those under secular ownership, particularly bearing in mind that the laity received communion only in bread.

In fact, there were few religious motivations in the establishment of vineyards in this period: secular factors prove far more important in explaining the spread of viticulture throughout Latin America. Wine was a normal part of the diet in Spain and it is testimony to the settlers' desire to replicate Spanish culture and diet as much as possible in New Spain that they quickly planted European crops, notably European vegetables, fruit, cereals – and vines.

The settlers could, of course, have imported wine from Spain. But the cost of transportation (including long distances over land once it reached the New World) made it much more expensive than the local product, and it could not be shipped in regular and adequate amounts to supply the increasing settler populations. There were also immense practical problems because of the instability of sixteenth-century wine, and much of the wine shipped failed to reach its destination in good shape. Although Spanish wine, mainly from Andalusia and Malaga, was exported to Mexico, it was seldom transshipped to the farther-off colonies on the west coast of South America.

Not only were these colonies too far off to make importing wine from Spain viable, but local conditions in a number of colonies were extremely favourable for viticulture. The climate and soil in some of the Peruvian river valleys proved so suitable that as much as 40,000 hectares of land were in vines by the 1560s, only twenty years after the first vines were planted. One of the main Peruvian wine regions was the Moquegua Valley, in the far south of the colony. It flourished not only because of excellent growing conditions but also because it was close to markets in silver-mining communities. The early techniques of wine-production in Peru were reminiscent of ancient Rome.[6] The grapes were crushed in large vats that each held an average 12,000–14,000 litres, and the unfermented juice was directed through channels into large earthenware jars (*tinajas*) that had a capacity of between 350 and 400 litres. The jars were partially buried to control temperature and minimize the risk of cracking during fermentation. Vineyards tended to be small holdings, and in the early period slaves, both African and Andean, were used for labour. The colour of Peruvian wine was described as 'red or claret, for it is not completely red like Spanish *vino tinto*'.[7] The quality of the wine was questioned even at the time. One early visitor to Peru was not optimistic about the prospects for viniculture there: 'There are many great vineyards in these valleys, where large amounts of grapes are gathered. No wine has yet been made from them, and I cannot, therefore, testify to its quality; but as the land is irrigated, it will probably be weak.'[8] The wine certainly had no more durability than its European counterpart, and it was noted that in one area the brother of one Spanish administrator who controlled the official wine trade sold bad wine, 'some of it vinegar', to Indians.[9]

None the less, Peruvian and other Latin American wine producers rapidly succeeded in establishing a flourishing industry to the extent that wine and silver became the two most profitable sectors of several regional economies. This colonial success upset Spanish wine-producers, and they were effective enough as a lobby that in 1595 Philip II issued an edict that restricted further vine-planting in Spain's colonies. (Monasteries were exempted.) This was the first of a number of attempts to protect Spain's domestic wine industry from colonial entrepreneurs. What upset the Spanish wine-makers was not competition from colonial produce on the home market, for wine made in the Americas was not exported to Spain. Their objections rested on their failure to realize hopes of supplying the expanding colonial market. Over the long term these attempts to stifle Latin American wine production failed, even when heavy taxes were later imposed. The royal edicts might have been observed to some extent in Mexico, where environmental conditions were less suitable for viticulture in any case, but they were clearly ignored in the more distant colonies of South America where vineyards, and later brandy distilleries, flourished.

Of the three regions that stood out as wine producers in the seventeenth and eighteenth centuries, Chile and Argentina have remained major producers, while Peru's industry declined steeply after the phylloxera epidemic of the late nineteenth century. During the eighteenth century, however, Peru was a major producer, and some regions produced massive amounts of wine, either for consumption as wine or for distilling into brandy. From the late seventeenth century, demand for brandy grew rapidly in Latin America. It had the attraction of being more alcoholic than wine and the advantage of surviving the often rough journey that exports had to undergo: although wine and brandy was shipped by sea along coastal routes, much was also carried overland on the backs of llamas and mules.

Peruvian wine-makers responded to demand with enthusiasm. An idea of the scale of Peruvian production can be gained from the fairly conservative estimate that the Moquegua region alone exported between 6 and 7 million litres of wine a year in the 1780s, most of it in the form of brandy.[10] Actual production must have been quite a bit higher. (For comparative purposes, in the 1990s only ten *countries* produced more than that volume of wine annually.) By the early eighteenth century Spanish miners ranked brandy higher than wine, and it was said that 'even the "most regular and sober persons" invariably drank a glass of brandy daily at 11 a.m. to strengthen the stomach and whet the appetite.'[11]

Chilean wine production was developed first in the north, then later in the middle of the country, around Santiago. Not only table wine was produced, but also muscatel, a sweet dessert wine that was exported to Peru. Argentina's wine production developed slowly, in part because the restrictions imposed by the Spanish government were more observed there than in Peru and Chile. Not until the eighteenth century did viticulture extend to the Spanish territories in North America. As had so often been the case in Latin America, viticulture accompanied the Jesuit missionaries, even if it was later extended under secular ownership. Wine was made at the Laredo mission in Baja California by 1701, but it reached the region that is now California even later. By 1760 there were fifteen missions in southern California, at least five of which were producing wine.

The determination of the Jesuits to make wine was thoroughly tested, for although the climatic conditions made viticulture viable the wine-making itself was far from straightforward. At Mission Santa Gertrudis, a mile-long irrigation ditch had to be cut through rock. There was a shortage of containers suitable for fermenting wine; some were bought or bartered from visiting ships, but in one case, reminiscent of the practice in Peru, reservoirs were cut into the rock and sealed with pitch once the wine had been poured in.[12]

Vines spread northwards through California with the missions, and there are reports of vineyards in the San Diego area in 1769. None the less, during the 1780s the mission there was complaining about being reliant on irregular shipments from Spain and Mexico. Viticulture did not reach the region to the north of San Francisco, now the heart of the California wine industry in the Napa and Sonoma valleys, until the 1820s. The most important of the eighteenth-century Californian vineyards was located at San Gabriel mission, near modern Los Angeles. In the 1790s it was producing 35,000 gallons of wine a year and considerable quantities of brandy. Even so, the mission vineyards did not constitute a wine industry, and it was not until they were secularized by the Mexican government in 1830, and privately owned vineyards were planted, that large-scale viticulture became a feature of California's agricultural economy.[13]

The rest of North America followed a different line of development in terms of its wine production. Wild vines grew throughout much of the continent, from Canada in the north to the Gulf of Mexico in the south, and from the Atlantic coast to the Midwest of the United States. Many early explorers were struck by the abundance of these grapes and were convinced that they would produce good wine. In 1524, for example, Giovanni da Verrazzano was impressed by the vines he found at Kitty Hawk, off the coast of what is now North Carolina. He noted 'many vines growing naturally, which growing up, took hold of the trees as they do in Lombardy, which if by husbandmen [farmers] they were dressed in good order, without all doubt they would yield excellent wine.' Sixty years later, in the same area, Walter Raleigh wrote that 'here were great stores of great red grapes very pleasant.' Much further to the north, Jacques Cartier came upon wild vines on an island in the St Lawrence River, and named it Bacchus Island.[14] The grapes in question were of natives of many varieties, most of them probably of the muscadine species. There is no evidence that these grapes were ever fermented by native Americans, and in fact the indigenous populations of eastern

North America seem not to have made alcohol from any product. The grapes clearly represented a real temptation to the earliest settlers, however, and before long attempts were made to produce wine from them.

By one account, now called into question, the first wine made in what is now the United States was produced in Florida by Huguenots, Protestants who fled religious persecution in France during the sixteenth century. Some of them had been involved in viticulture in France, because many Protestants lived in a region in the southwest, a broad swathe from Nîmes through Montpellier and Montauban to Bordeaux, that included important wine-growing areas. Refugee Huguenots established a settlement at the mouth of the St John's River in northern Florida in the 1560s and were reported to have made twenty hogsheads of wine from native grapes in the first year. The report on their wine-making came from an Englishman, John Hawkins, who found the Huguenots in desperate conditions and helped them by providing them with food. Hawkins seemed more irritated than impressed that the settlers had put their efforts into making wine rather than providing other necessities. According to Huguenot accounts, however, any wine they had was European.[15]

Whether or not the Huguenots produced wine in Florida, they were soon expelled by Spanish settlers. Spaniards settled in what is now South Carolina, and by 1568 they had planted a vineyard there, but it is not clear whether the vines were native or imported *vinifera* varieties.[16] If the French did not produce wine earlier in Florida, then it is likely that these Spaniards were the first to try to make wine in North America.

English colonists were not far behind in their determination to introduce viticulture. In the first permanent English settlement, at Jamestown in Virginia, there were attempts to cultivate native vines within two years of the community's founding in 1607, and during the following decades the inhabitants were under constant pressure to make wine. In 1619, for example, each householder was instructed to plant and maintain ten vines a year and to learn the art of vine-dressing. To facilitate this, eight French wine-makers were brought to the colony and attempts were made to bring more skilled workers, not only from France but also from Germany.

In 1622 every household in Jamestown received, on the king's command, a manual on cultivating vines and making wine. It was written by John Bonoeil, a Frenchman who had never visited America but who clearly fancied himself as having a good eye for potential centres of viticulture. Bonoeil made the dubious recommendation that native grapes should be used and that they should be boiled in water before fermentation, presumably to make them more sweet. He wrote: 'I have oftentimes seen such wine made reasonable good for the household. And by this means every man may presently have wine in Virginia to drink.'[17] Further acts making viticulture mandatory in Virginia were passed in 1623 and 1624, with the later requiring each household to plant twenty vines for each male over the age of twenty.

The enthusiasm of the English government for wine production in Virginia did not arise simply from altruistic concern that the settlers should have enough wine for their own consumption. The English hoped to emulate, in their American colonies, the success that the Spanish had had in their acquisitions in Central and South America. In the seventeenth century England was utterly dependent on continental Europe for supplies of wine, as it also was for two other highly valued commodities, olive oil and silk. If its new colonies could provide these products, England would be able to free itself from reliance on states (notably France, Spain and Italy) that were its economic rivals and, from time to time, its political enemies.

But these aspirations were disappointed. The environment in eastern North America – climate, soil, plant diseases, insects – was inhospitable to imported vines, and native varieties resisted vinification. Although some wine-making ventures had short-term success for a few years, all eventually foundered. As early as 1622 some Virginian wine was sent to London, but it spoiled en route, either because it was inherently unstable or because it was fouled by the barrels in which it was shipped. The colony's representatives reported that the wine had done more to harm the reputation of the colony than to advance it. The fate of wine at this period was finally sealed not only because viticulture was difficult in Virginia but also because tobacco grew so well there. Farmers readily planted this profitable crop in preference to the hardship and financial uncertainty associated with growing vines.

Rather than blame the poor native vines or the climate and diseases that killed imported varieties, responsibility for the failure of the Virginia wine experiment was fixed on the French wine-growers. They were said to have concealed their skills and to have been more interested in growing tobacco than vines. This did not dampen the enthusiasm of the first Virginians for consuming wine, however, and in 1623 the governor placed price controls on Spanish wines and complained that Spaniards were dumping in Virginia 'rotten wines which destroy our bodies and empty our purses'.[18] Dreams of establishing a massive wine industry in Virginia – one big enough to supply the English market – slowly died, but attempts to grow vines and make wine in the eastern regions of North America continued. When the Puritans landed at Plymouth Bay in 1621 they reported, in a manner reminiscent of Leif Ericsson, that they saw 'vines everywhere'. They are often said to have made wine from these grapes for the first Thanksgiving,[19] but there is no evidence of it. The *Mayflower*, which carried the first Puritans to Plymouth, had large stocks of alcohol, mainly beer and spirits, although the settlers faced a perilous shortage of it soon after they landed.

It is important to remember that the association of 'puritan' and abstinence from alcohol developed only in the nineteenth century. The seventeenth-century Puritans, like all their contemporaries, consumed alcohol as an integral part of their daily diet, not only because it was nutritious but also because it was safer than the often-polluted water that was available. Beer made from products as diverse as corn and pumpkin was brewed in Puritan households for private consumption as well as by 'common brewers' who made supplies for wholesale or retail sale. As for wine, there were early but unsuccessful attempts to plant vineyards. Not only was wine part of the culture of better-off English, but the Puritans used it in their religious services. The well-known preacher Increase Mather referred to wine as a 'good creature of God', while warning that no one should 'drink a Cup of Wine more than is good for him'.

The *Arbella*, which brought Puritans to Boston in 1630, carried three times as much beer as water and 10,000 gallons of wine, and the colonists made wine from local grapes in their first summer. The quality was so poor, however, that they asked the authorities in England to send out French viticulturalists to provide them with some expertise. Governor John Winthrop obtained an island in Boston harbour on condition that he establish a vineyard, and he optimistically agreed to pay the rent in wine. Eight years later the arrangement was modified to allow him to pay in apples. These earliest attempts to make wine set the disappointing tone for many decades.

It is easy enough to understand why early settlers in North America were so optimistic about the possibilities of making wine, and why they remained optimistic in the face of continual failures. On the eastern seaboard they encountered a land where vines grew wild and in abundance, and the Puritans, if not others, must have been reminded of the men who were sent by Moses to reconnoitre the Promised Land and who returned with a massive bunch of grapes. Even if these native American grapes proved unsuitable for wine, it seemed inconceivable that European varieties would not grow in the new land.

What the early colonists did not appreciate was that exotic vines would almost inevitably succumb to the harsh winters, the insects, and various funguses, moulds and other plant diseases to which the American vines were resistant. Optimism overcame experience time and again, however, as individuals insisted that the colonies had all the conditions necessary to become the site of a great wine industry. It was on the same latitude as many great European wine-producing areas, and all that was necessary was to crack the secret and end the succession of bad luck. Each group of immigrants, it seems, had to ride this rollercoaster of hope and despair before giving up.

It was not only the English colonists who were enthusiastic about the idea of making wine in their new world. Dutch settlers planted vineyards in the New Netherlands in the 1640s, but when the English took the colony in 1669 there was no sign of local wine-production. Swedes who settled along the Delaware River also tried their hand at viticulture, a project encouraged in the instructions given to the Swedish governor. A settlement of Pietists in Germantown, Pennsylvania, intended to specialize in wine, and later arrivals from the Rhineland contributed their expertise. All these attempts foundered.

In Pennsylvania, William Penn's vision of a new land included vines and his vision of a new society included wine. Within a year of arriving he reported having drunk wine reminiscent of a good claret but made from native grapes by a local Huguenot. Penn noted that vines probably grew best where they grew naturally, and he planned to experiment with indigenous vines 'and hope the consequence will be as good wine as any

European countries of the same latitude do yield.'[20] This would have pitted Penn's wines against those of Burgundy, but there is no evidence that he ever experimented with the local varietals. Instead, Penn planted 200 acres of French and Spanish vines in eastern Pennsylvania, though his own tastes, which ran to 'canary, claret, sack, and Madeira', were furnished by imports.

Even more concentrated efforts were made in the Carolinas, where native vines seemed to grow in particular abundance. Land on south-facing slopes in northern Carolina was designated for vineyards, and great expectations of viticultural success were voiced, but in the end little was started, let alone achieved. In 1670 vineyards planted near modern Charleston yielded good harvests, but their suitability for wine was questioned: 'some [grapes are] very pleasant and large but being pressed the thickness of their outward skin yields a kind of harshness which gives us reason to fear . . . that they will hardly ever be reclaimed or with very great difficulty.'[21] The colony's council asked for vines to be sent from Europe, along with skilled vignerons.

Among all the settlers, the French Huguenots had the best record, and they were reported as having made wine in several localities. In 1680, following another wave of religious persecution in France, the first organized group of Huguenots arrived in South Carolina in order to foster the production of oil, silk and wine. Using European and native vines they produced some wine, samples of which were sent to England where it was 'well approved of' by the 'best palates'.[22] The Huguenots must have had some luck in the first years, however, either because the weather was mild or diseases of the vine were temporarily at bay. Within a decade it is evident that no wine was being produced in the area.

While all this energy and time was being spent on trying to grow vines for wine in the American colonies, the settlers needed supplies of alcohol. Ale was widely consumed, in part because it was generally safer than water to drink, and it was brewed in the colonies. Towards the end of the seventeenth century distilled spirits began to make their presence known, particularly rum made from the sugar of the West Indies. Of the three main types of alcohol, wine was the most problematic. It was proving difficult to produce it locally, so all supplies had to be shipped from Europe. It was still unstable, however, and much of the wine that travelled across the Atlantic arrived in poor condition, giving the colonists ample supplies of vinegar. This in itself was a constant incentive to succeed at viticulture.

The keen interest that colonists had in promoting viticulture did not stop their leaders from expressing traditional concerns about drinking habits in their communities. As we have seen, Puritans thought that wine was good in moderation, but precisely what 'more than was good for' a man was difficult to define, and getting people to accept limits presented real problems. In Massachusetts wine was considered more problematic than cider and beer, but less harmful than spirits like whiskey and rum. Various measures were adopted to try to limit drinking to what was needed for a reasonable diet. The aim, of course, was to prevent drunkenness and the varied social and religious problems it gave rise to.[23]

The steps taken in Massachusetts included tight licensing laws that promoted cider and ale as the staple drinks. In 1677, for example, only seven of the twenty-seven men and women licensed to sell alcohol were permitted to sell wine; the majority could sell only beer and cider. Laws were also passed to forbid drinking to anyone's health, providing drink as part of wages, and furnishing rations of drink above and beyond wages. In 1645 a definition of excessive drinking was established: half a pint of wine per person on any occasion.

Such measures apparently did not achieve the results the Puritan legislators wanted, for wine continued to be consumed in substantial quantities. Nor were the culprits the labouring classes, for they could be counted on to drink rum and ale. It was the better-off who consumed wine, particularly on occasions such as weddings and funerals. At the 1678 funeral of Mrs Mary Norton in Boston, the mourners consumed 51½ gallons of Malaga wine. Seven years later mourners paid their last respects to the Reverend Thomas Cobbett by consuming one barrel of wine and two of cider, the latter with spice and ginger because of the cold weather.[24]

Later in the seventeenth century Massachusetts authorities tried to price alcohol, especially wine and rum, out of the reach of ordinary citizens. By 1698 the tax on wine was six to twelve pence a gallon, compared to only eighteen pence a *barrel* on cider, beer and ale. Wine was, however, spared the more drastic measure taken against rum and other distilled liquors when in 1712 their sale from taverns was banned entirely.

The seventeenth century in America thus witnessed some of the same ambivalence towards wine that had long been evident in Europe: a keenness to produce and drink it combined with profound suspicion of its effects on health and public order. They continued into the eighteenth century, when settled Americans and new arrivals persisted in their attempts to produce wine. Despite the sad history of American wine during the seventeenth century, hopes remained alive and even buoyant in the next century that the land would yet support a thriving wine industry.

None were more hopeful than the founders of Georgia in the 1730s. Like their Virginia counterparts a hundred years earlier, they conjured up Mediterranean images of silk and wine: 'Plantations of regular Rows of Mulberry-Trees [on which silk-worms feed], entwined with Vines, the Branches of which are loaded with Grapes.' Georgia was supplied with vines from Madeira and Burgundy, and by the late 1730s half an acre of land near Savannah was in vines. Samuel Wesley, brother of the theologian John Wesley who spent some time in Georgia evangelizing, wrote rhapsodically of what he imagined Georgia wine would be like:

> With nobler Products see thy GEORGIA teems,
> Chear'd with the genial Sun's director Beams
> That the wild Vine to Culture learns to yield,
> and purple Clusters ripen through the Field.
> Now bid thy Merchants bring thee wine no more
> Or from the *Iberian* or the *Tuscan* Shore;
> No more they need th' *Hungarian* Vineyards drain,
> And *France* herself may drink her best *Champain*.
> Behold! at last, and in a subject Land,
> Nectar sufficient for thy large Demand:
> Delicious Nectar, powerful to improve
> Our hospitable Mirth and social Love.[25]

The reality was as far from the image as Hungary was from Georgia. It is notable, though, that Wesley assumed wine would be made from native grapes, for what records there are of wine-making in Georgia generally refer to wild vines. Some were described as having 'a pleasant sweet flavour and taste', but there was agreement that they had little durability. One lot 'grew sour, and would not keep, tho' very pleasant to drink when new, and of a fine colour'. Attempts to cultivate vines and make wine in Georgia continued throughout the century, but despite sporadic small-scale successes – a small vineyard said to have flourished here, a few bottles of palatable wine produced there – the bright vision of Georgia as a wine colony gradually dimmed.

Attempts to produce wine continued in the other colonies through the eighteenth century. One venture was based at the optimistically named New Bordeaux, South Carolina, where a number of Huguenots established vineyards from the late 1760s. The leader of this group was Louis de St Pierre, who not only wrote a manual on viticulture, but actively sought official sponsorship of vineyards in the colony. St Pierre himself was granted 5,000 acres, much of which he planted in vines. Others in the area, Huguenots and Germans, also developed vineyards. One German, Christopher Sherb, produced small amounts of wine (80 gallons in 1769) for the local market. A similar venture, this one based in Florida, involved a fleet of eight ships that in 1767 imported an impressive company of 1,500 south Europeans – Greeks, Italians, Minorcans and Corsicans – together with thousands of European vine cuttings. By the time the American Revolution broke out, however, nothing had been heard of any vineyards producing wine.

But nowhere was the quest for wine pursued more earnestly than in Virginia. There were promising signs in the first decades of the eighteenth century when Robert Beverley planted three acres of native vines and produced red and white wine. In 1715 he made 400 gallons, and in 1722, 750 gallons. His best wine was said to taste rather like claret and to have the strength of port. Such successes, few as they were among the many attempts, kept hope alive to the point that Virginia's governors committed thousands of pounds to sponsoring vineyards. It is worth noting that viticulture in the colonies was frequently supported from the public purse, an indication of the importance attached to wine.

At one time, in the 1770s, no fewer than three significant wine ventures in Virginia were the recipients of official blessing and subsidies. In 1769 the assembly passed an act setting up André Estave with land, a house and slaves to establish a vineyard of native and exotic vines. The venture quickly went sour, however. Not only did many of Estave's slaves run away, but the vines were struck by frost in 1774 and by hail the following year. By 1777 his land had been sold off. In 1773 the assembly guaranteed

Robert Bolling £50 a year for five years to produce wine from imported vines.

The third recipient of public funds was Philip Mazzei, a Tuscan. He had planned to bring 10,000 French, Italian, Spanish and Portuguese vines, along with fifty European peasants, to Virginia, but in the end he recruited only ten vineyard workers. In 1775 Mazzei planted 1,500 of his vines near Thomas Jefferson's estate at Monticello, and half of them took root and produced grapes. But when he made wine in 1775 and 1776 it was from the grapes of native vines, not of the European stock. This was the only wine to come from Mazzei's venture, and his praise of it – that it was better than ordinary Italian wine or the wine made around Paris – was pretty half-hearted.[26]

Viticulture continued to attract venturers in other colonies, too. Wine was apparently made in Louisiana in 1775, and some claret or burgundy-style wines were sent to George III. Louisiana also saw the first hybrid varietal that drew on *vinifera* and native vines, the alexander grape. The hybrid, the apparently spontaneous product of an unknown native and one of the European vines originally imported by William Penn, made a wine that was said to have been very good in the February and March following the vintage, but which had gone off very soon after that.

In Pennsylvania Benjamin Franklin was an important supporter of viticulture. In the 1740s Franklin wrote instructions on making wine, and while he was the colony's agent in London he continued to promote viticulture schemes. One recognition of his work was a 1767 gift of a dozen bottles of Pennsylvania wine made from native grapes by a Quaker, Thomas Livezey. Franklin wrote that the wine 'has been found excellent by many good judges' in London, and that his own wine merchant wanted to know how much of it was available and at what price.

The English, in fact, demonstrated continuing interest in American viticulture. In 1758 the London Society for the Encouragement of the Arts, Manufactures and Commerce (later renamed the Royal Society of Arts) offered a £100 prize for the first colonist to produce five tuns (about 1,250 gallons) of acceptable red or white wine, but there was no winner by the time the offer was withdrawn in 1765. In 1762 the Society offered prizes of £200 for the largest vineyard of at least 500 vines planted north and south of the Delaware river by 1767. In 1765 the northern prize was won by Edward Antill for his 800-vine property near

New Brunswick, New Jersey. Antill had planted European vines but despite his optimism regarding the quality of the wines his vines might eventually produce, he abandoned viticulture soon after winning the prize.[27]

Attempts to cultivate vines in the eastern regions of North America thus produced meagre results throughout the eighteenth century. Some plans came to nothing, others resulted in vineyards that failed, others produced grapes but no wine. In many instances these were personal ventures that died when individuals died or lost interest in viticulture. North American wine was no match for locally made spirits. Compared to the handful of vineyards that were sporadically reported as having produced a barrel of wine here or a few gallons of indifferent wine there, breweries and distilleries sprang up everywhere. While viable vineyards might be counted in dozens, it is thought that there were as many as 2,579 distilleries in the United States by 1792.[28] One estimate of alcohol consumption in the 1790s suggests that an average American over the age of fifteen consumed about six gallons of absolute alcohol a year, about twice the volume consumed in the United States in the 1990s. Well over half the alcohol would have been in the form of beer, about a third in the form of distilled spirits, and less than a sixtieth in the form of wine.[29]

As in the non-viticultural regions of Europe, wine was consumed in the American colonies by the better-off, for whom it was integral to social functions. In the newly founded United States of America, the social tone was set by those who occupied the pinnacle of political power. George Washington, Benjamin Franklin and Thomas Jefferson all showed an interest in viticulture. When the Constitutional Convention met in Philadelphia in 1792, Washington led a delegation to look at a nearby vineyard that held out promise of success.

Franklin addressed wine on a number of occasions, always to praise it as a God-given boon. If it was true, he wrote, that truth is in wine, then men before Noah 'having nothing but water to drink, could not discover the truth. Thus they went astray, became abominably wicked, and were justly exterminated by water, which they loved to drink.' Noah, however, recognized the pernicious effects of water, 'and to quench his thirst God created the vine, and revealed to him the means of converting its fruit into wine.'[30] Franklin later penned a drinking song on this theme. It concluded:

> From this Piece of history plainly we find
> That water's good neither for body nor mind;
> That Virtue & Safety in Wine-bibbing's found,
> While all that drink Water deserve to be drown'd.[31]

Franklin pursued thoughts along similar lines when writing in 1779 to the abbé Morellet, one of the lesser lights of the French Englightenment. Morellet had suggested that the real reason for the American Revolution was not to achieve liberty from the English crown but rather to escape from English beer and embrace French wine. In his response Franklin wrote that the proof of God's intention that humans should drink wine was the placement of the elbow. Were it located higher or lower on the arm, he pointed out, it would be impossible to lift the wine glass directly to the mouth.

Thomas Jefferson clearly enjoyed wine as much as Franklin, but he expressed his appreciation in far more serious ways. While ambassador to France in 1787–88, Jefferson had toured much of Germany, Italy and France and had paid special attention to wine regions. Among those he visited were the Rhine, Champagne, Burgundy, Beaujolais, the Rhône, Piedmont, Bordeaux and the Loire. He tasted the wines extensively and recorded detailed notes that show his familiarity with some of the most famous vintages of the time. Jefferson lost none of his enthusiasm when he returned to the United States. He imported vine cuttings from a number of the best vineyards, including Château d'Yquem, but eventually gave up on European vines and by 1809 acknowledged that if wine was to be produced in America it would have to be from indigenous vine stock. Jefferson imported wine from Europe for his own cellar, and the best available French wine was served at banquets in the White House. The importance Jefferson attached to wine is demonstrated in the design of his house at Monticello, where a dumb-waiter was installed to bring wine directly from the cellar to the dining room.

The American Revolution soon had an effect on wine. It became common for candidates in elections to buy alcohol for voters, a practice well established in England and elsewhere. American politicians tended to buy imported wine for well-off voters but spirits or cider for those lower down the social scale so as to demonstrate a patriotic attachment to alcohol produced in the United States.

It was in the late eighteenth century that voices began to be raised in America against certain kinds of alcohol. One of the loudest was that of Dr Benjamin Rush, a signatory of the Declaration of Independence. Rush denied that distilled alcohol of any kind or in any amount could be beneficial. He described the effects of alcohol addiction on the body and insisted that drinking led inevitably to crime, financial disaster, immorality and the breakdown of the family. Even so, Rush, like many who were concerned by the social and personal effects of alcohol, treated wine differently. Wine, he wrote, could promote 'cheerfulness, strength, and nourishment, when taken only in small quantities, and at meals'. In 1802 Rush even bought shares in the Pennsylvania Vine Company, a venture that aimed to make wine.[32]

The special place of American wine was reflected in some official policies. In 1791 legislation was passed that exempted American wine from general taxes on alcohol. Jefferson supported the move enthusiastically and expressed the common view that wine was far preferable to spirits for common consumption: 'No nation is drunken where wine is cheap; and none sober, where the dearness of wine substitutes ardent spirits as the common beverage. It is, in truth, the only antidote to the bane of whiskey.'[33] This notion, that many of the problems associated with alcohol would be solved if people drank wine instead of spirits, was taken up by many social reformers in the nineteenth century.

For viticulture in the eastern regions of North America, the eighteenth century ended much as the seventeenth began: with a lot of official encouragement but very little domestic wine. After almost two centuries of experiments and ventures, many of them with official support, viticulturalists were still wrestling with the same issues: whether to try to make wine from native vines or from European stock, and how to enable the exotic vines to survive the perennially fatal onslaught of frost, hail, insects and diseases. Meanwhile, on the east coast the Spanish missions were advancing viticulture north to the regions that are now the heart of the American wine industry.

It is ironic that North America, where it proved so difficult to make wine, should have been so often perceived as a place where viticulture could thrive, while South Africa, which proved so hospitable to grapes, was at first overlooked as a site for wine production. Like the Portuguese before them, Dutch navigators underestimated the colonial potential of southern Africa when they first landed at the Cape of Good Hope in the seventeenth century during their single-minded search for spices. The Dutch had no interest where there were no spices, and when the Dutch East India Company established commerce in spices in the East Indies (now Indonesia), they sponsored a settlement at the Cape simply as a stage for revictualling ships on the long voyage from Europe to southeast Asia. The first mention of wine in the region occurred when it was used as a trading commodity: in 1595 a French ship stopped at Mossel Bay to take on food and exchanged Spanish wine for cattle supplied by the native inhabitants.

The eventual spread of viticulture to southern Africa in the mid seventeenth century was not due to official secular or church sponsorship, as had been the case in Latin America, but to the determination of one man, the doctor Jan van Riebeeck. He had visited the Cape of Good Hope in 1648 to rescue a group of shipwrecked sailors, and because of this experience was sent back four years later to set up a station that would eventually become Cape Town.

Vines are not native to southern Africa, but van Riebeeck was impressed by the similarity of the climate to wine regions in Europe and requested cuttings to plant near the Cape: 'they ought to grow as well and successfully here on the hillsides as they do in Spain or France,' he wrote.[34] The first shipment of vines arrived in 1655, their origins now unknown, and a year later more vines reached the Cape. The second shipment can be identified as having come from France. Other vines followed as the Dutch government developed an interest in fostering viticulture in its most southerly possession so that it could provision the Dutch settlements in Asia. The voyage from Europe to the Dutch East Indies took upwards of twelve months, and it would be a real advantage to be able to take on wine and other supplies at the Cape rather than carry them during the entire trip.

At first van Riebeeck cultivated his vines in a nursery, but in 1658 he planted his own vineyard of 1,200 vines. It was devastated after a raid by natives, but van Riebeeck replanted in 1659, this time with between 10,000 and 12,000 vines. In the same year the first wine was made and van Riebeeck wrote jubilantly in his journal, 'Today, praise be to God, wine was made for the first time from Cape grapes, namely from the new must fresh from the vat.'[35]

This was a beginning, but developing the Cape wine industry was a hard-fought struggle. In many respects the settlers in South Africa had an easier time of it than their counterparts on the eastern seaboard of North America. They did not have to contend with the dubious blessings of masses of native vines: there was no question but that South African wine would be made from exotic stock. Moreover, because there were no native vines there were no indigenous mildews, funguses and rots to afflict the immigrant vines; such diseases would arrive later. The southern African climate was also generally more suitable, even though some Cape crops were lost to heavy rain, hail and strong winds. Vine-growers also had to contend with wild animals that were partial to the young shoots of the vines and to birds that on several occasions consumed almost the entire harvest on the vine.

Van Riebeeck's viticultural evangelism also came up against the general indifference of the Cape settlers towards wine. Even by the end of the seventeenth century there were only a few hundred free burghers in the colony, and most were drawn from the social strata in The Netherlands in which wine was not widely consumed. Although the quality of Cape grapes was widely praised, it was generally accepted that the wine they produced was mediocre at best. Much of the responsibility for the gap between potential and reality was placed at the feet of the free burghers, who were portrayed as negligent in their wine-making methods.

Despite disappointing early results – one taster noted that Cape wine 'irritated the bowels' – vineyards spread throughout the Cape region as settlers planted vines, most using one of the muscat varietals. The Cape began to ship wine to Dutch colonists in the East Indies. As early as 1686, just three decades after viticulture was established in the Cape, the first quality controls were applied. The Dutch East India Company council decreed that no grapes could be pressed for wine until they had been certified by the colony's commander as 'of the requisite maturity'. This suggests that wine-makers had been using underripe grapes and making wine that must have been thin and acidic.

The sponsor of this regulation was one of the early Dutch commanders of the Cape settlement, Simon van der Stel, whose name lives on in the

Stellenbosch wine region. Van der Stel was responsible for a veritable revolution in viticulture and viniculture at the Cape. Not only did he insist on the importance of waiting until grapes were ripe before they were harvested, but he also emphasized the importance of cleanliness during wine-making. He himself experimented with a range of grape varieties on what was to become his famous Constantia estate on the Cape peninsula, established in 1686.

Within a few years the Constantia estate comprised more than 100,000 vines, making it by far the largest in the colony, and van der Stel employed the most modern equipment then available. There is no evidence that the commander had any experience of wine-making before his arrival in the Cape. From 1688, however, he was able to draw on the considerable viticultural expertise that arrived in the form of some 150 Huguenots who had fled religious persecution in France after Louis XIV revoked the 1598 Edict of Nantes giving Protestants limited rights. The Huguenots, many with wine-making experience, first sought asylum in The Netherlands, but the government encouraged them to move on to the Cape colony.

The Huguenots were granted land at Stellenbosch, Paarl and Franschhoek. Among the innovations for which they were responsible was the introduction of additional grape varieties, including perhaps the chenin blanc, adding to the muscat, cabernet sauvignon, syrah and pinot noir that were already being cultivated. The Huguenots made up almost a third of the Cape's European population, and with this influx of skilled workers the wine industry, located in favourable environmental conditions and having a stable market in the East Indies, flourished.

An important factor in its success was its ability to use slave labour. One description, by Lady Anne Barnard, of grape-treading at Constantia in the late eighteenth century gives a highly romanticized view of work conditions: 'What struck me most was the beautiful antique forms, perpetually changing and perpetually graceful, of the three bronze figures, half naked, who were dancing in the wine press beating the drum (as it were) with their feet in perfect time. Of these presses, there were four with three slaves in each.'[36] Slaves were so plentiful that owners were said to station them throughout the vineyards to pick off any insect that landed on their vines.

Even so, the reputation of Cape wines remained poor, and after one particularly bad shipment to the East Indies in 1687 an order was issued forbidding further exports. They continued nevertheless, and the order was finally revoked in 1717. It was not just the quality of the wine that was at issue, but also the containers used for shipping. The wood available at the Cape was not suitable for barrels, and when wine was transported in teak casks it was found to take on some of the reddish-brown colour from the wood. In 1725 a thousand bottles were sent out for filling with wine, but the results were no better. Yet despite problems of quality and shipping, the Cape wine industry grew. By 1752 some 3.9 million vines were in production, and in that year alone the Cape exported 642 leaguers of wine (about 440,000 litres) to the Dutch East Indies.[37]

Although it became essentially an exporter of inexpensive and low-quality wine, the Cape produced one of the most famous of all New World wines. In the late eighteenth century the Constantia vineyard was replanted, particularly with muscat vines, and a dessert wine known as constantia was produced. Both white and red were made, but it was the red that enjoyed greatest popularity in Europe, particularly in England. Its sweetness was achieved by leaving the grapes on the vine as long as possible, although they were not botrytized. Late harvesting was made possible by the warm climate and the absence of diseases, which meant that growers did not have to pick grapes as soon as they were ripe for fear they would be exposed to frosts or mildew. Such was the fame of constantia that there were even attempts to plant the grapes from which it was made in Beaune.

With the British seizure of the Cape of Good Hope from the Dutch in 1795, and its inclusion in the British Empire in 1814, wine exports rose. War in Europe had cut British imports of French wine and Cape producers were able to increase shipments, particularly after preferential tariffs were granted. At once, the Cape vineyards became the oldest in the British Empire. Britain had lost its American colonies only two decades earlier, but from a viticultural point of view they seemed like a lost cause in any case. The acquisition of the Cape colony seemed to offer Britain the supplies of wine that would free it of reliance on powers like France and Spain, and almost immediately it imposed measures to improve quality. Lord Horatio Nelson clearly thought that wine was one of the principal advantages of Britain gaining the Cape, for although he doubted its strategic value he acknowledged that it was 'an immense

1. The earliest evidence of wine

The earliest evidence of wine was found during excavations in Hajji Firuz in the Zagros mountains of western Iran. This nine-litre jar is the oldest known vessel to contain residue of wine and dates from 5400–5000 BC. This and five other jars had been set into the floor of the 'kitchen' of a mudbrick building.

2. Drinking wine in Assyria

The Assyrian King Assurbanipal and his queen are shown banqueting and drinking wine under a trellis of vines. This is a relief from the royal palace at Nineveh, dating from the seventh century BC.

3a and 3b. Making wine in Ancient Egypt

Wall-paintings of about 1400 BC depict wine-making in Ancient Egypt. Successive panels show (a) the grapes being picked and then trodden to extract the juice, and (b) the wine being placed in pottery jars for fermentation and conservation.

4. The krater of Vix

This massive 1100-litre krater, used by Greeks to mix wine and water, was found in the sixth-century tomb of a Celtic princess in Burgundy, France. Its size and delicate form of construction almost certainly rule out its use as anything but a decorative object.

5. The symposium of Ancient Greece

This scene, on a decorated kylix (a shallow wine cup), shows four men wearing garlands and reclining, drinking and talking at a symposium. A servant boy is replenishing the kylix of one of the participants.

6. The wine god

Bacchus, the Roman god of wine, better known to the Greeks as Dionysus, is often depicted in the revelry that is now implied by words like 'bacchanal'. Here he is shown in a less tumultuous mood, but the wreathing of his hair with vine leaves and grapes (which is typical of images of Bacchus) generously hints at the wild disorder with which he and his followers were associated.

7. BYO at the time of the Norman Conquest

The Bayeux Tapestry's portrayal of the conquest of England by William of Normandy in 1066 shows the Normans bringing a barrel of wine as part of their provisions. The text reads, 'They draw a wagon with wine and arms.' Wine was a normal part of military rations, but the Normans might also have been anxious about the availability (and quality) of English wine.

8. Christ in the wine press

This late medieval representation of Christ crushing grapes is a vivid evocation of the merging of wine and blood in Christian doctrine and ceremony.

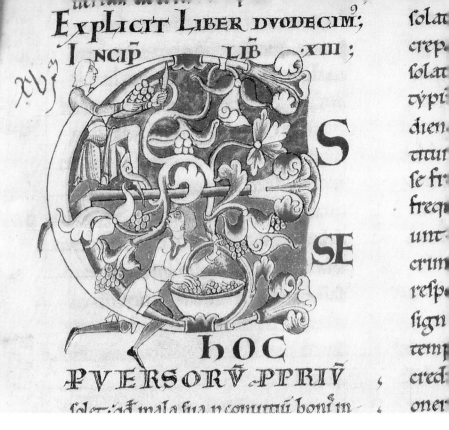

9. Monks celebrate wine
Part of a manuscript from the Abbey of Cîteaux, one of the largest vineyard-owning religious houses in Burgundy. The letter E is decorated with scenes of the grape harvest.

10. Vintage during the Middle Ages
A scene from an early sixteenth-century Flemish book of hours that depicts grapes being brought from the vineyard and pressed.

11. Shipping and sipping wine

The arrival of the year's new wine at the port of Antwerp was an important occasion. Antwerp was a major centre for the reshipment of wine from southern and western Europe to markets in northern Europe. This early sixteenth-century Flemish illustration of the month of October shows barrels being unloaded and merchants tasting the new vintage.

12. Family tree, with grapes

The age-old link between the grapevine and fertility is made clear in this sixteenth-century representation of the 'tree of consanguinity' as a vine.

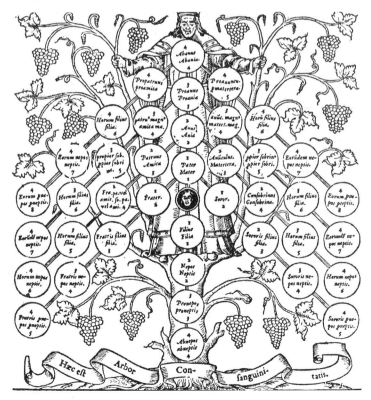

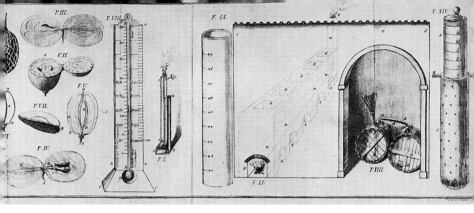

13. Science in the service of art

The eighteenth century witnessed a more scientific approach to viticulture and wine-making. Among the researchers was the Italian Adamo Fabbroni, whose *On the Art of Making Wine* included diagrams detailing the constituent elements of grapes, instruments used in wine-making, and the process of fermentation.

14. The heady wine of Revolution

The French Revolution destroyed the division of society into three orders (clergy, nobility, and the rest of the population). Outside this wine-shop, called 'Au 3 ordre reunis' (an ungrammatical rendering of 'The Three Orders Reunited'), three pairs of people amuse themselves: a priest drinks wine with a soldier; a man wearing a hat decorated with the red, white and blue cockade of the Revolution swings his companion; and a third couple (the man is perhaps a noble) hold each other affectionately.

15. Wine fraud, nineteenth-century style

Widespread adulteration and fraud in the wine industry inspired this satirical view of the manufacture of 'genuine port' from brandy, cyder, 'Red Cape' (red wine from Cape Colony) and additives such as alum and tartar.

[Genuine Wine Manufactory.]

16. Bullish about wine in the Bear state

In this representation of the growth of California's wine industry in the late nineteenth century, Liberty pops a cork from a bottle of sparkling wine while the Californian bear holds out a coupe (the shallow glass long used for such wine) in readiness. Cases of wine representing better-known Californian varietals occupy the foreground, while the head of the barrel shows the state seal.

Champagne advertisement (left)

LAURENT-PERRIER

"SANS-SUCRE"   "CHAMPAGNE"

CHAMPAGNE   COMPETITION

Supplied to
H.M. THE KING OF THE BELGIANS.
H.R.H. THE DUKE OF SAXE-COBURG GOTHA.
RT. HON. THE EARL OF DURHAM.
RT. HON. THE EARL OF DUNRAVEN.
PRINCE DE ROHAN.
H.E. THE MARQUIS HOYOS.
H.E. HUBERT DOLEZ.
THE CHEVALIER THIER.
LORD ERSKINE.
RT. HON. VIS. CURZON.
LADY SYBIL TOLLEMACHE.
SIR GEO. NEWNES, M.P.
SIR CHAS. NUGENT,
etc., etc.

Supplied to
H.M. THE KING OF GREECE.
H.R.H. THE DUCHESS OF TECK.
COUNTESS OF STAMFORD AND WARRINGTON.
COUNTESS OF DUDLEY.
THE COMTE DE GABRIAS.
VIS. DE CORDAS.
BARON D'UNETHORN.
LORD GREY DE WILTON.
LORD GRESHAM.
HON. LYONEL TOLLEMACHE.
MDME. ADELINA PATTI-NICOLINI.
COL. LOCKWOOD, M.P.
CAPT. COMBE,
etc., etc.

Laurent-Perrier
"SANS-SUCRE,"
Is supplied by all Wine Merchants throughout the World.
It is found at all the most important Hotels and Restaurants in Great Britain, Her Colonies and Possessions, the United States, Germany, France, Holland, Belgium, &c.

VINTAGES
1889, 1892, 1893,
"SANS-SUCRE,"
(Gold Label).

GRAND VIN
SANS-SUCRE
LAURENT PERRIER & C
Maison fondée en 1852
Bouzy près Reims

Laurent-Perrier
"SANS-SUCRE,"
Is supplied by all Wine Merchants throughout the World.
It is found at all the most important Hotels and Restaurants in Great Britain, Her Colonies and Possessions, the United States, Germany, France, Holland, Belgium, etc.

VINTAGES
1889, 1892, 1893,
"SANS-SUCRE,"
(Gold Label).

PRIZES of the Value of about £6000

17. Inventing and promoting champagne, the wine for all seasons

Laurent-Perrier's 'sans sucre' reflected the trend towards dry champagne and away from the very sweet styles that had been common earlier in the nineteenth century. This advertisement stresses the famous clients of the house and lures newer, and presumably less wealthy, customers with prizes.

Vin Mariani advertisement (right)

EMILE ZOLA
The Well-Known French Writer.

EMILE ZOLA Writes:
Vin Mariani--The Elixir of Life, which combats human debility, the one real cause of every ill--a veritable scientific fountain of youth, which, in giving vigor, health and energy, would create an entirely new and superior race.
EMILE ZOLA.

Never has anything been so highly and so justly praised as

MARIANI WINE, the FAMOUS FRENCH TONIC for BODY, NERVES and BRAIN
FOR OVERWORKED MEN, DELICATE WOMEN SICKLY CHILDREN
Vin Mariani is indorsed by the medical faculty all over the world. It is specially recommended for Nervous Troubles, Throat and Lung Diseases, Dyspepsia, Consumption, General Debility.

MALARIA, WASTING DISEASES AND LA GRIPPE.
Sold at all Druggists.   Refuse Substitutions.

VIN MARIANI GIVES STRENGTH.
SPECIAL OFFER.—To all who write mentioning LESLIE'S WEEKLY, we send a book containing portraits and indorsements of EMPERORS, EMPRESS, PRINCES, CARDINALS, ARCHBISHOPS and other distinguished personages.
MARIANI & CO., 52 WEST 15TH STREET, NEW YORK.
Paris—41 Boulevard Haussmann; London—83 Mortimer Street; Montreal—28-30 Hospital Street.

18. The great cure-all for bodily and social ills

Vin Mariani was a wine-based tonic that was endorsed by prominent men and women, including the Pope and – as shown here – Émile Zola. The health benefits of wine were being increasingly questioned when this advertisement was published in 1896. Although the claims made for the tonic's effectiveness seem extravagant, they were not out of line with advertisements for other patent medicines.

19. The French republic, wine and indivisible
A poster for Bastille Day 1901 links the French Revolution of 1789, the French nation and wine. From the early nineteenth century, the French began to regard wine as their national beverage, a position that led many to regard anti-wine temperance campaigners as anti-French.

20. Purifying the church of wine

Arguing that the wine in the Bible was really unfermented grape juice, many temperance supporters called for the removal of wine from communion. 'Unfermented wine' (surely a contradiction in terms) was largely resisted by the clergy, but this did not stop producers from touting its popularity.

21. 'Wine is the most healthy and hygienic of beverages'

This quotation of Louis Pasteur became a mantra for the wine industry in nineteenth- and twentieth-century France as it fought the enemies of alcohol. This advertisement in a viticultural periodical – an excellent case of preaching to the converted – presents medical authorities to the effect that wine is as nutritious as milk, bread, good meat and eggs.

22. Phylloxera, Italian-style

Phylloxera struck Italy later than France, but it quickly affected many of the nation's vineyards. Here, Italian workers use large syringes to inject carbon bisulphide into the earth to protect vines against phylloxera. The effectiveness of this method proved to be limited.

23. Wine – the 'smartly correct' choice

This 1941 advertisement promotes wine as an accompaniment to food. Reflecting residual uneasiness about alcohol even after the repeal of Prohibition, it stresses that wine helps people stay 'on the moderate side'. It also insists that there is no shame in serving American wine – just as well, because once the United States entered the Second World War in 1941, wine imports from Europe virtually dried up.

LET
THE
MOOD
TAKE
YOU TO **BORDEAUX**

24. Just lie back and think of Bordeaux?

For centuries bordeaux projected the image of a serious, masculine wine, a special preserve of English upper-class males who insisted on calling it 'claret'. In the more competitive market environment of the 1990s, Bordeaux wine-makers shed this image as readily as this couple shed their clothes, and began to promote bordeaux as youthful and fun to drink.

25. Tasting Wine at Vinopolis
A formal wine tasting at Vinopolis, the massive permanent wine exhibition in London that opened in 1999.

26. In the cellars of Vinopolis
One of the many exhibition areas at Vinopolis; a reconstructed Roman amphitheatre in the Rhône Room.

tavern'. The Cape lived up to this sneering expectation, and proved to be an important source of wine for British tables well into the nineteenth century.

Just as Constantia was making its impact on the British market at the end of the eighteenth century, a new wine region was being established further away from Europe than any before. In 1788 Captain Arthur Phillip, the first governor of the British colony of New South Wales in what was to become Australia, wrote to his superiors in London: 'In a climate so favourable the cultivation of the vine may doubtless be carried to any degree of perfection, and should no other articles of commerce divert the attention of settlers from this part, the wines of New South Wales may perhaps here after be sought with civility and become an indispensable part of the luxury of European tables.'

Over time, two centuries' time, Captain Phillip's confidence was borne out, but over the short term it proved more difficult than he had imagined to cultivate wine in Australia. Vines were included among the plants aboard the ships of the First Fleet that arrived in 1788, and within days they were planted in a location that is now downtown Sydney. The summer weather there was too warm and humid, however, and a second vineyard further west was established. By 1790 Phillip reported having 2,000 vines but a modest harvest: 'Last year produced two good bunches of Grapes which may be mentioned as being the first this Country has produced, tho' being neglected they decayed on the Vine.' Captain Watkin Tench described these pitifully few grapes as being 'of moderate size, but well filled out; and the flavour high and delicious'.

The 1791 vintage was more plentiful (it could hardly have been less) but apparently still inadequate for wine-making, and for some reason even the 150 kilograms of grapes gathered in 1792 were not crushed and fermented. When Peter Schaffer made wine in 1795, it was probably the first wine produced in Australia. Schaffer's first vintage was about 400 litres of wine made from grapes cultivated on less than a tenth of a hectare. It was described as 'tolerably good' and 'better than at the Cape'. But such encouragement fell on deaf ears, for however favourable southeast Australia might have been for viticulture, it lacked a market, the prime ingredient for a wine industry. The early settlements of Australia were populated by men and women from those social classes in

Great Britain that were not familiar with wine. The drinks they were used to were ale and spirits, and those were the beverages they made. The immigrants who were accustomed to drinking wine were few and could easily be supplied by wine from the Cape. In the first decades of the nineteenth century, rum (a term then covering a range of spirits) was the drink of choice in the Australian colonies, and so widely was it consumed that it became a form of currency: goods and services could be paid for in spirits, as could the labour of convict workers. Lacking a viable market of any kind, viticulture in Australia foundered and did not take root until the nineteenth century.

SEVEN

WINE, ENLIGHTENMENT AND REVOLUTION

Europe in the Eighteenth Century

The eighteenth century opened on a short-lived optimistic note for one major French wine region. Not only had there been a spurt of planting in parts of the Bordeaux region, but in 1697 the important English market was again opened to Bordeaux's quality wines after decades of on-off trade relations between England and France. But political volatility did not end with the seventeenth century, and in 1703 war between France and England closed the English market once again, for seven years. This time, French wine producers seem to have overcome the ban on their wine by the ingenious subterfuge of allowing the English to 'steal' it and pay the French wine-makers or merchants for it indirectly. This was accomplished by having ships laden with French wine sail close to the English coast where they were seized by English privateers. The wine was then taken to London where it was auctioned. The privateers were given a major part of the proceeds, with most of the rest going to the crown and a small portion paid to the tavern-owner where the auction took place. There is no hard evidence that these seizures were rigged, but so much premium French wine was captured and auctioned in this way that it is more than reasonable to suspect that the privateers must have had an arrangement with Bordeaux's merchants.[1]

Although this would have been an unusual arrangement – the wine-producers and merchants would have received a fraction, perhaps a quarter, of the price their wine attracted at auction – there is no other viable explanation for the vast amounts of premium wine that were transported close to the English coast where it was vulnerable to seizure. In May 1705, for example, 200 barrels of Haut-Brion and Pontac wine went under the auctioneer's hammer in London. In June, 230 barrels of Haut-Brion and Margaux were sold, and soon afterwards a further 288 barrels of Haut-Brion, Pontac and Margaux. These premium wines fetched about £60 a barrel, more than twice the sum offered for ordinary clarets seized by privateers. The proceeds from these three lots sold in the spring of 1705 alone were more than £40,000, and even if the privateers received half and paid Bordeaux's merchants half that to send the wine their way, the sums remitted to Bordeaux were not insubstantial. It would certainly have been more profitable than selling premium wine at low prices on the local Bordeaux market, as producers had been forced to do during earlier bans on exports to England.

The wine auctioned off in London was subsequently sold on the English market, where one of the final purchasers was John Hervey, the Earl of Bristol. His accounts for the period 1703–10, when French wine was banned, include the following: £27 10s. 'for a hogshead of Margoose [Margaux] clarett' in December 1703; £16 10s. 'for 3 chests of wine from Avignon', perhaps Châteauneuf-du-Pape, in June 1704; £80 'for 3 hogsheads of wine, 2 of Obrian [Haut-Brion] and 1 of white Langoon [Langon]' in July 1705; and £56 'for 2 hogsheads of Obrian wine' in May 1707.[2] Clearly the embargo did not deprive some consumers of their favourite wines.

As peace between France and England approached in 1709, the Bordeaux authorities decided to withhold export licences from the Dutch merchants who had dominated the trade in the seventeenth century. Despite the fact that the 1708 vintage was poor, the Bordeaux wine trade seemed to be heading for a new period of prosperity. But there was a sudden reversal of fortune, for the following winter was devastating for the vines in many parts of France. In January 1709 heavy snow fell and then temperatures plummeted far below normal, reaching –16°C in Montpellier and –18° in Marseilles, while in Paris the temperature did not rise above –20° for ten days. Throughout France, rivers froze. Then temperatures rose, melting the snow and causing floods, before plummeting again, reaching –23° in Paris.

The freezing cold and rapid fluctuations in temperatures killed vines throughout France and effectively ruined the 1709 vintage. Not only that, but much of the 1708 vintage, which was still in cellars when the bad weather struck, froze in its barrels. As the wine expanded it burst the barrels and then froze in red or yellow shards that protruded between the staves.

The result was a short-term disaster with long-term positive consequences. Production from 1708 to 1710 was low everywhere. For example, the vineyard of the Abbey of St Denis near Paris produced about 35,000 litres of wine a year in 1706 and 1707, but only 7,500 litres in 1708, an abysmal 3,750 litres in 1709, and 8,300 litres in 1710. The price of wine (and of other crops that were also destroyed) shot up. Many small wine-makers were ruined, having no wine to sell and no money to buy the grain and other goods they needed simply to survive.

What followed was an eerie echo of the devastation of the vineyards around Pompeii when Mount Vesuvius erupted in 79 AD. Just as Italian farmers had then raced to plant vineyards in order to profit from the shortage and high prices, so from 1710 onwards investors bought up land around Bordeaux and engaged in an orgy of planting. By about 1720 the destroyed vines had been replaced, but the planting continued in areas where other crops had previously been cultivated. By 1724 Claude Boucher, the Intendant (royal governor) of Bordeaux, noted more in alarm than admiration that, 'For ten leagues around Bordeaux you see nothing but vines. The same mania has taken hold on the rest of the province.'

When this had happened in Roman Italy the Emperor Domitian had issued an edict banning further planting and ordering the ripping up of many vineyards in other parts of the empire. The planting 'mania' in Bordeaux and elsewhere provoked a similar response. In 1722 the Parlement of Metz, whose jurisdiction included the vineyards of the Moselle, ordered the ripping out of all vines planted since 1700 in locations where vines had not grown before. In Burgundy, the Parlement of Dijon was inclined in the same direction but decided in 1725 to wait for the king to act, and in 1731 the nearby Parlement of Besançon ordered recent plantings in its region to be ripped out. In Bordeaux new planting was forbidden in 1724, and all vines planted since 1709, except those planted in the traditional areas and those in the best new locations in the Médoc, were ordered destroyed.

In 1731 the royal government took comprehensive action and forbade the planting of any new vineyards anywhere in France without the express consent of the king. The reasons given were fear of grain shortages if too much land was converted to viticulture and anxiety that overproduction of wine would depress prices and bankrupt the increasing number of peasant families depending on wine for their livelihoods, rendering them unable to buy food. On the face of it there did seem grounds for concern. In 1724 the vineyards around Paris produced more than 8.5 million litres of wine, twice the annual average of the previous ten years.[3]

There is a question whether these edicts really reflected fears about the grain supply or whether they aimed to restrict competition to established wine-growers. There is no doubt that French governments were chronically worried about grain, often less out of concern for the well-being of ordinary people and more because they knew that food shortages almost invariably led to riots and the breakdown of order. The best way to guarantee social peace in this period was to ensure that bread was available in plentiful amounts at affordable prices.

The royal edict did protect the established vineyards from competition from newcomers, although it is notable that the Intendant of Bordeaux exempted vineyards newly planted in what were reputed to be choice locations. Perhaps this was simply a sensible exception to make in the interests of quality, even if it enraged proprietors whose aspirations to profit from the wine-boom were threatened. One was the political philosopher Montesquieu, who owned vineyards in the Graves and Entre-Deux-Mers districts and who in 1725 bought land near the famed Haut-Brion estate. Montesquieu denounced the king's edict as irrational and insulting: irrational because it stopped the French from exploiting the massive demand for their wine, and insulting because it denied them the right to use their wealth and property as they wished.[4]

In the end the protests were moot, for as in Rome so in France the edict to rip up vineyards was widely ignored. Planting continued, although at a more sedate pace, and when permission did have to be obtained it could be purchased from royal officials. Finally, a 1756 inquiry showed that land under viticulture had increased without causing a grain crisis, and three years later the government annulled the 1731 edict.

The drive to plant vines seemed irresistible, in any case. Wine could be an excellent commercial product, not only for wealthy investors making high-quality wine, but also for small peasant wine-makers who served the mass market with low-quality, inexpensive vintages. Even though wine-growing entailed risks and was dependent on the vagaries of weather, plant disease and the market, it was a seductive opportunity to which an increasing number of peasants surrendered. Viticulture could support a family on an acre of land, unlike the twenty to thirty acres a grain-growing family needed to survive, although many peasants tried to manage with even less; around la Rochelle most peasant vine-growers cultivated less than half an acre.

Over the longer term the terrible winter of 1709 proved to be a watershed for French viticulture and wine-making. The need to replace so many vines gave growers the opportunity to plant different varieties from those that had been destroyed and to give more thought to matching varieties and locations. Until then, French vineyards had grown a chaotic profusion of grape varieties that contrasted starkly with the disciplined and limited spectrum of varieties now distributed (and enforced by appellation laws) among French wine-growing regions. More attention was also given to care of the vines themselves.

In Bordeaux, land under viticulture expanded steadily during the eighteenth century, thanks largely to noble landowners. Not the lazy, backward-looking group they have often been portrayed as, nobles were to the fore in bringing land under viticulture and adopting techniques that would produce wines best suited to consumer tastes, especially in the important English and Dutch markets.

The small, wealthy elite of Bordeaux nobles (whose families were mostly ennobled relatively recently in the preceding century), quickly purchased the best sites in the Médoc district. We have noted the Pontac family's success with its Haut-Brion vineyard, and other nobles were rapidly associated with equally famous estates. Many of the noble-owned vineyards were extended during the eighteenth century, but the role of noble proprietors was evident much earlier. In 1744 the Subdelegate of Bordeaux wrote that over half his jurisdiction was planted in vines and that 90 per cent of this land was owned by nobles and wealthy bourgeois.[5] That proportion increased during the century as wealthy owners found ways of forcing smallholders to sell. Peasants, whether they were pro-prietors, tenants or sharecroppers, were almost always disadvantaged because only residents of Bordeaux were able to bring wine into the city untaxed. Nobles, who kept residences in Bordeaux, thus escaped the duties that raised the price of wine, while peasants had to charge more for what might be an identical vintage.

Wine was the main source of landed income for many of Bordeaux's noble families. In 1755, sixty-eight noble magistrates earned almost three-quarters (73 per cent) of their landed income this way. Even a small property could contribute a significant amount as long as the wine was of a quality to command high prices. Councillor Castelnau, for instance, had only twenty acres of vines, which produced a total of twenty-five barrels of wine. But each barrel sold for 900 livres in 1755, returning him a nice income of 22,500 livres. That was twice what was required annually for a comfortable living that included summer and winter residences, four to six servants, a coach, quality clothes, good food and wine, entertainment and travel.[6] Others did even better. The Comte de Ségur, who owned the Lafite and Latour properties, drew an annual income of between 100,000 and 180,000 livres, although he reported much less to the tax authorities.

There were, of course, expenses in running a vineyard. Most of the noble proprietors employed workers whom they paid at a daily rate or whole families who received so much a year per acre of vineyard they looked after. Workers were not well paid, however, and their wage-rates did not change between 1750 and 1772 even though the cost of living rose steadily during the period.

To the northeast, the vineyards of Alsace began to recover in the eighteenth century from the devastation and commercial disruption of the Thirty Years War.[7] Land was more carefully cultivated and the oak forests so important for barrels and presses were put under strict management. As population increased and the local and more distant markets for wine grew, viticulture expanded. Around Ammerschwihr the land in vines increased from 321 hectares in 1721 to 465 in 1762, and overall in Alsace it doubled or trebled during the course of the century. The 1731 royal edict against new plantings was no more observed here than elsewhere. No variety was dominant. In 1750 the Weinbach estate at Kientzheim, which was owned by the Capucin religious order, cultivated almost 17,000 vines, of which 7,700 were raenschling, 3,000 rottraminer, 3,000 muscat, 2,000 pinot noir, 700 riesling and 500 tokay and chasselas. From the late seventeenth century a number of communes promoted noble varieties over others, but they encountered resistance on the part of growers. The same mixing of varieties was encountered elsewhere. A vineyard near Besançon reported muscat, plousard, bregin and gamay.[8]

Everywhere, in fact, replanting continued through the eighteenth century. The diary of a bourgeois who lived near Cahors recorded plantings, harvests and the price of wine in the last quarter of the century. In March 1787 he noted that, 'we have planted half the plot of land at Arnisac . . . which had been uncultivated for twenty years since the old vines were entirely wiped out by the extraordinary cold of the years 1765 and 1767.'[9]

Many of the wealthier proprietors took pains to improve the quality of their wines during the eighteenth century, yet they were still dependent on the weather to determine the size and, to a large extent, the quality of grape harvests. Overall, harvests were generally good from 1710 until 1766, but there were some notable exceptions. In 1754, for example, the vineyards around la Rochelle were destroyed by a combination of a harsh winter, worms in the vines and a summer drought. In 1765 the same region lost half its wine to worms and weather.

More disasters followed in the twelve years from 1767 to 1778 as a succession of cold springs, hail and wet summers was delivered. Of the twelve harvests, three were poor and eight were very poor, and in four of those years the yield around Paris was less than half the quantity that had been harvested in the 1750s. One owner noted in October 1771, 'The vines are producing virtually nothing, as much because of the awful winter followed by the heavy rains that ruined the grapes that had had so much promise, as because of the dry July that damaged them further.'[10] Producers reported frozen grapes and berries so green they were difficult to crush. Some producers even went so far as to try to improve the weak wine of one vintage by mixing it for a week with the press-cake (the dried grape residue left over after pressing) from the following year.[11]

The price of wine was very sensitive to the balance of supply and demand, and it rose in response to these shortages. At Argenteuil, for example, wine that had cost 66 livres in 1767–8 commanded 93 livres in 1778.[12] In the 1780s, the decade that closed with the outbreak of the French Revolution, conditions improved and 1785 produced record yields. But the quality was poor and the oversupply depressed prices in Argenteuil to 15 livres, less than the value of the barrel the wine was stored in. The volatility of the market caused great financial distress, especially among small producers. When prices were high because harvests were low, they had no wine to sell. When they had plenty of wine, there was no market for it. Peasants who relied on wine for their income supported the French Revolution in 1789 in the hope that it would change their circumstances.

The eighteenth century saw the growth of wealthy social groups as increased commerce and the spread of the professions inflated and enriched the middle classes. They represented a broad range of wealth, but they embraced a relatively luxurious lifestyle. Not only did their material living conditions improve, but they were willing to spend considerable amounts on food and drink, and their diet differed more and more from that of the masses. During the eighteenth century the consumption of coffee in Europe rose from 2 million to 120 million pounds (55 million kilograms), a year, while chocolate increased from 2 million to 13 million pounds, and tea rose from 1 million to 40 million pounds.[13] The increase in the rate of consumption of these luxury imports was much higher than the increase in population, but even so, by the end of the century, 13 million pounds of chocolate would have provided each inhabitant of western Europe with only about a quarter of a pound a year. It can hardly be true that these were products of mass consumption, and there is little doubt that the lion's share of coffee, tea and chocolate was consumed by a small minority of the population.

These new drinks were part of a broader change in the diet and tastes of better-off Europeans. The arrival of sugar from the West Indies was another element, and once it became more familiar to Europeans, its consumption rose rapidly. They began to use sugar to sweeten tea, coffee and chocolate, whereas these beverages (chocolate was usually taken as a drink) had been consumed unsweetened in the cultures in which Europeans had first come across them.[14] The change of behaviour was remarked upon in the first decades of the seventeenth century: 'Gentlemen carouse only with wine, with which many mix sugar – which I never observed in any other place or kingdom to be used for that purpose. And because the taste of the English is thus delighted with sweetness, the wines in taverns (for I speak not of merchants' or gentlemen's cellars) are commonly mixed at the filling thereof, to make them pleasant.'[15]

If we take into consideration the development of stronger alcohols, like distilled spirits, and sweeter alcohol like the hopped stouts and porters that came on to the market in the late 1600s and early 1700s, we can appreciate that at some levels Europeans were drinking beverages that were much stronger-tasting and generally sweeter than ever before. It would have been surprising if tastes in wine had not changed in response to the shift in the drinks spectrum. After brandy, porter, chocolate and sweetened tea, a glass of light claret such as the English had cherished since the Middle Ages might well have tasted watery, flat and insipid. Indeed, a number of eighteenth-century commentators held tea to be superior to wine: 'This delicious nectar has all the good effects of wine without the ill; a Liquor that warms without Inflammation, and exhilarates without intoxicating.'[16] Little wonder that tastes began to move toward fuller-bodied and sweeter wines.

The well-off minority who bought expensive imported beverages like tea and chocolate also represented a market for high quality wines and spirits, and one of the trends of the 1700s was the emergence of premium alcoholic drinks to satisfy this demand. Wine-makers and distillers who did not produce for this market turned their efforts to producing low-quality and inexpensive wines for mass consumption, thereby contributing to the growing gastronomic gap that separated the rich from the poor.

For all that French wine-producers expanded production during the eighteenth century, they did not recover their position in the prosperous English market. Although there remained strong demand in London and other cities for the richer, fuller-bodied French red wines, the dominant source of good and basic wine was Portugal. Portuguese wine-makers had got their foot in the English door in the late 1600s when, as discussed earlier, England placed a series of embargoes on French wines; but in 1703 that door was thrown wide open to Portuguese wine imports by a new trade agreement.

This pact, the Methuen Treaty, specified that the tariff on Portuguese wine would never be more than two thirds of that levied on French wines. In return English textile makers gained favoured access to the Portuguese market. The actual ratio between tariffs applied to Portuguese and French wines varied, but it was a constant barrier to French exports. In 1713 Portuguese wine was charged duty of £7 a barrel, but French wine was struck with a levy of £20. The roughly one-to-three ratio had narrowed to about one to two by the 1770s (Portuguese wine paid £30–£50 a tun, French wines £60–£90) but it clearly priced many French wines out of the English market.

On the positive side, the Methuen Treaty resulted in the rapid expansion of the Portuguese wine industry and of imports of Portuguese wine to England. From 1717 to 1777 the Portuguese shipped a steady ten to twelve thousand barrels of wine a year to England, for an overall annual average of 11,600 barrels during the whole period. This represented two thirds of all the wine England imported. The next largest source of English imports, Spain, contributed a quarter of the imports, and France delivered a mere 634 barrels a year on average, or 4 per cent of England's wine imports. The 4 per cent consisted of high-quality wines, but it left the bulk of French wine-producers to find other markets for their ordinary and poor-quality wine. The bulk of it was consumed internally: France's population, and therefore its market, rose by a third during the eighteenth century.[17]

Not all the Portuguese wine consumed in such quantities in eighteenth-century England was the type of sweet wine now known as port. Port-wines at this time came in a range of styles from dry to sweet, although the tendency was to produce increasingly strong wines as the century progressed. In the early 1700s, Portuguese producers added ten to fifteen litres of brandy to each 450-litre pipe of wine (about 3 per cent), but the proportion of brandy rose to 10 and then 17 per cent toward the end of the century. By 1820 it had stabilized at 22 per cent.

So rapidly did the English appetite for port grow that by the 1730s the merchants of the Douro were unable to meet the demand. As a result they began to fabricate wines from vintages that were inferior and did not have the qualities the English sought in their port. To make these wines acceptable, merchants began to blend wines, mixing deep-hued vintages with pale and strong wines with weak, add sugar and alcohol for sweetness, use elderberries to give more colour, and employ spices like pepper, ginger and cinnamon to provide additional flavour.

The resulting concoctions were soon discovered and denounced in England as being dangerous to health, and as a result port imports to England fell precipitously. In 1728 England had imported 116,000 hectolitres of port, but in 1744 imports declined to 87,000 hectolitres and in 1756 to a mere 54,900 hectolitres. Moreover, the bottom fell out of the price of port on the London market: a pipe of the wine that had fetched £16 in the late 1730s could be bought in 1756 for a sixth of that, £2 10s.[18]

The Portuguese government, recognizing a commercial and economic disaster in the making, reacted swiftly by creating a body to supervise and regulate the Douro wine industry. The General Company of Vineyards of the Alto Douro reduced the area under viticulture and fixed the geographical limits within which Douro wine could be made. This was the world's first officially delimited wine region. The government also created mechanisms for supervising all stages of wine-making, from planting vines to shipping and selling the end product. It also tried to remove temptations to fraud by ordering the ripping out of all elderberry plants in the region.

It was impossible to eliminate every dubious practice – dried elder-berries could be obtained by anyone who wanted to give his wine a little more depth of colour – but the decisive action of the General Company soon restored confidence in port. By the 1770s imports to England had rebounded to 160,000–180,000 hectolitres a year, and in 1799 an amazing 440,000 hectolitres were shipped. In 1799 the population of England was about nine million, so the port imported that year provided a little under five litres for every person. The point was, of course, not only that children did not drink port, but also that only a small minority of men did. Not only did they consume more than five litres a year; many drank more than five litres a week, for the eighteenth century produced what became known as 'three-bottle men', men who could down three bottles of port in a single sitting.

As a feat it is not quite what it seems, for eighteenth-century port was somewhat less alcoholic than its modern counterpart, the bottles held less than 75 centilitres, and they would have contained a certain amount of undrinkable sediment. Even so, emptying three of these bottles was an achievement of sorts, and there were those (including the playwright Sheridan and the prime minister William Pitt the Younger) who over-achieved and were reputed to be 'six-bottle men'. This is to say nothing of the classical scholar Dr John Porter, who was said to drink thirteen bottles of port a day. The prestige accorded those who could drink vast quantities of alcohol was part of a culture of heavy drinking that seems to have become widespread among English men of substance in the second half of the century. The phrase 'drunk as a lord' seems to have become entirely literal in its force. In 1770 the *Gentleman's Magazine* listed ninety-nine ways of calling a man drunk, including the genteel 'sipping the spirit of Adonis' and the cruder 'stripping me naked'.[19]

Port was not the only alcoholic beverage that gentlemen drank, nor did they all drink to get drunk. Even so, one wonders whether it was necessary to be as coy as Cyril Jackson, Dean of Christ Church, Oxford. In 1799 Jackson paid his wine bill of £73 6s. 6d. and wrote to his wine merchant, 'Allow me . . . to thank you for the French Brandy which has reached me very safe – But indeed you are too liberal – for I very much doubt whether you will ever be able to replace to yourself what you bestow so abundantly upon your friends – For myself I confess to you that it is something so very much beyond anything that I have ever tasted before, that I keep it sacredly to be used only in case of illness.'[20]

While port was making its name as the staple of the English wine market and select brandies were distinguishing themselves, certain French wines were achieving fame in their own right. In Bordeaux and Burgundy especially, specific districts, and within them individual estates and vineyards, became widely reputed. Wealthy vineyard proprietors were able to draw on the massive amount of research carried out on wine under the influence of the Enlightenment. Scientists of various kinds – agronomists, botanists and chemists among them – turned their learning to all aspects of viticulture and wine-making in an attempt to improve on traditional techniques and practices. The Academy of Bordeaux encouraged the writing of treatises on viticulture and wine-making and in 1756 invited works on the theme, 'What is the best way of making, clarifying and conserving wines? Is the method of clarifying them without eggs as good or better than using eggs?'[21] At the same time the Academy of Dijon took up the question of the quality of Burgundy wines. In 1777 a correspondent suggested that it sponsor a competition for suggestions on the best ways of promoting the trade in wines of superior quality.[22]

Those who had the motivation and the resources to improve their wines paid attention to all stages of the process from planting vines to conservation of the finished product. They began to select grape varieties more carefully and to use older vines to produce fuller-flavoured berries. During the harvest they picked only the ripe grapes, and they took more care with fermentation and both barrel- and bottle-ageing. Although only the wealthy proprietors could afford the luxury of methods such as rejecting grapes that had not ripened sufficiently, it is surely no exaggeration to say that vineyard proprietors did more for the quality of Bordeaux wine in the first half of the eighteenth century than had been done in the preceding six centuries.[23] By the middle of the eighteenth century the names of the great Bordeaux wines were already well known, prominent among them Haut-Brion, Lafite, Latour and Margaux. Much of the production of high-quality bordeaux was exported to England, but cheaper French wines were pretty much priced out of the English market by the Methuen Treaty. The finer Bordeaux wines were able to absorb higher duties into their prices and still sell successfully because their quality was recognized as substantially superior to any wines produced in Portugal or Spain.

In Burgundy, too, there was a tendency toward the consolidation of superior wines, and wines from vineyards such as Romanée and Montrachet attracted the highest prices, the most sure guide to reputation if not always to quality. But Burgundy wines still did not have the prestige of their Bordeaux counterparts. The difference was that while the best bordeaux were exported to the prosperous English market where they fetched high prices, the best burgundies (along with fine wines from Champagne and Anjou) were shipped to Paris. It was not until the eighteenth century that the growth of a prosperous bourgeoisie in France's largest city produced the demand for quality wines from Burgundy and other regions that the London market had created for Bordeaux wines.

It was a measure of the difference between the two markets that the extra one paid for fine burgundy in Paris was less than the premium applied to bordeaux in London. In Paris, wines from districts such as Clos Vougeot, Chambertin, Beaune and Nuits sold for only about 50 per cent more than ordinary wines, while those from Romanée and Montrachet fetched about a third more again.[24] This was a much narrower price range than that which benefited Bordeaux wines on the English market.

Just as fine wines were developed in Bordeaux and Burgundy in the 1700s, premium quality brandy entered the market. The Charente region began to distil all its white wine production as its position as a brandy region took off. Charente exported fewer than 7,000 barriques of brandy a year in the early eighteenth century, but by 1728 it shipped 27,000, by 1780 50,000, and by 1791 87,000. Although at first marketed as a beverage for seamen, soldiers and the poor, and originally distilled from the worst and excess wines, brandy soon appealed to the upper social classes, and a hierarchy of brandies became quickly apparent. By the 1720s brandy from the Cognac district of Charente was selling at 9½ livres a barrique, 2 livres more than brandy from the area around Nantes and Bordeaux.[25] White wines from Cognac produced a higher-quality brandy with a distinctive aroma, and quality was improved by ageing in the barrel for five to ten years and blending older with younger vintages.

But only a few proprietors anywhere had the resources to make premium wines, whether table or fortified. Most wine-makers produced for the mass market, where price was far more important a consideration than quality. Samuel Pepys and his drinking companions might have waxed eloquent about Haut-Brion, but it is unlikely that French workers commented at length on the aroma and taste of the cheap reds they bought by the pint. At most they probably noticed depth of colour (or its absence), for that seems to have been regarded as a reliable guide to a wine's strength.

Both the producers of high-quality wines and makers of mass wines paid attention to grape varietals, but for different reasons: makers of quality wines wanted grapes that gave them rich, full-bodied or sweet wines, while makers of wine for the mass market wanted vines that gave high yields and large volumes of wine to sell. The market for these wines grew steadily as a result of the rapid increase in Europe's population from the 1720s and 1730s, the spreading popularity of wine, and the increasing number of taverns and wine shops.

The desire for high-yield vines led to the widespread planting of gamay in the region around Paris. Not only were gamays more productive than most other vines, but they ripened sooner, an important consideration for viticulture in northern regions. The end result might not have been very praiseworthy (gamay-based wine was described as 'harsh and lacking body, warmth, and bouquet'), but even unfertilized vineyards would produce a lot of it and it made more financial sense to sell a lot of wine cheaply than a small quantity at a high price.

Despite the studies sponsored by the academies and the treatises of agronomists, chemists and others, and despite the efforts by a few proprietors to improve the quality of their wine, most wine-makers followed traditional methods. Vineyards tended to be small holdings, and most vignerons lacked the resources to be able to adopt the new methods that were recommended or to take the risks that experimentation involved. Compared to the techniques of planting, pruning and vinifying reported from the prestigious estates, a description of wine-making in the Toulouse region makes chastening reading. There the vines were not well planted or pruned, and the soil was cultivated only twice a year. The grapes were often picked too early, crushed by foot in large vats, left for months in the open air, and then poured into dirty and usually unseasoned casks. It was generally too acidic to compete with wines from nearby Gaillac, Montpellier or Bordeaux, and it was sold locally.[26] This only serves to reinforce the image of the huge gap that existed not only between the premium, proprietor-designated wines and the rest, but also between simple but good-quality wines and the inexpensive product that was consumed by the mass of the people.

In spite of the sluggishness with which many changes in wine-making were embraced, the eighteenth century saw important developments in the scientific understanding of many aspects of viticulture and the making and conservation of wine. In order for long-distance trade to succeed, producers and shippers had to confront the problem that had dogged them for centuries: how to ensure that wine did not deteriorate. The problems lay with both wine and containers. Wines were too often unbalanced and low in the alcohol needed to preserve them, and the failure to clarify and stabilize them predisposed them to early degradation. It is a measure of the durability of wine at this time that one contemporary expert wrote: 'with respect to age, wine is either old or new or middle-aged. For us, new wine is that which has aged two or three months, old is that which has aged a year, and middle-aged wine is that which, having aged four months, has not yet aged a year.'[27] If wine was thought to be old a year after its harvest, then the eighteenth century had not improved much on the classical period, 2,000 years earlier, which defined old wine in the same terms.

Storage and transportation in wooden barrels only hastened the tendency of wine to decline rapidly. The barrels were porous, allowing the contents to evaporate and air to penetrate, and in order to prevent wine from being exposed to air, barrels had to be topped up regularly. Needless to say, once wine began to be taken from a barrel for consumption, what remained was exposed to increasing amounts of air and it began to deteriorate at an accelerated pace.

Bottles had the potential to solve the problem of exposure to air, and by the early 1700s the most expensive French wines were being exported in corked bottles. The cost put these wines beyond the reach of any but the wealthy, however, and the consumers in Britain were deprived of bottled imports when in 1728 parliament banned the importation of wine in anything but barrels. Wine could be bottled on arrival in Britain, but by then it had already been at risk for months. In addition, bottling at this later stage increased the opportunities for adulteration and fraud.[28]

Various other means were employed to extend the life of wine, but their application was sporadic and inconsistent. German and Dutch shippers sterilized the insides of barrels by burning sulphur and went to great pains to ensure that barrels were kept as full as possible. They also treated the wine itself, racking it off its lees and fining it by adding egg whites or fish bladder (isinglass). The Dutch had also been to the fore in adding brandy to wine in order to increase the alcohol content.

As new techniques to preserve wine were examined and adopted, an old standby – adding lead to wine – finally fell into disrepute. This method can be traced back to ancient times, and right through the seventeenth century lead and its various compounds were used to balance acidity in wine and as a preservative. Lead not only adds a sweet taste to wine but contributes properties that inhibit the growth of bacteria. Until antibiotics were discovered, doctors often used lead ointments to treat open wounds.

During the seventeenth century there was growing suspicion that lead might be responsible for a number of illnesses generally known as colic, a term that covered a wide range of gastro-intestinal ailments. Specific manifestations were known as 'Devonshire colic' and 'Poitou colic': cider-makers in Devon sweetened their product with lead, and the wine-makers of Poitou used lead oxide to sweeten their wines to make them more competitive with their neighbours in the Loire valley to the north. Depending on the seriousness of lead poisoning, which was what this form of colic must have been, symptoms included extreme stomach pain, complete constipation, jaundice, loss of control in the hands and feet, blindness, loss of speech and paralysis. Many cases were fatal. It is more than likely that in the early stages, manifested by stomach pains and constipation, sufferers might have consumed even more wine because of its reputation as being beneficial for digestive problems. Here was a clear case of the cure killing the patient.

In the late seventeenth century a German doctor, Gockel, identified lead in wine as the cause of many illnesses among his patients, and as a result the use of lead compounds to correct wines was forbidden in Württemburg in 1696. But it was not until the eighteenth century that there was widespread acceptance that lead was dangerous, and even so, the use of lead to sweeten wine persisted. A late-eighteenth-century English cookery book included, in a recipe for wine, 'a pound of melted lead in fair water'.[29] In 1750 the Paris authorities discovered that 30,000 muids (about 8 million litres) of spoiled wine had been brought into the city to be made into vinegar. Suspicious at the amount, far more than the usual 1,200 muids brought in each year for that purpose, the police discovered that the wine was being treated with yellow oxide of lead to sweeten it for sale as wine.[30]

It was in the context of the search for a means to stabilize and preserve wine that sugar made its entrance into viniculture. Regular supplies of sugar were among the benefits Europeans derived from their overseas empires, and consumption of sugar was one of the principal signs of a shift in European taste. Sugar was an obvious additive for sweetening wine. And, added to juice before fermentation, it could also produce a higher alcohol content, which in turn produced more durable wine.

The use of sugar as a means of sweetening, strengthening and preserving wine is frequently attributed to Jean-Antoine-Claude Chaptal, a chemist (and later minister of the interior under Napoleon) who advocated the technique in works published in 1801. So closely is Chaptal associated with the technique that adding sugar to must at the time of fermentation is known as 'chaptalization'. The process was, however, known and practised well before Chaptal popularized it. The article on wine in the *Encyclopédie* (1765), the great eighteenth-century compilation of knowledge, warned against using lead and recommended sugar as a sweetening agent. Indeed, a succession of French scientists, agronomists and others recommended sweetening wine with sugar or substances such as honey and sugar-syrup so as to make fermentation occur as quickly as possible.

But it was the chemist Pierre-Joseph Macquer who boiled the issue down to its essentials: if the problem with underripe grapes was that they lacked enough sugar and produced a wine that was too acidic to be palatable, the solution was not to accelerate fermentation but rather to raise the proportion of sugar in relation to acid. Macquer tested his theory by pressing underripe grapes to obtain a sour, mouth-puckering juice, adding sugar, and letting the must ferment. The wine was stored in a barrel for a year, and when Macquer drank it, in October 1777, he reported that it tasted as good as any wine from a respectable vineyard in a good year. There was nothing syrupy about it, no sign (for this was the concern) that it tasted artificially sweet.[31] Indeed, Macquer saw nothing artificial about adding sugar to wine. He saw himself as merely being guided by nature and, in adding sugar to must, simply compensating for nature's deficit when it came to underripe or low-sugar grapes.

Chaptal acknowledged earlier writers on the subject in his publication. His work arrived on the scene at a critical moment, however, just as the French Revolution was giving way to the Napoleonic period. Efforts to hasten the recovery of France's economy and commerce, both of which had suffered during the Revolution, included attempts to promote the wine industry. In 1803 Napoleon's government distributed to wine-growers a booklet entitled *The Art of Making Wine According to the Method of Chaptal.* This was a work of synthesis that drew not only on scientific work but also on the experience of wine-makers themselves, for Chaptal had sent questionnaires to prominent producers asking them about their techniques. Chaptal's book was a clear statement of the best advice for wine-makers that could be given at the end of the eighteenth century. It summarized what was known about soil, and pointed out the benefits of light, porous, friable soils such as were found in the best areas of Bordeaux and Burgundy. It also noted more obvious points, such as the need for plenty of sunshine and the disadvantages of too much rain.

But the book's strengths lay in its advice regarding techniques of fermentation, racking and preservation, for here lay the essence of Chaptal's approach. He recognized that unlike milk and water, wine was not a natural product. It was made by a natural process, but the final result depended on the intervention of the wine-maker.[32] If good-quality wine was to be made, producers had to adopt the most appropriate methods and that meant they had to abandon many traditional practices and learn others. Their textbook would be Chaptal's manual, a classic product of the Enlightenment that insisted on the primacy of reason over tradition. It was particularly useful in France where, after the Revolution, many vineyards were owned by proprietors with relatively little vinicultural experience. As a comprehensive, commonsense guide to wine-making, however, it proved to be immensely influential far beyond the borders of France.[33]

The growing concern for quality and for differentiating acceptable from unacceptable methods of making wine had far-reaching consequences. It led finally to a radically different notion of what wine was, and a new sense of the balance between the contributions of 'nature' and 'man' (as human intervention was long known) in the making of wine.

Wine, as we have seen, is a word that over the centuries has covered a multitude of products. One is tempted to write 'a multitude of sins'. Wines have been heated, boiled and cooled, they have been blended, they have been mixed with everything from salt-water and honey to spices and herbs, they have been strengthened with alcohol, and coloured with berries and dyes. And they have all been called wine. In the eighteenth century these practices continued, and it was not until the twentieth that tight regulations began to define wine: in 1907 a French law defined wine as being made only from grapes or grape juice.

Because of the flexible definition of wine up to this time, there was relatively little concern for the precise constituents of the beverage. Although, as we have seen, the authorities stepped in to prevent certain forms of blending and adulteration, they were for the most part concerned with three activities. First, wine should not contain additives that were harmful to the consumer. Second, wine should not be misrepresented as to its provenance or character – cheap French wine should not be passed off as good-quality Spanish wine, even if it could be manipulated to taste and look like it or if a customer was ignorant or gullible enough to buy it. Finally, and this was where it was difficult to draw lines, wine should not be fabricated beyond a certain point. Wine-makers or merchants could deepen the colour of red wine by exposing it to skin contact as long as possible (extended maceration) or by blending lighter wines with darker, but they could not use berries or other substances. Similarly, wine might be sweetened or flavoured by the addition of cane- or grape-sugar but not other substances. These issues raise the question of the extent to which wine is a 'natural' or an artificial product, and there are still divergent positions on the degree of human intervention that ought to be permitted. For example, wine-makers in Burgundy are legally permitted to add sugar to their wines but those in California are not.

Attention to these issues could arise only from the emergence of high-quality designated wines and the increased concern for reputation that accompanied it. If consumers were going to pay the high prices these wines commanded, they wanted to ensure that they were buying the genuine article, not some cheap wine that had been manipulated to look and taste like it. In those times, when there was far less official surveillance and regulation of vineyards and wineries and of the transportation and sale of wine, there were ample opportunities for counterfeiting wines of all kinds. Even where regulations were in place they were frequently flouted in practice. In eighteenth-century France, for example, carters who transported wine were required by law to carry full documentation detailing its provenance, quality, price and destination, but in practice merchants were far too concerned about keeping the value of wine confidential to commit this information to writing, whether or not the law demanded it.[34]

It was in the context of increasing concern for quality during the eighteenth century that the first major scandals struck the European wine industry. And just as market forces were critical in determining the characteristics of quality wines, so the markets reacted against perceived abuses in wine-making and forced wine-producers to put their houses in order. The first big scandal has already been mentioned: the adulteration of wine by producers and merchants in the Douro region in the 1730s and 1740s so as to meet what was clearly irresistible demand from the English market. Blending and colouring on a large scale provoked a market reaction against port until the Portuguese government forced regulations on the Douro wine industry and restrictions on the additives and processes that could be employed to alter the taste, colour and alcoholic strength of the wine.

Other scandals followed. Towards the end of the century, growing demand for high-quality brandy led some distillers of Charente down the same path as the wine-producers of the Douro, and they began to blend local brandy with inferior imports from Languedoc and Catalonia. In order to protect their reputation the region's brandy producers formed an association in 1791 to regulate their industry.[35] There were also concerns about the misrepresentation of Burgundian wine. In 1764 a Dijon lawyer denounced merchants and foreign buyers for substituting second-rate wines for best quality and for blending wines from the south with wines from Burgundy.[36]

These concerns were quite different from the more general worries that the authorities had long had about commercial infractions (like selling short measures or misrepresenting the provenance of a wine) and adulterations that were harmful to consumers' health. In 1794, for example, the Paris authorities analysed scores of wine samples from sixty-eight of the city's wine merchants and concluded that only eight of them could be called wine. Most had additives ranging from water and cider to brandy and natural and artificial colourants such as beetroot and wood. This investigation took place during the Revolution, when times were often difficult for producers, merchants and tavern-owners, but there is no reason to believe that such practices were not common throughout the eighteenth century.

As worrying as this survey was, and as laudable as were the city's efforts to protect the interests of consumers, the authorities were not concerned with specific wines as such or with protecting the reputations of individual estates. The measures taken by producers in the Douro and Cognac regions, and the apprehensions expressed in Burgundy, on the other hand, were signs of increasing concern for the quality of wines from specific regions and districts, and thus evidence of the growing importance of their reputations.

It is clear that many of the developments in wine in this period were driven by an increasing demand emanating from all social levels. In England the 'three-bottle men' derived a kind of cachet from their oenological excesses, but heavy drinking of one sort or another was diffused throughout the whole society. Samuel Johnson was undoubtedly exaggerating when he wrote that 'all the decent people in Lichfield got drunk every night, and were not the worse thought of', but heavy drinking was not uncommon. The Essex shopkeeper Thomas Turner wrote of one bout of drinking: 'We continued drinking like horses, as the vulgar phrase is, and singing till many of us were very drunk, and then we went to dancing, and pulling wigs, caps, and hats; and thus we continued in this frantic manner, behaving more like mad people than they that profess the name of Christians.'[37]

But in England it was gin, rather than wine, that captured the masses, at least in London. Gin was developed in The Netherlands, a nation that for centuries managed to convey an image of Calvinist sobriety while dominating the trade in alcohol, providing the motive force behind the distilling industry and developing the wine industry in key regions of France, Spain and Portugal. Gin, a specifically Dutch alcohol, was a spirit flavoured with juniper berries. Known as *eau de genièvre* in French, it was generally called geneva (giving it a misleading link with what was, ironically, another centre of Calvinism), and when English soldiers encountered it they abbreviated the name even more to gin.

The popularity of gin took off in England when the periodic embargoes against France in the late seventeenth and early eighteenth centuries deprived the English not only of French wine but also of brandy. Imported and locally produced gin began to fill the alcoholic void. By 1727 consumption had reached five million gallons, and six years later London alone was producing eleven million gallons a year. What can only be described as a gin craze quickly developed, and by the early 1730s an estimated 7,000 dram shops, which sold only distilled alcohols, were providing for London's population. William Hogarth's etchings of Gin Lane, showing men and women lying insensible in the streets, evoked the horror that was expressed at what was portrayed as widespread drunkenness and social breakdown.

A series of official campaigns against gin and other spirits were mounted between the 1720s and 1750s. They aimed to curtail consumption by raising the taxes on spirits, in the hope that higher prices would reduce consumption, and by raising the licensing fee that dram shops had to pay.[38] What is notable is that the horror at the effects of spirits on society rarely spilled over to wine, while beer was thought to be innocuous. Hogarth's portrayal of Beer Street depicts happy and prosperous people before gin wrought havoc on their lives. As we shall see, in the nineteenth century, too, temperance advocates made an explicit and clear distinction between spirits and other forms of alcohol.

Despite temporary 'successes' such as gin's in the English market for alcohol, wine enjoyed increasing popularity during the eighteenth century, and the extraordinary growth of wine-production in the 1700s was made possible by the expansion of the markets for wine. Much French wine was shipped across the Atlantic, but this should not obscure the strength of domestic demand. In many regions of France wine was a staple of the daily diet, whether of the small producers, who drank weak, insipid piquette so as to save all their marketable wine for sale, of the working classes, who drank the mass-produced, inexpensive vintages, or of the better-off, who could afford wines from first-ranked estates or from areas gaining reputations.

Wine was part of fashionable dining, and many accounts detail the wine consumed at banquets and other occasions that attracted the better-off members of society. Voltaire hosted sumptuous dinners at his home in Ferney. Wine was often delivered in casks and bottled on arrival, and Voltaire's orders included thousands of bottles and corks. His wines included beaujolais (his favourite), burgundy (which he used to top up the barrels of beaujolais), and Spanish wine from Malaga. Another account of fine dining is Giacomo Casanova's description of a meal for the French ambassador to Venice, the abbé (later Cardinal) de Bernis and his mistress: 'We drank only Burgundy, and we emptied a bottle of "oeil de perdrix" champagne and another of some sparkling wine for gaiety.'[39]

The cellars of nobles provide insights into wine consumption at this level. The Duke of Tavanes kept mainly beaune and médoc in 240-bottle lots plus several hundred bottles that included Smirna, Cyprus and Tokaj wines. Wine was expensive, but not outrageously so. Accounts from one of the duke's 1784 food and drink orders showed wine as the least expensive item: Muscats, Malaga, Rhine and Bordeaux wine cost a total of 14 livres, far less than the duke spent on turkey with truffles (21 livres) or a pot of Rocquefort cheese (32 livres). In 1784 the duke's total cellar was valued at only 1,000 livres, at a time when his annual food budget was five times that.[40]

For his part, Claude-Philippe Fyot de La Marche, First President of the Parlement of Dijon, went through 760 bottles of wine between February and June 1761, 571 of them ordinary wine and 189 fine wines. (He also consumed 113 bottles of beer and 19 bottles of liqueur.) Most of the fine wines were local burgundies, including Chambertins, Vogueots, and Montrachets, but there were representatives from nearby

Switzerland and one each from Greece and Spain. President Fyot's household consumption for the four- to five-month period averaged five to six bottles of wine a day.[41]

But there was a strain of hostility towards luxury in the eighteenth century. A royal representative in the Toulouse region deplored the growing and 'enormous production' of wine there, which he blamed on 'the luxury that is introduced into all households'. The comment betrays the bias of a class that would reserve 'luxuries' like wine to itself, for the sort of wine common people in Toulouse drank was thin and acidic.[42] The philosopher Jean-Jacques Rousseau was another who expressed suspicion of high living. 'If I am given milk, eggs, salad, cheese, brown bread and ordinary wine I am sufficiently entertained.' Such a diet might have been modest for someone of Rousseau's standing, but it would have been luxurious for the mass of the French population in the eighteenth century. Moreover, the wine Rousseau called 'ordinary' was far superior to that consumed by most peasants and workers.

If connoisseurs expected the common people to drink wine, they did not expect them to have demanding palates. Voltaire cultivated his own vineyard for his staff and commented that 'my own bad wine, which is by no means unwholesome, gives them drink.' Yet despite their lower status, some of Voltaire's servants did apparently aspire to their employer's own tastes in wine, for he complained on one occasion that the carters had drunk fifty bottles of Malaga wine from one order.[43]

The interest of the better-off citizens of Europe in wines is reflected, too, in continuing references to wine in travel literature. A late-eighteenth-century guide to Russia and eastern Europe noted that vines grew only in the southern provinces, but that in St Petersburg people (that is, wealthy people) drank the best English beer and wines from Burgundy, Bordeaux and Champagne. Hungarian wines were described as excellent: 'they are strong, very alcoholic, and they warm the blood.' Special mention was made of the most popular wine: 'the wine of *Tockay*, especially that of *Torzal*, and the one called *Essence of Tockay*'.[44]

Much of the texture of past drinking cultures is lost to us, for we often have difficulty penetrating the privacy of the home, where so much drinking, among the upper ranks of society especially, took place. But among the lower social levels much drinking was public, carried out in taverns and bars under the watchful eyes of the police and other authorities who associated these establishments with dubious morality and outright criminality. Police, court and other records provide us with insights into public drinking, particularly in Paris, France's largest single market for wine.[45]

Although the flow of wine into Paris was closely regulated because it was taxed at the city gates, it is unclear how much wine entered each year. Paris took all the 40 million litres produced by the surrounding region, and evidently two or even three times more again from elsewhere in France. Between 60 and 80 million litres were accounted for each year, but to that we must add a 'dark figure' to allow for smuggling. The tax officials themselves conceded that about a sixth of the wine that entered Paris evaded them, but they had every reason to underestimate their inefficiency and the success of smugglers.

The official amount was enough for each of Paris's half million inhabitants to have about three litres a week, and if we double that to allow for illicit supplies, they would have about six litres. That volume becomes more substantial when we consider that wine-drinking was concentrated among adult males, and that the eighteenth-century population was more heavily weighted towards children than it is today. If adult males represented a quarter of the population and half as much untaxed wine as taxed wine was available, men had access to as much as eighteen litres of wine a week, although of course one must take into account wine consumed by women. Tavern-keepers sometimes let customers drink on credit, and some of their records show consumption of two litres a day and more. Quite clearly a labourer paid by the day could not drink such quantities. In the early nineteenth century a labourer would have to work four hours to pay for two litres of beer but eight and a half hours for two litres of average-quality wine.

These quantities, equivalent to three bottles of wine a day, are high, but they underscore the place of wine as an everyday drink, not one reserved for special occasions. More, wine was nutritious. Moheau, a prominent political economist, wrote that it was 'an excellent beverage for the poor, not only because it is a food but also because it is a very good protection against decay [antiseptic]'.[46] There is no hint of the argument, often made later, that the poor were poor because they squandered what little money they had on wine; wine was a food and it was as appropriate to spend money on it as on other items of the diet.

The ordinary people of Paris – artisans, day-labourers, domestics, shopkeepers, soldiers – did their drinking at the hundreds of taverns (*cabarets*) located within and outside the city walls; outside the walls, wine could be sold more cheaply because it was not subject to the city tax. The same was true of inhabitants of other cities. Lille, for example, had 296 taverns for 58,000 people in the 1760s, about one for every two hundred men, women and children.[47]

Public drinking was largely confined to adult males as they gathered in groups to drink and eat and play board games, sometimes to dance and be entertained by musicians. Living in cramped accommodation, with families squeezed into one or two rooms, men found an alternative space in bars. It was not a matter of seeking privacy, which the taverns certainly did not offer, but alternative companionship. Taverns were places of sociability, as important in their own way as family and neighbourhood, and wine was the currency of social exchange. Drinking together reinforced relationships and sealed agreements, and to refuse an invitation to a drink was an insult.[48]

The mixture of alcohol and large groups of males was always volatile, and brawls over games, intrusions into personal territory and perceived insults were not uncommon. In 1791 a conflict erupted at la Morienne in Lille when a drunk man went outside to vomit. He left behind his wife and during his absence a soldier tried to lift her skirts. The husband returned and, after a fight, he was killed by a sabre thrust.[49]

If there is such a thing as a typical group in an eighteenth-century Paris tavern, it was represented by three or four men at a table with a pitcher of wine. They were men of the same class, even of the same occupation and rank. For the most part journeymen masons drank with journeymen masons, master tailors with master tailors, coachmen with coachmen. The *cabaret* might have looked like a place of social promiscuity, but the rules of sociability were closely drawn and finely observed.

It was above all male, for although women were admitted to *cabarets* and could drink there, they were grossly underrepresented. Some men brought their wives, but they were in the minority, and overall there appears to have been a bias against women in such places. In some instances, when a married woman needed to speak to her husband and he was in a *cabaret*, she came to the door without entering and he went to the door without leaving.[50]

Quite often, a woman found in this predominantly male space was assumed, by male drinkers and the police alike, to be a prostitute. One wine merchant complained that the police had closed his *cabaret* for serving women, even though they were perfectly respectable. In fairness it might be pointed out that the police seem to have suspected all customers of *cabarets*, male and female, of being engaged in suspicious or outright criminal activities. Prostitution was the specific assumption they made about women and it is another example of the links men made between women, wine and immorality.

It was much the same in the *guinguettes*, the taverns situated for tax advantages outside the city wall, despite the romanticized image provided in 1789 by Étienne Chevalier, a wine-grower who was a member of the legislature:

Wine is the basis of the survival of the poor citizen of Paris. When bread, meat, and other foods are too expensive, he turns to wine; he nourishes and consoles himself with it. How many poor families go and eat at the *guinguette* in winter! There they find honest and inexpensive wine, food infinitely less expensive than in Paris; there they have light and warmth and they save their own wood, coal, and candles. These advantages enable them to tolerate more calmly the rigours of winter and poverty.[51]

It is notable that Chevalier portrayed wine not as a terrible opiate that ruined family budgets but as a means of survival and comfort. But as a wine-producer he had, of course, an interest in presenting wine in the best possible light.

It is impossible to say how often men visited their local tavern or travelled further afield for the cheaper wine outside the city walls. It was common for working men to start and end the day with a glass or two of brandy; wine, like beer, was consumed during the day. Throughout the working day, which was less disciplined by time than it is now, men took breaks and went to the nearest tavern to have a drink with friends and workmates. Small merchants transacted business with their suppliers over a pitcher of wine. The taverns' busiest time, however, was between eight and ten at night, after men had finished work. Weekends were also busy, particularly Sundays when wages were generally paid.

What of the wine that these men and the fewer women consumed? Given the social level of the *cabarets*' customers, we should assume that the wine was inexpensive and of quite poor quality. Quite often, the wine must have been on the verge of turning to vinegar, and tavern-keepers in Paris, like their counterparts everywhere else, did what they could to make their wine drinkable. Among all the conversations captured by the records, there is no hint of artisans sitting around their table, comparing notes on the colour, aroma, taste or finish of the wine. Wine at this level was a commodity like bread.

Eighteenth-century attitudes towards wine consumption were, as we have seen, positive, but there were the usual warnings about excessive drinking. The *Encyclopédie*, which expressed enlightened opinion and emphasized the importance of rationality, declared that 'drunkenness is always a fault against which one must be on guard; it is a breach of natural law which orders us to maintain our reason.'[52] The authorities themselves showed a general tolerance, and there is no evidence that they picked up drunks in bars or on the street unless there were some other reason to do so. Drunkenness in these cases was an element in a more serious offence. On the other hand, manuals given to priests to guide them when faced with circumstances like drunkenness suggest a recognition that alcoholism was a problem. Those who were unable to hold their drink were to be advised to abstain entirely. No exceptions, like accepting a friend's invitation to a drink, were acceptable. But those who could not give it up were to be allowed to drink moderately as long as they sincerely promised to try to overcome their habit.

The eighteenth century manifested all the personal and social problems associated with excessive drinking. Many women obtained a legal separation of their property when their husbands' drinking threatened them with financial ruin. Such women complained that a husband was 'often seized by wine' or 'surrendered himself to wine and women and neglected his business'. A steady stream of alcohol runs through the records of separations in eighteenth-century France. Men came home 'drunk', 'seized with wine', and assaulted their wives and children. In 1785 one Marie-Louise Bonnaire described to a Lille court the violent mix of her husband and wine. The court records read:

About five years ago he came back from the tavern and when she made representations to him he became angry, seized the fire-tongs and struck her on the head. About fifteen months ago, coming home full of wine, he started by punching her,

then ripped the handle off a frying-pan . . . About three and a half months ago
he talked to a scoundrel passing through town, then took him to the tavern of
Frédéric Bonnaire where they drank five bottles of wine. Coming home totally
drunk, he called her a slut . . .[53]

Some men blamed their spousal violence on the wine, saying that they
could remember nothing of the episode. In such cases the courts did not
treat drunkenness as a mitigating circumstance. In other cases men
justified their violence on the ground that their wives had been drinking
and had compromised their honour by behaving immorally. Wine was
also employed to help remedy the ill it had caused: in one case neighbourhood women administered wine to a woman, 'to bring her back to
consciousness', after she had been beaten senseless by her drunk husband.
Such were the sombre corners, undoubtedly far more frequent than their
representation in the written record, of the bright images of conviviality
and companionship most often associated with *cabarets*.[54]

Wine was part of everyday life on many levels, and it accompanied all
manner of relationships in their rich diversity. It lubricated and eased
social contacts and it corroded relationships just as easily. In wine-growing
areas wine was a medium not only of social but also of commercial
exchange. A vineyard-owning notary in Besançon paid his debts in this
liquid currency: a few setiers of 'good, old wine' to the school-master, a
barrel to the owner of his apartment, another to the shoe-maker.[55]

The French Revolution of 1789 is more associated in the popular mind
with violence and political turmoil than with the equally dramatic marks
it left on France's social and cultural landscape. In 1789 lists of grievances
(*cahiers de doléances*) addressed to the king were drawn up by communities across France, by the clergy and by nobles. These lists set out
perceptions of the problems facing localities, regions, social classes, or
France more generally, and suggested solutions. Most dealt with financial, legal and constitutional issues, but many involved the production
and consumption of wine. Although the most frequent complaints were
about the taxes on wine, for fiscal issues were the catalyst of revolution,
there was also concern about the quality of wine and about the extent
of wine-drinking and its social and economic effects.

The hamlet of Mennetou-sur-Cher near Orléans, for one, wrote that the tax on wine 'is perhaps the most harmful to all people and the least profitable to the king'. It was bad enough that vine-growers paid taxes on land but worse that they then had to pay more on every barrel of wine they took to market. Other restrictions they complained of were not being able to top up a barrel of the previous vintage with new wine and not being able 'to send a bottle of wine to the home of some unfortunate who needs it and to whom a charitable soul would want to give it' without incurring a charge by some zealous tax officer. In view of the 'amount of land in vines in France, in every town and parish', Mennetou's inhabitants suggested a simple tax on vines, scaled according to their quality, with another tax on each barrel of wine sold.[56]

Other communities demanded that all taxes on wine be simply abolished outright. Wine-growing communities sought recognition of the losses they had suffered when cold weather had killed their vines or when their vineyards had been washed away by rivers in flood. For their part, the parishes of Vouzon and Lamotte-sur-Beuvron (near Orléans) complained that the taxes on wine led to criminal activity and all manner of evil in rural areas:

How many clandestine wine-shops there are in the country! Often they are the refuge of that type of person who, having lost their minds because of drinking so much wine, are reduced to a level below animals so that they surrender to the passions that rule them: from which follows assaults, violence, loss of health, changes in character, and scorn for decent people who hate to see wine-sellers profit by allowing and even encouraging drunkenness.[57]

Through these varied complaints there emerges no sense that wine was priced out of the range of consumers. In fact for much of the decade that preceded the Revolution, wine prices were low, about two sous a pint rather than the three sous that had prevailed for much of the later eighteenth century. The problem for wine-growers was that grain prices rose far more than the price of wine, leaving producers with incomes below what they needed to pay for grain, the staple food. Poor grape harvests in 1788 and 1789 did push the price of wine up, but it was a dubious benefit for producers, because the cold weather that reduced yields also killed off vines in many regions.

Whether they were producers, merchants or consumers of wine, the French were clearly dissatisfied as the Revolution approached. None were more so in this respect than the ordinary people of Paris, the artisans, labourers and small merchants who were frequently to become involved in Revolutionary activities. The spread of wine-drinking in eighteenth-century France meant that it was regarded as a necessity, and the taxes on it were resented as much as or more than the duties on other commodities.

Wine was taxed not when it was purchased but as it entered towns and cities. Wine sold in Paris, whose half-million inhabitants made it by far the nation's largest single market, was subjected to customs duties at gates in the city walls and at posts on the River Seine. When the taxes were first imposed centuries earlier they were relatively light, but over time they had risen faster than the cost of living, and by 1789 the cost of wine was effectively tripled by the tax applied to it. The tax was levied by the barrel, regardless of the quality and value of the wine, so that, in relation to retail price, low-quality and inexpensive wine attracted a much higher tax than better-quality vintages. In essence, poor wine-consumers subsidized their wealthy counterparts.

The residents of Paris and other towns adopted a range of subterfuges to avoid paying these taxes. Barrels of wine were hidden under other produce as carts passed through the customs posts, while smaller quantities of brandy in pitchers were concealed under the voluminous skirts of female smugglers. Tunnels and channels – lined with wood, iron, lead, and leather – were constructed so that contraband wine flowed under and through city walls. When one was discovered and closed by the authorities, another was drilled to take its place.[58]

More permanent and open ways of avoiding the taxes were the *guinguettes* that were set up just outside the walls of Paris, where wine was tax-free because it had not entered the city. Any Parisian willing to walk a few kilometres was rewarded by wine at a quarter or a fifth the price charged in the city itself. It is hardly surprising that these establishments did a roaring trade, not only on Sundays but throughout the week. These taverns, less constrained for space than their urban counterparts, were often large, barn-like buildings with gardens where in the summer patrons could sit and drink. One of the more popular *guinguettes*, Le Tambour Royal, sold almost one and a third million litres of wine a year.

The popularity of this tax-free wine came into sharp relief when plans were announced in 1784 to extend the perimeter of the walls. This would have had the effect of enclosing the bars and thereby dramatically raising the price of the wine they sold. It was expected that new *guinguettes* would spring up outside the new walls, but they would be even further away from the concentrations of urban population.

Construction of the new city walls began in 1784 (though it was suspended for a time three years later). Rather than defeat Parisians, the new barriers posed a challenge which wine merchants and consumers rose to meet, and before long a vigorous smuggling campaign was under way. Tunnels were drilled through the new wall, and wine poured through them to merchants who sold the contraband at low prices on the other side. Tax officials had discovered and closed eighty such pipes by 1788. Buildings were constructed just outside the new walls with windows looking over them, and at night balloons filled with up to five litres of wine were tossed to recipients inside the city. Riots and disturbances were created to distract guards and allow shipments of wine to slip through the customs barriers.

By July 1789, however, political tensions had combined with a deterioration of living conditions (the price of bread had spiralled to unprecedented heights), and Parisians turned from evading the customs barriers to attacking them. The first episode of Revolutionary violence in Paris was not the famous storming of the Bastille prison on 14 July, but rather a series of attacks in the preceding days, when most of the customs barriers around Paris were destroyed or burned. This was not wanton and random violence but careful targeting of institutions that threatened the lives of the urban poor, the livelihoods of growers and the profits of large and small merchants alike.

The Revolution that developed from these first events was initially disappointing for wine-drinkers: the new city authorities needed revenue to run the city and promptly decreed that the taxes on wine and other products entering Paris should continue to be collected. The new walls that had been started in 1784 were completed in 1790. The next year, however, the Revolutionary government abolished all such indirect taxes throughout France. Soon after midnight on 1 May 1791, the day this law came into effect, a convoy of hundreds of carts carrying some two million litres of wine entered Paris to scenes of jubilation, and began dispensing its cargo at the bargain price of three sous a pint. Huge quantities of brandy were sold off in the same way, and similar scenes were played out elsewhere in France. How better to celebrate the suppression of the detested indirect taxes?

The price of wine rose during the 1790s in response to shortages caused by poor harvests, but it remained well below pre-Revolutionary levels. Even when indirect taxes were reintroduced in 1798, the tax on wine was only 3 to 4 per cent, a much lower rate than had prevailed earlier.

Consumption was only one respect in which the Revolution affected wine. Although agriculture generally stagnated during the Revolution, viticulture seems to have thrived, and the land surface in vines increased in many regions. But overall, the spread of viticulture was not staggering: one estimate puts the increase in land in vines at only 6 per cent between 1788 and 1808, but this might be too low. National wine production rose dramatically from an average 27.2 million hectolitres a year on the eve of the Revolution to 36.8 million in the period 1805–12, an increase of a third in less than twenty years.[59] To have increased the volume of wine produced to that extent with only a modest extension of land under viticulture, vine-growers must have improved their yields considerably.

Of the many areas that witnessed extensive vine-planting, one was the Corbières region of Languedoc, an area now with its own appellation. At the end of the Revolution, in 1802, the inspector-general of forests for the region reported that 'the only sector of agriculture which seems to have prospered is wine-growing; the area has considerably increased over the past ten years, and the consumption of local wines has replaced foreign imports.' In nearby Narbonne, the first site of viticulture in Roman Gaul, an official reported in 1792 that much of the arid land had been left uncultivated before the Revolution but that already most of it had been planted in vines. Statistics were gathered only after the Revolution, but they show an increase in land in vines in the Narbonne district from 10,111 hectares in 1788 to 15,790 hectares in 1812, an increase of more than 50 per cent.[60] Net expansion in other regions was much smaller. In Burgundy the area in vines rose from 17,658 hectares in 1786–8 to 20,548 in 1826–8, a growth of 16 per cent in thirty years.[61]

Several factors explain the expansion of viticulture during and after the French Revolution. First the Revolution did away with many of the restrictions that had been imposed on the ways peasants used their land. As we have seen, before the Revolution the French government had discouraged viticulture for fear that it would encroach on land planted with grain, the basic food resource. This was reinforced by landlords and the Church requiring payments of dues and tithes in the form of grain, effectively forcing peasants into grain production.

Peasants who did grow vines were subject to taxes and obligations that cut deeply into their revenues. The church tithe ranged from 3 to 10 per cent of production, depending on the locality. In most places peasants were forbidden to own their own presses but had to use the seigneur's and pay in kind for the privilege. Again, the rate depended on the locality, but it ranged from 5 to as much as 30 per cent of a peasant's produce. Not only was the seigneur's monopoly of wine-presses expensive, but it was also inconvenient and sometimes ruinous. The seigneur had the right to press his grapes when they were at their peak of maturity, often forcing the peasants, who had to wait their turn, to press grapes that were either underripe or beginning to rot. As a final injury, peasants were forbidden to sell their wine at certain times, giving the seigneur sole access to the market when prices were highest.[62]

When the Revolutionaries abolished many of these obligations, which were holdovers from the feudal system, peasants were able to plant and harvest their crops as they wished. Viticulture was the most attractive, because in good conditions it offered the best returns for owners of smallholdings. A single farmer could cultivate an acre of vines without having to hire extra labour.

The French Revolution not only facilitated the extension of viticulture but, directly and indirectly, it also stimulated the demand for wine. The abolition of internal customs duties meant that wine could be shipped from one region of France to another without incurring punitive excise costs on the way. Meanwhile, the suppression of the indirect taxes on wine reduced its retail cost. To the extent that price had been a brake on wine consumption before the Revolution, domestic demand must have increased appreciably during the 1790s. The state assisted sales by becoming a major customer, purchasing wine for the massive Revolutionary armies; by 1793–4 France had between 800,000 and a million men under arms. Besides providing wine for men on active service, the government also ensured that military hospitals were well provisioned.

The wars of the Revolutionary period, which began in 1792 and continued more or less continuously until the defeat of Napoleon in

1815, had variable effects on France's wine trade. Some regions in southwestern France that before the Revolution had imported wine from Spain found their supplies interrupted and turned instead to the local wine, which was being produced in greater quantities. French wine exports were affected far less than might be imagined given that France's enemies tried to impose a commercial blockade. Exports to England, for example, were hardly affected. The British navy permitted neutral ships to carry French goods to neutral countries, but they had no difficulty calling at a British port en route and off-loading quality wine.[63]

In short, the French Revolution provided the conditions for the expansion of viticulture and the market for wine. The increase in production is clear, and there is no evidence of overproduction. The fact that the price of wine rose by almost two thirds between 1776–89 and 1801–5 speaks of strong demand, either because consumption spread socially and geographically or because per capita wine consumption rose. It helped that when price limits were applied to basic goods from 1793, wine was included. In September 1794, for example, the price of a bottle of old wine was set at ten sous, one sou more than new wine. (Wine was classified as old at Christmas in the year following the vintage, that is, about fifteen months after it was harvested.)[64]

It is possible that drunkenness became more common as wine became more accessible, for in many communities the authorities moved to limit the hours that wine could be sold. Alternatively it might have been that the Revolutionary authorities adopted and insisted on more austere standards of behaviour, for they imposed closing times that were generally earlier than those set under the Old Regime. In the 1790s one town in Burgundy forbade the sale of wine after 8 p.m. (except to travellers and others staying in taverns) because late-night drinking had led to riots and scenes 'contrary to the good morals and virtues that are distinctive of republicans'. Other communities forbade sales after 9 p.m., and several went so far as to ban the sale of wine after the sun had set, although some allowed an extra hour's drinking during the summer months.

Workers and vine-growers were said to be among the most susceptible to drunkenness. They were alleged to drink to excess so that they fell ill and could not work, and as a result were often reduced to begging or sending their children to beg. Wine-growers were reputed to be not much better. They were described as drinking on credit throughout the year, only to have tavern-keepers seize their crops as payment and render them unable to pay their taxes and provide for their families.[65]

Wine was also problematic in a political sense during the Revolution. The social associations of fine and ordinary wines meant that wine could not be regarded as a politically neutral commodity. A print published early in the Revolution showed figures representing the three estates of the nation (the clergy, the nobility, and the Third Estate that comprised everyone else), toasting the new regime with wine. The noble is portrayed holding a fluted glass typically used for champagne, the cleric holds a glass with a round, bulb-like base and a stem that was appropriate for burgundy, and the commoner, in Revolutionary clothing, holds a goblet of the kind used for ordinary wine.[66]

It was this ordinary wine that flowed so freely in political festivities. Toasts to Liberty, Equality and Fraternity were common, and on some notable occasions fountains of wine were constructed. *The Marseillaise*, a military song of the Revolution that became France's national anthem, experienced a number of oenological rewritings. In one, the second line 'Le jour de gloire est arrivé' ('The day of glory has arrived') became 'Le jour de boire est arrivé' ('The day of drinking has arrived'). It is possible that Revolutionaries favoured red wine for their festivities because it was more in keeping with the Revolution: white was the colour of the hated Bourbon dynasty.

Beyond colour, however, lay quality, and implicitly the ground was prepared for an attack on fine wine. Like powdered wigs and frock coats, luxury wines such as champagne and the quality wines of Burgundy and Bordeaux became regarded by extremists as signs of aristocratic decadence. The point was accentuated in early 1794, during the radical phase of the Revolution, when local authorities were instructed by the government in Paris to draw up an inventory of fine wines in the houses of individuals who had been identified as enemies of the Revolution: those who had emigrated, or who had been charged or convicted of political crimes. A list of 'liqueurs, foreign wines, and fine wines of all kinds' that 'the desire for luxury of their former owners had brought together', was to be drawn up in the expectation that they might be 'used advantageously in exchange for basic necessities'.[67] It is not clear whether the intention was to sell or barter the wine inside or outside France.

But lest we think that this period promoted poor-quality wines for the common people, we should recall that the Revolutionary governments were overwhelmingly comprised of men from the middle classes. If they could not afford the most expensive wines, they would almost certainly not have purchased the cheapest. Throughout the Revolution, France remained hierarchical in taste as it was in politics, although there were attempts to narrow the distance between the extremes. A number of treatises were published during the Revolution proposing methods of viticulture or wine-making that would improve the quality of wines generally.[68] Nor, when price controls on basic commodities were established, did any spirit of oenological egalitarianism prevent the authorities from setting differential maximum prices according to quality and reputation. In 1793 in the district of Beaune, top-quality red wines like Volnay and Pommard were priced at 560–570 livres a queue (456 litres), while wines of Savigny were capped at 340 livres and those from Monthelie at 250 livres. The maximum prices for passetousgrains and for gamay wines were 200 and 180 livres respectively.[69]

Moreover, achievements in viticulture were recognized by prizes, and in 1794 an official circular noted that recognition was due to Bacchus himself, 'he who instructed his contemporaries in the arts of planting vines and harvesting'.[70] In 1799 eight of the ten prizes awarded in the Savigny commune in Burgundy went to vine-growers for achievements such as having 'vines perfectly cultivated with no diseased plants and with an abundant crop', and for being 'an excellent grower, hard-working and choosing his vines well', and 'a good grower and a good son, taking care of his very aged father who was one of the best vine-growers in Savigny'.[71]

The Revolution also saw changes in the ownership of many vineyards, first when the property of the Church was nationalized and later when land belonging to individuals convicted of emigrating or other political crimes was confiscated. Some of the rural land that was seized was under viticulture, and its sale by auction, starting in 1790, gave buyers from all social groups the chance to participate in a profitable sector of the economy. Of the major wine regions, Bordeaux was less affected than Burgundy because a smaller proportion of its vineyards was owned by the Church.

The sale of nationalized land was designed to raise money to pay off the debts the Revolutionary governments had inherited from the monarchy. Sales were by auction to encourage high prices, and the rules forbade the breaking down of properties into smaller lots or the forming of consortia of small buyers so that they could bid collectively. This method of sale favoured the wealthy, and most of the beneficiaries of these land sales were well-off bourgeois who lived in towns. Ownership of many good vineyards was transferred from the Church and nobility to investors, businessmen and professionals in nearby cities. Few peasants, except for those who were exceptionally prosperous, were in a position to purchase land at these auctions. In a single day in March 1795, at one of these auctions in Burgundy, one individual purchased ten parcels of land, all in vines, in the district of Gevrey-Chambertin. The successful bidder was one Jean Aubert, described as a '*cultivateur vigneron*' living in Dijon. He bid a total of 6,625 livres for the vineyards, all in a locality then, and now, considered one of the best in Burgundy.[72]

A number of famed estates went under the hammer. One was Romanée-Conti, seized from the last Prince de Conti and auctioned off in July 1794. The long catalogue entry aptly portrays the awe with which the estate was already regarded in the eighteenth century, when its wine commanded five or six times the price of other distinguished wines from the Côte de Nuits:

It is a vineyard famed for the excellent quality of its wine. Its situation in the vineyard territory of Vosne is the most advantageous for the perfect ripening of the grapes; higher to the west than to the east, it receives the first rays of the sun in all seasons, being thus imbued with the impetus of the greatest heat of the day . . . We cannot disguise the fact that the wine of La Romanée is the most excellent of all those of the Côte d'Or and even of all the vineyards of the French Republic: weather permitting, this wine always distinguishes itself from those of the other *terroirs* of predilection; its brilliant and velvety colour, its ardour, and its scent charm all the senses. Well kept, it always improves as it approaches its eighth or tenth year; it is then a balm for the elderly, the feeble and the disabled, and will restore life to the dying.[73]

This description is interesting for several reasons. It was written during the Terror, the most radical phase of the Revolution, and in fact during the most radical phase of that period itself when executions of nobles were at their peak. The timing might well explain the references to the health benefits or medical properties of the wine. There is no doubt that it was politically more appropriate to highlight the social benefits of Romanée-Conti for 'the elderly, the feeble and the disabled', than to suggest that it might be enjoyed as a luxury by the wealthy few. The final claim can be discounted as the hyperbole of the copy-writer. Paradoxically, the vineyard was known simply as La Romanée until the Revolution; '-Conti' was added by its new owner, one Nicolas Defer, a resident of Paris.

In some respects the French Revolution was beneficial to viticulture and to wine in France. Vine-growers were emancipated from the constraints under which they had laboured during the Old Regime. The amount of land under vines increased, and it is likely that yields also rose during this period, while the abolition of indirect taxes on wine must surely have broadened or deepened the market. Against these generally positive developments, the hostility sometimes expressed toward fine wine probably made little dent in supply or demand, and the transfer of individual vineyards from clerical and aristocratic owners very likely made little difference to the quality of the wine they produced. The national and local authorities promoted viticulture and the production of good-quality wine and in this respect set the tone for the increased intervention of the state in what was now recognized as a major French industry.

EIGHT

TOWARDS AN AGE OF PROMISE

Uncertainty and Prosperity, 1800–1870

As the nineteenth century opened in Europe, Napoleon had begun the campaigns that would by 1812 give France an empire that extended across three quarters of the continent. These wars and French domination affected wine in a number of ways. The wine trade was disrupted when Napoleon set up the Continental System to prevent trade between Europe and Britain. The System was designed to foster commerce (and interdependence) among the European states, almost all of which France either occupied or dominated, and to ruin Britain economically and force it to sue for a favourable peace.

The Continental System failed, not only because British maritime superiority enabled it to find new trading partners elsewhere, but also because, by smuggling or official connivance, European states continued to trade with Britain in order to protect their own economic interests. Even the French continued to sell wine and brandy to Britain, for home consumption and also for re-export to Scandinavia and the Baltic region. Between 1807 and 1816 some 4,478 barrels of French wine entered Britain each year, representing an eighth of total annual wine imports. The great bulk of British wine imports were Portuguese (50 per cent) and Spanish (23 per cent).[1]

In view of French breaches of their own trade embargo, it was ironic that the refusal of the Portuguese, for a century Britain's main supplier of wine, to abide by the terms of the Continental System attracted a response from France. French troops and their Spanish allies invaded northern Portugal, including the principal wine region along the Douro, between 1807 and 1809, and the British landed forces in 1809. Actual damage to the vineyards as a result of hostilities was minimal because the vineyards were located in difficult and broken terrain above the

Douro, which was unsuitable for much formal military activity. In 1808 the Portuguese successfully used this topography against the French by firing from among the vines in the high, walled vineyards on to French troops who had crossed the Douro and tried to move along the roads bordering the river.[2]

At a broader level the war disrupted the Douro wine-makers in scores of large and small ways that complicated their lives and work. Conscription drew off skilled vineyard workers, foreign troops occasionally looted cellars, all but a few of the important British merchants resident in Porto left when the French arrived, and the shipping of wine to export markets became increasingly risky. Even so, there were fewer interruptions in production and trade than might have been expected. Whatever decline there was in exports was partially offset by the increased consumption of wine locally by foreign troops, and it is probable that service in Portugal accustomed men to drinking wines that they later sought out when they returned home. But with the declining influence of British merchants on the spot in Porto, prices for Portuguese wine began to rise, and in years of poor harvest, like 1811, prices rose even more quickly. From that year, facing higher prices and the suspicion that some of the wine was of dubious quality, English demand for Portuguese wines began to decline.

In other wine regions it was not so much war as French conquest that had an impact on wine. Napoleon saw territorial domination as an opportunity not only to benefit France, but also to confer the advantages of new French institutions and practices on foreign states so as to bring them up to the French level of civilization. This was France's 'civilizing mission'. One of these aims was to undermine what was left of the economic power of the Church. Wherever the French found archbishops, bishops and religious houses owning land, including vineyards, they confiscated the estates and sold them to secular owners, just as the Revolutionaries had done in France in the early 1790s. Thus in 1803 the French authorities confiscated about a quarter of the vineyards of the Mosel region, including some of the best, and sold them to secular owners. For instance, the estate of Kloster Eberbach was expropriated from the Cistercian Order, which had planted vines there in the twelfth century, and sold to the Duke of Nassau. In parts of Italy, including Piedmont, the same policies were applied and there, too, it was the wealthy rather than the peasantry who gained ownership of vineyards.[3]

It might be that the role of the Church, and of monasteries in particular, in medieval viticulture and wine-making has been exaggerated, but none the less their ownership of vineyards was a continuity over the centuries from the early Middle Ages. With the sale of many religious vineyards in Burgundy to secular owners in the eighteenth century, the confiscation and sale of Church land during the French Revolution, and the extension of these policies by Napoleon to much of Europe outside France, that continuity came to an end.

In 1815 the Napoleonic wars also came to an end, and political and economic conditions stabilized. Losing the war did not have a harmful impact on French viticulture, which continued the expansion that had begun before the middle of the eighteenth century. By 1828 French vineyards covered some two million hectares and accounted for 40 per cent of the world's wine production. In contrast, Italy (which today produces more wine than France) could boast only slightly more than 400,000 hectares, a fifth of France's area. Larger than Italy's were Austria (625,000 hectares) and Hungary (550,000 hectares).[4]

Elsewhere, wine-makers who looked forward optimistically to a new era of prosperity after the Napoleonic wars must have been disappointed when the grape harvest of 1816, the first full year of peace, was devastated in many regions by very cold temperatures. Appetites for wine are not affected by such setbacks, however, and the wine business did its best to recover speedily from the quarter-century of political turmoil that had begun with the French Revolution. Even before hostilities in Portugal had completely ended, for example, British merchants began to return to Porto to supervise their business interests and maximize their chances of remaining the main wine supplier for the profitable English market. Demand had declined from 1811, but the merchants, now joined by George Sandeman (founder of one of the pre-eminent port merchant companies), hoped that peace would revive the market and lead to a renewed period of prosperity for Portuguese wine.

They were frustrated in this aspiration by a shift in English drinking patterns during the first half of the century. Although the country's population increased rapidly, doubling between 1800 and 1850, demand for wine stayed more or less constant. Beer, which was improving in quality, and spirits provided for the rest. Even within the wealthy and middle-class wine-drinking population, however, there were shifts in preference, possibly a result of increased awareness of the dangers of excessive drinking and of the influence of the emerging temperance movement. Port lost much of its market to lighter wines, such as inexpensive Spanish imports, and many drinkers who wanted higher alcohol content in wine shifted from port to sherry. From providing more than half England's wine in 1800, port fell to under a third by 1830.

Some of the wine Portugal no longer exported to England was directed to its colonies. Angola became the recipient of considerable volumes of wine and distilled spirits in the late 1700s and the 1800s. In the ten-year period 1798–1807, for example, an average of 282 pipas of wine (about 140,000 litres) was shipped from Lisbon to Luanda each year. By the 1860s the total alcohol exported to Portugal's West African colonies reached 23 million litres, most of it in distilled form which better withstood the voyage and the heat.[5]

What the Douro lost was gained by Jerez. Sherry, most of it sweet, made up a fifth of English wine imports between 1814 and 1824, but amounted to two fifths in the period 1826 to 1840.[6] Britain was the destination of nine tenths of Spain's sherry exports, although British merchants re-exported some of it to other markets. This export boom had repercussions in Jerez itself. The area in viticulture grew by 50 per cent between 1817 and 1851 and 50 per cent again by 1870. These new vineyards, many owned by large merchant companies, produced the vast volumes of cheap sherry that were shipped to England. Over time the price of the traditional, expensive sherries produced by peasants declined (from about 110 to 40 pesetas a butt between 1865 and 1880). Many peasants were forced to sell, and by the end of the nineteenth century most Jerez vineyards were controlled by large companies such as Duff, Garvey and Byass.

Spanish viticulture also surged ahead outside Jerez. It is estimated that the country's area in vines increased fourfold during the nineteenth century, and by the 1890s Spain was producing more than 20 million hectolitres of wine a year. In Catalonia alone, production in 1890 was six times the 1860 level. The result was that wine constituted a growing proportion of Spain's exports: a third by value in the late 1850s alone.[7]

In Europe generally there were shifts in the patterns of alcohol-consumption. Industrial spirits – liquor distilled from sugar-beet and molasses rather than grapes – became increasingly popular in much of central, eastern and northern Europe where vines were either marginal or could not be cultivated at all. Thus Germany and Scandinavia became significant producers of grain-based alcohol like schnapps. Spirits also became popular in some wine-producing countries, such as France, especially among workers in the northern industrial cities. The appearance of mass-produced alternative alcoholic beverages did not necessarily lead to reductions in wine-production, however, and for the most part, the volumes of European wine available for the market rose during much of the nineteenth century. The populations of most states rose steadily during the 1800s (France was an exception), so that even if the proportion of wine-drinkers fell, the numbers increased in absolute terms.

The growth of wine-production was not steady, and it suffered a severe setback two thirds of the way through the 1800s as a result of the phylloxera epidemic, but over the long term the increase in production was clear. For example, France annually produced 51 litres of wine per capita in 1840, 60 litres in 1859, and 77 litres per head in 1872, a stunning increase of 50 per cent in just thirty years.[8] Most of the increase was in the less expensive, poorer-quality wines, but there were even more notable increases in the regions associated with better-quality wines. The Bordeaux region produced some 1.9 million hectolitres of wine each year in the late 1850s, 4.5 million hectolitres annually ten years later, and more than 5 million hectolitres a year by the mid 1870s.

There were equally important changes in the organization of the French wine industry during the 1800s, and in fact it is in this period that we can properly begin to refer to it as an 'industry' in the modern sense. Most wine production and markets in France fell into one of two broad categories. The first consisted of premium wines made in relatively small quantities for the luxury markets, many of them outside France. The example of Bordeaux is obvious, but Burgundy also participated in this way, shipping more than 200,000 hectolitres of wine a year to Paris by cart and canal in the early part of the nineteenth century.[9] The second category, much larger but less regulated and visible, was made up of the ordinary wines produced on a small-scale and artisanal basis to provide for local and regional markets.

These were hard times for many wine-growers, however, because production of wine (35–40 million hectolitres a year) exceeded domestic demand. Prices fell by a quarter between 1800–1820 and 1820–50, and vignerons' earnings were low. Exports were relatively low at between 1 and 1½ million hectolitres a year, and high domestic taxes on wine raised the price of wine in France itself. A group of producers from Beaujolais complained that 100 hectolitres of wine sold in Paris for an apparently generous 5,800 francs, but that when one took into account the costs of growing the grapes (200 francs), barrels (750 francs), transportation (700 francs), merchant's commission of 10 per cent (580 francs), and above all direct taxes (93 francs) and indirect taxes (2,675 francs), there remained only 802 francs for the vineyard-owner and his vigneron to share between them.[10]

Later in the century, wine-production was not only greater but it had been reorganized to become what has been called 'a vast wine-producing complex', comparable to the massive textile and metal industries that had grown up in northern France.[11] Several developments drove this transformation. First, land under viticulture increased substantially during the Revolutionary and Napoleonic periods and continued to increase in the nineteenth century. From just under 2 million hectares in 1850, French vineyards occupied almost 2.6 million hectares in 1875, an increase of almost a third. Most of the expansion was in the south, particularly in Languedoc. In 1800 that vast region had only 65,000 hectares in vines, but by 1869 the Hérault alone had 226,000 hectares of vineyards.[12]

Second, there were improvements in productivity across the board as increases in the volume of wine easily outstripped the expansion of land used for viticulture. Growers in the south of France especially extended their vineyards beyond the hillsides and began to plant vines on the plains and rolling land, where they were easier to grow and more accessible for pruning and harvesting. High-yielding varietals like grenache were planted by the million and gamay vines made progress in the Val de Loire and in the outlying districts of Burgundy. Such was the concern of burgundy-producers that in 1845 a congress of vignerons in Dijon reissued Duke Philip the Bold's 1395 condemnation of gamay as a 'disloyal' vine that produced foul wine.

Third, the all-important markets of the north became more easily accessible to the expanding vineyards of the south. Most French wine was consumed domestically, and the extension of railways gave producers much easier, faster and above all cheaper access to the populous urban markets. France was a highly centralized nation, and all railways led to Paris. From the capital, the steel lines radiated out in all directions and soon penetrated, like the roots of a vine, into the main wine-producing regions. Dijon, at the north end of Burgundy's Côte d'Or, was linked to Paris by rail in 1851 and as a result enjoyed a short-lived market advantage until the line to Bordeaux was completed two years later. By 1856 wine from the massive vineyards of Languedoc was being shipped to northern markets by train, and by 1875 France had a comprehensive network of railways and a national wine market.

It was not only the fact of rail transportation that made a difference, but also the variable rates offered by the rail companies. The costs of moving freight were not strictly correlated to distance, and this strengthened the competitive position of vineyards furthest away from Paris and other major markets. They paid less per unit of freight than regions closer to the markets. As a result of the buoyancy of the wine industry in the Midi, the vineyards around Paris went into decline. In the valley of the Oise, for example, land in vines declined from 2,285 hectares in 1852 to just 811 hectares ten years later. This was indicative of the rapid decline of marginal wine-producing regions, a trend that would be intensified by the phylloxera epidemic a decade or two later.

Parisian taste did not change as soon as wine became available from the south. Wines from Burgundy retained the loyalty of many Parisians until the late 1860s, when a poor harvest in Burgundy forced many consumers to look for alternatives. Increasing consumption in Paris also made new sources of wine necessary. Parisians consumed a growing share of the national output: 86 million litres in 1840 but 300 million litres by 1872, a rise that far outstripped the growth of the capital's population. The rise in consumption was probably stimulated, as well as sustained, by the availability of inexpensive wines from the south.

Changes in international commerce also assisted the French wine trade. The loss of France's satellites at the end of the Napoleonic wars deprived wine-producers of some markets, but they began to export significant quantities to the Americas, especially to Argentina and, from the 1840s, to the United States. The high level of American imports was short-lived, however, and sales of French wine there fell during the 1860s through a combination of the Civil War, the emergence of the California wine industry, and American protectionist policies. It is possible, too, that the decline of demand in the United States, as in England at about the same time, was due in part to the influence of the strengthening temperance movement. As we shall see, however, wine was far less a concern of temperance advocates than spirits, and some even praised wine as a safe alternative to other alcohol.

In Europe, Germany and The Netherlands were major importers of French wine, the better Bordeaux vintages going to Germany, cheaper wines to The Netherlands. In terms of volume England remained a minor customer for French wine through the first half of the century, and then mainly for premium bordeaux. An 1860 treaty between Britain and France dramatically reduced the tariffs on wine, however, and sales of the less-expensive clarets began to rise just at the time that exports to the United States started to fall off. Even though English wine-drinkers remained by and large faithful to Iberian wines, consumption of French wine increased eight-fold between the mid 1860s and the mid 1870s.

English drinkers might well have been encouraged to drink French wine not only because prices fell but also because they believed it was good for them. In a series of articles published in a medical journal in the 1860s, then in a bestselling book, Dr Robert Druitt argued for the particular health benefits of French wine. Much more than wine from Spain or Portugal, he wrote, French wines (bordeaux or burgundy) were ideal for children, the old, the sick, and for anyone who needed to use their brain.[13]

The writing of doctors like Druitt echoed the works of Greek and Roman authors who, two thousand years earlier, had linked the quality of wines with their therapeutic properties. But during the first half of the nineteenth century it became clear that there was increasing interest in defining quality for other purposes. A consensus on the ranking of Bordeaux wines had emerged as early as the first two decades of the 1800s, as wine-writers agreed that a handful of estates (Margaux, Latour, Lafite, Haut-Brion) were consistently producing wines that stood apart from the rest. In 1855, the ranking was made explicit and considerably more detailed for the Universal Exhibition in Paris, and later it became not only official but also so permanent that it has remained virtually unchanged in a century and a half.

*

Greater attention to quality was also evident in a number of Italian wine regions, and it was during the nineteenth century that several wines, including barolo, chianti and barbaresco, began to stand out from the mass of their undistinguished peers. Wine was produced throughout the peninsula and was consumed by all social groups, but, with a few exceptions, Italian wines were poor quality and were marketed locally. Unlike France, Italy had not developed a range of premium wines; the better-off consumers imported quality wines, especially bordeaux and burgundies, even in regions such as Piedmont that now produce their own fine wines. Nor had Italy (unlike Spain and Portugal) developed foreign markets for its ordinary wines, partly because Italy had been marginalized when the focus of European trade had shifted from the Mediterranean to the Atlantic.

There were several reasons for the relatively late emergence of quality Italian wines. Until it was unified in 1860–61, the Italian peninsula was made up of many small states, some of which were independent, while others, including Venetia and Lombardy, belonged to larger entities like the Austrian Empire. Different systems of weights and measures, together with the tariffs imposed by each state on goods from others, prevented the development of a national market for wine. Nor did any individual state have a sufficient mass of well-off consumers who could support the production of fine wines locally. Long-distance international trade was ruled out because Italian wines travelled very badly. Some attempts had been made to export barolo to England in the eighteenth century, but even after it was clarified, slightly fortified, and even covered with a film of olive oil to protect it from the air, little of the wine seems to have reached its destination in good condition.[14]

The few exceptions to the undistinguished wines of northern Italy included barolo from Piedmont and valpolicella from Venetia, both of which found limited markets outside their own regions, particularly in Vienna. But like wine exporters everywhere, their fortunes were often tied to political influences in the form of import duties. In 1833 the Austrian government lowered the tariff on Piedmontese wine, but thirteen years later, under pressure from Hungarian wine-growers, it more than doubled the rate of duty, with the result that the price of barolo rose and sales fell.

Politics touched the history of northern Italian wines in the nineteenth century more directly than elsewhere. The middle of the century saw a growing desire within the Italian political elites to throw off foreign domination and to unite the politically fractured peninsula into a single nation. Two of the leading statesmen of unification, which was all but achieved by 1861, were Camillo Cavour and Baron Bettino Ricasoli, agronomists who took a particular interest in developing viticulture in their respective regions, Piedmont and Tuscany.

Ricasoli is widely regarded as having created the wine we now know as chianti. Respectable wines were made in the Chianti district before the nineteenth century, and although they had found a limited market in England in the seventeenth and eighteenth centuries, they had been pushed out by French and Portuguese competition. By the early nineteenth they were sold only locally. Ricasoli's improvements, starting with his own estate at Brolio, set the tone for the more general transformation that not only distinguished chianti from other regional wines but also gave it a quality that enabled it to compete with foreign wines.

In 1851 Ricasoli toured vineyards in France – in the Rhône, Beaujolais and Burgundy regions – to study their methods of viticulture and wine-making. But his mind was constantly on the potential of his own district. After tasting an 1846 beaujolais he noted in his journal, 'A good wine, but little taste and no aroma, not sharp, a golden red colour, and supple. Wine from Chianti is superior in taste and aroma; but it is inferior because it is still a little bitter, and its colour gives the wine density but deprives it of an attractive appearance.'[15]

Among the innovations that can be credited to Ricasoli is the selection of a restricted number of grape varieties from which to make chianti: sangiovese above all, but also canaiolo, malvasia and trebbiano. Although Ricasoli experimented with other varieties, including many he brought back from France, Tuscan vineyards were increasingly restricted to those that have become identified with chianti. Ricasoli also modified harvesting habits and made it incumbent on the peasants who grew vines on his estates to determine the best date to start picking. It was on this decision, he pointed out, that 'the good reputation of the wines of Brolio depends'.

But Ricasoli did not believe that good wine reflected no more than successful viticulture, and he paid close attention to vinification. He abandoned open fermentation vats for closed, and improved clarification techniques. On the other hand Ricasoli maintained the technique known as *governo*, in which the unfermented juice of grapes that have been dried for a month or two is blended into wine that has just finished fermenting. The effect was to restart fermentation and increase the alcoholic strength of the wine. Although *governo* is now employed far less widely, it was common practice in Tuscany throughout the nineteenth century.

Ricasoli's innovations produced not only more wine but better wine. By the 1870s, production at Brolio was a fifth greater than it had been in the 1830s, and 70 per cent of it was designated as being of first-class quality. The achievement was won at the expense of good relations with his tenants, over whose traditional practices and feelings he had ridden roughshod. When he died they condemned him, perhaps appropriately, to spend eternity wandering the woods of Chianti on a white horse.[16] At the same time, the whole region benefited from the elevated status that chianti gained and its increasing success in international markets, not to mention the wider national diffusion that the unification of Italy made possible.

The recovery of chianti from decline in the late 1700s to a reputable wine a century later was part of a more general transformation of Italian wine during the nineteenth century. One notable trend was a shift from sweet to dry. Barolo and barbaresco started the century as sweet wines and ended it much drier. It was in the 1820s that Sicily began to produce dry wines as well as the strong sweet wines for which it had long been known.

More attention was paid to quality in Germany's wine regions during the nineteenth century as they became part of a larger market in which they were forced to compete directly with one another. The creation of a customs union (Zollverein) in 1834 reduced the tariff barriers that had protected the mediocre wines of the individual German states. Better wines chased the poor from the market, a process that was accelerated by improvements in transportation, especially the spread of railways. The result was that while some German wine regions flourished, others failed. Württemberg's and Franken's vineyards declined by about 50 per cent during the century, and Baden's suffered under an onslaught of imported wine from Bordeaux. The wines of the Rhineland increased their sales in Prussia, while Prussia's own vineyards, which had produced only poor-quality wine for cities like Berlin and Dresden, went into decline. It was a parallel to the decline of the vineyards of the Paris region once the wines of the Midi became available.

The trend towards improvement was not simply a result of the changed economic and political environment, however, for German wine-producers began to pay more attention to techniques of wine-making and to quality controls. Growers' associations were established in all the wine regions, and later in the century state-sponsored institutes for viticultural research were set up. The states also began the long and difficult process of delimiting regions and establishing criteria for appellations. Some of these systems were based on straightforward criteria of grape varietals, but others achieved a completely unworkable complexity. In the 1830s, for example, the Palatinate adopted a system with more than sixty-five grades of quality.

As the large producers refined their products and introduced new techniques, the much larger number of small producers found themselves relegated to providing for the mass market, where they had to compete with foreign imports. Their response was to form cooperatives, which not only provided a communal press and vinification facility, but also helped individual producers obtain credit to improve their properties and vine stock. The cooperative movement began in 1869 in the Ahr region, and by the early 1900s there were more than a hundred cooperatives, the core of the hundreds more that were formed during the twentieth century.[17]

A particular trend was evident in Germany's Mosel region, where in the late eighteenth century producers had begun to leave grapes on the vine until they had started to dry or even until they were affected by botrytis, or noble rot. Gradually a vocabulary developed to describe the various degrees of late harvesting, the state of the grapes, and the method of selecting grapes for wine. These terms are familiar to modern wine-drinkers because they are the categories of sweetness by which German wines are now officially ranked: *Spätlese* for late-harvested grapes, *Auslese* for bunches of grapes selected for possessing concentrated sugars, and *Beerenauslese* for the practice of selecting individual grapes because of their ripeness. Other categories, like *Trockenbeerenauslese* (selecting individual grapes from bunches on account of their raisiny quality) and *Eiswein* (ice-wine) would follow later.

Overall the total size of Germany's vineyards remained steady during the nineteenth century, although there was some loss following the arrival of phylloxera. But unlike France's population, which stagnated, Germany's shot up during the 1800s, doubling every fifty years. This created a widening gap between the supply of and demand for wine. Even though the great bulk of alcohol consumed in Germany was beer and spirits, the demand for wine began to exceed production, and by the turn of the century Germany, once an exporter of wine, had become an importer. In the years before the First World War, Germany imported an annual average of 330,000 litres of wine from France and 88,000 litres from Italy.[18]

Although Europe's wine industry generally grew during much of the nineteenth century, it had to adjust to changing conditions. Overall production rose steadily in many regions, but drinkers' tastes changed, with other alcoholic beverages cutting into wine-markets or preventing wine-consumption from spreading. The temperance movement, which is discussed in the next chapter, began to make its presence felt in many countries, but not always to the disadvantage of wine. The experience of the fifty or sixty years following the defeat of Napoleon suggested that wine was in a new social and cultural environment, and that more changes were yet to come.

Some of those changes were the result of the greater theoretical knowledge of wine. From the end of the eighteenth century scientists began to delve more deeply into what were then, and would remain for many decades, the chemical and biological mysteries of wine. The critical process of fermentation by which wine was made was scarcely understood, and neither were the principles of conservation. It was recognized that fermentation varied according to environmental conditions and that exposure to air and summer heat could spoil wine, but wine-makers and merchants carried out their operations according to traditional methods. This did not mean that there were no innovations along the way. Burning sulphur in barrels as a means of conserving wine became more widely practised from the seventeenth century onwards, as did the addition of alcohol in the form of spirits. Italian producers poured a layer of olive oil on wine to protect it from the air. But what was still lacking was the kind of understanding that would enable the basic processes of wine-making to be improved in order to increase a wine's general quality and durability.

In the final decades of the eighteenth century some progress was made towards an understanding of fermentation. On the eve of the French Revolution (of which he would become a victim in 1794), the scientist Antoine-Laurent Lavoisier published an important work that defined fermentation as a chemical process. Lavoisier's experiments with wine convinced him that fermentation was a chemical reaction in which sugar was converted to alcohol, carbon dioxide and acetic acid. It was, he argued, fundamentally a rearrangement of the essential elements of sugar such that there were equal amounts of oxygen and carbon dioxide in the end product as there had been in the sugar that was fermented.[19]

This explanation of fermentation as a chemical process was largely accepted until it was challenged in the mid-nineteenth century by the great French scientist Louis Pasteur. Pasteur's interests in wine were many and varied. He came from the Jura region of France which produced (and still produces) distinctive wines, including *vin de paille*. Pasteur unashamedly promoted Jura wines in particular – he used them in many of his experiments – but he was a supporter of wine more generally. His statement that wine was 'the healthiest and most hygienic of drinks' was widely exploited by the wine industry not only to publicize its product but also to defend it against those who suggested that wine might be harmful to the health.[20]

What gave Pasteur's pronouncement its credibility was not only his fame as a scientist, but also the fact that he worked extensively on wine. It is estimated that he devoted only some three or four years in the late 1850s and early 1860s to wine research, but his findings fundamentally re-shaped wine-production in France and elsewhere. The most important contribution was to suggest that fermentation, rather than being simply a chemical process, was also a biological one. This conclusion emerged from the area of research for which Pasteur is best known: the role of bacteria in human and animal disease and the means of preventing the spread of diseases. Pasteur discovered that fermentation occurred when an organism (yeast) attacked the sugar in must, and that wine turned to vinegar when it succumbed to bacteria that were present within it.

Central to Pasteur's work on wine was the role of oxygen. He determined that fermentation occurred best when it took place without oxygen, making it a form of 'life without air'. The question of oxygen was also at play in the degradation of wine. Pasteur discovered by experimentation that the exposure of wine to oxygen allowed the growth of bacteria (acetobacters) that turned the various acids in wine to acetic acid, or vinegar. The process of pasteurization, heating as a means of killing bacteria, began to be used (though far from universally) as a way of killing the bacteria that were detrimental to the quality and keeping properties of a wine.

Although the work of scientists like Pasteur would eventually become fundamental to the transformation of wine-making, it did not measurably affect wine-making methods in the nineteenth century. Most producers, particularly in Europe, were owners of small vineyards who persisted with traditional methods that demanded no explicit scientific understanding of the process involved. Fermentation occurred year after year, whether it was a chemical or a biological process, and the wine that was produced was never intended to age gracefully for decades but was meant to be consumed within a year.

Attempts were made, none the less, to disseminate new information on wine to producers, for example in Chaptal's *The Art of Making Wine*, discussed in Chapter 7. But it is impossible to say precisely how influential Chaptal's book was. Most vineyards were small lots owned by peasants, many of whom were illiterate, and smallholders were financially least able to make the changes advocated by Chaptal. Even when new techniques did not involve expenditure, they entailed risk. Operating as they did on the margins of subsistence, many producers were unwilling to deviate from the methods that provided them a living, even if it was from wine that experts in Paris judged inferior.

The attitude of these small producers was fairly expressed by Honoré de Balzac in *Lost Illusions*:

The bourgeois – I mean monsieur le marquis, monsieur le comte, monsieur this that and the other, claim that I make junk instead of wine. What use is education? You figure out what it means: Listen: these gentlemen harvest seven, sometimes eight barrels to the acre, and sell them at 60 francs a barrel, which makes at the most 400 francs an acre in a good year. Me, I harvest 20 barrels and sell them at 30 francs, total 600 francs. So who are the fools? Quality, quality! What use is quality to me? They can keep their quality, the marquises and all. For me, quality is cash.[21]

This would be a defensible attitude if wine were viewed simply as a profitable crop to supply a mass market. From the point of view of producers of premium wines for the high end of the market, however, it summarized all that was wrong with the French wine industry. Even so, the wines with the highest social reputation gained their cachet partly through their rarity, a quality that was most easily gauged against the much-scorned and mass-produced wines. Premium wines needed *vins ordinaires* in order to maintain their distinction.

Beyond the scientific endeavours of Pasteur and others, there were attempts to understand wine more systematically at other levels. The nineteenth century saw the publication of dozens of works that attempted to survey the wines of Europe and the world. This was, in effect, the beginning of the genre of literature broadly known today as wine-writing, a category that covers everything from writing on the historical and technical to the financial and aesthetic aspects of wine. Commentaries on wine and assessments of specific wines, the kind of wine-writing that is today to be found in mass-circulation magazines and in newspaper columns, developed during the nineteenth century.

It was only in this period that wine-writers shook off the slavish adulation of Ancient Greek and Roman wines that had until then passed for wine appreciation. Until the late eighteenth century, commentaries on wine tended to hark back to ancient times and to decry the quality of modern wines in comparison. A striking example was one 1775 work that purported to compare ancient and modern wines, but which devoted almost all its pages to the former.[22] Even Adamo Fabbroni, whose book was the first modern approach to wine-making, was familiar with the classical authors, and he easily integrated references to them throughout his work.

This tendency was only to be expected in the late eighteenth and early nineteenth centuries, when there was a revival of interest in Greece and Rome, as shown by the popularity of neo-classical architecture and art and the obsession with classical literary criticism. In this cultural environment it is, perhaps, not surprising that wine-writers thought of ancient wines as the benchmarks against which modern wines should be assessed. At the same time it was also a pointless exercise, for while it is possible to compare a classical text with a modern one and discuss their relative merits, it is impossible to taste an ancient wine.

Within a few decades, however, wine-writers were imbued with the spirit of progress that is often seen as characteristic of the age. They began to take modern wines seriously and to study them in their own right, without glib comparisons to the imagined qualities of wines that had been produced two thousand years earlier. Their positive outlook for wine meshed well with the work of scientists who publicized the ways in which modern wine could be improved. Equally important, they were able to admit the prospect of improvement in its own terms, not as an attempt to return to standards supposedly attained by Greek and Roman wine-makers, nor by writing off modern wine as worthless.

Two wine-writers, a French wine-merchant and an English journalist, set the new tone and standard of wine-writing. In 1816 André Jullien published a wide-ranging book that dealt not only with the main wine regions of France (although that was his emphasis) but with those of Europe more generally and of other parts of the world.[23] Jullien's breadth was astonishing, and he provided information designed not only to assist wine-drinkers in developing their cellars, but also to give comparative viticultural information that would assist wine-producers.

In 1833 what might be considered the English equivalent of Jullien's work, Cyrus Redding's *History and Description of Modern Wines*, was published.[24] His was a global survey of wines, but Redding also devoted chapters to practical matters such as the conservation and adulteration of wines. If we believe Redding, adulteration and deception were practised on a grand scale with the wines imported to England. This applied particularly to fortified wines, whose 'spirituous strength' could mask adulteration and deceive even very experienced tastes. 'Any attempt to fabricate Romanée-Conti would not thus easily answer, because the fineness, delicacy, and perfume of this wine are not to be copied.'

Redding blamed the English for this situation: they so much preferred spirits and fortified wines to 'pure' wines that their palates were dulled to the point where they could hardly tell genuine wine from the fraudulent beverages they were sold. He was scathing in his comments:

The inhabitants of the United Kingdom swallow above a quart of wine a head, man, woman, and child, and more than a gallon of spirits annually, to say nothing of oceans of malt liquor, beside home-made wines, cider, and perry. As the fondness for spirit increases, that for wine diminishes. The cuticle on the hand of a blacksmith is hardened by the hot iron, and cannot distinguish objects by the sense of feeling; in the same manner the stomach of the spirit-drinker is lost to the healthy freshness of wine, being too cold and unseasoned for his seared stomach, while adulterations or coarse mixtures of the grape remain undiscovered.[25]

The growth of consumer-centred wine-writing signalled a more sophisticated and educated approach to wine-drinking among the European middle and upper classes. Guides such as Jullien's and Redding's were not written for peasants and urban workers. These large social groups might have consumed large volumes of wine in some parts of Europe, but they bought at the inexpensive end of the price spectrum and they invariably bought only enough for their immediate requirements. They no more had cellars full of ageing wine than they had savings accounts or pension plans.

The expansion of the middle classes and the growth of bourgeois prosperity throughout much of the nineteenth century (sometimes called 'the bourgeois century') brought with it a new appreciation of commodities. This was the beginning of a recognizable consumer culture, accompanied by mass production, thanks to industrialization, and advertising. There were great celebrations of commodities in the form of international exhibitions, such as the 1851 Great Exhibition in London and the 1855 Universal Exposition in Paris. For our purposes there was one important difference between these two celebrations of materialism, and that is that while alcohol was banned from the London exhibition, it was a feature of the Paris show. The organizers of the latter saw it as an opportunity to showcase the best French wines as well as wines from other parts of Europe and from as far away as Australia.

It was for the 1855 Paris exhibition that the *cru* system of ranking Bordeaux wines was created. Napoleon III requested a classification of the best Bordeaux wines, and the Syndicat des Courtiers de Commerce, the association of wine merchants, obliged within a matter of days. A total of fifty-eight red wines were divided into categories: four first growths (*crus*), twelve second growths, fourteen third growths, eleven fourth growths, and seventeen fifth growths. Twenty white wines were classed as either first or second growth, and a twenty-first (Château d'Yquem) was given the unique status of 'Premier cru supérieur'.

The Bordeaux classification has been contentious since it was drawn up, not only because it was based on the price that individual wines fetched on the market at that time, but also because it omitted a number of Bordeaux districts. Among the red wines, all were from the Médoc except for Haut-Brion. The list might have been a good guide to bordeaux in the mid nineteenth century, but what could not have been predicted then was that the rankings would retain such authority for so long. The classification has proved so rigid that only one wine has successfully challenged its ranking: in 1973 Château Mouton-Rothschild was elevated from second to first growth. The other criticism of the 1855 classification is that it has systematically excluded wines that deserve to be included.

Purveyors of these and other fine wines, in France especially, portrayed their products not only as natural but also as the culmination of long traditions. The apparent contradiction was resolved by suggesting that what was traditional was natural by the very fact of its longevity and permanence. What was new must, in contrast, be artificial and would prove to be transient. Traditions can, however, be constructed by various means in order to legitimate practices and to give commodities an added appearance of respectability, and there are few better examples of the invention of tradition than the process that some wines underwent in this period.

Prime among the inventors of tradition were the Bordeaux winemakers who began to use the word 'château' in the names of their estates. Wine that was known as simply Margaux or Haut-Brion in the eighteenth century became labelled as Château Margaux and Château Haut-Brion in the next. In part the change reflected the invention of lithography in 1798, which made it possible to mass produce labels, but the addition of 'château' was a decision independent of this.[26]

There was nothing deceptive or intrinsically wrong with introducing the château reference, for there were châteaux on the properties where the vineyards were located. But the buildings and estates were not known by these names before the late 1800s. In the 1850 edition of his 1833 survey, Cyrus Redding listed among Bordeaux 'wines of the first class' only one 'château', and that was Margaux.[27] In the 1855 classification, only five wines bore the title 'château', while an English list of about 1870 conferred 'château' on only four: Haut-Brion, Lafite, Latour and Margaux.[28] By the twentieth century all the classified wines bore the château title.

The wines from the estates surrounding the châteaux were now associated directly and explicitly with the buildings, some of which were quite ordinary dwellings to which a turret had been added. The practice distinguished these wines from others, and their proprietors from the mass of wine-producers. It associated them with aristocracy and thereby with tradition and lineage, in so far as nobles are commonly assumed to have roots that run back to the Middle Ages. (The designation of some grape varieties as 'noble' and the reference to botrytis as 'noble rot' are other expressions of the aristocratic associations of wine.) This would have been a dubious enough proposition even in the eighteenth century, when many Bordeaux vineyards were planted or purchased by nobles: most of the new proprietors belonged to recently ennobled families. It was even more dubious in the nineteenth century, however, when the owners of many of the 'château' vineyards had purchased them during or after the French Revolution. Some owners were from families that had been granted nobility during the Napoleonic empire in the early 1800s, others were foreign nobles, and many were not nobles at all. A number – nobles and commoners alike – were businessmen who regarded their vineyards simply as commercial operations. The Marquis de las Marismas, who purchased Château Margaux in 1836, was one of several Paris-based bankers who bought famous vineyards in the Médoc in the mid nineteenth century but showed little interest in them beyond their profitability.[29] When Haut-Brion was sold in 1825, it was owned two thirds by a stockbroker and one third by a wine-merchant, and when it was sold again in 1836 the purchaser was a Paris banker.[30]

The appeal of the château name later spread beyond Bordeaux into the Loire, the Midi and elsewhere in France. It quickly found its way outside Europe as well, as far as Australia, where in 1879 the name of the Tabilk vineyard in Victoria was changed to Château Tahbilk.[31] Perhaps this was the idea of the manager appointed two years earlier, François de Coueslant, whose name certainly resonates with the affectation of château. 'Château' would later be associated with other vineyards in Australia as well as in Canada and elsewhere.

In a sense, it was fair enough to point to the château, the actual structure, as the repository of a vineyard's tradition, for it was virtually the sole continuity over time. Château Margaux, completed in 1817, has been described thus:

The house is in the image of the vintage. Noble, austere, even a little solemn . . . Château Margaux has the air of an ancient temple devoted to the cult of wine . . . Vineyard or dwelling, Margaux disdains all embellishments. But just as the wine has to be served before it unfolds all its charms, so the residence waits for the visitor to enter before it reveals its own. In each case the same words spring to one's lips: elegance, distinction, delicacy and that subtle satisfaction given by something which has received the most attentive and indeed loving care for generations. A wine long matured, a house long inhabited: Margaux the vintage and Margaux the château are the products of two equally rare things: *rigour and time*.[32]

Owners came and went, as did vines, but the château stayed put. It might be argued that the terroir of Château Margaux also endured more or less unchanged, but how could that complex relationship be expressed on a label? (Few château labels show vines.) The château, solid, permanent, resisting change, stood four-square for tradition, and the lineage and stability embodied by the château on the outside of the bottle represented the consistent and reliable quality of the wine it contained.

The château label was directed first and foremost at the upper echelons of wine consumers, and in France that represented only a small section of the wider market for alcohol, a market that was divided in a number of ways. Even though wine, like beer, was considered a food, men were far more likely than women to drink. It is often difficult to ascertain drinking patterns in the past, especially in the privacy of the home, but it seems certain that men drank alcohol far more frequently and in larger quantities than women. Second, there were class distinctions. They were most evident in the quality of wine consumed, but in general it is safe to say that the upper and middle classes throughout France drank wine, and that wine-drinking among peasants and workers varied by region.

Throughout the nineteenth century France's drinking culture began to divide more and more clearly into a wine-drinking south and a spirits-drinking north. There were two reasons for this. Wine tended to be less expensive where it was produced and, as northern vineyards contracted during the 1800s, that meant the south. The exception seems to have been Paris, where wine drinking might have been more common because it had been a tradition for centuries.[33] In contrast, spirits of all kinds were manufactured in the newer industrial cities of the north, and they became the drink of choice for urban workers. In the first half of the century spirits were distilled from grape juice, but after the phylloxera epidemic created a shortage of grapes and pushed up the price of juice, alcohol (known as 'industrial spirits') was almost entirely made from products such as sugar beet and molasses.

At mid century, insights into wine consumption at the level of individual families were provided by the French social scientist Frédéric Le Play, who studied family budgets as part of broader research into family forms and behaviour. One of Le Play's case studies, the family of a master-bleacher of Paris, spent almost 300 francs a year on alcohol, almost all of it (290 francs) on wine from Burgundy. Le Play observed that 'the wine, purchased in barrels, is put in bottles by the head of the family. The whole family drinks wine at the midday and evening meals; it observes . . . no days of abstinence.'[34] Another Parisian family, its head a carpenter, consumed ninety litres of wine a year (in baskets of ten one-litre bottles), plus a litre of brandy 'for socializing with friends or relatives', and another five or six litres of brandy with friends outside the house, presumably in taverns.[35] In these cases the consumption of wine or wine and brandy was clear. The southern French families studied by Le Play consumed only wine. A family of peasants in Béarn drank wine from Gers, but only on special occasions or at times of hard physical labour.[36] The family of a peasant soap-maker of lower Provence consumed 320 litres of wine from their own property and also made a liqueur from grapes and brandy, in effect a fortified wine.[37]

Le Play's research extended beyond France and was suggestive of drinking patterns elsewhere. As we might expect, the family of a typographer of Brussels consumed mainly beer, but we might be surprised at how little: over a year the typographer drank ten litres of beer and one of brandy. The total spent on alcohol was seven francs, the same as the family spent on salt and pepper for a year.[38] In contrast the nine-member family of a share-cropper of Tuscany went through 712 litres of wine from their own harvest and another 458 litres of piquette. Le Play reported that the family ordinarily drank weak wine, but sometimes, 'especially at times of intense labour, good wine which they kept specifically for these occasions. In former times they never lacked [good wine] which was also used on festive occasions; now they are keeping the good wine because, following the diseases of the vine, its price has increased.'[39] As final examples, the family of a share-cropper of Castile, in Spain, drank each year twenty litres of piquette fortified with grape-based brandy, while industrial workers in the silver factories of Chemnitz, in Germany, consumed brandy, wine and beer in varying proportions.[40]

As anecdotal as Le Play's data are (the families were case studies within a broader research project), it is evident that wine was part of the diet not only of the middle and upper classes of nineteenth-century Europe, but also of the masses of the population. The reported per capita consumption does not seem to have been high (it is not always clear which family members drank the alcohol), but generally speaking it seems to have been higher in wine-producing regions like southern France, Tuscany, the Rhineland and Spain than in the northern industrial centres. Calculating units of alcohol (higher per litre of brandy than of wine) would give quite different results, of course.

In France the major exception to the northern preference for spirits was Paris, where wine remained the staple alcohol of all classes, especially after the railways brought in increasing quantities of cheaper wine from the south. Per capita consumption seems to have declined in the first half of the nineteenth century, although it is difficult to obtain accurate statistics because much of the wine consumed by Parisians was drunk in taverns outside the city's precincts, where it was cheaper. The best estimate is that the average adult Parisian male consumed between 100 and 175 litres of wine a year, but even at the high end that estimate is well under the figures generally accepted for the eighteenth century. By 1865, however, per capita consumption of wine had risen to 225 litres a year, along with 80 litres of beer and 12 litres of various spirits.[41]

The increase in alcohol consumption by Paris workers from the 1850s onwards was part of a more general shift in diet, for they also ate increasing amounts of bread and meat. It was said that Paris workers were regarded by their provincial counterparts as gourmets and connoisseurs. In the 1880s the president of the carpenters' union cited increased consumption of wine as evidence of improvements in workers' conditions during the previous forty years. Workers could now drink wine at noon, he boasted, and where they used to drink a quarter-litre they were now drinking a litre.[42] Not everyone, however, thought that increased alcohol consumption (even when that alcohol was wine) was the best measure of improved living standards. Concern was expressed at some trends that were noticed, such as the tendency for workers to replace breakfast with a glass of white wine or brandy.

It was not only at the mass-market level that the production and consumption of wine rose during the nineteenth century. An unambiguous sign of the buoyancy of the trade in luxury wine was the expansion of champagne production: in 1800 in the region of 300,000 bottles a year were produced, but by 1850 20 million bottles were being produced, and in 1883 production reached 36 million bottles. As production rose, champagne was increasingly exported from France. It was fitting that England, which had first welcomed Champagne's sparkling wine in the seventeenth century, remained the single largest consumer, but the United States quickly became a major market. The Mumm company alone shipped 420,000 bottles across the Atlantic in 1877, but twenty-five years later they shipped 1.5 million bottles. American sales of champagne quadrupled in the first decade of the twentieth century.[43]

As champagne became a mass-marketed wine, consumed conspicuously by the world's elites, it underwent quite fundamental changes in methods of production and character. The essential element of the Champagne method, which sets it apart from other ways of making sparkling wine, is that the wine is fermented in the bottle in which the consumer receives it. It was a method that exposed two major problems. The first was how to prevent the bottles from exploding under the pressure of the carbon dioxide that built up during fermentation. Modern champagne has about six atmospheres of pressure, which is to say that the pressure inside the bottle is six times greater than the pressure outside. Until heavy, thick-walled bottles with a deep punt (the indentation in the bottom of a wine bottle) were designed, many exploded.

The second problem was how to rid the bottle of the sediment that resulted from the fermentation. Early in the nineteenth century the wine was decanted and recorked, but in the process much of the pressure (and thus the bubbles) was lost. Some time in the second decade of the 1800s, however, the process of riddling was devised in the champagne house owned by a young widow, Nicole-Barbe Clicquot-Ponsardin, now far better known as la Veuve (Widow) Clicquot. Riddling involves gradually turning a bottle of champagne upside down during fermentation so that the sediment of dead yeast cells settles in the neck of the bottle. When the bottle was opened the sediment, under pressure, shot out, an event called disgorgement. The bottle could be topped up and recorked far more quickly than was possible when it had to be decanted, and only a little of the pressure was lost.

Veuve Clicquot managed to keep riddling and disgorgement a secret for only a few years, and by the 1820s the techniques were being employed by other champagne-makers. The combination of being able to maintain pressure in the bottles and to manufacture bottles that could generally be counted on to withstand the pressure within them, provided the preconditions for the growth of the champagne industry. Removing the cork from a bottle of champagne was now certain to produce the noise that became synonymous with joyous celebration. It is a sign of the arrival of industry status that while six of the most famous champagne makers were in business before 1820 (Veuve Clicquot Ponsardin, Heidsieck, Moët, Perrier-Jouët, Louis Roederer and Taittinger*), three more started producing in the 1820s (Joseph Perrier, Mumm and Bollinger), and many others followed during the next three decades.

Not only was the champagne of 1900 in much greater supply than champagne of 1800, but it tasted and looked quite different. For most of the century champagne was made as a sweet sparkling wine, with the sweetness adjusted to the markets in which it was sold. Russians demanded the sweetest champagne (about 300 grammes of sugar per litre), while the English preferred a much drier style with between 22 and 66 grammes of sugar. The French themselves fell in the middle of this spectrum. The trend toward drier champagnes began in the 1850s after an English wine merchant persuaded Perrier-Jouët not to sweeten their 1846 vintage champagne. His thinking was that the English market was already crowded at the sweet end by such wines as port and madeira, and that a dry champagne could claim a unique place in the market. By the 1870s dry (Brut) champagne was being generally exported to England.

---

* Other champagne houses founded before 1820 included Billecart-Salmon, Gosset, Henriot, Jacquesson and Ruinart.

Although slightly sweeter versions were still more popular in France and some other European markets, no champagne produced at the end of the nineteenth century had anything like the sugar content of its forebears of the early 1800s.

As for its appearance, in the first half of the century champagne was not the light yellow-gold colour we are now familiar with, but ranged from a pinkish-tawny hue often referred to as *œil de perdrix* ('eye of a partridge'), to amber and even brown. Some of the pink tone was obtained from skin contact with the black grapes in the champagne blend, but amber was contributed by the practice of including cognac in the liquid with which each bottle was topped up after disgorgement. In some cases colour was obtained from boiled elderberries, a practice reminiscent of some of the more shady episodes in the history of wine.

No wine region was more conscious of tradition in the nineteenth century than Champagne because it needed to invent one. The region's wine itself was reinvented in the nineteenth century to become a mass-produced wine, using methods that owed much to new industrial tech-niques, and having a new appearance and taste. Champagne was, in many respects, a product of the new industrial world. Despite the carefully nurtured and promoted associations with aristocracy and royalty, cham-pagne was for the most part consumed by the increasingly numerous and prosperous middle classes that wanted to share what it could of the upper-class lifestyle.

Unlike the merchants of premium Bordeaux wines, whose advertising was carefully understated, the merchants of champagne rallied enthusi-astically to the new advertising media. Champagne became a thoroughly modern commodity whose image was carefully designed to appeal to the widest possible spectrum of markets. In a period when posters became the advertising medium par excellence, champagne bottle-labels became mini-posters. Some of these associated champagne with sports and leisure activities, like hunting, horse-racing and rowing. One label showed a young woman cyclist, her hair flying provocatively loose in the wind, pursued by two young male cyclists; the label bore the similar-sounding phrases 'Grand Vin des Cyclistes. Fin de Siècle.' Other labels linked champagne to love, marriage and baptism, which, in the late nineteenth century, was considered the appropriate sequence of these events. Some labels were designed for special occasions, like the 1892 anniversary of

Christopher Columbus's arrival in the Americas and the 1889 centennial of the French Revolution.[44]

Champagne-makers did not shy away from contemporary politics, but they catered to a wide spectrum of positions. One of the 1889 French Revolution labels showed an uplifting Revolutionary scene that would appeal to the left and liberals, while another depicted Marie-Antoinette, whom conservatives considered a martyr. Some champagne houses linked their product to French national character and designed labels with flags, soldiers and battles. On the eve of the First World War one house simply changed the soldier's uniform and flag according to the country to which the champagne was being shipped.[45] During the Dreyfus affair, the notorious case of a Jewish army officer wrongly convicted of espionage that aroused a wave of anti-Semitism in France, one champagne manufacturer came out with a 'Champagne Antijuif' (anti-Jewish Champagne). Presumably it was to be consumed by anti-Semites as they celebrated the successive convictions that Dreyfus suffered until he was finally pardoned.

In short, the labelling and advertising of champagne, the image that the producers showed to the world and the associations they wished to be made with their wine, were flexible and volatile. Just as it is said to be the one wine that successfully accompanies all foods, champagne was portrayed as the one wine that could be consumed by anyone on any occasion – it could be drunk at the joyous solemnity of a wedding, at a picnic break from cycling, at a political banquet, or it could be broken over the bow of a ship at a launching ceremony.

Yet against this unstable image, so much in tune with the frenetic life led by so many middle-class people at the turn of the century, there was another, countervailing tendency in the presentation of champagne: an emphasis on its traditions, history and its natural character, all qualities that contrasted with the dominant trends and values of the late nineteenth century. At a time of political change and the growth of liberal and even democratic institutions, the champagne houses, like the proprietors of château-wines in Bordeaux, stressed their lineage and their associations with aristocracy and royalty.

Most champagne labels generally carry only the name of the house, like Bollinger, Piper-Heidsieck, Billecart-Salmon and Moët et Chandon, in the style of nobility and royalty. Some alluded to lineage explicitly, like Jacquesson et Fils, and only a handful bore explicit evidence (like Pol Roger et Compagnie) that they were corporate entities. When champagne was sold to nobles and royal houses, the labels frequently bore their crests. It was helpful that one of the centres of champagne production had strong royal connections: Reims was the site of the coronations of French kings from the ninth to the eighteenth centuries.

Champagne manufacturers invoked their exalted customers as much as the qualities of the wine itself in their promotions. In the late 1890s an advertisement for Laurent-Perrier's 'Sans-Sucre' ('Without Sugar') listed as clients the kings of Belgium and Greece, the Duke of Saxe-Coburg Gotha, the Duchess of Teck, the Earl of Durham, the Prince of Rohan, Lord Grey of Wilton, and an assortment of other nobles, knights and military officers. The advertisement sent the clear message, however, that anyone could join this elite, at least to the extent that they enjoyed champagne. It stated that Laurent-Perrier was 'supplied by all Wine Merchants throughout the World', and the advertisement announced a competition (something no self-respecting aristocrat would stoop to enter) with prizes valued at £6,000.[46]

During the nineteenth century the champagne industry even helped to invent its own history by popularizing the story of Dom Pierre Pérignon, a monk of the Abbey of Hautvillers, near Epernay, from 1668 to 1715. Pérignon was involved in wine-making at the abbey and is credited with improvements in such areas as pruning vines and blending wines. It is possible, too, that he furthered the processes of making and preserving champagne by introducing corks and using stronger English bottles. It is often difficult to distinguish fact from fiction in the case of Dom Pérignon, but it is clear that he did not 'invent' sparkling wine in any meaningful sense. The reactivation of fermentation (the 'second fermentation') in the bottle was a function of seasonal temperature changes, not of human intervention or invention. Although the wine was eventually made deliberately, it was neither discovered nor invented at one point in time, and certainly not by one person.

Yet that was the role attributed to Dom Pérignon by one Dom Grossard in 1821. Grossard had been a monk at the Abbey of Hautvillers before it was suppressed during the French Revolution, and his exaggerated account of Pérignon gave importance to the abbey as much as to the former monk. Grossard might have been ignored had his story of

Pérignon's achievement not so well served the need of champagne producers for a tradition to balance the changes in colour, taste and production methods to which champagne was subjected from the 1820s. By the second half of the nineteenth century the story was widely accepted as fact, and Dom Pérignon had become famous as the founding father of fizz. The story had been further embellished, so that now Pérignon was reputed to have been blind but possessed of such keen senses of smell and taste that his ability to blend wines was unmatched.

The champagne industry was quick to adopt and disseminate this version of its beginnings. It fitted well into the representation of champagne as having a long history that was replete with spiritual connotations: we have already seen how Dom Pérignon, on first tasting champagne, is supposed to have exclaimed, 'I am drinking the stars!' It surely did the image of champagne no harm at all to have these celestial links, particularly when it came to be a feature of all manner of events where divine benevolence was invoked: marriages, christenings, inaugurations and the launching of ships. Much later, in 1937, Moët and Chandon named one of its premium champagnes 'Dom Pérignon'.

Champagne was also portrayed as a natural beverage, despite being, in its nineteenth-century form at least, very much a product of the industrial age. When Pommery made its first champagne in the brut style in 1874, it named the vintage 'Pommery Nature'. In a sense it was more natural than the sweeter version because less sugar was added, but it was essentially no more natural than any other champagne.

A final feature of nineteenth-century champagne we might note was its relationship to women. In general, wine-drinking was associated with men, and the red wines of Bordeaux and Burgundy were resolutely male in their cultural representations. Associations with nobility and lineage were implicitly male, because nobility, like royalty in France, passed through the male line. Champagne was quite different in that it explicitly appealed to men and women alike. Women were depicted on many labels, and when Laurent-Perrier advertised its elite clients they included women such as the Countess of Dudley, the Countess of Stamford and Warrington, Madame Adelina Patti-Nicolini and Lady Sybil Tollemache. They were not as numerous as male clients, but they were there, prominently displayed on the poster.

Women were also more prominent in the champagne houses than in other regional wineries. Undoubtedly the best known was La Veuve Clicquot, whose name replaced that of her husband on the label of her champagne after his death, and has been retained since. Clicquot was not merely the owner of the business, of course, but is often credited with devising the *pupitre*, the rack in which champagne bottles are held while being riddled. La Veuve Pommery is less famous, even though she took over the business after her husband's death in 1858, promoted the export market for her wines, and oversaw the first dry champagne in 1874. Her name did not grace the labels of Pommery champagne, however, except for special blends called 'Louise Pommery'.

The appeal to women and men, to the middle classes and the aristocracy and royalty, the portrayal of champagne as appropriate on almost any occasion, placed champagne in the mainstream consumer trends of the nineteenth century. At the same time, the propagation of the Dom Pérignon story, the invention of other traditions, and the stress on its elite consumers were counterweights to the modern trends from which the champagne houses profited enormously. The few champagne houses in existence in 1800 did have a history of catering to a small, wealthy, elite clientele. As they, and the other houses founded in the 1880s, reached for the mass market, they achieved the difficult feat of harmonizing two images that were intrinsically contradictory.

As European wines confronted the new industrial societies that emerged in the nineteenth century, wine-makers across the Atlantic and in the southern hemisphere contended with a host of different problems. For the United States it was not a question of how best to age wine or to advertise it, but how to make wine on a commercial basis at all. The experience of the seventeenth and eighteenth centuries could have cast nothing but pessimism on many aspiring wine-makers, but they persisted in experimenting with locations and grape varieties until they succeeded. Success was also due in part to the fact that so many of those who tried their hand at viticulture were newcomers to America whose baggage included incredulity that wine could not be made in what generation after generation of immigrants saw as a promised land.

Their naïvety was shared by the various legislatures that made land grants to help what in many cases were the most unpromising petitioners who sought to establish vineyards in the most unsuitable locations. One such enterprise was launched by several hundred former military officers and civilian officials of Napoleon's regime, who had sought exile in America after their emperor was defeated in 1815. Two years later they formed the French Agricultural and Manufacturing Society to grow vines and olives on 92,000 acres, provided to them by Congress, on land in present-day Alabama. Whether the congressmen were being soft-hearted or soft-headed is not clear, but there is no evidence that these French immigrants had any previous experience in agriculture. The required skills clearly did not come with the nationality, and perhaps it was misplaced nationalism that led the French to persist with *vinifera* vines and ignore native varietals. In any case, during the ten years of the experiment, the former officers and officials applied to their vines and olives the same competence and flair that had cost them the Empire. By 1828 the vineyard was deserted.[47]

It was a newcomer from Switzerland who is credited with first making wine in substantial quantities in the United States. Jean Jacques Dufour studied the struggling vineyards of the eastern seaboard before deciding to plant his own in Kentucky. In 1799 he set up a joint stock company, the Kentucky Vineyard Society, and planted 10,000 vines representing thirty-five varieties in what he called First Vineyard. Although the vines flourished initially, most succumbed in their third year to black rot, mildew and perhaps other diseases as well. Dufour noticed that two of the varieties – both native hybrids even though Dufour believed they were *vinifera* varieties – had survived. He replanted with them, but again they began to wither.

Apparently convinced that location was the problem, Dufour obtained land in Indiana Territory, at a community that would eventually be known (after the Swiss wine-producing commune, Vevey) as Vevay. A number of Dufour family members emigrated from Switzerland to work the vines in this Second Vineyard, and by 1808 they were producing 800 gallons of wine a year. Production rose steadily and peaked at 12,000 gallons with the 1820 vintage. There is disagreement as to the quality of the wine and confusion about its benchmark. Dufour had boasted that the Ohio River, on which his vineyard was located, would soon rival the Rhine and the Rhône, but when the wine was made its makers advertised it as 'superior to the common Bordeaux claret'. Other palates disagreed, but whatever its merits, Dufour's wine did sell commercially. It fetched $2 a gallon in Cincinnati but could be bought for half that at the winery door.[48]

Indiana was also the site of the vineyard cultivated by the inhabitants of New Harmony, a utopian community established by German immigrants on the banks of the Wabash River in the early 1800s. After trying but failing with German varietals like riesling and sylvaner, they succeeded in producing wine for sale from hybrids. By 1824 the vineyards covered twelve acres and the red wine was said to be locally popular, although outsiders' descriptions of this 'Wabaschwein' pronounced it as having a 'strange taste', lacking body and tasting insipid.

These early vineyards, among the first successful such enterprises in the United States, established the Indiana-Ohio-Kentucky area as a leader in American viticulture. When the 1860 census reported on wine production in the United States, it set total national production at 1.6 million gallons. The census probably understated the volume of wine being produced in California at that time, but it attributed 568,000 gallons, more than a third of the nation's wine production, to Ohio, with another 180,000 gallons to Kentucky-Indiana. The region, no longer so readily associated with wine, thus accounted for close to half the wine reported in the United States in 1860.[49]

Location was not really the obstacle to successful viticulture and wine-making during the first decades of the Republic. Rather, it was the tendency of successive wine-makers to re-invent the wheel, oenologically speaking. Each aspiring wine-maker, it seems, had to plant *vinifera* vines first and have them fail before trying with hybrids or native varietals. Some pioneers, as we have seen, did not move to the second stage and simply gave up when their *vinifera* vines withered. It was a not unreasonable decision on some levels, because there was an entrenched sense of cultural inferiority in American wine-drinking society that abhorred the very idea of drinking wine made from anything but *vinifera* varietals. When one wine-maker was urged by President Jefferson to pursue his work with a native grape, he replied that Americans were not ready for such wine. As soon as they learned that it was made from native grapes, he said, they found fault with it, even though they might have been praising it until then.[50]

The wine-maker in question was John Adlum, who is credited with having demonstrated that good wine could be made with native grapes.

The varietal was the catawba, probably a *labrusca–vinifera* hybrid, and it was catawba wine that Jefferson described in 1809 as comparable to a chambertin. Adlum's later wines were far less reputable. He planted a vineyard in Georgetown in the District of Columbia in 1816 where he made a wine he called 'Tokay'. It contained some brandy, and Adlum was alleged also to add juice from wild grapes now and again.

Yet despite mediocre practical achievements, Adlum became a recognized authority on making wine from non-*vinifera* grapes. In 1823 he published *A Memoir on the Cultivation of the Vine in America, and the Best Mode of Making Wine*. Some of its advice, such as fermenting at almost boiling point, was less than helpful, but the essential theme of the book – that good wine could be made with native grapes – was important. Until American viticulturists learned this lesson, their efforts to make wine were bound to be attended by more failure than success.

Southern states also contributed to the development of American wine in the first half of the nineteenth century, but on the whole their successes were few and small. In the 1820s the legislatures of South Carolina and Georgia received petitions for assistance to establish vineyards as a way to help their sagging agricultural economies. They showed more restraint than some of the northern and the federal legislatures, however, and probably saved the region's taxpayers money.

Individually, the various attempts to make wine in the first decades of the nineteenth century were modest. A survey in 1825 listed sixty vineyards with a total of 600 acres throughout the United States. Another survey five years later showed 200 vineyards covering 5,000 acres. Such a leap in five years seems unlikely, but the general trends were right: that as the century progressed more vineyards were planted than failed. Moreover, the size of vineyards expanded, as is suggested by the average size of 10 acres in 1825 and 25 acres in 1830. With size came economies of scale and the potential to develop financially viable wineries.

One of the first commercial producers was Nicholas Longworth, who from the early 1840s made wine from his catawba vines on the Ohio river near Cincinnati. Longworth's still whites became popular, but what promoted him to commercial success was his sparkling wine. In the best tradition of the Dom Pérignon story, Longworth made the first batch of sparkling wine by accident, but after years of experimentation he began to turn out considerable volumes, all made by what was then the new (and was to become known as the 'traditional') method. Longworth experienced many of the same problems as wine-makers in Champagne itself. In one year 42,000 of 50,000 bottles undergoing second fermentation exploded, although Longworth collected the spilled wine and distilled it into brandy.

In time the problems were solved and Longworth's sparkling catawba shared the market with the French champagnes that were imported in increasing volumes to the United States. The wine list of one Cincinnati hotel showed Longworth's at $2 a bottle, the same price as Heidsieck and a little less expensive than Mumm ($2.50). In the section devoted to 'Hocks', this wine list offered white wines made from catawba grapes at $1.50 a bottle, less than a Rudesheimer at $3 a bottle. For comparative purposes we might note that the hotel was selling Château Lafite at $3 a bottle.[51]

Cincinnati's wine-drinkers rallied to the wines of Longworth and other producers, and they found support in other markets as well. Samples were sent to the 1851 Great Exhibition in London, and even though wines were not permitted to be exhibited, the catalogue mentioned them with equivocal approval. 'With many persons,' the catalogue said, 'the taste . . . is very soon acquired, with others it requires considerable time.'[52] Three years later, on home ground at the New York Exhibition, Longworth's Isabella sparkling wine won unqualified praise and took the award for the best American wine.

Thanks to Longworth and other producers in the region, the area around Cincinnati became the heart of the American wine industry in the 1850s, to the extent that by 1860 almost a third of the nation's wine was made in Ohio. Already in that decade, however, vineyards were succumbing to a variety of diseases, notably black rot and mildews, whose causes growers did not understand and which they were therefore unable to prevent or cure. The social and political dislocation of the Civil War, which broke out a few years later, compounded the difficulties already faced by wine-makers in the region and slowed the growth of the young industry.

War did not inhibit the wine industry everywhere in the United States, however, and during the 1860s wineries flourished in some of the viticultural regions of New York state. The first vineyard in the Finger Lakes area, the Pleasant Valley Wine Company, began operations in 1860 and by 1864 was producing 30,000 gallons of sparkling wine. Wine regions developed on Long Island, on the banks of the Hudson River and along the south shore of Lake Erie.

North of New York State, some of the Canadian colonies were also beginning to produce small quantities of wine. The first known wine was made by Johann Schiller, a retired German soldier, near Toronto as early as 1811. The vine stock was probably obtained from Pennsylvania, and Schiller made no more than enough for his own and perhaps his neighbours' requirements. In the 1860s, however, his property was bought by Count Justin M. de Courtenay, who formed a company and sold wine under the Clair House label. De Courtenay had made wine earlier in Lower Canada (Québec) but it had not been well received and he moved to Upper Canada (Ontario). Clair House was more successful (or Ontario drinkers less discriminating), and samples were exhibited in 1867 in Paris. A Toronto newspaper reported that the French judges had found them similar to beaujolais, and added misleadingly (probably counting on its readers' ignorance) that beaujolais 'is known to be the best [wine] in France'.[53]

A number of vineyards sprang up on Pelee Island in Lake Erie, now a designated Ontario wine district. One vineyard was planted with catawba vines in the 1860s to supply an Ohio winery, but from 1893 it also provided grapes for the sweet wine made by a Canadian company, Brights. In 1866 three Kentucky investors formed a company called Vin Villa, the first commercial winery on Pelee Island, and it was followed by others soon after. The major Ontario wine district, on the Niagara Peninsula, developed more slowly, although there were 5,000 acres of vineyard by 1900. The vines were mainly concord, which is not versatile as a wine grape, and much of the product was grown for fresh fruit and later juice and jellies. In 1868 the concord was crossed with another variety to produce what was called the niagara grape, and in the 1880s it was extensively planted in Ontario to make white wine.

By 1890 there were thirty-five wineries in Ontario and six in other parts of Canada, including Québec and British Columbia. In the western part of the country, the Okanagan Valley in British Columbia was the site of the vineyard planted by the Oblate religious order.[54] By the turn of the century Canada's was a fledgling wine industry that was impeded, like much of that in the eastern United States, by reliance on varietals that were generally difficult to make into anything but mediocre wine.

In many regions of North America, whether in Ontario or the southern US states, enthusiasm and optimism were greater than the immediate prospects of viticultural success. During the late 1850s the American South had experienced a veritable planting mania. A Southern Vine Growers' Convention was formed, and it even called a meeting of all vine-growers in the United States to discuss common problems. Although largely ignored by northerners (this was on the eve of the Civil War), the Convention met and discussed a number of the problems at the heart of the developing American industry. It called for a clearer categorization of varietals, for example, and a new system of labelling wines. Most American wines at that time were labelled by varietal, but the Convention proposed labelling, in descending order, by state, specific location and grower. The optimism and national vision that motivated the Convention faded with the southern wine industry. Georgia, where wine production declined after the war, was typical among southern states.

Far off to the west, however, a wine industry emerged from a history that was quite independent of the viticultural traditions of the eastern half of the United States. Unlike the succession of British, French, Swiss, German, Dutch and other immigrants who fretted over their withering *vinifera* vines in the east, the Spanish Jesuits had cultivated the *vinifera* varietal that became known as 'mission' and successfully made wine in commercial quantities. As Spain's colonial power declined, Mexico won independence in 1821, and parts of its northern territory – including what became New Mexico, Texas and California – were eventually annexed by the United States. These regions therefore entered the union with a tradition of viticulture and instantly became its oldest wine-producing regions.

In the southwest, Spain's New Mexico province held much promise for viticulture. The wine from the El Paso region (widely known as 'Pass Wine') had a good reputation, and when the territory was annexed by the United States in 1848 many of the first administrators regarded wine as the key to the region's economic prosperity. Vines had been the only revenue-producing crop while the province was in Spanish hands, and praise for El Paso wines was often unbridled. One soldier from an 1846 expedition wrote that they were 'superior, in richness of flavor and pleasantness of taste, to anything of the kind I ever met with in the

United States, and I doubt not that they are far superior to the best wines ever produced in the valley of the Rhine, or on the sunny hills of France.' A military surveyor reported that El Paso wines 'compared favorably with the richest Burgundy'.[55] But demands that the US government tap this viticultural wealth found no response in Washington, and the vineyards of what is now Texas and New Mexico declined, to be revived commercially only in the late twentieth century.

In California wine-making was linked primarily to the mission stations, but because they made far more wine than was needed for religious purposes they sold to the local market and might even have exported their wine by coastal shipping to South America. Actual production volumes are not known with any certainty, but it is thought that in the 1820s the important San Gabriel mission, located near Los Angeles, had 170 acres of vines and produced about 35,000 gallons of wine a year. Much of this was distilled into brandy, but San Gabriel also made two red wines (one dry and one sweet) and two whites, one of them fortified. The mission also made a beverage known as 'angelica' (after the nearby town) by adding brandy to unfermented or barely fermenting must and producing something similar to mistelle.

During the mission period southern California, especially the Los Angeles region, was far more important than the north, but even the south's fledgling wine industry was threatened when in 1833 the Mexican government adopted a policy of secularizing the vineyards. In protest the Jesuits adopted a scorched-earth policy with truly biblical overtones, and ripped out most of their vines. Those vineyards that survived suffered years of neglect so that, for all practical purposes, mission wine had disappeared by the middle of the century. Wine production continued in the region, however, because some commercial wine-making by secular proprietors had begun before the mission vineyards were destroyed. Several entrepreneurs established vineyards around Los Angeles, still a tiny community, and by the 1830s (when the mission vineyards declined) they were cultivating between 50 and 100 acres. The first winery to operate on a commercial basis was set up by a French immigrant with the apt name Jean-Louis Vignes. A native of Bordeaux and from a family of coopers, Vignes clearly knew what he was doing, and by 1840 he was not only producing wine and brandy from thirty-five acres of vines, but even sold some in Santa Barbara and San Francisco. Vignes's vines were predominantly of the mission variety, although he also experimented with other European grapes.[56]

Vignes was followed by other wine-makers, and by 1850 a veritable industry based on Los Angeles had sprung up. The town's population was still under 2,000, but it boasted some hundred vineyards that were clearly exporting beyond the locality. One producer, Matthew Keller, is reputed to have become the first American wine millionaire, and even if that is an exaggeration it is suggestive of the potential profitability of California wine. But Keller and others ran into problems of overproduction and quality. There were no regulations or quality controls on wine. When Keller asked his wine-maker in 1878 how a certain sherry had been made, he was informed: 'All I know about it now is that it was made of white wine, Spirits, Grape Syrup, Hickory nut infusion, Quassia, Walnut infusion and Bitter aloes, the proportions I could not tell to save my life. At the time I made it I noted down on *cards* the contents of each vat, so that I could continue to make it if it turned out well, but when I received your letter saying it was no account I tore up the cards.'[57] This was a recipe for neither good wine nor long-term commercial success.

Companies were set up in the 1850s not only to produce their own wine but also to buy from other vineyards and distribute California wines. One was Sainsevain Brothers, owned by the nephews of Jean-Louis Vignes who had bought their uncle's business. They attempted to diversify by making a sparkling wine, but it was a poorly conceived venture and led to the decline of their business. In contrast, Kohler & Frohling, a company founded by two Germans, flourished. They not only made wine from other vineyards under contract, but also controlled the picking and crushing so as to ensure quality through the whole process. Kohler and Frohling introduced new varieties to southern California and began to wean the industry from its almost exclusive reliance on the tried-and-trusted mission varietal.

This company's other main achievement was in selling California wine outside California. San Francisco became an important market (it took 130,000 gallons of Los Angeles wine in 1861, for example), but Kohler & Frohling had agents in Boston and New York City and by 1860 were shipping $70,000 worth of wine out of the state. California wines were generally well received in the east, and by the late 1860s almost three quarters of a million gallons of the state's angelica, port and white wine were being consumed there.[58] This success unnerved the producers of Ohio and New York, and they accused the Californians of adulterating their wines, using fraudulent labels, and even passing off eastern American wine as Californian.

The wine boom in southern California was echoed by another in the north of the territory in the 1850s when vineyards began to proliferate in the Sonoma and Napa valleys. Impetus to the development of viticulture there was provided by the discovery of gold, which inflated California's non-native population from about 14,000 in 1848 to 224,000 in 1852. The Gold Rush was quickly followed by a Grape Rush, as many prospectors turned their properties, which had proved free of gold, into vineyards. They included John Sutter, the Swiss whose discovery of gold had sparked the Gold Rush. An idea of the planting frenzy is given by the number of vines in Santa Clara County: 30,000 in 1855, 150,000 in 1856 and 500,000 in 1857.

Many of the proprietors of the new vineyards had no more experience as wine-makers than they had had as prospectors, and they seemed headed for the same success in wine as in gold. Many were undoubtedly saved from ruin by the California State Agricultural Society, which dispatched visiting committees to vineyards. In a short time the valleys north of San Francisco were producing volumes of creditable wine and planting a range of European varieties that had not been planted in vineyards around Los Angeles. At the Thompson brothers' vineyard in the Napa Valley, for example, some forty-five different varietals were being propagated by the late 1850s. Within a decade the northern California vineyards overtook those in the south. In part the reasons were better climate and soil, but the fact that the Napa and Sonoma valleys were close to the large San Francisco market was also important. Southern California wines, made more expensive by the costs of transportation, began to lose ground in this important market.

Even so, it would be a mistake to think that northern California wine was an excellent product at this time. It received very mixed reviews, and even those who praised it recognized the need for improvement. To this end the governor of California struck a three-man commission in 1861 to examine the best ways of encouraging quality viticulture in the territory. One of the commissioners, a Hungarian immigrant called Agoston Haraszthy, has often been called the father of Californian wine-making. Haraszthy was a volatile entrepreneur who planted vineyards in Wisconsin and other parts of California before settling in Sonoma. His Buena Vista vineyard was substantial, having 14,000 vines and another 12,000 in its nursery in 1857, and his wines won prizes at state fairs. But although Haraszthy's achievements were not inconsiderable, he was no great innovator. Despite frequent claims, he did not bring superior varietals to California and he was not responsible for introducing the zinfandel vine which is now so closely identified with the region.[59]

As the nineteenth century drew to a close, California produced more and more wine and the north consolidated its dominance over the south. There was a short-lived revival of vineyards around Los Angeles as investors hoped to profit from the phylloxera epidemic that seemed about to force Europe to import wine. But the vines of southern California were afflicted by their own disease which put an end to many ventures, some of which were already facing financial problems. Instead of cultivating grapes for wine, many southern California farmers turned to growing them for raisins. Although wine never disappeared from the southern region, it found itself eclipsed by the north.

At the turn of the century California's wine industry was well established, but it was largely in the hands of many relatively small-scale proprietors. There had been attempts by entrepreneurs to start gigantic enterprises, but most had failed. In the 1880s Leland Stanford, a former governor of the state and founder of Stanford University, planted thousands of acres of vines at his Vina Ranch on the Sacramento river. He installed irrigation, imported wine-makers from France, and constructed presses and storage facilities, but the results were disappointing. Although some Vina wine was made, most was distilled into brandy, and even though that was reputed to be as good as cognac, the whole venture was a failure in Stanford's eyes.[60] Instead of being dominated by large-scale enterprises, Californian wine-making remained dispersed among one or two hundred producers who drew grapes from about 750 vineyards.

These grapes were largely unchanged from earlier in the century, too. Mission was the predominant variety for red wines – although zinfandel was increasingly used for better-quality reds – and chasselas was the main white. Other varieties were beginning to make their mark, however, and more certain vine identification and classification helped, although many vines labelled riesling were probably not the genuine article. None the less, California wines exhibited at the 1893 Columbus Exposition in Chicago included riesling, cabernet, semillon, barbera and malbec. By the late nineteenth and early twentieth century the sweet wines that had predominated in the earlier 1800s had given way to dry styles, even though sweet wines still accounted for 40 per cent of the total as late as 1910.

The volume of wine produced in California shot up at the turn of the century. Production varied from year to year, of course, but the trend was clear. The state produced 10 million gallons of wine in 1880, 18 million gallons in 1886, 44 million gallons in 1902, 31 million gallons in 1905 and 45 million gallons in 1910.[61] The bulk of it was consumed in California itself as wine or brandy. Although export markets opened up in the east as well as in South America, the Pacific and England, they accounted for only about 5 per cent of production by 1900. The obstacles to exporting included the costs of transportation and the risks of wine being spoiled as it crossed the United States by train. Wine-drinkers in the eastern states could buy European wines at roughly the same price as Californian, and the Californian wine-makers failed to develop a market for their higher-quality wines.

The California Wine Authority, established in 1894 to consolidate production and marketing, began to sell wines under its Calwa label, and it had some success despite losing ten million gallons of wine and its building during the 1906 San Francisco earthquake. It sold a variety of fortified wines and table wines (including a red sparkling wine). Harrods, the exclusive London store, advertised a Calwa zinfandel as 'most wholesome and bloodmaking', a description that was probably compelling at the time.

Its wine might have been healthy, but California's wine industry was by then starting to feel the effects of change in the status of wine in the United States. Per capita wine consumption, which had peaked at a little over half a gallon a year in 1880, was down to a third of a gallon in 1900. Rather than being regarded as healthy, wine was associated in some quarters with illness. An 1897 article on 'popular errors' in living complained that Americans ate too much: '. . . the anteprandial cocktail, the stimulus afforded the appetite by a bottle of good wine . . . [result in] the consumption of an amount of food that simply overwhelms the assimilative organs.'[62] This was part of a shift of opinion – medical as well as lay – against the belief that wine was a healthy drink with therapeutic properties. Even more dangerous to wine was the rise of the prohibition movement, which was far more of a threat than the temperance movement. The latter had been generally tolerant of wine, but the prohibitionists reviled wine as much as any alcohol. Worse, they eventually succeeded in having Prohibition enacted in state after state and eventually, in 1920, throughout the country.

One sign of impending change was the invention and growing popularity of grape juice. Drawing on scientific work on fermentation, Dr Thomas Welch discovered that by heating freshly pressed grape juice to 140° Fahrenheit he could kill the wild yeasts and prevent any fermentation from taking place. Grape juice was marketed as a safe alternative to wine and, to add insult to injury, it was sold in the US in burgundy bottles as 'Dr Welch's Unfermented Wine'. In Great Britain, where Welch hoped to attract port-drinkers, grape juice bore the label, 'Unfermented Port Wine'. By 1907, a million gallons of grape juice were being sold each year in the United States.

It was ironic that research designed to improve wine was used to undermine it, but the growing popularity of grape juice and the declining consumption of wine suggested underlying weakness in the apparently robust American wine industry. Within a few years it, and the alcohol industry generally, had proved unable to prevent the Prohibition movement from achieving its goal of legislating the end of commercial wine-making, brewing and distilling in the United States.

In the New World wineries of the southern hemisphere, producers battled with different problems, prominent among them their sheer distance from major markets. In the early nineteenth century the colonial dominance of Spain and Portugal in Latin America waned and the wine industries they had promoted found themselves in a new political environment. There was little effect in Peru and Chile, where the Spanish had allowed virtually unrestricted viticulture because they could not guarantee successful shipping of Spanish wine that far. It was a different situation in Mexico, where restrictions had been imposed so as to protect as much of the colonial market as possible for Spanish wines. Instructions periodically transmitted from Madrid, to the effect that new vines should not be planted in Mexico and that existing vines should be ripped up, were widely ignored. None the less the policy had a dampening effect on Mexico's own wine industry.

For similar reasons virtually no wine was produced in Brazil in the colonial period. Apart from in a few regions, Brazil's climate is unsuitable for viticulture, but what might have been attempted was deterred because the Portuguese colonial authorities wanted to ensure an export market for domestic wines. In the late eighteenth century these restrictions were intensified and Portuguese wine-producers were granted monopolies over the supply of wine to Brazil. The Douro region, for example, was given exclusive access to the wealthy Rio de Janeiro market, although only second-quality wines were exported there.[63] The effect of this policy was to raise the price of wine to five times its price in Portugal, and disputes over wine policy were part of the general conflict between local politicians and Lisbon that eventually led to Brazil's independence.

Chile and Peru, the largest Latin American producers in the early 1800s, relied mainly on the mission grape that the Spanish had planted everywhere along the west coast of the Americas where grapes would grow. Wine-makers in both countries were producing what by most accounts were respectable wines (and a great deal of brandy), and quite reasonably they saw no need to change their grapes or their methods. The first signs of change came in 1851 when a Chilean landowner, Silvestre Ochagavia Errazuriz, planted a variety of French vines in his vineyard south of Santiago. They included merlot, cabernet sauvignon, malbec, sauvignon blanc and riesling, the varietals that were to become the basis of Chile's modern wine industry.

On the other side of the Andes in Argentina, wine remained a small business based on the mission grape. From mid century, Italian immigrants helped to introduce European varietals, and the important Mendoza region was replanted with European vines in the late 1800s. Even there, however, viticulture remained fairly marginal, and until it was linked by rail in the 1880s Mendoza's wine-producers were isolated from their most obvious markets.

Overall, Latin American vineyards developed steadily but unspectacularly during the nineteenth century. Because of persistent difficulties shipping wine by sea over long distances they made little impact on the wider wine world, although they were mentioned in contemporary surveys of wine. Cyrus Redding's encyclopedic work praised Latin American wines in general, although it is clear that he relied on the accounts of others for his assessments. Argentinian wines, he wrote, were promising whenever owners paid attention to cultivation, and at Mendoza a 'very good second-class wine' was made. Redding also praised Chilean and Peruvian wines, noting that 'those of Chili [sic] are thought the best, the muscadine being remarkably good'.[64] Another guide, however, placed most Latin American wines on a narrow spectrum of mediocrity, listing them as common (Bolivia), middling (Brazil and Paraguay) and ordinary (Buenos Aires, Chile, Cuba and Plata (Uruguay)). Peru's wines were given a comparative accolade: 'good'.[65]

Across the Pacific Ocean in Australia, viticulture had made hardly any impact by the end of the eighteenth century, but during the first decades of the nineteenth the foundations were established for what has become one of the world's influential wine producers. The beginnings, like those in many other regions, were not promising. For some time attempts to grow vines were only marginally successful, and the little wine that was made was inauspicious. In 1801 two French prisoners of war were put in charge of a vineyard at Parramatta, near what is now downtown Sydney. They planted 12,000 vines and in 1803 made their first wine, but it was considered so poor that the governor of the colony concluded that the prisoners knew little of vines or wine.[66] It is not clear whether they had falsely claimed to be wine-makers, whether the authorities had assumed from their nationality that they must know about wine, or whether they were indeed capable wine-makers working with the wrong grapes in difficult circumstances.

It was in light of this and earlier failures that in 1803 a Sydney newspaper published the first Australian article on viticulture. It gave advice on viticulture and wine-making, but it was clearly no more than a translation of a European article. There was so little awareness of viticulture that none of those who translated, edited and typeset the article remembered that the seasons in the Southern Hemisphere were different from those in the Northern, and so the article recommended pruning vines in January and February – mid-winter in Europe, but summer months in Australia.

The first wine-maker to produce on what might be called a commercial basis was Gregory Blaxland, who by 1816 was making wine from pinot noir and pinot meunier grapes. The Royal Society of Arts in London, the same body that encouraged American viticulture, offered a medal for the best wine of at least twenty gallons made from grapes grown in New South Wales, and in 1822 Blaxland entered his wines. They were awarded a silver medal and grudging approval, but when he submitted another batch of wine six years later it was judged 'decidedly better', and he was awarded a gold.[67]

Australian wine was boosted in the 1820s by the arrival of James Busby. Busby was a wine enthusiast who had toured vineyards in France before going to Australia and who established vineyards in New South Wales. He might or might not have produced wine (the evidence is unclear), but no one worked harder at that time to promote viticulture in the young colony. In 1831 Busby returned to Europe and toured the wine regions of Spain and France, collecting vine samples and information. The vines – in all he brought 362 different varietals back to Australia – were planted in Sydney's Botanical Gardens. He disseminated his knowledge in an influential 1833 work, *Journal of a Tour through Some of the Vineyards of France and Spain*.

On a more practical note, Busby took ten gallons of some Australian wine with him to England, half in a small cask and half in bottles. Some of the bottled wine had spoiled by the time it reached its destination, possibly because the bottles had not been washed thoroughly, but the cask wine made the trip safely. Some was served at a dinner given by a 'very eminent Oporto wine merchant', who reported that it resembled burgundy. Busby brought some of the wine back to Australia and found it 'perfectly sound ... a well flavoured and strong-bodied wine'.[68] To any Australian wine-maker who dreamed of supplying the European market, it was very good news to learn that Australian wine could travel around the world and be none the worse for it.

Busby helped establish the foundations of viticulture in New South Wales, and in the 1830s vineyards sprang up around Sydney and further north in the Hunter Valley. The names of some of the pioneers grace labels today. By 1836 George Wyndham was producing 7,000 litres of wine and in the 1840s Dr Henry Lindeman was planting his first vines. Viticulture quickly became established as a minor form of agriculture in New South Wales. By 1850 there were more than a thousand acres of vineyards, half of them in the Hunter Valley. Even so, it was a commercially marginal industry. Wine was expensive in relation to other kinds of alcohol, and the social make-up of the colony included few members of the classes associated with wine-drinking. Rum, gin, brandy and beer were far more popular.

As the other Australian colonies were founded, vineyards were soon planted in them. A few dotted Tasmania, but they declined during the nineteenth century and experienced a renaissance only in the last decades of the twentieth. Viticulture was much more extensive in Victoria, where it would later be boosted by a number of Swiss immigrants. More than 150 acres were in vines by 1850, some around what is now Melbourne and others in the Yarra Valley to the north. Vines were planted in far-off Western Australia, too. The first wine was made in 1834, but the local market was limited and viticulture remained a minor activity until the rest of Australia discovered the products of the Margaret River region.

In South Australia, however, things moved much more quickly. Vines were planted around Adelaide within months of the colony's being settled in the 1830s, and by 1840 the first commercial vineyard had been planted from cuttings of the vines James Busby had brought from France and Spain. There is some debate as to who actually made the first South Australian wine – a matter of some importance because of the prominence of the state's wine now – but we do know who exported wine first: one Walter Duffield, who daringly sent a case of his Echunga Hock to Queen Victoria in 1845.[69]

Another of Australia's great names, Dr Christopher Penfold, arrived in South Australia in the 1840s and set up a medical practice on his estate, which he called 'The Grange'. He brought with him vine cuttings from southern France, including many of the grenache variety. These he planted and made into wine, but initially he provided the wine only to his patients and on prescription. Wine is rich in iron and was the perfect remedy for the anaemia that many poor immigrants developed on the voyage from Europe to Australia. That same decade, a pivotal one for Australian viticultural history, saw Lutherans from Silesia settle the Barossa Valley to the north of Adelaide. Among the important events was the planting of Rhine riesling vines by an immigrant, Johann Gramp, at his property on Jacob's Creek. Vineyards soon spread throughout the

Barossa Valley, sustained by a steady flow of immigrants and by the development of a strong local market for the wine.

But this market was exceptional, and it was partly the more general lack of interest in their product at home that probably motivated some Australian wine-producers to publicize their wines in Europe. European wines were also the benchmark against which all wines were judged, and praise by European connoisseurs must have been the ultimate goal of any antipodean wine-maker. Some took advantage of the great industrial and agricultural exhibitions to display their wares. The first, the Great Exhibition held in London in 1851, did not, as noted above, permit the exhibition of wines, but either through ignorance or in the hope that it would be displayed despite the prohibition, some wine was sent from vineyards at Camden, in the Hunter Valley. The exhibition catalogue cited the ban on alcohol to explain why 'the specimens sent over are not found in this collection', but it none the less devoted considerable space to a description of the vineyards and the techniques of viniculture:

One of these is a hogshead from the first vineyard, made from a grape, imported from France called 'La Folle,' mixed to the extent of about one-third with another sort from Madeira, called the 'Verdeilho' ... In the process of manufacture the grapes were crushed by being passed through a machine of simple construction, which reduces them thoroughly without bruising the stalks ... The wine was fermented in large vats of hewn stone containing from 800 to 1,600 gallons ... It was then drawn off into large store casks, containing 400 gallons ...

The exhibition catalogue also described the taste of the wines, which suggests that even if the samples were not exhibited, they did not go to waste. They were said to have 'A certain dryness and bitterness peculiar to the wines of New South Wales, to which the palate becomes accustomed; but with age this bitterness passes off.' The catalogue suggested keeping the wines at least three years before drinking, and concluded its tasting notes with the supercilious comment that the wines 'are very wholesome, and are extensively used by persons who have acquired a taste for them'.[70]

Australian wine-makers had more success in Paris four years later. Wines were prominent at the Universal Exhibition of 1855, not least because the French wanted to demonstrate their pre-eminence in an endeavour that was attracting more and more participants. Like other New World wines, Australia's had to fight a European assumption that only European (and often only French) wines could achieve standards of excellence. At the 1873 Vienna Exhibition the French judges, tasting blind, praised some wines from Victoria but withdrew in protest when the provenance of the wine was revealed, on the grounds that wines of that quality must clearly be French. At the Bordeaux International Exhibition a number of Hunter Valley wines won gold medals, but their brilliance was dulled by faint praise. The best Australian red wines were not thought to be as good as the best or even the ordinary wines of France, and judges commented that they were good raw material that could easily be improved.[71]

Even so, Australian wines continued to win high honours in French competitions, and this should have told their producers something. The aroma of a Victorian syrah exhibited at the 1878 Paris Exhibition was likened to Château Margaux and its fullness compared to good burgundy. 'Its taste completed its trinity of perfection.'[72] At the 1882 Bordeaux International Exhibition one Australian wine won a gold medal 'first class', and at the 1889 Paris International Exhibition another won a gold medal 'against the world'.[73] At this time Australian wine-makers accepted not only that French wines were the best in the world, but also that the aim of non-French wine-makers should be to make wines in the same style as the French and other European wines. Little if any thought was given to developing new names for the distinctive wines, and they were called 'burgundy', 'bordeaux', 'hock' and 'sherry'. It would be a hundred years before New World styles were accepted in their own right in the New World itself, and even longer before the European names were abandoned in favour of varietal descriptions.

In the second half of the century, wine production in the Australian colonies soared. For example, the Bendigo region of Victoria had 50 hectares of vineyards producing 6,825 litres of wine in 1861, nearly 200 hectares and 53,000 litres eight years later, and about 220 hectares yielding 275,000 litres by 1880. By then about a hundred wineries were operating in the region. Two of South Australia's main wine regions were developed in the later nineteenth century. By the mid 1880s Thomas Hardy had planted more than 600 hectares in McLaren Vale and was producing almost half a million litres of wine a year. Soon after, the more isolated Coonawarra region was being planted. Starting with twenty-six vineyards originally planted in 1891, the region quickly attracted wine-makers.

Australia's wine industry and culture also began to mature. For example, an association of Hunter River vineyards was formed in 1847. Despite the fact that French, German and Swiss immigrants played such an important role in the development of the early wine industry in Australia, many of the pioneer wine-makers were British, and to some extent the Hunter River association aimed to overcome their cultural inexperience: 'We happen to have emigrants from a country which does not produce wine; our knowledge of its growth and manufacture, therefore, is only the result of our reading and limited experience in this.'[74] The association would allow wine-makers to share information and hold exhibitions, and it seems to have achieved its aims. A consensus developed that syrah and semillon vines were most suitable for the region, and the first wine show was held in Sydney in 1850.

Wine-making techniques evolved, too. Wine was a cottage-industry product early in the 1800s. Grapes were destemmed by hand, crushed by foot and fermented in open vats. By the last decades of the century large presses were being used and the must was being cooled in order to control fermentation in the often warm Australian autumn. American oak staves were imported by the thousand and barrels assembled in Australia. Seppelt's winery alone kept six to ten coopers employed full-time making barrels for the millions of litres of wine produced in the Barossa Valley by the end of the century.

The success of the Australian wine industry depended, of course, on markets. Most of the Hunter Valley production (which reached 273,000 litres by 1860) was sold in the locality, but in the 1860s attempts were made to market the wine in the potentially large Sydney market. It was the development of wine-drinking in the urban areas that enabled the New South Wales wine region to develop as quickly as it did. By 1895 some four million litres of wine were made in the colony, the bulk of it also consumed there. In South Australia the leading edge of marketing was dominated by the Thomas Hardy company. By the 1880s Hardy had opened a wine bar where lunch, consisting of a sandwich and a glass of chilled claret, could be had for five pence. In 1893 the corporate presence of Hardy's, the largest South Australian producer at over

1,750,000 litres in 1895, was marked by a massive (for the time) head-quarters in Adelaide that housed a laboratory, blending vats, storage for more than a third of a million litres of wine and stables for the horses and carts used to transport the wine.

By then, Hardy's was exporting considerable quantities of red wine to Great Britain.[75] They and other Australian wine exporters were able to benefit from faster steam ships that exposed their freight to the damaging effects of travel and heat for shorter periods. Wine was part of a broader commerce in food that developed in this period: as early as 1881, frozen meat was shipped from New Zealand to Britain.

By the turn of the century, Australia's vineyards were producing twelve million litres of wine a year and the industry seemed to be thriving. In 1901, however, when the existing states federated to form modern Australia, the tariff barriers between them fell. South Australia was best placed to take advantage of the new open market, and soon it was flooding the urban markets of Victoria and New South Wales with table wines as well as the increasingly popular fortified wines and brandy. Many smaller wineries, some suffering the effects of phylloxera, sold out to the larger South Australian companies such as Seppelt. Many independent producers survived phylloxera and acquisition by the emerging wine conglomerates, but in the first years of the twentieth century Australia's wine industry was dramatically different from the series of small pioneering enterprises that had been established in the colonies only a few decades earlier.

In Britain's other antipodean colony, New Zealand, wine production was far more sluggish. Grapes were grown in 1819 in the north of the North Island, but it was only in the 1830s that wine is known to have been made. The wine-maker was the oenologically irrepressible James Busby, who emigrated across the Tasman Sea in 1833 and planted vineyards so promptly that he was able to serve his wine to the captain of the French ship *Astrolabe* when it visited New Zealand in 1840. The captain described it as 'a light white wine, very sparkling, and delicious to taste, which I enjoyed very much'.[76] The first resident bishop brought more vines, and Catholic missions began to make wine in the 1840s, as did the residents of Akaroa, a small French settlement in the South Island.

It was in the 1890s, however, that the first signs of wine as a serious activity appeared. The government invited the viticultural adviser to the Victorian government to study viticulture in New Zealand and to comment on its likely success. Following a favourable report, in 1898 the government set up an experimental vineyard at Te Kauwhata to grow different varietals. Even more important was the arrival in New Zealand of large numbers of immigrants from Dalmatia, then part of the Austrian Empire, some of whom had vine-growing experience. At first many were employed digging kauri gum (the hardened resin of the kauri tree), but by the early 1900s they had migrated to the Henderson area, just north of Auckland, which was to be for many years New Zealand's main wine-producing district.[77]

In South Africa, the history of the wine industry was closely linked to politics. The British defeated the Dutch in 1795, and in 1814 a convention in London formally incorporated the Cape Colony, as South Africa was known, into the British Empire. In the first few years of British rule not a great deal changed. There was a general sense that Cape wine was good but that it could be improved, but virtually the only wine exported to England was the exceptional constantia. At a pound a gallon, it was expensive even in South Africa, but it cost much more on the London market. Concern about the quality of ordinary Cape wine crystallized after a group of soldiers died after drinking some that had been adulterated, and the local authorities appointed official wine-tasters for a brief period in the first years of the 1800s.

The position of wine-taster was revived in 1811, when the colony's governor wanted to increase exports of South African wine to Britain by taking advantage of the trade disruptions that resulted from the European wars. The governor sent samples of eight wines and brandies to the Colonial Secretary and urged him to encourage wine production at the Cape so as to provide for the Royal Navy and for British domestic consumption. As a quality control, all export wines had to be submitted to the official taster for his inspection and approval. Wine had to have aged for at least eighteen months before it could be exported. To these controls the government added incentives in the forms of medals for vine-planting and wine quality.

But South African wine did not find a great deal of favour in Britain.

There were complaints by merchants and consumers about its quality, although it is alleged that some of the criticism was organized by parties close to French and Portuguese wine interests. One wine-trade book damned the wine-makers for carelessness. It alleged that harvesting was left to emancipated slaves who failed to separate ripe from unripe fruit and threw everything, stalks, stems and any earth clinging to them, into the vat. No care was taken over fermentation or the vats themselves. It concluded that 'the dogged, obstinate disposition of the Dutch could not be more fully displayed than in their total indifference to the character of their wines.'[78] These Dutch seemed a far cry from their compatriots who earlier had sponsored the development of wines in Europe. The influential Cyrus Redding, however, suggested that the problem lay not with the wine-makers but with shipping. South African red was 'a sound, good wine', he wrote, but asked, 'Who would believe this, from the specimens tasted in England?'[79]

Given the generally jaundiced views of Cape wine, it seems that all that propped up the British export market was its price: South African wine sold relatively inexpensively because it was subject to the low preferential tariffs on goods from the Empire. When the punitive tariffs on French wine were dropped in 1861, the bottom fell out of the market for Cape wines. From the million gallons sold in 1859, Cape wine exports to Britain plummeted to 127,000 gallons in 1861 and just over 30,000 gallons three years later.

This devastating blow forced South African wine-makers to reassess their position. They complained bitterly that because their wines had to travel through warm temperatures to reach Britain they were at high risk of spoilage unless fortified to at least 26° proof. But wine of that strength was saddled with a tariff much higher than French table wine, which in addition cost much less to ship. When the British government refused to budge on tariffs, many Cape wine-growers simply abandoned their vineyards.

Viticulture was given a new lease of life, however, with the discovery of gold and diamonds in the Transvaal and Cape province. New prosperity boosted the domestic demand for wine and brandy, and vineyards began to grow. There had been 13 million vines in 1859 but by 1891 there were 79 million. In the 1880s the government began to take the colony's wine more seriously. An experimental wine farm was set up, foreign experts were hired, and efforts were made to educate wine-makers in basic techniques of hygiene and fermentation. Still, however, the problem of transportation remained, and wine sometimes started fermenting again as it passed through the tropics. The wine shipped to the 1889 Paris Exposition, according to one account, 'did untold injury to the fair name of the Cape Colony as a wine-producing country'.[80]

NINE

A TIME OF TROUBLES

Wine and its Enemies, 1870–1950

Two thirds of the way through the nineteenth century, as the production and consumption of wine were expanding throughout the world and increasing attention was being given to higher-quality wines, the industry ran into a series of crises that left it reeling for almost a century. Phylloxera threatened to destroy almost every vineyard in the world; widespread adulteration and fraud affected wine in many regions; after phylloxera was conquered, overproduction and slumping prices threatened the livelihood of growers; anti-alcohol movements gained strength to the point that in the United States Prohibition was enacted; two world wars drained labour and destroyed export markets; and tariff barriers raised prices while economic depressions reduced demand. No sooner was one challenge overcome, it seemed, than another took its place, and it all added up to what looked like a new dark age for wine.

Of these challenges, the anti-alcohol movement had been growing for many years before it reached its peak in the decades either side of 1900. Concern at the personal and social effects of alcohol had, of course, been voiced as long as alcohol had been available, but it was not until the nineteenth century that an organized movement began to challenge what by then had become an industry. It was in the 1820s that scientists proved that fermented beverages such as wine, beer and cider contained alcohol: until that time it was thought that such drinks included the constituent elements of alcohol, but that alcohol was produced only by distillation, not by fermentation. The discovery that wine contained the same alcohol as rum and brandy, even though in lower quantities by volume, eroded some of the more indulgent views of wine.

Another important milestone was reached in 1849 with the recognition of alcoholism as a medical condition. First described by a Swedish doctor,

Magnus Huss, alcoholism was soon accepted by the medical profession throughout the world as including a wide range of physical and mental symptoms. Alcohol quickly became regarded in a more suspicious light. Not only could morally undisciplined individuals abuse it to become intoxicated more or less frequently, but there were some who had no control at all. Drunkenness might have tragic results for the individual and his or her family, but alcoholism also had additional social consequences. By the early 1900s alcoholism, which had been defined only half a century earlier, was being blamed for many of the problems that faced western societies.

These problems were associated with the huge social and cultural changes that the western world experienced in the nineteenth century: industrialization, the growth of cities, the expansion of the working class with its unions and socialist ideologies. All seemed to threaten the existing social, political and religious order and to bring in their wake epidemics of antisocial behaviour: crime, prostitution, family breakdown and gambling, as well as insanity and suicide. Alcohol was implicated in all. Men were depicted as drinking away scarce family resources in bars before returning home drunk, penniless and abusive, and of using alcohol to seduce women. Alcohol was said to lubricate the slippery slope towards prostitution and to be an active agent leading to insanity, murder and suicide.

Anxiety about the dangers of alcohol and the directions of social change galvanized the anti-drink campaign: by the last decades of the 1900s it was the largest sector of the broad-based movement for social reform that was active in every western country. Within the campaign were two broad streams. One was the teetotal or prohibitionist wing, which campaigned for a total ban on the production, sale and consumption of alcohol. For prohibitionists, all forms of alcohol were an unmitigated evil that was responsible for most of the ills that faced individuals and society. Among their more extravagant allegations were that alcohol made people more vulnerable to cholera and that particularly heavy drinkers were at risk of spontaneous combustion. Temperance literature recorded many eye-witness accounts of drinkers who had died from internal conflagration. Reports described blue flames and smoke bursting from the mouth and nostrils, and in some cases, it was said, no more than the charred remains of these drinkers were found. Readers of some of this literature were assured, among other things, 'that in northern countries flames frequently burst from the stomachs of persons in a state of intoxication'.[1] As sensational as these cases were in highlighting the terrible consequences of drinking, most of the efforts of the anti-alcohol campaigners went to educating the public on the diseases and social scourges that resulted from drinking and to trying to persuade legislators to prohibit the production and sale of alcohol.

The other stream of the anti-alcohol movement comprised the advocates of temperance, represented by mass organizations like the Women's Christian Temperance Union, which campaigned for restrictions on production and sale but allowed the moderate use of alcohol. For them, the main culprits were whisky, rum and other distilled spirits, and they often made exceptions for wine and beer as long as they were not consumed in excessive quantities. This distinction had been established by one of the earliest temperance writers, the American doctor Benjamin Rush. He suggested in the 1780s that if consumed in moderate quantities and with food, wine (or beer or cider) promoted 'cheerfulness, strength, and nourishment'. But excessive consumption of stronger drinks led drinkers first to idleness, then illness, indebtedness and crime, and eventually to death by suicide, disease or execution. Rush implied that while wine could be consumed in moderation, there was something inherent in spirits that led to their being consumed to excess.[2] Hard liquor was treated by nineteenth-century anti-alcohol activists rather as cocaine has been in more recent times.

But even after wine was recognized as alcoholic, most advocates of temperance were tolerant of it, and even some teetotallers, who were in principle absolute abstainers, made a unique if grudging exception for it. Most American temperance societies began by banning only the consumption of 'ardent spirits' while permitting wine in moderation, but some moved quickly to a more inclusive prohibition. Two temperance groups in Virginia forbade their members wine as early as the 1820s when they learned that it contained alcohol. They were also concerned that some of their members were fortifying wine with spirits and even pretending to drink wine by colouring brandy with pink grapefruit juice.[3]

Tolerance of wine, even support of wine-production, was one of the paradoxes of the temperance movement. It is possible, of course, that in places like the United States, where for the most part wine was consumed only by the better-off minority, that the sheer imbalance in rates of consumption of different alcohols seemed to make wine less problematic. All reports suggest that in the first third of the nineteenth century high levels of drinking were common in the United States. The annual per capita consumption of spirits was 7.5 gallons, about three times the 1985 level.[4] In comparison, wine was drunk in small quantities, and drinkers consumed less than 10 per cent of their alcohol in the form of wine.

One clear reason for the special status accorded to wine everywhere was the continuing recognition of its therapeutic or medicinal properties, and a number of fervent supporters of the temperance movement were both doctors and wine-makers. They included Dr Henry Lindeman and Dr Christopher Penfold, both leading lights of the Australian wine industry whose names grace labels today.[5] In America, Dr Benjamin Rush invested in a vineyard as he wrote on the dangers of alcohol. These men were not hypocrites, seeking to profit from what they believed evil; like many supporters of temperance, they thought wine fell into a different category altogether.

So widespread and entrenched was the use of wine by doctors that many prohibitionists had difficulty with this argument. Some made an exception for the consumption of wine for medicinal purposes, when it could be administered in controlled circumstances and on rare occasions. Others, however, refused to believe that alcohol could do anyone any good, and accused doctors of promoting drunkenness in their patients when they prescribed them wine. One wrote that 'the downfall of many a man or woman has dated from the first dose prescribed by a heedless or mercenary physician'.[6]

Beyond the medical argument for treating wine distinctly was its positive role in religion, especially Christianity. Most anti-alcohol campaigners had religious affiliations, and many were able to justify moderate wine-drinking by pointing to biblical example. But this was unacceptable to teetotallers, for whom alcohol was alcohol whatever its form, and they devised ways to explain away the positive references to wine in the Bible. One was to argue that, while the Bible did indeed allow wine in certain cases, the greater knowledge of alcohol provided by nineteenth-century science made the biblical approval obsolete. This was not a widely supported position, because it opened the way to the possibility that other biblical doctrines, like divine creation, might also be discarded in light of modern scientific discoveries. The second major approach to wine was a 'two-wine theory' that postulated that there were actually two different wines in the Bible. One was good and one was bad, with the good wine being not wine at all but unfermented grape juice. This theory must have been made more credible by the appearance of Dr Welch's grape juice, marketed as 'unfermented wine'. A campaign was mounted in England to have the Anglican Church replace wine with unfermented juice at communion, but it was unsuccessful. Even though many clergy supported the anti-alcohol movement, they were unwilling to go so far as to let it interfere with the tradition of serving wine.[7] Some American churches began to use unfermented juice, but by the middle of the century only about 7 per cent of New York congregations had done so. The Methodist Episcopal Church, a leading supporter of temperance, declined to endorse juice until 1880.[8] The Catholic Church, of course, had long ceased providing the laity with wine at communion.

Many of the anti-alcohol movements were active in countries where wine was neither widely consumed nor a major industry. Wine was a minority drink in the United States, Britain, Canada, Australia and New Zealand, and although some of their wine industries were becoming regionally important, they had yet to make an impact nationally. It was in these countries that the temperance lobby was more successful in persuading legislators to restrict the availability of alcohol, including wine. In the major wine-producing countries of Europe, where wine was also much more widely consumed, temperance movements had far less impact, even though they went to great lengths to exclude wine from the scope of their activities.

In France the object of most anti-alcohol agitation was the industrial alcohol produced by distilling grain, sugar beet and other products, a process deemed more artificial and less natural than the alcohol derived from fermenting grapes and other fruit. Industrial alcohol was colourless, odourless and flavourless, making it a perfect base for liqueurs and aperitifs flavoured with herbs and essences. The major attraction of these drinks was that they were less expensive than wine, but the shortage of wine and the spread of adulterated and fraudulent wine as a result of the phylloxera epidemic also helped push drinkers toward such alternative forms of alcohol.[9]

Industrial alcohol became popular just as alcoholism was recognized as a medical condition, and researchers and anti-alcohol campaigners quickly drew a link between the two. Rather than thinking of alcoholism as a long-standing problem that had just been defined or named, doctors thought that it was a new disease. It was confidently asserted by the Académie Française in 1853 that, 'France has many drunkards but, happily, no alcoholics.'[10] Wine and other fruit-based alcohols had been consumed for centuries without producing an epidemic of alcoholism, and they could safely be excused responsibility. The increasing consumption of industrial alcohol was demonstrable, however, and it seemed the obvious explanation for what within a few decades was recognized, even within France, as a plague.

However misleading this link was, it seemed to exculpate wine from responsibility for the worst kinds of social problems. Instead of targeting all forms of alcohol as equally dangerous, French scientists, social commentators and activists focused only on industrial alcohol. Even within that category, some were thought to be worse than others. One was absinthe, a high-alcohol, greenish-coloured beverage flavoured with wormwood that was reported to have had effects that were not so much intoxicating as hallucinogenic.[11] French workers developed a particular affinity for absinthe, and by the 1890s it had displaced beer and brandy to become, after wine, the second most popular drink in Paris.[12]

There was some debate whether there really was any difference between the various forms of alcohol. Chemists reported that alcohol was the same thing whether it was derived from distillation or fermentation or from grain or grapes, and some insisted that in fact industrial alcohol contained fewer impurities than fruit alcohol. But many doctors and hygienists, not to mention the powerful wine lobby, were adamant that fermented fruit alcohol was not only not dangerous but that beverages made from it were healthy and hygienic. Wine was the most common of these drinks, but also included were apple-based calvados and cider, pear-based poiré and brandy made from grapes (notably cognac). Unlike most distilled alcohols, wine and grape-based beverages were portrayed as natural products that embodied their *terroir*, the natural environment in which vines grew. This emphasis on the vine and viticulture, rather than the work of wine-makers in controlling the colour, taste and alcoholic strength of wine, made it seem more a product that emerged effortlessly from nature, unlike the bottles of industrial alcohol that rolled off the production lines of huge, urban distilleries. Fermentation, it was stressed over and over, was a natural process, unlike distillation which was artificial. As it was portrayed by its producers, wine reinforced the late-nineteenth-century trend toward 'natural' foods and drinks that included cereals and grape juice.

Wine was regarded so positively in France that the main temperance organization actually called for an increase in wine-production and for more efforts to ensure that wine was protected from 'adulterations and falsifications that deprive wine of its natural qualities and make it harmful to public health'. In other words, wine was healthy, and it became harmful only when additives, like essences, aromas and industrial alcohol, were used to modify it, a practice that spread during the phylloxera crisis.[13]

Nor was there any doubt, except among the most hard-line teetotallers, that wine possessed health-promoting properties. Wine had traditionally been used as a remedy for all kinds of maladies, but now doctors came to the support of wine in a more scientific way by emphasizing the therapeutic properties of specific wines. In England in 1877, Dr Francis Anstie, editor of the *Practitioner* and a physician in London's Westminster Hospital, published highly detailed instructions for using wine. He criticized his colleagues for dispensing it willy-nilly, without matching wine-type to malady. Levels of alcohol, acid, sugar and ash content made some wines inappropriate for some illnesses, he advised, and doctors should carefully distinguish between strong wines (such as port, sherry and madeira) and light wines that had less than 10 per cent alcohol. Among Anstie's recommendations were old sherry for typhoid fever, burgundy for dyspepsia, port for 'simple anaemia' or anorexia, and a 'generous and potent wine' to help the elderly suffering from sleeplessness and digestive problems. As a general tonic to maintain good health, Anstie recommended a daily intake of half a bottle to a bottle, but he warned against mixing drinks: 'adherence to one drink, and generally one *wine*, is almost a necessity for the purposes of health.'[14] In France, Louis Pasteur's description of wine as 'healthful and hygienic' was widely quoted by the wine industry, and in 1903 the French parliament legally designated wine as a healthy and hygienic beverage.

The medical standing of wine is shown by its having continued to be served in hospitals as part of treatments and convalescent regimens. In a twelve-month period in 1870–71, one hospital in Darmstadt, Germany, went through 4,633 bottles of white and 6,332 bottles of red Rhine wine, 60 bottles of champagne, a few dozen bottles of superior white wine and red bordeaux, and about 30 dozen bottles of port.[15] In 1898 some three million litres of wine were served in Paris hospitals alone.[16] These endorsements underscored the health-giving properties of wine if consumed in moderation. What constituted moderation in wine-drinking was, however, as much debated in the nineteenth century as it had been earlier. One medical writer suggested that an active male might well drink between one and a half and four litres of wine a day (two to five standard bottles). The general sense, however, was that one litre a day was not problematic, as long as it was consumed with food.[17]

But the days of wine as a widely prescribed medicine were numbered. By the turn of the century new drugs and treatments had begun to appear. Painkillers like aspirin, together with a host of sedatives, tranquillizers and antibiotics, entered the medical arsenal. They were the result of scientific research and could be mass-produced by the industrial processes that were both a boon and a threat to wine. More to the point, the new medicines were clinically tested and were often launched on to the market with testimonials, however exaggerated, as to their marvellous curative properties. The value of wine was of a different order. It was 'a harmless stomachic, diuretic, and sedative, gently beneficial in virtually all ailments',[18] and did not stand up to the increasingly rigorous demands of doctors and patients. Like powdered herbs, plants and the other stuff of folk-medicine, wine was pushed off the pharmacy shelf as doctors reached for more modern remedies to cure their patients' ills.

At a time of deepening nationalism, it is not surprising to find French defenders of wine arguing that their product was an expression of the very soil in which the vines grew. One denounced water-drinking in ringing nationalistic terms: 'Young men or sad old men may advocate water as the only healthy drink and hurl anathemas at those who enjoy the pleasures of a glass of old wine or fine cognac. No! In our beautiful France, a country of wine, joy, openness and happy temperament, let us not talk about abstinence. Your water, your Lenten drinks, your Ceylon tea, fig or acorn coffee, your lemonade and camomile, be hanged. You are not only bad hygienists, but bad Frenchmen.'[19] Anti-wine activism was depicted as alien to France. One of the most important teetotal movements, the Croix Bleue, was based in Switzerland, giving rise to the sneering comment that abstainers were 'Geneva clergymen with high collars and skin yellowed from not drinking wine'. Here was a restatement of the old belief that wine gave colour to the complexion.

To most French temperance advocates, as it was to many in other countries, wine was not only not part of the alcohol problem. It was part of the solution. In Australia, Dr Henry Lindeman saw spirits as the cause of alcoholism and wine as an antidote to the malaise, while earlier, in the United States, Thomas Jefferson had argued that 'no nation is drunken where wine is cheap'.[20] Water was not a viable substitute for alcohol. Throughout Europe, France included, few communities had access to adequate supplies of water that were not contaminated by human, animal or industrial waste. If drinkers could be persuaded to switch from industrial alcohol to wine, they would benefit from a pure, natural beverage. Alcoholism would decline, and with it the social ills for which it was blamed.

So entrenched was the denial that wine was a form of alcohol as open to abuse as any other kind, that official French statistics on the consumption of alcohol often omitted wine. Because of the greater consumption of industrial alcohol in the north, the contrast was often made between an alcoholic north and a sober south. Indeed, when wine was left out of calculations, per capita consumption of alcohol in the north was higher, but when wine was factored in the south easily out-consumed the north.

The preference for wine over distilled spirits also reflected class prejudices. Industrial alcohol was less expensive than wine and was therefore popular with workers. Wine was consumed widely in the south of France but in the north (with the exception of Paris) only by the better-off. It is telling that doctors – all middle or upper class – stressed the different physical effects of wine and industrial alcohol. They acknowledged that wine could have harmful effects on the liver but they insisted that industrial alcohol damaged the brain. Industrial alcohol thus contributed to mental and intellectual degeneration and served to reinforce notions of the poor as brutish and stupid. In contrast, liver complaints and ailments such as gout that were attributed to wine had a kind of cachet as manifestations of good living. Even excessive wine-drinking was excused. Wine was said by apologists in France to produce a characteristic

French kind of drunk, one who was witty, vivacious and intelligent. Excessive consumption of other forms of alcohol produced inebriates who were boorish at best and dangerous at worst.

The French temperance and anti-alcohol movements had little influence on government policy, although they achieved a ban on the sale of absinthe in 1914, just before the outbreak of the First World War. But even that ban was justified not so much by any sense of the social or personal consequences of absinthe-drinking as by fear of the effects it might have on military efficiency. The production, sale and consumption of wine were never threatened by French temperance campaigners, but instead it was promoted by them as the cure for the nation's alcohol-related ills.

The impact of temperance campaigns varied immensely from country to country. France and the United States represent its extremes: there was little temperance legislation in France, while in the United States the constitution was amended to prohibit the sale and consumption of alcoholic beverages. In between lay a variety of codes that more or less effectively restricted the availability of alcohol. Sometimes wine was included, sometimes not. As early as 1838 a Massachusetts law tried to deter liquor sales by requiring purchasers of spirits to buy a minimum of fifteen gallons at a time and to take them off the premises; wine was exempted. The German temperance movement actively encouraged the production of wine and beer as alternatives to schnapps, the alcohol considered that country's real problem.[21]

It is the American temperance movement that has attracted most attention from historians because of its astounding success. During the nineteenth century various American states passed laws restricting alcohol in one way or another. There was a wave of legislation from 1851 when Maine prohibited all intoxicating liquors. It was followed in the next four years by twelve states and territories as well as by individual municipalities. When the town of Evanston, Illinois, was founded in 1855, it declared itself 'dry'. But not all the prohibitions were total. For example, Virginia legislated prohibition but allowed residents to purchase limited quantities of beer, spirits or wine (one gallon) a month. Laws did not stop people drinking, of course, and it seems that per capita alcohol consumption actually increased in proportion to rising number of jurisdictions with anti-alcohol laws. As the authorities discovered when prohibition became national in 1920, it was easier to legislate abstinence from alcohol than to enforce it.

From the 1870s, the American prohibition movement went into high gear, with the founding of the National Prohibition Party, the Women's Christian Temperance Union and, in the 1890s, the Anti-Saloon League. By supporting 'dry' candidates at the state level, these societies were able to influence legislation so that by the time the prohibition amendment to the Constitution was passed in 1919, a majority thirty-three of the then forty-eight states had already passed laws prohibiting the alcohol trade – in spirits, beer and wine – within their borders.

The temperance and prohibition movements were thus a more serious threat to the wine industry in the United States than elsewhere. In Europe, anti-alcohol campaigners were regarded like most other pests in the vineyard: annoying, sometimes worrying, but eventually manageable. One of these challenges was presented by widespread powdery mildew (oidium), a fungus native to North America that was found in Europe in the 1840s. Its symptoms are powdery-looking spores on short stalks that infect grapes, preventing them from colouring properly and growing to full size. Not only does oidium reduce yields, but the affected fruit has characteristic off-flavours, and while it did relatively little damage to American vines, it was devastating to *vitis vinifera* varieties like chardonnay and cabernet sauvignon. French vineyards were widely affected in the 1850s and the vintage of 1854 was disastrous, the smallest since 1788. Only after that experience did French wine growers begin to apply sulphur as an effective fungicide.

The outbreak of powdery mildew was bad enough, but it was nothing compared to the phylloxera epidemic that threatened to kill all Europe's vines and wipe out the whole wine industry in a matter of years. The phylloxera is a small, yellow aphid, about a millimetre long, that feeds on the roots of the vine. As it consumes the sap it infects the root, which swells into 'galls', rather like the swellings (buboes) that occur on humans infected by bubonic plague. As sap ceases to circulate, the infected root shrivels and dies, leaving the vine without sustenance. The green leaves turn yellow, wither and fall.

Each female phylloxera lays hundreds of eggs, and with up to seven generations each summer the number of aphids reproducing increases rapidly. As they exceed their food supply on one root they move to others on the same vine, then move up the trunk and to the leaves. From there they migrate to other vines through cracks in the soil and by the action of the wind, but the most common cause of the spread of phylloxera is humans. The aphids are transferred from one area to another on soil attached to boots, tools and machinery, in irrigation water, and carried on rootlings. The progress of decline may be rapid or slow, depending on factors such as the condition of vines and soil composition. Vines that are affected by other problems are more rapidly killed by phylloxera, but vines growing in sandy soils appear to weather infestation much better. Depending on conditions, vines can produce long after being infected, although most die within a few years.

Phylloxera was indigenous to eastern North America. Native vines developed tolerance of it, for even though infected vines developed swellings like reddish bubbles on their leaves, the vines survived. It was not so with European vines, and many of the exotic vines planted in North America from the seventeenth century onwards had quite possibly failed as much because of phylloxera as of the climate. Because of the recognized superiority of *vinifera* vines, there was no interest in importing American vines to Europe for making wine. But in the mid nineteenth century scientific interest in botany led to the widespread exchange of plants of all kinds across the globe. There was no awareness of the dangers this traffic posed to indigenous flora, and no quarantine restrictions were imposed.

Among the plants brought to Europe from the United States between 1858 and 1862 were large numbers of vines. They were distributed throughout Europe – to scientific establishments in France, England, Portugal and Germany, including wine regions like Bordeaux and Alsace – and it is thought that phylloxera was present on the roots of such vines. In 1863 the first reports of infestation began to appear, both in England and in the south of France, and before the decade was out dying vines were reported throughout the wine regions of France. The southern Rhône Valley and Bordeaux were first affected, which suggests that there might have been two separate sources of infection, and by 1880 most of southern and central France was suffering from the disease. By 1890 virtually all France's wine regions showed evidence of it.[22]

A commission established in 1868 studied affected vines in the southern

Rhône and quickly identified the tiny yellow aphid as the culprit. The leader of the commission, the natural scientist Jules-Emile Planchon, recognized the phylloxera as an aphid that caused swellings on oak leaves. He named the species that fed on vines *phylloxera vastatrix*, meaning 'the devastator'. It might have seemed unnecessarily dramatic at the time, but the aphid's new name was to prove all too appropriate.

At first there was resistance to the implications of the discovery. Growers preferred to blame more familiar problems, like the weather and soil exhaustion, and some scientists thought phylloxera was an effect rather than the cause of the problem. Some religious commentators insisted that the failing vineyards were evidence of God's wrath. The Old Testament was full of threats that God would destroy vines if his people disobeyed his laws. The fact that French birth rates were falling more rapidly than those in any other European country (to the point that French population actually declined in the 1860s, at the very time of the phylloxera outbreak) revived age-old links between wine and fertility. In this case, the issue was the failure of both.

Not until 1869, when a national commission studied the problem, was there general acceptance that phylloxera was killing the vines, and by then the problem was largely out of control. French wine production fluctuated wildly, but throughout the 1860s and 1870s it generally lay between 50 and 60 million hectolitres a year. By the 1880s it settled at little more than half that – about 30 million hectolitres annually – and production did not recover until 1900. Land under viticulture decreased by almost a third, from 2,500,000 hectares before the outbreak to 1,730,000 hectares in 1900,[23] and not all of this area was in full production. In specific localities the effects were often worse. Hérault, which with some 220,000 hectares of vines in 1882 had the largest area of vineyards of any département, was left with only 90,000 hectares ten years later. The Gard lost an even greater proportion, losing more than four fifths of the 88,000 hectares of vines it boasted before phylloxera struck.

The official response to the disaster, which threatened to obliterate what had become a major domestic and export industry, was hesitant and slow. In 1870 the attention of the French government was, understandably enough, distracted from the vine problem by the war with Prussia which resulted in the defeat of France and a revolution in Paris the next year. Moreover the viticultural disaster itself unfolded slowly.

The infection spread gradually across France, and even the initial decline in production, although worrying, was not unprecedented. In 1870 the government offered a reward of 20,000 francs for a cure for phylloxera, but it was a sign of increased concern that it was raised to 300,000 francs four years later.

Suggestions flowed in, ranging from the potentially useful to the absurd, and almost half the 696 proposed remedies were tested. Flooding the vineyards in winter was found to control the aphids temporarily, but it was impossible on hillsides. Some of the most promising approaches involved injecting the soil with insecticides. Of these the most successful proved to be liquid carbon bisulphide, a powerful chemical that killed not only the aphids and other living organisms but also, in some tests, the vines themselves. It provided an immediate solution, and, although it did not prevent reinfestation once it had dissipated, a programme of pumping the insecticide into the soil was begun.

The other main approach involved grafting European vines on to the rootstocks of phylloxera-tolerant American vines. There were concerns, however, that the grapes from such vines would have what is referred to as the 'foxy' taste of the American grapes. There was also resistance on the grounds that it was American vines that had caused the problem in the first place. Many producers wanted an absolute ban on American vines, not a programme that would introduce millions of them to French soil, whether or not they had French tops.

In 1878 and 1879 laws were passed that attempted to limit the spread of phylloxera by implementing different policies in each of three broad viticultural zones. In the worst-infected south, French and American vines could be planted. In a broad central zone, where phylloxera infestation was as yet moderate, American vines were prohibited and chemical insecticides were to be used. In the north, which was thought to be phylloxera-free, nothing was to be done and American vines were strictly prohibited. Yet these policies were impotent against the spread of phylloxera. Not only did the aphid breed prolifically and overcome almost all obstacles placed in the way of its migration, but the measures were often ineffective. Insecticides were only temporarily successful, and the effectiveness of any policy relied on universal compliance. If only one small vineyard or part of a vineyard was not treated, it provided a source for the reinfestation of all others in its region.

At an international congress on phylloxera held in Bordeaux in 1881 the idea of grafting French vines on to American rootstocks was adopted as the best measure against phylloxera. A programme of grafting began, and by 1900 more than two thirds of the vines growing in France had American roots. Owners of small vineyards were initially slow to participate, not least because of the expense and the disruption to production caused by ripping up and replacing vines. Fears that American rootstock would pass on undesirable tastes to the European vines proved unfounded, but some regions held out against the programme anyway. Burgundy forbade the use of American vines for grafting until 1887, when widespread grafting by wine-growers forced the authorities to capitulate.

But the treatment had side-effects. Huge quantities of American rootstock had to be imported, and much of it turned out to be infected with a new disease, downy mildew, which reduced yields and produced weak wine. A treatment was devised quickly at the Faculty of Science of Bordeaux, and a liquid mixture of copper sulphate and lime was sprayed on the affected vines.

As the French wine industry languished in the doldrums of low production, the high prices that the scarcity of wine led to encouraged the manufacture of wine from other products, such as imported raisins. A popular book entitled *The Art of Making Wine from Raisins* appeared in 1880 and rapidly went through a number of printings. Raisin-based wine, sometimes blended with cheap red wines from Languedoc, accounted for more than a tenth of the wine consumed in France in 1890. The French also began to expand viticulture in Algeria, their North African colony, and the land planted in vines there increased twentyfold between 1880 and 1900.

Although French vineyards have received most attention in terms of the effects of phylloxera, the louse had an impact throughout Europe and the wider world of wine. The use of American rootstock in huge quantities actually had the effect of spreading phylloxera to previously uninfected regions, where it began to kill ungrafted vines. Throughout southern Europe, in Spain, Italy and Greece, vineyards were ruined and many were never replanted because their owners could not afford the necessary American rootstock. Italy, Spain and Portugal briefly profited from the outbreak of phylloxera in France because they were able to export considerable quantities of wine, but their vineyards were in turn affected. Phylloxera made its first appearance in Spain in 1878, in the southern Malaga region. This was the source of wine known as 'mountain', a sweet, fortified wine popular in Britain and the United States during the first half of the nineteenth century. By the later 1800s mountain's popularity was declining as sherry and port dominated the sweet and fortified wine market and as tastes generally shifted towards dry wines. Phylloxera dealt an almost fatal blow to the already troubled Malaga wine industry, for by 1891 it had destroyed more than 90 per cent of the vines and infected most of the remainder. When other regions also succumbed – like Jerez, Malaga's rival, in 1894 – it was alleged that the louse had travelled with Malaga's vineyard workers who had migrated in search of work.[25]

Phylloxera became a general problem in Italy by the 1880s. The spread was slowed by the comparative isolation of many Italian vineyards and because the style of viticulture encouraged firmly pressed ground, which made it difficult for the aphids to reach the deep roots. Gradually, however, the disease spread, and by 1888 the government introduced legislation to deal with it. Because their vines were infected later, Italians and Spanish growers were able quickly to apply the lessons the French had been slow to learn, and they began replanting with grafted vines. The progress of phylloxera in Italy was far more moderate than in France, and in 1912 just under four million of the country's four and a half million hectares of vines were still not affected.[26]

At the time that it was cutting a swathe through Europe's vineyards, phylloxera was also killing vines in other parts of the world. It had reached California by 1873, though it is unclear whether it was carried on French *vitis vinifera* or American concord vines. By 1880 some 600 acres of vines had been destroyed in Sonoma, but growers were reluctant to admit that it posed a serious threat to their livelihoods, even when the evidence – withering vines – was plain to see. By 1900 a mere 2,000 acres of vines remained productive in the Napa Valley, and by 1915 it estimated that at least a quarter of a million acres of vineyards had been lost in the preceding decades.[27] Phylloxera hit Australia in the 1870s, first in Victoria and in the next decade in New South Wales. The Victorian government pursued a number of policies, first favouring the destruction of affected vines, which led to a massive reduction in vineyards in some districts, then encouraging replanting so the region would not lose ground to other colonies. Quarantine restrictions imposed by South Australia protected that state's vines.

One by one, virtually all the world's wine regions, great and small, succumbed to phylloxera. Most recovered after replanting with grafted vines, although vineyard areas after the epidemic were usually smaller than before. Some regions never really recovered. The vineyards of Peru, for example, began a long period of decline as a result of infestation, and only in the 1970s was serious attention given to replanting and reviving the industry that had been so important in the seventeenth and eighteenth centuries. Ironically it was Chile, Peru's neighbour to the south, that was one of the notable exceptions to phylloxera infection. Vines were imported from Europe in 1851, before the arrival of phylloxera there, so that Chile's vine stock was not diseased. It is arguable that Chile's isolation also played a role (although isolation did not spare New Zealand's vines), and it is also possible that the qualities of Chile's soil and the practice of irrigation made it less hospitable to the devastating aphid.

The phylloxera epidemic was undoubtedly a deadly threat to the world's wine industry. Had grafting not been discovered as a countermeasure the disease might well have wiped out *vinifera* vines for all practical purposes. It is a chastening lesson in the environmental consequences of an unregulated traffic in plants and insects around the world. For one or two decades it severely disrupted wine production and trade and, by implication, the consumption patterns that had developed during the first two thirds of the nineteenth century.

It is only a slight exaggeration to say that the history of wine can be divided into two periods, BP and AP: Before Phylloxera and After Phylloxera. The phylloxera epidemic had dramatic immediate and longer-term implications for virtually all aspects of viticulture and winemaking. In the short term it encouraged fraud as merchants and winemakers tried to eke out scarce supplies of grapes, and claims of adulteration gave rise to more coherent regulations governing wine. Losses to phylloxera effectively ended viticulture in some areas, profoundly altered ownership patterns of vineyards, and encouraged hybridization.

The immediate effect of the phylloxera crisis in any region was to reduce land in viticulture and the amount of wine available to the market. Wine merchants imported wine from other European countries and North Africa, and blended French with foreign wines. By the 1880s millions of hectolitres of wine from Italy, Spain and Portugal were being imported, much of it in the form of full-bodied reds for blending with the weaker French product. Even more was imported from France's African colonies. Algeria's vineyards expanded sixfold from 17,000 hectares in 1872 to 110,000 hectares in 1890. If phylloxera killed off much of the wine industry in South America, it helped to create another in North Africa.

Raisin-based wine was also made in large quantities. Hot water added to raisins and allowed to ferment produced a wine of about 10° of alcohol. It could be consumed as it was or blended with red wine from Languedoc. It is estimated that tens of millions of hectolitres of raisin wine were made in the 1880s and 1890s and that it accounted for about six per cent of wine sold in the early 1880s and ten per cent in 1890.[28] Merchants diluted wine with water to stretch meagre supplies, while some adulterated wine in various ways or fabricated wines from ingredients other than grapes, fresh or dried. The shortage of wine and rising prices for what was available drove some wine-drinkers to alternative forms of alcohol, notably beer and distilled spirits.

One region experienced a combination of troubles. Following the German victory in 1871, Alsace and Lorraine were annexed to Germany and Alsace became a German wine region. But its immense potential – it would have provided two-fifths of Germany's wine – alarmed producers in other parts of the country and they were successful in slowing the Alsatian response to phylloxera. The region's vine-growers were compelled to rip out all their vines and burn them, but they were forced to wait ten years before replanting. Even then, the vineyards were established on the plains rather than on the hillsides that had produced fine wines before the arrival of phylloxera, and instead of replanting the riesling vines that had brought Alsace fame, vignerons were permitted to use only hybrids. From making distinctive and fine wines, Alsace became a producer of little more than cheap wines suitable only for blending. In 1909 producers were permitted to try for quality by adding sugar and raising the alcohol content. But by the time Alsace rejoined France in

1918, after four years of war, its wines remained far inferior to those the region had begun to produce during the first two thirds of the nineteenth century.[29]

Wine was by now a commodity that could be traded globally, and the European disaster had repercussions as far away as California. British and American entrepreneurs began to show increased interest in California, and in one instance a massive half million dollars was invested in a wine company in the expectation that Europe as a whole would soon need to import wine from the New World. The optimism of many Californian producers, as they contemplated the ruined vineyards of Europe, was captured in the 1879 assertion by one proprietor: 'Whoever lives a half century hence, will find the grapes of California in every city of the Union; her raisins supplying the whole Western hemisphere; her wines in every mart of the globe, and then, with her golden shores, her sunny clime, her vine-clad hills and plains, will California, indeed, be the Vineland of the world.'[30] Half a century away from 1879 lay 1929 and anything but a vision of prosperity, but that could hardly have been predicted.

Over the slightly longer term, there was some restructuring of French vineyards that compensated for the loss of land under viticulture. Many proprietors replanted with new, high-yield vines, contributing to an overall increase in productivity towards the end of the nineteenth century. Between 1880 and 1920 the average yield of French vines trebled from 13.5 to 38.6 hectolitres of wine per hectare. In the 1880s some 34 million hectolitres of wine were available on the French market each year, but in 1900 the market was flooded by more than twice that, about 71 million hectolitres. At the same time the French population grew very sluggishly, so that there really was twice as much wine available on a per capita basis in 1900.

Increased productivity that more than compensated for loss of viticultural land, together with easier and cheaper transportation, led to a surplus and, predictably, to a decline of prices. From a high of 36 francs a hectolitre in the period of shortage after the phylloxera epidemic, the price of French wine fell to 15 francs by 1906.[31] The impact was most felt in those regions of the Midi where wine-grapes were virtually the sole crop. Most of the vineyards that were not replanted belonged to small producers who could not afford the American rootstock needed for replanting. The effect of the crisis was thus to eliminate many of the financially marginal wine producers. Thousands left the land entirely and joined the migration of rural dwellers to the cities, where they became workers in the emerging industrial economy.

Moreover, the means of dealing with mildew and phylloxera involved transformations in viticulture that made consumers, especially the important and wealthy English market, suspicious of French wine. Old vines had had a particular renown in the production of many great wines, but they had died and wine was now made from new stock. Worse, the new vines grew on American roots, and there was suspicion that the flavour of American wine would forever taint the great wines of Burgundy and Bordeaux. Behind this lay a particularly English snobbery about the United States: grafting noble European vines to American stock in the 1880s was no more acceptable than the idea of a British king marrying an American divorcee would prove to be fifty years later. This, together with the fear that wine might be tainted by all the chemicals now employed to keep pests at bay, depressed the market for French wine. The English found their consolation in scotch whisky, but French wine-growers had to wait for theirs until French wine rebounded after the Second World War.

At the turn of the century, then, French wine-makers were facing problems of critical proportions: overproduction, depressed prices, sagging export markets, and widespread adulteration and fraud. Not only did many merchants continue to blend quality with inferior wines, but the artificial 'wines' of the phylloxera period continued to find a market even after plentiful supplies of genuine wine were once again available. Wine-makers throughout France, especially in Languedoc, tried in vain to persuade their regional and national governments to take decisive action. In 1905 the inhabitants of Argeliers (Aude), led by a vigneron, Marcelin Albert, signed a petition stating: 'The undersigned have determined to pursue their just claims to the very end, to refuse to pay their taxes, and to demand the resignation of the elected officials, and they urge all the communes of the Midi and Algeria to follow their example to the cries of "Long live natural wine! Down with the poisoners!".'[32]

It is notable that there was no resentment at imports from Algeria (whose wine was regarded as French) and that the issue of overproduction was ignored entirely. Responsibility for the crisis was laid solely on the producers of fraudulent wine. A commission set up by the government in 1907 similarly failed to identify overproduction as the main reason for the slump in the wine industry. Indeed, the commission's report pointed out that vineyard area had declined in the late nineteenth century and overlooked the fact that increases in yields had more than compensated.

Frustrated at the failure of the government to deal decisively with the crisis that threatened their livelihoods, vine-growers in Languedoc began a campaign of protests. A series of rallies, each bigger than the one before, was held throughout Languedoc on successive Sundays during April, May and June 1907, culminating in huge demonstrations of nearly 300,000 people in Nîmes on 2 June and more than 600,000 in Montpellier a week later. On each occasion Marcelin Albert addressed the crowd in terms that evoked the French Revolution, calling for a 'Committee of Public Safety for the defence of viticulture'. This popular movement particularly affected the mayors of the region's communes, and by the middle of June half of them had resigned.

The government in Paris responded by increasing the tax on sugar, an essential ingredient in artificial wine, but it also acted forcefully against the protesting wine-producers. Arrest warrants were issued against Albert and other leaders of the vignerons' protests, and troops were dispatched to the troubled region. On 19 June 1907, clashes in Narbonne resulted in the deaths of five protesters. Learning of this the next day, sympathizers in Perpignan burned down the prefecture, the symbol of the national government.

The insurrection did not go much further, though, for the government, uncertain of the loyalty of locally recruited troops, made a number of concessions. Key among them was the law of 29 June 1907, which was passed hastily to appease the passions of Languedoc vignerons but which none the less contained provisions that would help solve some of the problems. Under its terms, producers had to declare the size of their crop annually, as well as the volume of their wine reserves (including fine wines ageing in warehouses and cellars). These declarations would give the authorities information on the volume of wine that the market would be subject to each year. The law also struck at artificial wine by setting limits on the amount of sugar that could be used in making wine and tried to encourage quality by prohibiting the sale of substances designed to improve defective wine. Further legislation in the following months regulated the wine trade and established a central agency for the repression of fraud. In September 1907 an important law defined wine as the exclusive product of 'the alcoholic fermentation of fresh grapes or of the juice of fresh grapes'. On a note of practicality, the government tried to reduce wine stocks in 1908 by buying two million francs worth in order to provide soldiers with a small daily ration.

French politicians could thus respond to producers' concerns about quality without dealing with the underlying problem of overproduction. The laws were, however, significant steps in the regulation of wine, for although aspects of wine-production and trade had been subject to legislation in many countries long before this period, it was in the early twentieth century that states began to introduce systematic and enforceable guidelines. The French were to the fore in this trend and in many respects established models that other states adapted to their own conditions.

One important series of regulations concerned delimited regions of production. A 1905 law against fraud had made it an offence falsely to portray a commodity as the product of a particular locality so as to increase its value. Starting in 1908, the government began to establish the limits of broad regions that produced distinctive alcoholic beverages, such as champagne, cognac, bordeaux, banyuls and armagnac. This was the beginning of the *appellation contrôlée* system, discussed later in the chapter, a complex of regulations that applied not only to wine but to other commodities such as cheese.

It might have been expected that any attempts to establish the boundaries of delimited regions would immediately give rise to complaints from districts that were excluded, and a major problem soon arose in the case of champagne. The appellation regulations for this wine specified that it should be made from grapes grown in designated districts in the départements of Marne and Aisne, but they excluded producers from the Aube entirely. Not only was this an insult, for the chief town of Aube, Troyes, was the historic capital of Champagne, but it also ignored practice: since the mid nineteenth century Aube producers had supplied the champagne houses of Marne with part of their white wine for blending. Echoing their counterparts in Languedoc, the vignerons of

Aube revolted in 1911, and the government capitulated, designating the département a 'second zone' of champagne.

Meanwhile the vignerons of Marne, who had no complaint about the original delimitation in their favour, declared war on merchants whom they accused of fraudulently using wine from other regions of France in their blends. Between December 1910 and April 1911, crowds of vine-growers stormed one cellar after another where they believed fraud was being perpetrated, and smashed the bottles resting in the riddling racks. Hundreds of thousands of litres of champagne were destroyed in the disturbances. Once again troops were brought in, but this time they were not deployed against the vignerons with fatal results, and legislation took the heat out of the protests.

The regulatory system that began to emerge in France in the early 1900s, the basis of the comprehensive rules that govern wine-production today, thus arose from the conditions prevailing after phylloxera was under control and as wine-producers tried to bring some semblance of equilibrium to production and demand. Regulations were not simply imposed on producers by politicians in Paris; as we have seen, in a number of cases the government was forced into legislative action by the direct pressure of producers themselves. They saw wine fraud not only as an issue of quality, reputation and consumer protection, but as a threat to their very livelihoods. Phylloxera had driven thousands of vignerons out of viticulture, and those who remained were that much more determined to stay.

The calm that settled over Champagne after the protests in 1910 and 1911 was short-lived, however, for the region was soon torn apart by war. The summer of 1914 had been very warm, and the vintage was expected to be a good one. The tens of thousands of vine-workers and vignerons called to military service that August believed they would be home in time to pick the grapes. But it was not to be so, and the grapes were gathered by women, children and men too old to have been called up.

True to expectations, the 1914 harvest was a massive one that produced vast quantities of wine – some 60 million hectolitres, almost 50 per cent more than the preceding year. In a spirit of patriotism and commercial calculation, Languedoc producers presented 200,000 hectolitres for distribution in military hospitals to boost the morale of the wounded (and presumably to hasten their recovery). By the time the wine was shipped, the optimism of summer had been cooled by hideous battles that cost enormous numbers of lives, and the conflict on the Western Front had settled into a drawn-out war of attrition.

There was a long historical tradition of supplying wine to the military, but during the nineteenth century it had been called into question by the growing alarm at the effects of alcohol. In the first years of the 1900s a number of armies carried out experiments to see how alcohol affected military performance. A German survey of soldiers who fired some 36,000 rounds over sixteen consecutive days showed that their marksmanship was not affected by alcohol – presumably a moderate intake.[33] The French military authorities seemed more realistic about the chances of preventing soldiers from drinking. Instead of comparing efficiency between those who drank alcohol and those who did not, French authorities compared the effects of beer and wine, and concluded that the impact of wine was less negative.

French military rations included only a small amount of wine, although soldiers were permitted to buy more when local conditions allowed. But the gift by Languedoc producers prompted the ministry of war to distribute wine to soldiers on a regular basis. Set at a quarter of a litre per day in 1914, the ration was increased to half a litre in 1916. By 1918 officers had the option of adding another quarter litre to their men's allowance, and soldiers were allowed to purchase a further quarter litre at subsidized prices. French soldiers thus had access to a litre of wine a day legitimately, and there were no doubt many opportunities to supplement this amount informally. (The military authorities fought a constant war against attempts to smuggle spirits into the war zone.) French forces at the front consumed some 12 million hectolitres of wine in 1917, and it was expected that they would have needed 16 million the following year had the war not ended. Thousands of rail tankers were pressed into service to ensure that the troops got their wine.

All this wine was requisitioned from producers by the government at prices that rose as wine supplies declined; the gift of wine in 1914 was an investment that paid many wine-growers handsome returns. Vignerons in Languedoc did very well from requisitions, but the government was not interested in paying premium prices for fine wine, and many producers in Bordeaux and Burgundy were forced to accept prices that were well below the costs of production.

Virtually all the wine distributed in the French army was red, because it was thought to be more masculine and more likely than white wine to put fire into soldiers' blood and breathe courage into their hearts. (Paradoxically, the experience of Australian soldiers gave the English language the word 'plonk', meaning cheap or poor-quality wine. It is believed to be a corruption of *vin blanc*, which the Australians pronounced 'van blonk', [34] making it probable that the Australians drank wine of a colour the French considered inappropriate for fighting men.) At the end of the war a French military newspaper, *The Echo of the Trenches*, gave wine some of the credit for victory: 'No doubt our brilliant generals and heroic soldiers were the immortal artisans of victory. But would they have been without the plonk [*pinard*] that kept them going to the end, that endowed them with spirit, courage, tenacity, and scorn for danger, and made them repeat with unbreakable conviction, "We will prevail".'[35] Here was the clinching argument against the opponents of wine: not only could wine save society from alcoholism and social decline, but it had saved the nation from defeat.

Yet it had been far from easy for French producers to meet the demands of the military. The 1914 harvest had been excellent, but the following year's production of 20 million hectolitres was only a third of the volume. The vines had suffered from a variety of diseases because of damp weather, and there was not enough labour available to treat them effectively. Horses, the main form of transportation, as well as other vineyard necessities became more and more scarce. The Algerian vineyards fared not much better, and demand in France (both civil and military) was met only by the importation of massive quantities of Italian and Spanish wine. The harvests of 1916 and 1918 were better (they averaged 40 million hectolitres), but they were still modest in relation to demand. The 12 million hectolitres consumed on the battle front in 1917 represented almost a third of 1916's production.[36] Scarcity on the home market was reflected in the rising price: a litre of wine that cost 20 centimes in 1914 fetched one franc ten centimes by 1918.[37]

The First World War did more than interfere with vineyards and harvests. During the conflict most European states reduced alcohol-production so as to concentrate labour and resources on war-related sectors of the economy and tried to reduce consumption so as to increase efficiency in the labour force. In England bar hours were reduced and beer was diluted, and similar measures were adopted in all the belligerent states. All but one of the Canadian provinces adopted prohibition policies in 1916 or 1917, and when Québec fell into line in 1919 it banned the sale of spirits but not of wine or beer. Just how effective the wartime policies were is not clear, although one book published after the war argued that, in England at least, they contributed to the 'national efficiency' that enabled the country to hold out longer than Germany.[38]

Unlike earlier conflicts, such as the Thirty Years War, when marauding armies devastated vineyards and fields, the First World War in northern Europe was largely stationary. The Western Front scarcely moved for four years after a stalemate was established by December 1914. At the same time, some of the most intensive fighting took place in Champagne, and many hundreds of hectares of vineyards were put out of commission – not only during the conflict itself but for some time afterwards because of the danger from the unexploded shells that littered the countryside. None the less, Champagne continued to produce its distinctive wine throughout the war, even though vine-growers and harvesters often risked their lives to tend and bring in the grapes. The first wartime harvest, in fact, is reputed to have been one of the century's greatest, not despite the war but, indirectly, because of it: the harvest was less organized than usual, and some grapes were picked when underripe and therefore acidic while others were overripe and therefore more sweet than usual.

But if war had less effect on French wine production than might have been imagined, labour shortages and the diversion of resources for the war effort meant that vineyards did not receive the care they required. The same was true, though much less so, in Italy (which entered the war in 1915), while Spain and Portugal were largely unaffected by the conflict. Portugal continued to ship wine to England and in 1916 was granted sole rights to use the words 'port' and 'madeira' on its wines, an early step towards the protection of regional names. In other respects, however, the conflict interfered with trade. For the duration of hostilities Germany and the Habsburg Empire ceased to be markets for French and Italian wines. The 1917 Russian Revolution saw the disappearance of the imperial court and nobility and, with them, about a tenth of the export market for champagne. Confronted by Bolsheviks who drank vodka and beer rather than imported wine, the Tsar might well have been deprived of the solace to be found in champagne when a ship carrying wine to the imperial court in 1916 failed to reach its destination after being torpedoed by a German submarine in the Gulf of Finland. Its cargo of champagne – 1907 Heidsieck – was salvaged in good condition in 1998.

In its effects on wine, the 1914–18 war was truly global, for there were even repercussions in New Zealand, as far away as it was possible to get from the conflict in Europe. Viticulture there was largely carried out by immigrants from Dalmatia, which was until 1918 part of the Austrian Empire with which the British were at war. In 1914 one New Zealand member of parliament stated that, while he had never seen the 'Austrian wine' produced by the Dalmatians, he believed it to be 'one of the vilest decoctions which can possibly be imagined', and that it was 'a degrading, demoralizing, and sometimes maddening drink to many people who use it'.[39] The government required wine-makers to be licensed, for which they had to prove they were of 'good character'. The new requirements, together with the internment of many Dalmatians for the duration of hostilities, reduced the number of wine-makers in New Zealand from seventy in 1913 to thirty-five two years later.

Throughout the wine-producing world immediately after the war there were attempts to return to normal, but conditions had changed. In France the war had cut deeply into a generation of French men, many of them vine-workers. The lists of names inscribed on war memorials in town squares throughout French wine-producing regions represented not only lost sons, brothers and husbands, but also hands that would no longer tend the vines and make wine. Wine-production was still labour-intensive, and the shortage of men threatened to slow the recovery of the industry.

The German wine industry was seriously affected by the war, and the area under viticulture continued to shrink. From 120,000 hectares at the turn of the century, Germany's vineyards had fallen to 102,000 in 1913, but between the world wars they fell to between 70,000 and 75,000 hectares. Even this steep decline, in part a result of losing Alsace to France, concealed the difficult times that wine-makers experienced, especially in the 1920s. Many of the most important viticultural areas on the left bank of the Rhine were occupied by French forces for ten years after the war, so producers were not free to market their wines. Consumption of wine, like that of other goods, was affected by the serious economic difficulties Germany experienced in the 1920s, especially the inflation of 1923 that made the Mark worthless and ruined many middle-class families. Finally, the Treaty of Versailles, the postwar settlement, required Germany to import 260,000 hectolitres of French wine each year free of tariffs. This flood of cheap wine undercut German production and drove many vine-growers off the land. It was not until the 1930s that German wine-producers were free of some of these constraints, and by then they were affected by the depression and the advent of the Nazi government.

In contrast to Germany, postwar France experienced a spurt of planting that by 1924 had added nearly 50,000 hectares of vines, many of them hybrids planted in the wider Paris region whose vineyards had contracted in the late nineteenth century. By far the fastest growth was in the south, however, where Languedoc vineyards increased from 170,000 to 270,000 hectares between 1920 and 1930. Production increased accordingly. The 1922 harvest produced a massive 72 million hectolitres, and production during the remainder of the 1920s was respectable, averaging 60 million hectolitres a year.[40] In addition, millions of hecto-litres of Algerian wine were sold on the French market. Despite the loss of so many young men, many in their prime drinking ages, per capita consumption of wine in France rose to 136 litres a year, compared with 103 litres in 1904. The oenological experience of French soldiers during the war had accustomed millions of men, many of them cider and spirit consumers before 1914, to drinking wine on a daily basis.

Increased consumption notwithstanding, France had a surplus of wine because many prewar export markets had shrunk or disappeared. The collapse of the Russian, Habsburg and German empires and the social and financial decline of their elites deprived producers of fine wines of many of their customers. The market for wine in Belgium seems to have been boosted by the wartime experience, but it was a small one that was still dominated by beer. The United States introduced Prohibition in 1920. The British demand for wine declined, particularly once the Great Depression struck after 1929. But even in the 1920s, whatever taste for French wine the war might have given British soldiers was dulled by its sheer cost back home. Import tariffs favoured the British Empire, and England was flooded not by French table wines but by Australian fortified wines. Because of the 1916 rule giving Portugal sole rights to certain names, the Australians sold their products as 'port-style' and 'madeira-style' wines.

The overall result of protective tariffs and depression was that between 1920 and 1940 European wine exports languished; France's were only half what they had been before the war. In the 1920s France shipped an annual average of 1.6 million hectolitres abroad, but in the next decade exports averaged only half that. These volumes drained little from the available surplus, and the crisis of overproduction was accentuated in bumper years. In both 1934 and 1935, 100 million hectolitres of domestically produced and imported Algerian wine flooded the French market. The glut caused by low exports and high production affected all types of wine, from the least to the most expensive. In 1934 only 4,559,030 bottles of champagne were exported, a mere third of the 13,583,719 shipped abroad in 1919. In the same fifteen-year period the number of bottles stored in cellars in Champagne doubled from 72 to 147 million.[41]

The interwar period in France thus saw a continuation of the series of crises that had begun with the phylloxera epidemic. But in retrospect the picture was not entirely bleak, for vine-growers, wine-producers and the government took steps to protect and strengthen the ailing industry, and policies enacted in the 1920s and 1930s set the stage for the recovery of French wine after the Second World War.

It was after the First World War that the cooperative movement accelerated, especially in southern France. In 1920 there were ninety-two cooperatives with a combined storage capacity of 120,000 hectolitres: twenty years later there were 838 with a capacity of 12 million hecto-litres.[42] The state assisted small producers who wanted to form cooperatives by providing legal advice and, more important, financial assistance in the form of grants to subsidize the capital costs of buildings and equipment. Governments of both left and right supported the cooperatives: the left because they were exercises in socialism, the right because they protected small proprietors from the pressures of the market.

Cooperatives were less common in regions noted for higher quality wines, but even there they were established in small numbers. When the small wine-growers of Vosne-Romanée (in Burgundy) faced a crisis soon after the war because they were able neither to sell their grapes profitably nor to make their own wine because they were too poor to buy or repair equipment, the mayor set up a cooperative that proved to be their salvation. Although this and most other cooperatives in Burgundy, Bordeaux, Champagne and Beaujolais were eventually disbanded, they enabled the owners of some small vineyards to survive the most difficult years of the century.

The other major development in France between the world wars was a series of laws that eventually led to the AOC (*Appellation d'Origine Contrôlée*) regulations that define the regions, grape varieties and other characteristics of about half the wine now produced there. Some legislation delimiting districts entitled to use certain appellations had been passed before the war, but from 1919 the process accelerated and became more inclusive. In 1919, for example, the courts were given authority to hear disputes over delimited areas, and their judgements also began to include grape varieties as criteria for defining coherent wine districts and types. By 1927 this trend resulted in a new appellation law that specified the permitted varietals in each case.

Until this point the laws said virtually nothing about yields, minimum alcohol levels, or methods of viticulture and viniculture, but these matters were dealt with in the comprehensive AOC legislation that was passed in 1935. Thereafter, no wine would qualify for AOC status unless it was made from specified grapes from a delimited area, and unless it conformed to other requirements considered appropriate to that wine type. Depending on the specific AOC, these criteria might include maximum yields, alcohol levels and the observance of particular growing and vinification techniques.

A national committee (composed of representatives of producers, merchants and the government) set up to grant AOC status became the forerunner of the Institut National des Appellations d'Origine (INAO), established in 1947 and still responsible for performing this task. During the late 1930s, until its work was effectively cut off by the Second World War, the committee fielded hundreds of demands for AOC status and complaints about its decisions.

Among those who faced not only adverse weather, insects and economic depression but also the new world of AOC designations and cooperatives were the producers of Monthelie, a small community in Burgundy whose land was almost entirely devoted to viticulture. Grain was so insignificant to Monthelie's economy that it was said locally that a chicken would die of starvation at harvest time. The records of the town's agricultural society provide unusually intimate glimpses into the world of ordinary producers in this period.[43] As early as 1919 Monthelie's vignerons complained about their exclusion from the Côte de Beaune appellation, and called the attention of the authorities to their fine wines. This was only the first shot in their campaign to have their wine recognized as having contributed to the reputation of their better-known neighbours like Meursault, Volnay and Pommard. Monthelie's wine-makers insisted in 1923 that their produce was 'the equal of these other wines, and that since time immemorial they have been sold under their own name as well as under more famous names like Pommard and Volnay'.

Monthelie's vignerons demonstrated concern for varietals, and in 1924 they argued that defining wines only by region had allowed other producers in the Beaune area to use gamay grapes. They appealed against a 1925 decision by the court in Beaune, which gave burgundy status to wine made from gamay grapes, as 'contrary to usage'. After the passage of the 1935 AOC law, Monthelie applied for its own AOC status, and provided the adjudicating committee with information on the district's position, soil and topography. Monthelie's producers undertook to limit their red grapes to pinot noir and some of its variants, and their whites to chardonnay and pinot blanc. They also agreed to standardize row-spacing, practise traditional vinification and ensure that their wine had a minimum 10.8 per cent alcohol. But they drew the line at having their vines trained in one single fashion and at setting maximum yields. Vines should be trained according to where they grew, the vignerons argued, and they declared they would not over-produce because to do so would lower the quality of their wine. Despite these efforts, Monthelie had not achieved AOC status when war broke out in 1939.

These producers also flirted with the idea of a cooperative. In 1921 they visited the cooperative set up in Vosne-Romanée, and their comments are a good corrective to the notion that cooperatives were more concerned with volume than quality. What Monthelie's wine-makers wanted in a cooperative was a powerful body that would fight not only for a more vigorous wine trade but would also combat fraud and ensure high quality. Nuits-St-Georges had a cooperative, they noted, and 'the prosperity that reigns in that district and the wonderful state of the vines' demonstrated the advantage of having such an organization in every commune.

Elsewhere in Europe, wine-production was affected not only by the same currents of economic uncertainty, but also by political upheaval. The seizure of power by Mussolini's fascists in 1922 helped viticulture because of the policy of self-sufficiency. The fascist regime aimed to increase Italy's wine exports. 'The vineyards are now almost everywhere being organized along essentially economic lines of cultivation,' the minister of agriculture noted, 'with more and more standardized products, better suited for foreign markets . . .' He added direly, 'The National Government has not failed to provide legislative measures against disloyal competition, in defence of our typical national wines, and to push them in foreign markets.'[44] But land-reclamation schemes and financial aid to farmers helped cereal-producers more than vine-growers, and the area under viticulture declined by between 5 and 10 per cent from the 1920s to the 1930s.

German wines were not as positively regarded by the Nazi regime installed in 1933. Adolf Hitler himself was a near-teetotaller. Although his public career began with an attempted putsch in a Munich beer-hall, he was not there for the beer. Nazi ideology regarded excessive drinking as immoral (drunkenness was a ground for expulsion from the Party) and alcoholism was considered a form of degeneracy. People diagnosed as alcoholics could be denied a marriage certificate, and between 20,000 and 30,000 were forcibly sterilized under Nazi race hygiene laws.

Official policies aimed to reduce alcohol consumption, but there was no wholesale attack on the alcohol industry during the Third Reich. Before the outbreak of war, at least, the state needed the jobs provided by the distilleries, breweries and vineyards, not to mention the taxes that alcohol generated. Indeed, wine producers even received some state assistance,[45] and wine-production remained steady during the 1930s. Perhaps it helped that the foreign minister, Joachim von Ribbentrop, had been a wine merchant before entering the Nazi government. Although figures during the war are uncertain, consumption of all forms of alcohol rose during the 1930s, and that of spirits almost doubled.[46]

Other European wine-producing states fared worse. The outbreak of civil war in Spain devastated vineyards in regions like Valencia and Catalonia, and throughout the country generally they were neglected. The industry began to recover only in the 1950s. The installation of a fascist regime in Portugal in the 1930s led to a programme of cooperativization, but the reorganization of the industry did not lead quickly to changes in quality.

While European producers adjusted to interwar conditions, their American counterparts faced a crisis that seemed as fatal as phylloxera. In 1920 the United States congress enacted the Eighteenth Amendment to the Constitution, which prohibited the production, sale and transportation of 'intoxicating liquor' throughout the nation. Any hopes that beer and wine might escape prohibition were dashed when liquor was defined as any beverage that contained more than half a per cent of alcohol. The only concessions to wine were restricted uses in religious ceremonies, for medicinal purposes and as a food flavouring. These exceptions provided loopholes for some breaches of prohibition – the religious and medical demand for wine seems to have risen dramatically – and a few wineries maintained operations, though on a much-reduced scale. But most, like breweries and distilleries, simply went out of business. American wineries produced 55 million gallons of wine (2 million hectolitres) in 1919, but by 1925 production had fallen by 90 per cent to under 4 million gallons.

Yet these statistics of commercial wine-production are misleading, for they mask what was probably a substantial increase in wine consumption during the period that Prohibition was in force. The Volstead Act, the legislation designed to enforce the Eighteenth Amendment, permitted individuals to make 'non-intoxicating' cider and fruit juices for their own consumption in their own homes. Although the river of wine that had poured from California's wineries was reduced to a trickle, the state's vineyards not only continued to grow grapes but even increased production. The grapes were shipped throughout the United States, either fresh, as juice, as concentrate or as dehydrated grape 'bricks'. Juice and grape flavourings (including port, sherry, claret, riesling and tokay) were sold in casks suitable for fermentation, and in major cities home delivery was possible. The bricks of dehydrated grapes carried the 'warning' that adding water and yeast would start fermentation and result in wine – just the information people needed to start making wine in their bathtubs. In addition, of course, much wine was made illegally on a commercial basis and supplied to restaurants, clubs and clandestine bars.

The actual impact of Prohibition on alcohol consumption is to some extent a matter of speculation, because production was no longer commercial and was therefore not recorded for shipping, taxation and other purposes. Although beer, wine and spirits were made illegally both in household and commercial quantities, it was beer that was hardest hit. Consumption had been increasing before Prohibition, but its sheer volume in relation to alcoholic content made it more difficult than wine and spirits to transport and conceal. Prohibition thus affected working-class beer-drinkers more than the better-off consumers of wine and spirits. The best estimates of wine consumption suggest that it declined immediately after the Eighteenth Amendment came into force, but rose once the market for grapes and grape-products was established. By the late 1920s wine consumption was probably twice the prewar level.[47]

When Prohibition was repealed, wineries returned to production but consumption in the United States fell. It was beer, the least expensive form of alcohol, that benefited most, but the effect of the Great Depression on incomes meant that sales of all kinds of alcohol stagnated throughout much of the 1930s. French producers, who had hoped that a newly 'wet' America would take some of their surplus wine, were as disappointed as California's wine-makers.

Elsewhere in North America, Prohibition boosted not only wine consumption but also commercial production. When Ontario banned the production of alcohol during the First World War it made a concession to the grape-growers' lobby and exempted wine made from Ontario-grown grapes by producers licensed by a provincial board. There were ten wineries in 1917, and such was the demand for licences to quench the province's thirst during Prohibition that fifty-seven more were granted permission during the next ten years. Despite a regulation that wineries could sell their wine only from stores on their properties and in minimum quantities of five gallons, there was strong demand for what was often a wretched brew of concord grapes, water, sugar and all manner of colorants and other additives. Consumption of domestic wine in Canada was a modest 221,985 gallons in 1921, but in 1930 consumption in Ontario alone exceeded two million gallons.[48]

The outbreak of another European war in 1939 meant another interruption in wine production and trade. France's exports fell 50 per cent in 1940, to just under half a million hectolitres, but for the rest of the war they rebounded to about a million hectolitres a year. Most of this wine went to Germany or to neutral countries, from where very small quantities were re-exported to traditional markets such as England. France's production from the German invasion in 1940 to the liberation in 1944 averaged 43 million hectolitres, a decline of more than a quarter compared to the late 1930s. One reason was the annexation of Alsace to Germany, but vine-growers throughout France also experienced the same shortages of labour, equipment and supplies that had reduced French production during the First World War.

By 1940 the wine-makers of much of the world had experienced as many as eight decades of adversity in the form of diseases, anti-alcohol pressure and legislation, and volatile economic and political conditions that had played havoc with production and trade. The Second World War was yet another blow to commerce, and many producers must have despaired of recovery. The heady days of growth and profit were now history, beyond the immediate experience of those involved in growing wines and making and selling wine. The vignerons of the small community of Monthelie recorded the catalogue of misfortunes of 1940: freezing weather in January, heavy rain in April, occupation by the German army in June, and the prompt confiscation of their wine reserves. Such, they recorded, 'is the balance-sheet of a particularly catastrophic year'.[49]

France's stocks of wine fell during the war, in part because of seizure by German occupation forces. The vignerons of Monthelie reported that the Germans had seized all the wine ageing in their cellars and had paid them in occupation currency, which they rightly suspected was not worth a great deal. In Bordeaux and Burgundy, stocks of wine were successfully concealed. At Château Haut-Brion, which was used successively as a French military hospital and a German airforce rest home, the entrances to the cellars were hidden behind piles of rubbish, but even then the wartime production was left intact by German forces.[50] Overall, however, French wine production slumped. The Vichy regime that governed those parts of France not occupied by Germany brought in new regulations that undid many of the laws introduced before the war to guarantee quality. The government's main concern was to stretch diminishing supplies, and to this end it permitted blending, lowered the minimum level of alcohol, and allowed the growing of grape varieties that had earlier been forbidden. A complex mechanism of rationing and price-fixing was put in place, and larger producers were required to turn over a proportion of their wine for distilling.[51]

The war of course also disrupted the wine trade, not only within Europe but in global terms. For example, Australia had been exporting some 16 million litres a year to Britain before the war – most of it in the form of fortified wine – but in 1940–41 exports fell to 7.5 million litres and by 1943 they were half that again. The reasons included an embargo on imported alcohol without a licence and the risks posed to shipping by German submarines. Most of the surplus was taken care of by the Australian domestic market. Helped by the presence of American soldiers based in Australia, consumption rose from 14.5 million litres in 1939 to 37 million litres by 1944.[52]

The Second World War was the culmination of decades of troubles that had plagued the wine industry of the western world. From the end of the nineteenth century to the middle of the twentieth, wine had been threatened by disease, prohibition, tariff barriers, economic depression and international wars. Recovery from such a long period of difficulty would not be rapid, but from the 1950s onwards the wine industry found itself facing a much more receptive environment, and decades later it had emerged into a period of relative prosperity and stability.

TEN

INTO THE LIGHT

A Half-century of Prosperity, 1950–2000

Prosperity is relative, and who could argue that the fifty years that followed the Second World War, compared to the catalogue of disasters during the eight decades that preceded it, were not a vast improvement for producers and consumers of wine alike? In the last years of the twentieth century, wine seemed to go from strength to strength. Rigorous appellation regulations were applied in almost all wine-producing countries and, despite some well-publicized scandals, consumers were entitled to have increasing confidence that the wine in the bottle they bought was the wine described on its label. Wine-makers throughout the world focused steadily on providing quality wines for an increasingly educated and demanding market, and wine consumption rose in parts of the world where it had previously been the least popular of the three main types of alcohol. Even the therapeutic properties of wine staged a come-back after a century in the shadows, as surveys and tests suggested that wine was not only part of a healthy diet but could actually help prevent certain diseases.

This picture of prosperity and optimism must, of course, be qualified. Beneath the success of wine lay many difficult years of economic restructuring by producers, some undertaken at their own initiative, some mandated by governments. The fundamental problem of overproduction, which had dogged the wine industry for decades, persisted. Moreover, despite advances in viticultural sciences, vines were still affected by diseases (including phylloxera) and consumption patterns swayed by economic cycles and shifts in taste. These years also saw advertising play a more important role as wine was consumed less as an integral part of the daily diet and more as an optional consumer product. The commercial success of wine and the creation of a new culture of wine-drinking owed a great deal not only to the higher quality achieved by producers, but also to successful marketing strategies.

The broad context for the changing place of wine in the western world was an economic environment that was for the most part positive. The fifty years after the Second World War witnessed a number of economic cycles, including periods of recession, high unemployment and inflation, but the overall trend was towards prosperity. Despite the fact that there remained millions of poor in Europe and North America, the benefits of this prosperity were spread much more widely than they had been in the first half of the twentieth century.[1] Yet although the growth of the middle class, which resulted from the redistribution of income between 1950 and 2000, might have created the potential for a widening wine market, it did not guarantee one. Wine consumption has risen in some societies, but it has declined or stabilized in others. Worldwide production, on the other hand, has increased, with the result that the chronic problem of overproduction has far from disappeared.

One of the most dramatic changes in the postwar period was the decline in consumption in countries that were historically the largest producers of wine. France, for example, witnessed a steady and precipitous decline in the second half of the 1900s. In the late 1930s per capita consumption of wine in France was 170 litres a year, a level that fell during the war years because of shortages. In the late 1940s consumption rebounded almost to its prewar level, reaching 150 litres in the early 1950s, but instead of rising or even simply stabilizing at that point, it began a long-term decline. By the 1970s it had fallen to 110 litres, and in the mid 1990s it was little more than half that level, at about 60 litres of wine per year for each inhabitant. In fifty years, per capita consumption of wine had fallen by 60 per cent.

Similar patterns, though less dramatic, occurred elsewhere. Italian consumption fell 45 per cent, from 110 to 60 litres a head, between the 1950s and 1990s. In the same period, per capita wine consumption declined by half in Chile, a third in Portugal and a quarter in Greece.

Statistics like these attribute the same level of wine consumption to children and adults and to women and men. Because adult males drink more wine (and alcohol generally) than any other group in all western societies, a shift in the age-structure necessarily changes per capita rates. Even if French men had continued to consume wine at the same rate during the 1950s and 1960s, per capita consumption would have fallen because of the larger proportion of children in the population resulting from the postwar baby boom. Since the 1960s, too, France has witnessed a large immigration of North African Muslims, the majority of whom abstain from all forms of alcohol. But even controlling for these variables, wine consumption has declined. Between the early 1960s and the mid 1980s, consumption by French people fifteen years and older fell by a quarter, from 127 to 97 litres of wine a year.[2]

The decline of wine consumption in much of continental Europe can be described and explained in various ways. One is a preference for quality wine: the decline in consumption of table wines (*vins de table*, the lowest-ranking French wine) has been far more rapid than that of AOC wines. From an average 100 litres a person in the 1970s, table wine consumption plummeted to under 20 litres in the late 1990s.[3] It goes without saying that AOC wine is more expensive, and the decision to spend more per bottle goes some way to explaining the decline in the volume of wine consumed. France is, however, a nation of remarkable regional variations, and there remained strong markets for table wine in the southeast, southwest and in Paris. These were the strong wine-drinking regions of the nineteenth century, when consumption among peasants and manual workers was particularly high.

Between 1950 and 2000, immense social changes took place in France and other major European wine-producing countries such as Italy, Spain and Portugal. Even though large numbers of their populations remain poor, an increasing proportion shared in the benefits of postwar prosperity and participated in the consumer economy that accompanied it. As lifestyles changed, so did the place of wine in it, although the precise mechanism here has not been satisfactorily explained. Wine ceased to be the integral part of the diet that it had been for centuries and became instead only one of several options. Most surprising is the decline of wine as the beverage that accompanied meals, for, to an extent that would have horrified those who in the mid 1900s defined wine as quintessentially French, their late twentieth-century compatriots became water drinkers. In part this reflected the improved supply of good-quality tap water since the 1950s, but commercially bottled spring water production has also soared to meet demand. In the 1950s a third of French people had a glass of water, not wine, at hand as they sat at the meal table, but that was true of three quarters of them in the 1990s. Wine was only one commodity among several that were available, and its share of family budgets fell as purchases of water rose.

One facet of the decline of wine as part of the everyday diet has been a redefinition of the relationship of alcohol to work. When wine was perceived not as a luxury or an optional commodity, but as a food that provided nutrition and energy, moderate consumption during work hours was not problematic. Concern about the relationship between drink and efficiency came to the surface during the First World War, when restrictions on alcohol were introduced, at least in part to ensure that workers in vital industries maintained high levels of production. At some point in the twentieth century, the incompatibility of work and drink became more generalized. If popular stereotypes carry any weight, however, there are class differences in what is acceptable. Executives may conduct business and make deals over meals accompanied by alcohol, but it is unacceptable for workers on an assembly line or clerks in an office to drink on the job. Many companies have policies that discourage or prohibit the consumption of alcohol by their employees at any time during the work-day. There is a world of difference between the workers at Venice's Arsenal dockyard, imbibing freely from the fountain of wine provided by their employer (see Chapter 5), and modern office workers drinking water from a cooler. The difference can be expressed not only in centuries but in cultures of drinking.

If wine has fallen from favour as an everyday beverage inside homes and in the workplace, it has also lost some of its appeal as a public drink in much of Europe. The most dramatic manifestation of this is the rapid decline in the number of cafés in France. Still one of the most common associations that foreigners make with France, the pavement café offering a glass of wine has become increasingly rare. It is estimated that before the First World War there were more than half a million cafés with the Class IV licence that permitted the sale of wine. That number represented one café for every 80 inhabitants, but by the 1990s there were only 160,000 such cafés, one for every 360. And even when people drank in cafés in the 1990s, they were less likely than in the past to drink wine. Young people, in particular, turned toward liqueurs and spirits.

There have been some countervailing influences on consumption. Throughout the late 1980s and 1990s, for example, evidence of the potential health benefits of drinking wine has been mounting. Wine came to medical attention for its role in explaining the 'French paradox', the fact that the French have a low rate of heart disease despite eating a diet that should predispose them to a high rate. The critical variable, many researchers argued, was wine. There has been continuing debate on this issue, much of it centring on whether other forms of alcohol are as beneficial as wine and whether red and white wines are equally effective. Estimates of the desirable intake of wine vary from one or two to four or five glasses a day. Although it is recognized that excessive drinking can be harmful to health, the consensus among medical authorities is that the regular consumption of wine in moderate quantities helps to reduce the likelihood of coronary disease and heart attack.[4]

It is said that when this news was first aired on American prime-time television in 1991, sales of red wine shot up to four times their normal level before settling down again. It is not possible to estimate the long-term influence of the health argument on sales of wine, but it seems clear that reports of the benefits of wine are more likely to raise consumption than lower it. At the same time it is evident that drinking wine or other forms of alcohol is dangerous during pregnancy or before operating machinery or driving a car. Campaigns against drinking while pregnant and drunk-driving must also have had an impact on consumption patterns, if not rates, but they are difficult to quantify with any precision.

Statistics of per capita consumption of wine and other beverages bear witness to a remarkable shift in drinking cultures during the second half of the twentieth century. The public drinking common to French urban workers, overwhelmingly men, who settled down to a few glasses of red wine with their workmates and neighbours, has given way to new patterns.[5] To some extent neighbourhood sociability has been replaced by a more intense sentiment of domesticity, manifested by people increasingly entertaining in their homes rather than meeting their friends in public places like cafés. It is easy to romanticize the past and to overlook the personal, family and social consequences of heavy drinking by males in cafés and bars, but it is none the less undeniable that a sea-change has taken place, not only in the amount of wine consumed in some important European wine-producing countries, but also in the contexts in which it is consumed.

Beyond continental Europe, levels of wine consumption have followed several patterns. In the United States less than two litres a year were drunk before the Second World War, but by the 1970s and 1980s the level exceeded eight litres. By the mid 1990s, thanks in part to higher federal excise taxes that raised the price of wine, consumption had fallen and stabilized at about seven litres a year. This is a low level by European and South American standards, but it is notable that wine has increased its share of the total alcohol intake of Americans. A similar pattern is evident in Australia, where consumption rose from 17 litres in 1980 to 21 litres in 1987, but declined to 19 litres in the early 1990s. This is the highest per capita rate of wine consumption in an English-speaking nation.

Although some countries, such as The Netherlands and Japan, began to consume more wine on a per capita basis, these increases were not enough to compensate for the losses elsewhere. The Netherlands ranked about twentieth in consumption (17 litres a head in the early 1990s) but its population was small, while the much larger Japanese population drank less than a litre of wine per person. Moreover, as world consumption of wine fell, production rose. California produced 28 million gallons of table wine in 1957, but its volume doubled in the next ten years and quadrupled in the next ten, reaching 197 million gallons by 1975. By 1996 the state produced 304 million gallons of table wine as well as 9 million gallons of fortified wine and another 19 million gallons of sparkling wine.

It was not only additional planting that was responsible for the rise in production. Mechanization, more effective disease control and improved varieties of vines all played an important role. Mechanization came relatively late to European vineyards, and although tractors were on the market between the world wars, few vignerons used them until the 1950s and 1960s. For the most part tractors were too large to fit between the rows of vines, especially during the summer when they bushed out, and vine-growers had to wait for the development of straddle-tractors (*enjambeurs* in French), which operate with their wheels on each side of a row of vines and the motor and driver perched high above the vines. They can be used for pruning and for spraying. Until they went into use, however, most growers used horses.

Mechanization was generally inappropriate for small producers, because the returns do not justify the capital outlay and operating costs.

It is estimated that a tractor is a profitable investment only for a vineyard larger than ten hectares,[6] but in the mid 1950s some 84 per cent of vineyards in the south of France were less than five hectares in size and a mere 6 per cent were larger than ten hectares.[7] In this situation the mechanization of viticulture was impossible, and it was not until small producers were driven out of business and larger units created that tractors and other machines began to be used extensively. In the Médoc, where vineyards were big enough to justify the use of tractors, the vines were frequently planted too close together. In 1956, when freezing weather killed off many of the vines, replanting in some vineyards was carried out so as to leave room for tractors to operate. In other parts of France and Europe vine-growers began to space vines sufficiently far apart to accommodate ordinary mass-produced tractors that were less expensive than the straddle models specifically designed for viticulture.

In addition to the savings that mechanization introduced, growers were able to increase their yields by using more effective measures against the wide range of diseases and pests that threaten vines and their fruit. Tractors fitted with sprays could deliver sulphur, lime and copper to as many as 35,000 vines a day, a task that would take an army of men and women spraying from tanks strapped to their backs. The number of times vines have to be sprayed depends on weather and infestation, but it generally ranges from ten to twenty times a year. In more recent years some growers have used aircraft and helicopters to drop sulphur, but they are less effective because the fungicides delivered this way do not reach the underside of the leaves. Sulphur, lime and copper are the three sprays traditionally used in France, and their use is even permitted in making organic wines. Synthetic chemical and biochemical products for disease and insect control became more widely available after 1950, but although they were initially used by some vine-growers, especially in the New World, there has been a tendency to abandon them in favour of the three traditional sprays.

The third major change that has helped increase production has been clonal selection. Selection of vines for the quality of their fruit has gone on for millennia, but with more recent advances it has been possible to breed varieties that produce wine of consistent quality and that are more resistant to viruses and other diseases. This may be done simply by encouraging the formation of grapes that are not so tightly packed in the bunch that they trap the moisture that can lead to the growth of fungi. The by-product of this, one that is not too far from the front of the grower's mind, is that new clones give a higher yield. The application of a range of viticultural techniques meant that crop yields generally rose in the last decades of the twentieth century, although the appellation regulations in some countries, such as France and Italy, specify maximum yields per hectare. This, combined with patterns of planting and falling levels of consumption, means that on a global basis more wine is being produced each year than the market can absorb.

For obvious reasons, rates of consumption and levels of production are of interest to producers and governments. They were especially important in the 1950s and 1960s when many wine-producing countries expanded the land in vines, increased wine-production beyond demand and began to accumulate considerable stocks of wine. From the late 1940s to the mid 1960s, worldwide production rose 45 per cent, from 193 million to 280 million hectolitres. Western Europe's production jumped by 43 per cent, Eastern Europe's more than doubled, and New World production increased by 57 per cent.

As production in Europe rose and consumption fell by an estimated two million hectolitres a year, a surplus quickly accumulated to the point where it became known as the 'wine lake'. Wine was not the only commodity whose production exceeded demand (the excess-food landscape included a 'butter mountain'), but it clearly could not continue without dire consequences. In the early 1980s the European Community (the earlier incarnation of the present-day European Union) imposed compulsory distillation on overproducers, a policy that lowered the level of the wine lake slightly but still left plenty of room for deep-draught vessels. Later in the 1980s the Community offered incentives to producers who ripped out their vines entirely. In a period of only five years, some 320,000 hectares of vineyards (a little under 10 per cent of Europe's total) were destroyed. Most of those affected were in Spain, southern France and southern Italy. Over the longer term the policy of reducing Europe's vines was successful in reducing viticulture from 4.5 million hectares in 1976 to 3.4 million in 1997. Production fell from 210 million to 154 million hectolitres in the same period, virtually eliminating the surplus.

Other countries also adopted vine-pull schemes. They were introduced, for example, in New Zealand, Argentina and some Australian regions in the 1980s. Argentina's land under viticulture had grown by a third in a short period, shooting from 190,000 hectares in 1963 to 250,000 hectares in 1977. The success of government incentives saw the area reduced to 178,000 hectares in 1989 and to below 150,000 in the 1990s. In 1985 the South Australian government subsidized the ripping out of vineyards that were inefficient and that grew grape varieties that were unfashionable and therefore commercially not viable. Between 1980 and 1988 the vineyard area of Australia declined by a sixth, from 64,000 to 54,000 hectares. But thanks to the success of the Australian wine exports during the 1990s, when they grew by 25 per cent a year to a total of 222 million litres in 1998–9, a programme of planting began once again. Elsewhere, producers in regions like California and South Africa were faced in the 1960s with quotas on the volume of grapes that could be used for making wine.[8]

Export numbers, per capita consumption and wine surpluses are understandably important to producers and governments, but the majority of drinkers are more interested in retail price and the quality of wine and the relationship between them. Beneath the statistics of consumption levels – whether they are rising, falling or stationary – lies a clear secondary trend: that average consumers are buying wine of better quality than ever before. At the wealthiest end of the market quality has historically been important, and that has not changed. Indeed, with the upward spiral of prices for fine wines of high repute, the wealthy have this market to themselves. Very few drinkers can now afford to purchase first-growth bordeaux and other French wines of equivalent rank. A bottle of 1989 Château Haut-Brion fetched an average US$423 at auction at the end of the 1990s; its retail price would be much higher and it would cost two to three times as much in any restaurant that included it on its wine list. At Sotheby's in March 2000, 12 bottles of Château Pétrus sold for US$24,150. Few non-French wines approached these heights, but many other wine regions had individual wines that commanded prices in excess of US$100 a bottle. They included a number of California cabernet sauvignons and Australian shirazes.

Below the elevated, and sometimes inflated, reputations of the most expensive wines, well-made wines that deliver good quality at a reasonable price have increasingly marginalized poor wine. The drive to quality by both large and small producers has not been so much a trickle-down effect, although emulation and ambition have certainly been factors. Rather, quality has risen under the pressure of consumer preferences and a wine market that was much better educated in the 1980s and 1990s than it had been in the 1950s and 1960s.

As quality has improved, a small number of producers have resisted some of the changes introduced during the twentieth century by making 'organic' wines. To be considered organic, which in Europe is a legal designation, wine must be made from vineyards that do not use chemical fertilizers, pesticides or fungicides. Motivated by a desire to farm in accord with nature as well as to avoid any in-wine residue, organic wine-makers also tend to use wild yeasts in fermentation and to avoid filtering their wine. In a particular form of organic viticulture, known as biodynamic, growers are guided in their planting, growing and harvesting schedules by the movement of the moon and stars and other natural phenomena. Although only a small proportion of wine-makers have adopted biodynamic practices, they include some of the best-known producers in some regions, such as Chapoutier in the northern Rhône. Moreover, as public concern has risen over the use of chemicals in agriculture and genetically modified foods, demand for organic wine has increased. Many supermarkets and stores have devoted special sections to them.

One of the important structural supports of quality during the postwar period was the spread of laws delimiting wine areas and types. The French had accomplished the basic work of their appellation (AOC) system during the 1930s, but it was elaborated after the war as region after region was granted its own AOC status. Other European states had already taken similar measures before the Second World War – some, like the delimitation of the Douro region in the eighteenth century, well before it. The drive towards quality wines in the postwar period, however, saw the development of concerted series of policies, a trend that was accelerated by the demands of importing countries as the global wine trade expanded.

In the early 1960s Italy developed the DOC (*Denominazione di Origine Controllata*) regulations that had been sketched out during the 1930s. These regulations were as comprehensive as the French AOC rules in that they not only defined regions but also specified grape varieties, maximum yields, levels of alcohol and even acidity and extract levels. In a number of cases the DOC regulations required producers to follow the practices in place when the law was applied and to refrain from any process that would change the nature of the wine in question. In 1963 an additional level of certification was introduced: the DOCG, which added '*e Garantita*' to the original words, guaranteed rather than merely regulated the character and quality of the wine. Conveniently indicated by a coloured band on the neck of the bottle, it was to set Italy's elite wines off from those designated merely DOC.

After chronic problems, including the classification of some decidedly ordinary wines as DOCG, Italy's regulations were revised in 1992 to provide a more reliable guide to quality. At the bottom were wines ranked as table wine (*vino di tavola*) without any geographical reference. One step up were wines classed IGT (*Indicazione Geografica Tipica*), or wines that were typical of a particular region. For superior wines the DOC and DOCG classifications were maintained, but each was sub-divided by the addition of '*vigna*', allowing a producer to specify a vineyard site. Finally, any winery was permitted to apply for its own classification as a 'wine that makes Italy proud', even if it did not satisfy the various DOC or DOCG criteria.

Beginning in 1971 and continuing through to the 1990s, German regulations built on the delimitation law of 1930. Reflecting the chronic struggle of German grape-growers to produce ripe fruit, the rules took a different direction from the French, Italians and other West Europeans. The grid of classification criteria did include region, but designations of quality emphasized the degree of ripeness achieved by the grapes used. All of Germany's more than 2600 vineyards, even the smallest, were classified as Einzellagen (individual sites) within thirteen broader regions such as Mosel-Saar-Ruwer, Pfalz, Rheingau and Baden. Vineyards can make wines of any quality, and the level achieved, determined by the ripeness of the grapes, is indicated on the label. The lowest qualities, made from the least ripe grapes, are *Deutscher Tafelwein* (table wine) and *Deutscher Landwein* (regional wine), but they make up only a small proportion of all German wine in any year.

Most German wine is categorized as *Qualitätswein* (quality wine) and must be tasted to ensure that it meets specified standards. Designating almost all Germany's production as quality wine makes the term meaningless, and the category is subdivided. At the lower level is QbA (*Qualitätswein bestimmter Anbaugebiete*), or 'quality wine from a specified region', the appellation under which most German wine is sold. QbA wine may be chaptalized, but that is not permitted of wine made from riper grapes and given the higher ranking QmP (*Qualitätswein mit Prädikat*), 'quality with distinction' or 'attributes'. QmP is in turn subdivided according to the ripeness of grapes into Kabinett, Spätlese, Auslese, Beerenauslese, Trockenbeerenauslese and Eiswein. Each has different criteria. The difference between Auslese and Beerenauslese, for example, is that wine from the first is made from selected bunches of grapes, while wine from the second is made from individual grapes selected for their ripeness. All QbA and QmP wines must be tested by a government board in order to get an official approval number (A.P.Nr.), without which they cannot be marketed.

Yields were not included in the German classification scheme until 1989, and even then they were extremely generous. In the Mosel-Saar-Ruwer region, for example, riesling producers were permitted 120 hectolitres per hectare, higher than any yield normally permitted under French appellation laws. In the 1990s more rigorous rules were imposed. Among other criteria, the maximum annual yield for QbA wines was set at the average of the preceding ten years. If producers wish to exceed these limits they can do so as long as they are prepared to market the product as table wine. Other reforms in the 1990s sought to give consumers more precise information on the source of grapes used in wines: whether they came from one or from several delimited vineyards.

Australia's system is the Label Integrity Programme (LIP) which originally required 80 per cent of wine to come from the region designated on the label, 80 per cent to be of the stated varietal and 95 per cent of the wine to be of the stated vintage. When wines are blended, the order of the varietals on the label must reflect their proportion in the wine, so that a blend labelled semillon chardonnay contains more semillon than chardonnay. Like other New World wine-producing countries, Australia negotiated an agreement with the European Commission so that its wine could be marketed in the lucrative European market. As of 1994 the minimum proportions of wine by region or varietal were raised from 80 to 85 per cent.

The one major wine producer to have lagged behind the trend in developing increasingly rigorous appellation laws is the United States, perhaps a reflection of the country's more lax regulatory system. In the late 1970s the concept of American Viticultural Areas (AVAs) was devised by the Bureau of Alcohol, Tobacco, and Firearms. An AVA is defined as a region that is set off from others by having particular geographic and climatic characteristics and a distinctive tradition of wine-production. The first Californian region to be granted the status was Napa Valley, in 1981, but by 2000 the state contained some eighty individual AVAs. Unlike more demanding appellation systems, AVA regulations made no reference to varietal or maximum yield. They prescribed only that 85 per cent of grapes come from a delimited region and that in varietal wines 75 per cent come from the specified AVA. One major difference between the American and European appellation systems is that AVA does not appear on bottle labels.

It has been argued that the rudimentary restrictions imposed by AVA rules reflect the youth of the American wine industry, and that it is unreasonable to impose rigorous criteria on districts that are still experimenting with varieties and where optimum crop yields have yet to be determined. But similar conditions did not prevent Canadian wine-makers from establishing an appellation system, the VQA (Vintners' Quality Alliance) in 1990. At first this was a voluntary agreement among Ontario wine-makers to ensure that bottle labels accurately reflected wine in terms of its geographical source, varietal and vintage, but it later extended to other regions of Canada. A voluntary system was not enough for the European Commission, however, and in order to facilitate access of Canadian wines to European markets, VQA regulations began to take legal force (first in British Columbia) in the 1990s.

Controlled appellation systems, which can be expected to cover the wine-producing world ever more comprehensively, have had a number of unanticipated results. Their aim was to provide consumers with certainty that the wine they paid for was the genuine thing: that a bottle labelled 'chianti' contained a wine made from a certain blend of grapes grown in a delimited region and vinified according to specified rules, and that wine labelled 'rioja' likewise satisfied the appropriate requirements. Guarantees of this sort largely exclude the possibility of producers innovating if they want to keep their appellation, and in most cases appellation is a valuable commodity in its own right, giving a wine readily recognized identity and in many cases a higher value on the market. To this extent wine-makers in Europe are more restricted by appellation regulations than those of countries like Australia and the United States.

One of the overriding problems with appellation systems is that they generally set out to indicate the character of a wine, not its quality. Quality is implied by the assumption that a wine made from specified grapes in a delimited area, grown and vinified as indicated by the appellation, will be of good quality. As a rule appellation status is a reasonable guide to quality, but it does not follow that non-appellation wines are necessarily inferior. There is a sense in which the appellation rules have had an effect similar to the 1855 Bordeaux classification. Classed growth wines might on the whole still be superior to those not in the classification, but many wines that are not classed are superior to many that are. Château Pétrus, for example, is recognized as one of Bordeaux's consistently great wines and it fetches considerably higher prices at auction than any other bordeaux, even though it is not included as a growth of any rank.

In the case of producers of appellation wines of extremely high reputation, it would generally be foolish to relinquish appellation status by introducing vines and wine-making practices not permitted by the rules of the particular appellation. The quality of wines aside, there is simply too much at risk commercially to surrender appellations like Gevrey-Chambertin and Saint-Emilion. Few producers have had the courage (or financial means) to ignore the appellation rules, even when they believed they interfered with their ability to make better wines. During the 1980s a number of producers in the central Italian region of Tuscany, following the example set by the wine Sassicaia in the sixties and seventies, ignored DOC regulations on permitted grape varieties and began to make wines from cabernet sauvignon, syrah and merlot grapes that swiftly won international acclaim. Unable to qualify for DOC status, their wines (often referred to in the English-speaking world as 'Super-Tuscans') were classified as common table wine, a designation that ought to indicate an inferior wine made according to no specified criteria. Under the 1992 revision of the DOC laws, however, individual producers have been able to apply for classification of their wines under a special 'wines that make Italy proud' clause.

A third weakness with appellation systems as they have evolved is that there are immense variations among wine-producing countries in the proportion of their wine that receives appellation status. In Germany virtually all wines (about 95 per cent) meet the requirements and taste-testing levels that earn Qualitätswein classification. In France, on the other hand, less than half the wine produced falls within AOC designations, although the proportion increased during the 1990s. The variation results from the different sets of criteria on which the respective appellation systems are based, but it causes confusion when appellation-status is equated with quality and raises questions about the relative rigour of the two systems. There are also big differences between appellations in individual countries. In France, for example, some AOCs cover vast expanses with a variety of climatic and other characteristics, while others are tightly defined. The AOC Côtes-du-Rhône, for example, covers some 40,000 hectares, but within its area lies one of the smallest AOCs, Château Grillet, which occupies less than four hectares of land.

Periodic scandals have also drawn attention to the fact that compliance with appellation regulations is often inadequately supervised. In the 1980s some Austrian wine was discovered to have been adulterated with diethylene glycol to give it body, while some Italian wine containing methanol killed three people who drank it. At about the same time a prominent German wine-maker was convicted of adding liquid sugar to his wine in contravention of appellation rules. In the 1990s a third-growth Bordeaux château in Margaux was discovered to have used grapes from a lower-ranked Haut-Médoc appellation in its second wine. It is impossible to know whether these and other scandals represent a much more frequent incidence of adulteration and misrepresentation. There is sporadic evidence of crop yields above the permitted limits, of more of a particular wine appearing on the market than was produced, and of the regular use of illegal additives in some regions.[9] But delimitation and appellation laws were introduced originally to deal with adulteration and fraud, and there is no doubt that such practices are far less common at the end of the twentieth century than at the beginning. The appellation laws and their enforcement agencies, together with practices like estate bottling (rather than bottling by merchants), and the regular chemical analysis of wines by private and state laboratories, have helped to improve the integrity of wine.

*

In the New World the emphasis on quality led to a reorganization of the wine industry. Immediately after the Second World War in regions like California and Australia, wine-production was largely in the hands of a few big companies. The largest Californian producer, Gallo, was a major winery before the war and consolidated its position during the 1950s and 1960s, by which time it already had the capacity to store 100 million gallons of wine. In Australia the wine market was long dominated by companies such as Penfold's, Lindeman's and Hardy, while in New Zealand Corbans and Montana were among the giants. In the small Ontario market, companies like Bright's and Jordan Valley held sway. In these and other regions there was a host of small wineries producing limited quantities of wine that was often (although not always) of better quality than that of the mass-market producers.

For the most part, the two sectors of the industry cooperated, although there were occasions when the bulk-wine makers objected to any suggestions that their wine was inferior. In the late 1950s, for example, Gallo and other large Californian wine-makers objected to references to 'premium' wine in the public-relations material issued by the Wine Advisory Board, an industry body that was responsible for promoting wine. The designation of some wines as 'premium' implied that other wines were not. Various compromises were tried in order to bridge the gap between the large-scale and the limited producers. The offending word 'premium' was removed in favour of a distinction between 'fine' and 'popular' wines, but even that was too much. By the 1960s official advertising campaigns treated all California wines as essentially the same, a solution that pleased the big producers but not the small wine-makers, for whom 'California wine' was 'synonymous with cheapness'.[10]

As an increasing number of consumers began to search for quality in wine, a number of changes took place. The smaller companies began to win a larger share of the market as their wines were seen as more artisanal and individual than the mass-produced wines of the large companies. Over time a number of the smaller companies became large producers in their own right, without forgoing their reputation for quality. Meanwhile the existing big companies themselves also began to focus more on quality without sacrificing quantity. They not only raised the overall quality of their bulk-produced wines but also began to make relatively (to their total production) small quantities of higher-quality wines. Many are sold under variants of the company name or under distinct names so that consumers know that they are paying more for a better wine. In the US, for example, Gallo sells most of its least expensive wines under the Carlo Rossi and Livingston Cellars labels, some middle-range wines as Turning Leaf, and higher quality products as Ernest & Julio Gallo and Gallo Sonoma.

During the 1980s and 1990s, when the drive for quality had begun to gather steam, a large number of new wineries was established, especially in the New World. Often very small-scale producers, many of them 'boutique wineries', these new vineyards were planted in regions where grapes had either not grown at all before or had not grown successfully. In the 1960s, wine production in the United States was overwhelmingly dominated by California, with minor industries established in New York State and Oregon. During the 1980s and 1990s, however, there seemed to be no place where grapes could not be grown commercially for wine, and by 2000 only two states – Alaska and North Dakota – did not have commercial vineyards. The results were very variable, but no producers in Texas, New Mexico or Maine could be under any illusion that unless they produced quality wine they would soon be driven out of business.

The geographical extension of wine-making affected other countries, too. In New Zealand the industry's centre of gravity shifted south from its original concentration around Auckland, in the northern half of the North Island. The discovery that excellent wines could be made in the South Island led to the planting of the massive Marlborough vineyards. Nor did the southward drift stop there, and vines were planted in the Central Otago region, making them the world's most southerly vineyards. In Australia scores of new wineries were set up in the established regions such as the Hunter, Barossa and Yarra Valleys, while little-known districts expanded and came to the fore. One was Margaret River in Western Australia, a continent away from Australia's main wine-producing areas in the southeast. In Canada, where wine-making had been concentrated in the Niagara area of Ontario, a major new region opened up to the west, in the Okanagan Valley of British Columbia, and boutique wineries appeared to the east, in Québec and the Atlantic provinces.

Many of the older, successful, small- and medium-scale wineries were bought out by larger companies, and although they have kept their labels and the identity of their wines, they are now part of large corporate entities. This process has gone a long way in Australia, where two holding companies, Southcorp and BRL Hardy, own dozens of wineries. Among those owned by Southcorp are Penfold's, Lindeman's, Seaview, Seppelt, Hungerford Hill, Rouge Homme, Killawara and Wynns Coona-warra Estate. The trend toward corporate ownership of what had pre-viously been independent wine-producers was by no means confined to the New World. One of the largest companies in the French wine business is Louis Vuitton Moët-Hennessy (LVMH), which also has extensive interests in perfume (Dior) and other luxury goods. In addition to owning several of the best-known champagne houses (Moët et Chandon, Veuve Clicquot and Krug) and extensive wine companies elsewhere in Europe and in Argentina and Australia, LVMH purchased the prestigious Château d'Yquem in 1999.

Corporate takeovers are nothing new in the Old World or the New, and nor was purchase of famous vineyards by business interests. Although wine is often referred to in quasi-religious terms – many wine-makers refer to their wine as expressing not only *terroir* but also their soul – it has historically been as much a commercial proposition as any branch of agriculture. Many of the classed-growth château wines of Bordeaux and the classified domaines of Burgundy have changed hands scores of times in the last 300 years and still maintained their integrity. The latest round of acquisitions is likely to make no greater difference.

Old World wines had to respond to a new environment in the last decades of the twentieth century not so much in terms of their commercial structure as in terms of the challenge posed by wines from the New World. For centuries it was assumed that the wines of Europe generally, and the wines of France especially, represented the pinnacle of the wine-maker's art. So implicit was this belief that wines made in the Americas, Australasia and South Africa generally bore the names of the European regions which they were thought to approach most closely. In many cases these designations were pathetic expression of pious hope, rather than any real sense in which California burgundy or Ontario sherry bore any resemblance to their European namesakes. Europe's wines were to New World producers as the wines of the classical world had been to wine-writers of the eighteenth and nineteenth centuries: benchmarks against which they judged their own wines.

But there was a critical difference, in that while classical wines could only be imagined, their tastes and other qualities judged by contemporary descriptions filtered through layers of prejudice, it was possible to put New World wines up against the old. This had, of course, been going on for more than a century, first as wine-makers from the far-flung parts of the globe sent samples of wine to societies offering prizes, to colonial secretaries who might offer encouragement or money, or to European wine cognoscenti. With the beginning of regular international exhibitions and later wine competitions, New World wine was regularly tasted in Europe. The results were mixed. Often, European judges were condescending, and sometimes when they discovered an excellent wine from outside Europe they simply refused to believe its provenance. Wine fraud was widespread, it is true, but what frequently underlay European judges' assessments of New World wine seemed to be nothing more than old prejudice, the belief that it was just not possible to make excellent wine outside Europe.

The situation had begun to change during the twentieth century, when Britain imported vast volumes of Australian table and fortified wines, but there remained resistance on the Continent, particularly in France. A critical moment occurred in 1976 when, to mark the bicentennial of the American Revolution, a comparative tasting of American and French wines was held in Paris. The tasting panel, drawn from the elite of the French wine establishment – merchants, restaurateurs, wine-writers and government officials – was presented with five Californian chardonnays and five white burgundies, followed by five California cabernet sauvignons and five red bordeaux. The tasting was carried out blind and there was utter consternation when the results were tabulated and showed that a Californian wine had won in both the white and red categories. This tasting might not have changed many French minds about the overall relative quality of French and Californian wines, let alone New World wines in general, but it reinforced the name that California was earning as a quality wine region.

The generally improving reputation of New World wines gradually earned them an increasing share of their own markets. Canadian wine-drinkers long spurned the products of Ontario, which they associated with poor-quality wines made from inferior hybrids or native varieties like concord. With the growth of small wineries making quality wines from *vitis vinifera*, as well as ice-wines from riesling and hybrids, Ontario wines captured an increasing share of the Canadian market. The same is true of domestic wines throughout the New World.

This trend has cut across established patterns of the trade in wine. The Old World still exports to the New in far larger quantities than the reverse, but the trade gap has narrowed, and the growing popularity of domestic wines in the New World has, in effect, deprived European producers of export opportunities they might have had. The result has been commercial tension between the two wine worlds, in particular over the reluctance of successive French governments, under pressure from the domestic wine lobby, to allow New World wines to be marketed freely in France. Of the major European wine-producing countries, Germany has been the most receptive to imports from countries like the United States and Australia.

There have also been largely successful attempts to prevent New World wine producers from profiting from the reputations that European wine regions had built up over centuries. Gradually, agreements were signed to prevent the use of regional names like burgundy, sherry, port, bordeaux, champagne and rhinewine by producers outside those regions. Some wine-makers have developed new names entirely. In California in 1988 the name 'meritage' was coined to refer to red or white wine made from the traditional blend of grapes used in making bordeaux. Within Europe itself, as in the wider world, sparkling wine can no longer be called 'champagne' unless it complies with the appellation rules – which include geographical criteria. Thus sparkling wine from Spain is sold as 'cava', and German wine as 'Sekt', while Americans and Australians make simply 'sparkling wine'. Meanwhile, the Alsatian grape variety that had long been called 'tokay' was renamed 'tokay pinot gris' to distinguish it from the Hungarian wine.

For the most part, New World wine-producers responded to the need to re-name their wines by abandoning references to regions. They began to describe their wines simply by the varieties from which they were made, and that is the dominant method by which most of their wines are now labelled. Unlike European delimited areas, which generally grow a very restricted range of varieties, New World wine regions typically draw on a broad spectrum. Certain districts, it is true, have become well known for varieties that grow particularly successfully there. They include Oregon for pinot noir, the Central Valley of California for zinfandel, the Hunter Valley in Australia for shiraz, and Marlborough in New Zealand for sauvignon blanc. But it makes no sense to describe a wine as an oregon, a central valley, a hunter river, or a marlborough, because each also produces wines made from different varieties.

The identification of wine primarily by varietal ran counter to the European tradition of stressing geographical location. Although regions are closely associated with specific varieties, either singly or in blends, and are now legally bound to them by law through the appellation regulations, it was the location – the *terroir* – that was the dominant identifier. It was expected that someone who purchased a Pétrus would know that it was made almost entirely of merlot with a little cabernet franc, and that a barbaresco was based on nebbiolo. Some well-known European wines, it is true, show the variety on their labels. Alsatian rieslings and gewürztraminers are examples, but the varietal is always secondary to the delimited region. From another perspective, Europeans did identify their wines by variety, but they did so indirectly by reference to AOC regions where only certain varietals were permitted. Anyone who knew the law was aware that a red wine labelled AOC Côte de Beaune was made from pinot noir grapes.

There is an irony in all this, because having banned the use of European regional names as ways of describing New World wines, European producers exporting to the United States, Australia, Canada and elsewhere began to abandon their own regional designations in favour of specifying the varietals from which they are made. Thus a number of burgundies exported have 'pinot noir' printed on their labels in larger letters that the Burgundy appellation, and many wines from the south of France have followed suit. It is unthinkable that the great classified wines would ever change in this way, but the trend reflects the imperatives of the global market and the growing influence of the New World.

The global market was also reflected in the transnational investments and collaborative ventures that during the 1980s and 1990s brought together wine producers from quite divergent backgrounds. One of the most interesting was the partnership of California wine-maker Robert Mondavi and Bordeaux proprietor Baron Philippe de Rothschild in creating a vineyard and winery to make their well-known Opus One wine. Other examples were simple investments, such as those by Moët and Chandon in sparkling wine production in Argentina and Australia. The flow of capital and expertise also went the other way. In the 1990s BRL Hardy, one of Australia's great wine conglomerates, bought vineyards in Chianti and Languedoc. The former was not successful and was soon abandoned, but the latter flourished in the La Baume estate near Béziers. La Baume makes millions of litres a year of red and white from grapes that it sources from its own vineyards and from local growers on contract. Moreover, it has introduced Australian methods of viticulture (like night harvesting) and viniculture that are often quite at odds with regional practice.

The Hardy winery in France is part of the more general influence that Australia had on the world of wine in the last decades of the twentieth century. Although Australia was responsible for only about 2 per cent of global wine production, its results have been impressive and it has established benchmarks for a number of varietals, such as chardonnay and shiraz. Moreover, Australians have innovated in canopy-management and other viticultural techniques and in wine-making, and they have a general attitude to their work that sets them apart from producers in Europe. Australian wine-makers travel the wine world as highly skilled seasonal workers, relocating to the northern hemisphere during the off-season at home. The exchange of expertise runs in all directions (French wine-makers work in Australian vineyards), and wine-makers throughout the world can now draw on a far wider range of knowledge and experience than ever before.

What was already a substantial world of wine expanded in some senses in the 1980s and 1990s as political changes had an immense impact on wine. When the communist system in the Soviet Union began to unravel in the 1980s, the reforming administration of Mikhail Gorbachev launched a campaign to reduce the production and consumption of alcohol. Widespread alcoholism was blamed for declining life expectancy as well as falling economic production and a host of social problems. The main culprit was said to be vodka, but the anti-alcohol campaign was comprehensive. Distilleries, breweries and wineries were closed down, as were retail outlets, bars and many licensed restaurants. Vine-yards in important regions like Georgia were ripped out and the total area in vines declined by about a quarter.

The result was an instant reversal of a trend which had seen alcohol-production increase steadily since the Second World War. In 1940 the Soviet Union had produced 2 million hectolitres of wine, but by 1960 the volume had quadrupled to 8 million before leaping to 27 million hectolitres in 1970 and 32 million hectolitres in 1980. Five years later output was back to 1970 levels. A similar pattern applied to other alcoholic beverages – especially fruit and berry wine and vodka – and pure alcohol, although the production of beer continued to rise gently in the first years of the campaign. The main category of alcohol to buck the trend was sparkling wine, which had been sold under the name 'Soviet Champagne'. Production rose from 37 million bottles in 1960 to 87 million in 1970, 178 million in 1980, and 258 million in 1988.[11]

The collapse of the Soviet Union in 1991 and the emergence of new independent states held out the promise that two of them would reinvigorate their wine industries: Georgia, which had been the heart of Soviet wine-production, and Ukraine, whose territory included the Crimean vineyards. The failure of the Soviet Union was preceded by the collapse of regimes throughout eastern Europe. Many of these states, such as Hungary, Romania and Bulgaria, had extensive vineyards that had been state-owned under the socialist regimes. In most cases the land was sold off to private proprietors and in the 1990s many began to produce higher-quality wines for the export market.

The other political event of the period that impinged directly on wine was the end of the apartheid government in South Africa and the cessation of international trade sanctions. South Africa's wine industry had continued to operate during the embargo, but because many potential markets were closed, production was below capacity and in many cases isolation from world markets meant that wineries had failed to reach the same levels of quality as other New World producers.

An important development that accompanied and reinforced the concern for quality throughout the western world was the growth of a consumer culture associated with wine. The development of this culture was made possible only by the expansion of what might be thought of as the wine constituency – those who are interested enough in wine to go beyond drinking it to thinking seriously about it. The evidence suggests that since the Second World War, and especially since the 1970s, this group has steadily expanded. From an elite of well-to-do men, many actively involved in the wine business, it now comprises a substantial part of the middle class, including many women as well as men, only a minority of whom are professionally associated with wine. The growth of this constituency was part of a more general growth of interest in food and drink.

This group of consumers began to sustain an extensive range of goods and services dedicated to wine. For example, the number of publications related to wine has increased steadily since the 1970s. Before then, wine magazines and periodicals were directed primarily at readers in the wine business. During the last three decades of the century not only have many shifted their emphasis to include consumers, but they have been joined by many more publications. Only the most prominent example is the influential *Wine Spectator*, which commenced publication in 1976. At the end of the century there were scores of periodicals devoted to wine, and hundreds of books dealing with all aspects of wine appear each year.

The growth of wine publishing has brought forth a new generation of wine-writers in various genres. Building on the tradition of Cyrus Redding and André Jullien in the nineteenth century and André Simon in the twentieth, they differed from their predecessors not only in the size of their readership, but also in their ability to make a living primarily from writing rather than involvement in the wine industry. Among the best-known wine-writers in English are Hugh Johnson, Jancis Robinson, Robert Parker and Oz Clark. Their books, which include encyclopedias, atlases, guides for buyers, and studies of regions, grape varieties and the science of wine-making, line the shelves of bookstores throughout the world. Going beyond the printed word, they give lectures, lead tastings, and have produced series of television programmes and CD-ROMS.

In addition to reading material, wine-drinkers can buy a wide array of paraphernalia: decanters, foil-cutters, corkscrews and other types of cork removers, thermometers, carafes, wine-preservation devices, temperature- and humidity-controlled cellars for home installation, and cellar books. Those who want to taste wine formally can buy tasting glasses, aroma wheels, sets of bottled aromas, and any number of how-to-taste guides. Those wanting to make their own wine can buy all the equipment together with juice, concentrate or fresh grapes, depending on where they live.

Opportunities for education in wine have expanded dramatically. There are a myriad wine appreciation classes and courses, tutored tastings, sommelier certification programmes, and professional degrees in everything from viticulture and wine-making to winery management and wine consultancy. A number of universities have become prominent in these fields, notably the University of California at Davis, Roseworthy Agricultural College in Australia and the University of Bordeaux. In most wine regions universities and colleges offer programmes in viticulture, viniculture and wine management, and in France a Université du Vin has been established at Suze-la-Rousse with the mission of studying all aspects of wine. In Great Britain the Institute of Masters of Wine began to offer the MW qualification in the 1950s, based on a rigorous examination that tests worldwide knowledge of oenology and viticulture.

Those who want to learn about wine less formally have the option of wine tourism. Not only are there organized tours of wine regions, but wine-makers' associations hold festivals and festivities to draw visitors to their localities and their cellars. Most wineries welcome visitors and will gladly sell wines at the cellar door. In larger cities wine and food festivals are regular occurrences. All these activities raise the profile of wine and help to sustain and widen its consumer base. The place of wine in economies at all levels is shown by the support festivals and tastings receive from individual wineries, chambers of commerce, and regional and national governments. Many wine regions boast museums of wine that display bottles, implements and other paraphernalia, and highlight the oenological history of their localities. In London, long one of the world's great wine markets, 1999 saw the opening of Vinopolis, a massive permanent exhibition of wine and wine culture and a centre for information on wine.

Underlying this consumer culture is, of course, the wine itself. Wine, like alcohol generally, has become more accessible in all markets. This is a function less of the broadening popularity of wine and more of the trend toward deregulation that has been a feature of many economies and marketplaces since the 1980s. Where wine was available from government liquor outlets in the 1950s and 1960s, it can now be purchased in privately owned stores and supermarkets. There is no more clear indication of the trend towards the mass market for higher-quality wines than the fact that supermarket chains, such as Tesco and

Sainsbury's in Great Britain, sell a number of them under their own label.

Limitations on access to wine appear from time to time, like the attempt in the US Congress in 1999 to halt mail-order sales across state borders. This was not only an echo of prohibitionist sentiment but also a reaction against the more positive attitude towards wine that had been developing. In the 1990s the US Bureau of Alcohol, Tobacco and Firearms, the federal body that regulates the alcohol trade, permitted wine-makers to print references to the potential health benefits of wine on their labels. The labels would not refer to the benefits as such but would invite drinkers to write for information on the effects of wine on health.

If this implied that drinkers could not only enjoy the taste of wine, but also benefit from it, they could select their medicine from a well-stocked pharmacy, for at no time in history have consumers had such a range of wines to choose from. American and British wine-drinkers can buy wine from almost all of the American states, as well as from producers throughout Europe, Latin America, Canada, parts of the Middle East, North and South Africa, Australia and New Zealand. The only wine Americans cannot legally buy, as long as their trade embargo lasts, is wine from Cuba. It is likely that the sheer range of wines now available has helped broaden interest in wine. Facing a shelf of wine from regions and districts as diverse as Anatolia, Rutherglen, Lake Erie North Shore, Lubbock and Puglia is like embarking on a mystery tour of taste. It is difficult not to feel the meaning of *terroir*, for each bottle represents a bit of the culture and history of its region of origin.

Throughout the western world, in short, unprecedented numbers of men and women have invested time and money in, and derived pleasure from, learning about wine. Their lessons have come from the page, from the screen, from travel, and – most profitably – from the glass. This trend has led to the creation of the solid market that is necessary for the continued production of quality wine. At the beginning of the new millennium all the wind seems to be in the sails of the wine industry. General prosperity in western economies has sustained a healthy wine market, producers are paying more attention to quality than ever before, interest in wine is more widespread than it has ever been, and wine is once again being hailed as a healthy beverage.

The very approach of the millennium brought one type of wine to the fore: champagne, the byword in celebration. Although a wide range of excellent sparkling wines, most made by the champagne method, were on the market, many people wanted the corks that popped at midnight on 31 December 1999 to bear the name of a famous champagne house, not of a producer of Australian brut or Spanish cava. During the 1990s the rumour spread that there would not be enough champagne to meet demand, and some individuals and restaurants began to stockpile supplies. Champagne's producers had foreseen the surge in demand, however, and took steps to ensure that adequate supplies would be available. Growers and the champagne houses agreed to produce enough grapes to make an average 270 million bottles of champagne a year during the second half of the 1990s. In addition, more than a hundred million bottles of reserve wine, kept for blending, were released for champagne production. As a result, the number of bottles of champagne put on the market each year rose steadily during the 1990s, from just over 200 million in the recession years 1991–2, to 300 million in 1999.

It was expected that demand for champagne would decline in the first few years of the twenty-first century, but by its very cultural significance, the sales of champagne are likely to be more volatile than those of many other types of wine. Paradoxically, volatility has been the constant in the long history of wine, as its fortunes have been shaped by politics and wars, by social and economic change, by shifts in taste and diet, and by its relationship to religion and medicine. The history of wine should convince anyone – producer, merchant or consumer – that wine is not a commodity that inspires complacency, and that its future will prove as fascinating as its past.

APPENDIX

HISTORICAL MEASURES OF WINE

Over the centuries, wine has been aged and shipped in a variety of containers of many different sizes. They ranged in volume from hundreds of litres to the standard modern wine bottle of three quarters of a litre. Containers varied in size not only over time, but also from place to place, such that a barrel from one part of Europe held more or less than a barrel from another region. At certain times attempts were made to standardize the volumes of certain containers, but it was not until the nineteenth century that fabrication techniques made reliable standardization possible. The conversion of old measurements of volume into new can, therefore, be only approximate. The conversions given in the text are as accurate as possible, but they are often no more than the best estimate among a range of possibilities.

The following list gives the approximate equivalents for the containers mentioned in the text.

amphora
Most classical amphoras contained between 22 and 30 litres. A working average is 25 litres.

barrel
This is more a generic term for a container than a guide to volume. The barrel of medieval Florence contained 45.5 litres, but the barrel of Pisa held 68 litres, and the English fifteenth-century barrel held 143 litres. The standard Bordeaux barrel which is now widely used, holds 225 litres (59 imperial gallons).

bottle
The size of glass bottles varied widely over time because each was individually blown. Standard modern wine bottles hold 75 centilitres (26 fluid ounces).

butt

A barrel fixed by English law at 573 litres (126 imperial gallons) in the fifteenth century. Modern sherry butts hold 491 litres (108 imperial gallons) of wine.

gallon

The medieval English wine gallon was equal to about three litres and by the eighteenth century it had risen to 3.8 litres. The modern imperial (British) gallon, standardized in 1824, is about 4.5 litres. An imperial gallon is approximately equal to 1.25 American gallons.

leaguer

Used in the calculation of Cape wine, it equals 682 litres or 150 imperial gallons.

litre

About 0.22 imperial gallons.

muid

A measure used widely in France where its volume varied from region to region. The Paris muid represented 268 litres in the seventeenth and eighteenth centuries, but it was much larger in Montpellier (730 litres) and Roussillon (472 litres).

pièce

A barrel in regions like Burgundy and the Rhône and Loire valleys. It equals 225–228 litres (59–60 imperial gallons).

pipe, pipa

Commonly used to measure Iberian wines, it varied from 454 to 573 litres (about 100–126 imperial gallons) in the early modern period. The modern port pipe holds 523 litres (115 imperial gallons).

tun

An English measure equal to two English pipes or butts: about 1146 litres or 252 imperial gallons.

SELECT BIBLIOGRAPHY

This bibliography lists only the main books that relate to the history of wine. Other books, articles in periodicals and manuscript sources are cited in the notes.

Adams, James du Quesnay, *Patterns of Medieval Society* (Englewood Cliffs, NJ: Prentice Hall, 1969).

Allen, H. Warner, *A History of Wine: Great Vintage Wines from the Homeric Age to the Present Day* (London: Faber and Faber, 1961).

Alsace: vignerons et artisans (Paris: Musées nationaux, 1976).

Amerine, Maynard A. and Vernon L. Singleton, *Wine: An Introduction* (Berkeley, CA: University of California Press, 1965, rev. edn Sydney: Australia and New Zealand Book Company, 1977).

Amouretti, Marie Claire and Jean-Pierre Brun (eds.), *La production du vin et de l'huile en Méditerranée* (Athens: Ecole française d'Athènes, 1993).

Aspler, Tony, *Vintage Canada: A Tasteful Companion to Canadian Wines* (Toronto: McGraw Hill-Ryerson, 1993).

Barr, Andrew, *Drink* (London: Bantam Press, 1995).

Barr, Andrew, *Wine Snobbery: An Insider's Guide to the Booze Business* (London: Faber and Faber, 1988).

Barrows, Susanna and Robin Room (eds.), *Drinking: Behavior and Belief in Modern History* (Berkeley: University of California Press, 1991).

Beeston, John, *A Concise History of Australian Wine* (2nd edn, Sydney: Allen and Unwin, 1995).

Berman, Constance Hoffman, *Medieval Agriculture, the Southern French Countryside, and the Early Cistercians: A Study of Forty-Three Monasteries* (Philadelphia: American Philosophical Society, 1986).

Blocker, Jack S. Jr, *American Temperance Movements: Cycles of Reform* (Boston: Twayne, 1989).

Blocker, Jack S. Jr, and Cheryl Krasnick Warsh (eds.), *The Changing Face of Drink: Substance, Imagery, and Behaviour* (Ottawa: Publications Histoire sociale/Social History, 1999).

Les Boissons: Production et consommation aux XIXe et XXe siècles (Paris: Comité des Travaux Historiques et Scientifiques, 1984).

Bourély, Béatrice, *Vignes et vins de l'Abbaye de Cîteaux en Bourgogne* (Nuits-St-Georges: Éditions du Tastevin, 1998).

Brears, Peter, *Food and Cooking in Seventeenth-Century Britain* (London: English Heritage, 1985).

Brennan, Thomas, *Burgundy to Champagne: The Wine Trade in Early Modern France* (Baltimore: Johns Hopkins University Press, 1997).

Brennan, Thomas, *Public Drinking and Popular Culture in Eighteenth-Century Paris* (Princeton: Princeton University Press, 1988).

Briggs, Asa, *Haut-Brion: An Illustrious Lineage* (London: Faber and Faber, 1994).

Briggs, Asa, *Wine for Sale: Victoria Wine and the Liquor Trade, 1860–1984* (Chicago: University of Chicago Press, 1985).

Brooks, Van Hyck, *The Wine of the Puritans: A Study of Present-Day America* (London: Sisley's, 1908, repr. Folcroft, PA: J. Folcroft Library Editions, 1973).

Burford, Alison, *Land and Labor in the Greek World* (Baltimore: Johns Hopkins University Press, 1993).

Busby, James, *A Manual of Plain Directions for Planting and Cultivating Vineyards* (Sydney: R. Mansfield, 1830).

Busby, James, *A Treatise on the Culture of the Vine and the Art of Making Wine* (Sydney: Government Printer, 1825).

Busby, James, *Journal of a Tour through Some of the Vineyards of Spain and France* (Sydney: Stephens and Stokes, 1833).

Butel, Paul, *Les négociants bordelais: l'Europe et les Iles au XVIIIe siècle* (Paris: Aubier, 1974).

Butler, Frank Hedges, *Wine and the Wine Lands of the World* (London: T. Fisher Unwin, 1926).

Cato, Marcus Porcius, *On Agriculture* (London: Heinemann, 1934).

Conroy, David W., *In Public Houses: Drink and the Revolution of Authority in Colonial Massachusetts* (Chapel Hill: University of North Carolina Press, 1995).

Conway, James, *Napa* (New York: Avon, 1990).

Craeybeckx, Jan, *Un grand commerce d'importation: les vins de France aux anciens Pays-Bas* (Paris: SEVPEN, 1958).

Crawford, Anne, *A History of the Vintners' Company* (London: Constable, 1977).

Croissance agricole du Haut Moyen Age: chronologie, modalités, géographie (Auch: Centre culturel de l'Abbaye de Flaran, 1990), 103–15.

Cushner, Nicholas P., *Lords of the Land: Sugar, Wine, and Jesuit Estates of Coastal Peru, 1600–1767* (Albany: State University of New York Press, 1980).

Dallas, Gregor, *The Imperfect Peasant Economy: The Loire Country, 1880–1914* (Cambridge: Cambridge University Press, 1982).

de Blij, Harm Jan, *Geography of Viticulture* (Miami: Miami Geographical Society, 1981).

de Blij, Harm Jan, *Wine: A Geographic Appreciation* (Totowa, NJ: Rowman and Allanheld, 1983).

de Blij, Harm Jan, *Viticulture in Geographical Perspective* (Miami: Miami Geographical Society, 1992).

de Blij, Harm Jan, *Wine Regions of the Southern Hemisphere* (Totowa, NJ: Rowman and Allanheld, 1985).

de Castella, Hubert, *Notes of an Australian Vine Grower* (Melbourne, 1882, repr. Melbourne: Mast Gully Press, 1979).

de Castella, Hubert, *John Bull's Vineyard* (Australia, 1886).

de Langle, Henry-Melchior, *Le petit monde des cafés et débits parisiens au XIXe siècle* (Paris: Presses Universitaires de France, 1990).

Dickenson, John and Tim Unwin, *Viticulture in Latin America: Essays on Alcohol, the Vine and Wine in Spanish America* (Liverpool: University of Liverpool, Institute of Latin American Studies, Working Paper 13, 1992).

Dion, Roger, *Histoire de la vigne et du vin en France des origines au XIXe siècle* (Paris, 1955, repr. Paris: Flammarion, 1977).

Le Vin (ed. Jean Bart and Elisabeth Wahl) *Dix-huitième siècle* 29 (Paris: Presses Universitaires de France, 1997).

Druitt, Robert, *Report on the Cheap Wines from France, Germany, Italy, Austria, Greece, Hungary, and Australia: Their Use in Diet and Medicine* (London: Henry Renshaw, 1873).

Duby, Georges, *Rural Economy and Country Life in the Medieval West* (London: Edward Arnold, 1968).

Dunstan, David, *Better than Pommard! A History of Wine in Victoria* (Melbourne: Australian Scholarly Publishing/Museum of Victoria, 1994).

Durand, Georges, *Vin, vigne et vignerons en Lyonnais et Beaujolais (XVIe-XVIIIe siècles)* (Paris: Mouton, 1979).

Enjalbert, Henri, *Histoire de la vigne et du vin: l'avènement de la qualité* (Paris, 1975).

Fabroni, Adam, *De l'art de faire le vin* (Paris: A.-J. Marchant, Year 10 [1801]).

Faith, Nicholas, *Château Margaux* (London: Mitchell Beazley, 1991).

Fournier, Dominique and Salvatore D'Onofrio (eds.), *Le ferment divin* (Paris: Éditions de la Maison des sciences de l'homme, 1991).

Francis, A. D., *The Wine Trade* (London: A&C Black, 1972).

Fuller, Robert C., *Religion and Wine: A Cultural History of Wine Drinking in the United States* (Knoxville, TN: University of Tennessee Press, 1996).

Gabler, James M., *Passions: The Wines and Travels of Thomas Jefferson* (Baltimore: Bacchus Press, 1995).

Galtier, Gaston, *Le vignoble du Languedoc méditerranée et du Roussillon* (3 vols., Montpellier: Causs, Graille, Castelnau, 1960).

Garlan, Yvon, *Vin et amphores de Thasos* (Athens: École française d'Athènes, 1988).

Garrier, Gilbert, *Histoire sociale et culturelle du vin* (Paris: Larousse, 1998).

Garrier, Gilbert (ed.), *Le Vin des historiens* (Suze-la-Rousse: Université du Vin, 1990).

Geraud-Parracha, Guillaume, *Le commerce des vins et de l'eau-de-vie en Languedoc sous l'ancien régime* (Mende, 1958).

Grace, V. R., *Amphoras and the Ancient Wine Trade* (Princeton: American School of Classical Studies at Athens, 1981).

Gruter, Edouard, *La naissance d'un grand vignoble: les seigneuries du Pizay et Tanay en Beaujolais au XVIe et XVIIe siècles* (Lyon, 1977).

Hagen, Ann, *A Handbook of Anglo-Saxon Food* (Pinner, Middlesex: Anglo-Saxon Books, 1992).

Haine, W. Scott, *The World of the Paris Café: Sociability among the French Working Class, 1789–1914* (Baltimore: Johns Hopkins University Press, 1996).

Halasz, Z., *Hungarian Wine through the Ages* (Budapest: Corvina, 1962).

Halliday, James, and Hugh Johnson, *The Art and Science of Wine* (London: Mitchell Beazley, 1992).

Heine, Peter, *Weinstudieren: Untersuchungen zu Anbau, Produktion und Konsum des Weins im arabisch-islamischen Mittelalter* (Wiesbaden: Otto Harrassowitz, 1982).

Hen, Yitzhak, *Culture and Religion in Merovingian Gaul, AD 481–751* (Leiden: Brill, 1995).

Hippocrates (London: Heinemann, 1967).

Hocquet, Jean-Claude, *Voiliers et commerce en Méditerranée, 1200–1650* (Lille: Presses Universitaires de Lille, 1979).

Hyams, Edward, *Dionysus: A Social History of the Wine Vine* (New York: Macmillan, 1965).

Hyams, Edward, *The Grape Vine in England* (London: Bodley Head, 1949).

James, Margery Kirkbride, *Studies in the Medieval Wine Trade* (ed. Elspeth M. Veale, Oxford: Clarendon Press, 1971).

Jeffs, Julian, *Sherry* (3rd edn, London: Faber and Faber, 1982).

Johnson, Hugh, *Hugh Johnson's Modern Encyclopedia of Wine* (2nd edn, New York: Simon and Schuster, 1987).

Johnson, Hugh, *The Story of Wine* (London: Mitchell Beazley, 1989).

Johnson, Hugh, *World Atlas of Wine* (London: Reed International, 1996).

Jones, Frank, *The Save Your Heart Wine Book* (Toronto: Stoddart, 1995).

Jullien, André, *Topographie de tous les vignobles connus* (Paris, 1816).

Kay, Billy, and Cailean Maclean, *Knee Deep in Claret: A Celebration of Wine and Scotland* (Edinburgh: Mainstream Publishing, 1983).

Kelly, Alexander, *The Vine in Australia* (Melbourne: Sands, Kellny, 1861).

Kennedy, Philip F., *The Wine Song in Classical Arabic Poetry: Abu Nuwas and the Literary Tradition* (Oxford: Clarendon Press, 1997).

Khayyam, Omar, *The Ruba'iyat of Omar Khayyam* (trans. Peter Avery and John Heath-Stubbs, London: Allen Lane, 1979).

Kinnier Wilson, J. V., *The Nimrud Wine Lists: A Study of Men and Administration at the Assyrian Capital in the Eighth Century BC* (London: British School of Archaeology in Iraq, 1972).

Lachiver, Marcel, *Vin, vigne et vignerons en région parisienne du XVII au XIXe siècles* (Pontoise, 1982).

Lachiver, Marcel, *Vins, vignes et vignerons: Histoire du vignoble français* (Paris: Fayard, 1988).

Langenbach, Alfred, *The Wines of Germany* (London: Harper, 1951).

Lapsley, James T., *Bottled Poetry: Napa Winemaking from Prohibition to the Modern Era* (Berkeley: University of California Press, 1996).

Laurent, Robert, *Les vignerons de la 'côte d'Or' au XIXe siècle* (2 vols., Dijon, 1958).

Lavalle, J., *Histoire et statistique de la vigne et des grands vins de la Côte-d'Or* (Paris: Dusacq, 1855).

Leipoldt, C. L., *Three Hundred Years of Cape Grapes* (Cape Town: Stewart, 1952).

Lender, Mark Edward and James Kirby Martin, *Drinking in America: A History* (New York: Free Press, 1982).

Lesko, Leonard H., *King Tut's Wine Cellar* (Berkeley: B.C. Scribe Publications, 1978).

Liddell, Alex, *Madeira* (London: Faber and Faber, 1998).

Lissarague, François, *The Aesthetics of the Great Banquet: Images of Wine and Ritual* (Princeton, NJ: Princeton University Press, 1987).

Loubère, Leo, *The Red and the White: The History of Wine in France and Italy in the Nineteenth Century* (Albany: State University of New York Press, 1978).

Loubère, Leo, *The Wine Revolution in France: The Twentieth Century* (Princeton: Princeton University Press, 1990).

Loubère, Leo, Jean Sagnes, Laura Frader and Remy Pech, *The Vine Remembers: French Vignerons Recall their Past* (Albany: State University of New York Press, 1985).

Lucia, Salvatore Pablo, *A History of Wine as Therapy* (Philadelphia: Lippincott, 1963).

Lucia, Salvatore Pablo (ed.), *Alcohol and Civilization* (New York: McGraw Hull, 1963).

Maguin, Martine, *La vigne et le vin en Lorraine, XIVe-XVe siècle* (Nancy: Presses Universitaires de Nancy, 1982).

Mahe, Nathalie, *Le Mythe de Bacchus dans la poésie lyrique de 1549 à 1600* (Berne: Peter Lang, 1988).

Mancall, Peter C., *Deadly Medicine: Indians and Alcohol in Early America* (Ithaca: Cornell University Press, 1995).

Margolin, J.-C. and R. Sauzet (eds.), *Pratiques et discours alimentaires à la Renaissance* (Paris: G.-P. Maisonneuve et Larose, 1982).

McGovern, P. E., S. J. Fleming and S. H. Katz (eds.), *The Origins and Ancient History of Wine* (Luxembourg: Gordon and Breach, 1996).

Le Ménagier de Paris (Georgine E. Brereton and Janet M. Ferrier, eds., Oxford: Oxford University Press, 1982).

Mendelsohn, Oscar A., *Drinking with Pepys* (London: Macmillan, 1963).

Murray, Oswyn and Manuela Tecuşan (eds.), *In Vino Veritas* (London: British School at Rome, 1995).

Nolleville, Jean, *Le vin d'Ay à l'origine du champagne* (Reims, 1988).

Olney, Richard, *Romanée-Conti: The World's Most Fabled Wine* (New York: Rizzoli, 1995).

Opperman, D. J., *Spirit of the Vine: Republic of South Africa* (Cape Town: Human and Rousseau, 1968).

Ordish, George, *The Great Wine Blight* (London: Dent, 1972).

Ordish, George, *Vineyards in England and Wales* (London: Faber and Faber, 1977).

Palmer, Ruth, *Wine in the Mycenaean Palace Economy* (Liège: Université de Liège, 1994).

Paronetto, Lamberto, *Chianti: The Story of Florence and its Wines* (London: Wine and Spirit Publications, 1970).

Paul, Harry H., *The Science of Vine and Wine in France, 1750–1990* (New York: Cambridge University Press, 1996).

Pinney, Thomas, *A History of Wine in America from the Beginnings to Prohibition* (Berkeley: University of California Press, 1989).

Pliny the Elder, *Histoire Naturelle* (Paris: Société d'Edition 'Les Belles Lettres', 1958).

Poo, Mu-chou, *Wine and Wine-Offering in the Religion of Ancient Egypt* (London: Kegan Paul International, 1995).

Prestwich, Patricia E., *Drink and the Politics of Social Reform: Antialcoholism in France since 1870* (Palo Alto, CA: Society for the Promotion of Science and Scholarship, 1988).

Price, Pamela Vandyke, *Wines of the Graves* (London: Sotheby's Publications, 1988).

Ray, Cyril, *Lafite* (New York: Stein and Day, 1969).

Raymond, Irving Woodworth, *The Teaching of the Early Church on the Use of Wine and Strong Drink* (New York: Columbia University Press, 1927, repr. New York: AMS Press, 1970).

Redding, Cyrus, *A History and Description of Modern Wines* (3rd edn, London: Henry G. Bohn, 1850).

Roberts, James S., *Drink, Temperance and the Working Class in Nineteenth-Century Germany* (Boston: George Allen and Unwin, 1984).

Robinson, Jancis (ed.), *The Oxford Companion to Wine* (Oxford: Oxford University Press, 1994, rev. edn 1997).

Robinson, Jancis, *Confessions of a Wine Lover* (London: Viking, 1997).

Robinson, Jancis, *Vines, Grapes and Wines: The Wine Drinker's Guide to Grape Varieties* (London: Mitchell Beazley, 1992).

Roche, Emile, *Le commerce des vins de Champagne sous l'ancien régime* (Châlons-sur-Marne, 1908).

Rorabaugh, W. J., *The Alcoholic Republic: An American Tradition* (New York: Oxford University Press, 1979).

Sadou, Roland, Giorgio Lolli, Milton Silverman, *Drinking in French Culture* (New Brunswick, NJ: Rutgers Center for Alcohol Studies, 1965).

Sagnes, Jean (ed.), *La Viticulture française au XIXe et XXe siècles* (Béziers: Presses du Languedoc, 1993).

Samuelson, James, *The History of Drink* (London: Trubner and Company, 1878).

Scheindlin, Raymond P., *Wine, Women, and Death: Medieval Hebrew Poems on the Good Life* (Philadelphia: Jewish Publication Society, 1986).

Sclegel, Walter, *Der Weinbau in der Schweiz* (Wiesbaden: Franz Steiner Verlag, 1973).

Seltman, Charles, *Wine in the Ancient World* (London: Routledge and Kegan Paul, 1957).

Sereni, Emilio, *History of the Italian Agricultural Landscape* (Princeton, NJ: Princeton University Press, 1997).

Serlis, Harry G., *Wine in America* (New York: The Newcomen Society in North America, 1972).

Seward, Desmond, *Monks and Wine* (New York: Crown, 1979).

Shiman, Lilian Lewis, *Crusade against Drink in Victorian England* (London: Macmillan, 1988).

Simon, André, *The History of Champagne* (London: Octopus, 1971).

Simon, André, *The History of the Wine Trade in England* (3 vols., London: Wyman and Sons, 1906).

Snyder, Charles R., *Alcohol and the Jews* (Carbondale, IL: Southern Illinois University Press, 1978).

Sournia, Jean-Charles, *A History of Alcoholism* (Oxford: Basil Blackwell, 1990).

Stanislawski, Dan, *Landscapes of Bacchus: The Vine in Portugal* (Austin: University of Texas Press, 1970).

Strabo, *The Geography of Strabo* (3 vols., London: Bell, 1912).

Stuller, Jay, and Glen Martin, *Through the Grapevine: The Real Story Behind America's $8 Billion Wine Industry* (New York: HarperCollins, 1994).

Sullivan, Charles L., *A Companion to California Wine: An Encyclopedia of Wine and Winemaking from the Mission Period to the Present* (Berkeley: University of California Press, 1998).

Sutcliffe, Serena, *Champagne: The History and Character of the World's Most Celebrated Wine* (New York: Simon and Schuster, 1988).

Tchernia, André, *Le Vin de l'Italie romaine: essai d'histoire économique d'après les amphores* (Rome: École française de Rome, 1988).

Thudichum, J. L. W., *A Treatise on Wines* (London: George Bell, 1893).

Todd, W. J., *A Handbook of Wine* (London: Jonathan Cape, 1922).

Tovey, Charles, *Wine and Wine Countries: A Record and Manual for Wine Merchants and Wine Consumers* (London, 1862 and 1877).

Ulin, Robert C., *Vintages and Traditions: An Ethnohistory of Southwest French Wine Cooperatives* (Washington, DC: Smithsonian Institution Press, 1996).

Unwin, Tim, *Wine and the Vine: An Historical Geography of Viticulture and the Wine Trade* (London: Routledge, 1991).

Vandermersch, Christian, *Vins et amphores de Grande Grèce et de Sicile, IVe–IIIe s. avant J.-C.* (Naples: Centre Jean Bérard, 1994).

Varro, Marcus Terentius, *On Agriculture* (London: Heinemann, 1934).

Vizetelly, Henry, *The Wines of the World Characterized and Classed* (London, 1875).

Warner, Charles K., *The Winegrowers of France and the Government since 1875* (New York: Columbia University Press, 1960).

Warsh, Cheryl Krasnick (ed.), *Drink in Canada: Historical Essays* (Montreal: McGill-Queen's University Press, 1993).

Weinberg, Florence M., *The Wine and the Will: Rabelais's Bacchic Christianity* (Detroit: Wayne State University Press, 1972).

Weinhold, Rudolf, *Vivat Bacchus: A History of the Vine and its Wine* (Watford: Argus Books, 1978).

Wheaton, Barbara Ketcham, *Savoring the Past: The French Kitchen and Table from 1300 to 1789* (Philadelphia: University of Pennsylvania Press, 1983).

White, Stephen, *Russia Goes Dry: Alcohol, State and Society* (Cambridge: Cambridge University Press, 1996).

Wilkins, John, David Harvey and Mike Dobson (eds.), *Food in Antiquity* (Exeter: University of Exeter Press, 1995).

Williams, Jane Welch, *Bread, Wine, and Money: The Windows of the Trades at Chartres Cathedral* (Chicago: University of Chicago Press, 1993).

Wine and Spirit Merchant: A Familiar Treatise on the Art of Making Wine (London: W. R. Loftus, n.d. [1864]).

Younger, William, *Gods, Men and Wine* (London: Michael Joseph, 1966).

NOTES

INTRODUCTION

1 Back label, Banrock Station Shiraz (Australia), 1998.

ONE ON THE TRAIL OF THE EARLIEST WINES

1 The best short description of this technique is Patrick E. McGovern and Rudolph H. Michel, 'The Analytical and Archaeological Challenge of Detecting Ancient Wine: Two Case Studies from the Ancient Near East', in Patrick E. McGovern, Stuart J. Fleming and Solomon H. Katz (eds.), *The Origins and Ancient History of Wine* (Luxembourg: Gordon and Breach, 1995), 57–65.

2 Patrick E. McGovern, Ulrich Hartung, Virginia R. Badler, Donald L. Glusker and Lawrence J. Exner, 'The Beginnings of Winemaking and Viniculture in the Ancient Near East and Egypt', *Expedition* 39:1 (1997), 5.

3 Virginia R. Badler, 'The Archaeological Evidence for Winemaking, Distribution, and Consumption at Proto-Historic Godin Tepe, Iran', in McGovern, Fleming and Katz, *Origins and Ancient History of Wine*, 45–56.

4 McGovern et al., 'Beginnings of Winemaking', 3.

5 Maynard A. Amerine and Vernon L. Singleton, *Wine: An Introduction* (second edn, Brookvale, NSW: Australia and New Zealand Book Company, 1977), 9.

6 William Younger, *Gods, Men and Wine* (London: Michael Joseph, 1966), 27.

7 R. J. Forbes, *Studies in Ancient Technology*, vol. III (Leiden: E. J. Brill, 1965), 61–3.

8 Vernon L. Singleton, 'An Enologist's Commentary on Ancient Wines', in McGovern, Fleming and Katz, *Origins and Ancient History of Wine*, 72.

9 Jane M. Renfrew, 'Palaeoethnobotanical Finds of *Vitis* from Greece', in McGovern, Fleming and Katz, *Origins and Ancient History of Wine*, 256, Map 16.1.

10 McGovern et al., 'Beginnings of Winemaking', 5.

11 Genesis 9:20–21. (*The Jerusalem Bible* is used throughout this book.)

12 William Ryan and Walter Pitman, *Noah's Flood: New Scientific Discoveries about the Event that Changed History* (New York: Simon and Schuster, 1998).

13 Ryan and Pitman, *Noah's Flood*, 212.

14 Ronald L. Gorny, 'Viticulture and Ancient Anatolia', in McGovern, Fleming and Katz, *Origins and Ancient History of Wine*, 150.

15 Badler, 'Archaeological evidence', 53.

16 Powell, 'Wine and the Vine in Ancient Mesopotamia: The Cuneiform Evidence', in McGovern, Fleming and Katz, *Origins and Ancient History of Wine*, 112–22.

17 Powell, 'Wine and the Vine in Ancient Mesopotamia', 105–6.

18 Jean Bottéro, 'Le Vin dans une civilisation de la bière: la Mésopotamie', in Oswyn Murray and Manuela Tecuşan (ed.), *In Vino Veritas* (London: British School at Rome, 1995), 30.

19 Bottéro, 'Vin dans une civilisation de la bière, 30.

20 Tim Unwin, *Wine and the Vine: An Historical Geography of Viticulture and the Wine Trade* (London: Routledge, 1991), 66–7.

21 Bottéro, 'Vin dans une civilisation de la bière, 29.

22 Unwin, *Wine and the Vine*, 66; David Stronach, 'The Imagery of the Wine Bowl: Wine in Assyria in the Early First Millennium BC', in McGovern, Fleming and Katz, *Origins and Ancient History of Wine*, 189–91.

23 J. V. Kinnier Wilson, *The Nimrud Wine Lists: A Study of Men and Administration at the Assyrian Capital in the Eighth Century BC* (London: British School of Archaeology in Iraq, 1972), 4, 44, 114, 117.

24 See A. C. Stevenson, 'Studies in the Vegetational History of S.W. Spain. II. Palynological Investigations at Laguna de la Madres, S.W. Spain', *Journal of Biogeography* 12 (1985), 293–314.

25 McGovern et al., 'Beginnings of Winemaking', 9–12.

26 Mu-chou Poo, *Wine and Wine-Offering in the Religion of Ancient Egypt* (London: Kegan Paul International, 1995), 7.

27 Dominic Rathbone, *Economic Rationalism and Rural Society in Third-Century AD Egypt* (Cambridge: Cambridge University Press, 1991), 246–50.

28 T. G. H. James, 'The Earliest History of Wine and its Importance in Ancient Egypt', in McGovern, Fleming and Katz, *Origins and Ancient History of Wine*, 205–10.

29 Leonard H. Lesko, 'Egyptian Wine Production during the New Kingdom', in McGovern, Fleming and Katz, *Origins and Ancient History of Wine*, 217.

30 James, 'Earliest History of Wine', 198–9.

31 James, 'Earliest History of Wine', 192.

32 Rathbone, *Economic Rationalism*, 258–9.

33 Lesko, 'Egyptian Wine Production', 222.

34 Leonard H. Lesko, *King Tut's Wine Cellar* (Berkeley: B. C. Scribe Publications, 1978), 23.

35 Lesko, *King Tut's Wine Cellar*, 40.

36 Unwin, *Wine and the Vine*, 73.

37 Poo, *Wine and Wine-Offering*, 32.

38 Lesko, 'Egyptian Wine Production', 229.

39 Unwin, *Wine and the Vine*, 66.

40 This position is argued forcefully in Unwin, *Wine and the Vine*, 77–94.

41 Unwin, *Wine and the Vine*, 60–61.

42 James, 'Earliest History of Wine', 203–4.

43 Younger, *Gods, Men and Wine*, 31; Patrick E. McGovern, 'Wine for Eternity', *Archaeology*, July–August 1998, 32.

44 Younger, *Gods, Men and Wine*, 31.

TWO DEMOCRATIC DRINKING

1 Ruth Palmer, *Wine in the Mycenaean Palace Economy* (Liège: Université de Liège, 1994), 14–19.

2 Albert Leonard Jr, ' "Canaanite Jars" and the Late Bronze Age Aegeo-Levantine Wine Trade', in McGovern, Fleming and Katz, *Origins and Ancient History of Wine*, 233–6.

3 Alison Burford, *Land and Labor in the Greek World* (Baltimore: Johns Hopkins University Press, 1993), 135.

4 Simon Hornblower and Anthony Spawforth (eds.), *Oxford Classical Dictionary* (Oxford: Oxford University Press, 1996), 1622.

5 Christian Vandermersch, *Vins et amphores de Grande Grèce et de Sicile, IVe–IIIe s. avant J.-C.* (Naples: Centre Jean Bérard, 1994). 37.

6 A. Trevor Hodge, *Ancient Greek France* (Philadelphia: University of Pennsylvania Press, 1999), 121.

7 Hodge, *Ancient Greek France*, 214–15.

8 Peter Jones and Keith Sidwell (eds.), *The World of Rome: An Introduction to Roman Culture* (Cambridge: Cambridge University Press, 1997), 182.

9 T. J. Santon, 'Columella's Attitude towards Wine Production', *Journal of Wine Research* 7:1 (1996), 55–9.

10 Cato, Marcus Porcius, *On Agriculture* (London: Heinemann, 1934), 105.

11 N. Purcell, 'Wine and Wealth in Ancient Italy', *Journal of Roman Studies* 75 (1985), 3.

12 André Tchernia, *Le Vin de l'Italie romaine: Essai d'histoire économique d'après les amphores* (Rome: Ecole française de Rome, 1986), 88.

13 Keith Nurse, 'The Last of the (Roman) Summer Wine', *History Today* 44 (1994), 4–5.

14 P. V. Stanley, 'KN Uc 160 and Mycenaean Wines', *American Journal of Archaeology* 86 (1982), 577–8.

15 Hesiod, *Works and Days*, ll. 609–17.

16 Cato, *On Agriculture*, 97–9.

17 Euripides, *Bacchae*, ll. 420–23.

18 François Lissarague, *The Aesthetics of the Greek Banquet: Images of Wine and Ritual* (Princeton: Princeton University Press, 1987), 81; H. Warner Allen, *A History of Wine: Great Vintage Wines from the Homeric Age to the Present Day* (London: Faber and Faber, 1961), 48–58.

19 *World of Athens: An Introduction to Classical Athenian Culture* (Cambridge: Cambridge University Press, 1984), 330.

20 Hugh Johnson, *The Story of Wine* (London: Mitchell Beazley, 1989), 64.

21 Purcell, 'Wine and Wealth in Ancient Italy', 1–19.

22 Thomas Braun, 'Barley Cakes and Emmer Bread', in John Wilkins, David Harvey and Mike Dobson (eds.), *Food in Antiquity* (Exeter: University of Exeter Press, 1995), 34–7.

23 Tchernia, *Vin de l'Italie romaine*, 59–60.

24 Tchernia, *Vin de l'Italie romaine*, 18–9.

25 Tchernia, *Vin de l'Italie romaine*, 16.

26 Hornblower and Spawforth, *Oxford Classical Dictionary*, 1622.

27 Cato, *On Agriculture*, 105.

28 Lesko, *King Tut's Wine Cellar*, 14.

29 *Digest*, XXXIII, 6, 11.

30 Tchernia, *Vin de l'Italie romaine*, 36.

31 Yvon Garlan, *Vin et amphores de Thasos* (Athens: École française d'Athènes, 1988), 5.

32 Strabo, *The Geography of Strabo* (3 vols., London: Bell, 1912), *passim*.

33 Tchernia, *Vin de l'Italie romaine*, 36.

34 Pliny the Elder, *Histoire Naturelle* (Paris: Société d'Edition 'Les Belles Lettres', 1958), book XIV, 20–76.

35 Lesko, *King Tut's Wine Cellar*, 14.

36 Wolfgang Rösler, 'Wine and Truth in the Greek Symposium', in Murray and Tecuşan, *In Vino Veritas*, 109.

37 Lissarague, *Aesthetics of the Greek Banquet*, 9.

38 Rösler, 'Wine and Truth', 106–12.

39 Burford, *Land and Labor in the Greek World*, 214.

40 John Maxwell O'Brien, *Alexander the Great: The Invisible Enemy* (London: Routledge, 1992).

41 Arthur P. McKinlay, 'The Classical World' and 'Non-Classical Peoples', in Raymond McCarthy (ed.), *Drinking and Intoxication: Selected Readings in Social Attitudes and Control* (Glencoe, IL: Free Press, 1959), 51.

42 Douglas E. Gerber, 'The Measure of Bacchus', *Mnemosyne* 41 (1988), 39–45.

43 Lissarague, *Aesthetics of the Greek Banquet*, 10.

44 Jean-Charles Sournia, *A History of Alcoholism* (Oxford: Basil Blackwell, 1990), 6–7.

45 Elizabeth Belfiore, 'Wine and *Catharsis* of the Emotions in Plato's *Laws*', *Classical Quarterly* 36 (1986), 421–37.

46 Jones and Sidwell, *World of Rome*, 213.

47 McKinlay, 'Classical World', 59.

48 Euripides, *Bacchae*, ll. 274–8.

49 1 Timothy 5:23.

50 Sournia, *History of Alcoholism*, 10.

51 *Hippocrates* (London: Heinemann, 1967), 325–9.

52 Hornblower and Spawforth, *Oxford Classical Dictionary*, 56.

53 Louis E. Grivetti and Elizabeth A. Applegate, 'From Olympia to Atlanta: A Cultural-Historical Perspective on Diet and Athletic Training', *Journal of Nutrition* 127:5 (1997), 863–4,

54 Hornblower and Spawforth, *Oxford Classical Dictionary*, 229.

55 Genesis 9:20–21.

56 Numbers 13:17–28.

57 Micah 6.15.

58 Joel 1:11–12.

59 Proverbs 20:1.

60 Isaiah 28:7.

61 Hosea 4:11.

62 John 2:1–11.

63 Mark 14:25.

64 Mark 14:24.

65 Sournia, *History of Alcoholism*, 13.

THREE WERE THE 'DARK AGES' THE DRY AGES?

1 Edward Gibbon, *The History of the Decline and Fall of the Roman Empire* (ed. David Womersley, London: Penguin Books, 1994), 238.

2 Tim Unwin, 'Continuity in Early Medieval Viticulture: Secular or Ecclesiastical Influences?' in Harm Jan de Blij (ed.), *Viticulture in Geographical Perspective* (Miami: Miami Geographical Society, 1992), 9.

3 Dan Stanislawski, *Landscapes of Bacchus: The Vine in Portugal* (Austin: University of Texas Press, 1970), 11.

4 Tim Unwin, 'Saxon and Early Norman Viticulture in England', *Journal of Wine Research* 1:1 (1990), 63–4.

5 Unwin, 'Saxon and Early Norman Viticulture', 64; Edward Hyams, *Dionysus: A Social History of the Wine Vine* (New York: Macmillan, 1965), 37.

6 Ann Hagen, *A Handbook of Anglo-Saxon Food* (Pinner, Middlesex: Anglo-Saxon Books, 1992), 94.

7 J. M. Wallace-Hadrill, *The Barbarian West, 400–1000* (London: Hutchinson, 1952), 153.

8 Georges Duby, *Rural Economy and Country Life in the Medieval West* (London: Edward Arnold, 1968), 42.

9 See Desmond Seward, *Monks and Wine* (New York: Crown, 1979), 25–35.

10 Pamela Vandyke Price, *Wines of the Graves* (London: Sotheby's Publications, 1998), 75.

11 Marcel Lachiver, *Vins, vignes et vignerons: Histoire du vignoble français* (Paris: Fayard, 1988), 45–6.

12 Younger, *Gods, Men and Wine*, 233.

13 Lachiver, *Vins, vignes et vignerons*, 52–3.

14 *New Cambridge Economic History of Europe* (Cambridge: Cambridge University Press, 1966), I, 68–9.

15 Lachiver, *Vin, vignes et vignerons*, 46.

16 Seward, *Monks and Wine*, 30.

17 Seward, *Monks and Wine*, 29.

18 F. W. Carter, 'Cracow's Wine Trade (Fourteenth to Eighteenth Centuries)', *Slavonic and East European Review* 65 (1987), 538.

19 Dietrich Lohrmann, 'La Croissance agricole en Allemagne au Haut Moyen Age', in *La Croissance agricole du Haut Moyen Age: chronologie, modalités, géographie* (Auch: Centre culturel de l'Abbaye de Flaran, 1990), 114.

20 Unwin, *Wine and the Vine*, 157.

21 Yitzhak Hen, *Culture and Religion in Merovingian Gaul, AD 481–751* (Leiden: Brill, 1995), 236–7.

22 Pierre Riche, *Daily Life in the World of Charlemagne* (Philadelphia: University of Pennsylvania Press, 1978), 177.

23 Riche, *World of Charlemagne*, 176.

24 Hen, *Merovingian Gaul*, 240.

25 John T. McNeill and Helena M. Gamer, *Medieval Handbooks of Penance* (New York: Octagon, 1965), 230.

26 McNeill and Gamer, *Handbooks of Penance*, 286.

27 *Qur'an*, sura 5, verse 92.

28 Philip F. Kennedy, *The Wine Song in Classical Arabic Poetry: Abu Nuwas and the Literary Tradition* (Oxford: Clarendon Press, 1997), 105.

29 Raymond P. Scheindlin, *Wine, Women, and Death: Medieval Hebrew Poems on the Good Life* (Philadelphia: Jewish Publication Society, 1986), 28–9.

30 Thomas A. Glick, *Islamic and Christian Spain in the Early Middle Ages* (Princeton: Princeton University Press, 1979), 80.

31 Scheindlin, *Wine, Women, and Death*, 19–25.

32 Kennedy, *Wine Song*, 141.

33 Omar Khayyam, *The Ruba'iyat of Omar Khayyam* (trans. Peter Avery and John Heath-Stubbs, London: Allen Lane, 1979), 68.

FOUR WINE RESURGENT

1 Thomas Pinney, *A History of Wine in America: From the Beginnings to Prohibition* (Berkeley: University of California Press, 1989), 3–4; Unwin, *Wine and the Vine*, 160–61.

2 Pinney, *Wine in America*, 3.

3 *New Cambridge Economic History of Europe*, I, 170, 297.

4 F. W. Carter, 'Cracow's Wine Trade', 548.

5 Emilio Sereni, *History of the Italian Agricultural Landscape* (Princeton, NJ; Princeton University Press, 1997), 121.

6 P. W. Hammond, *Food and Feast in Medieval England* (Stroud: Allan Sutton, 1993), 13.

7 The best treatment of the subject is Margery Kirkbride James, *Studies in the Medieval Wine Trade* (ed. Elspeth M. Veale, Oxford: Clarendon Press, 1971).

8 James, *Medieval Wine Trade*, 32.

9 Billy Kay and Cailean Maclean, *Knee Deep in Claret: A Celebration of Wine and Scotland* (Edinburgh: Mainstream Publishing, 1983), 9.

10 James, *Medieval Wine Trade*, 55–6.

11 Carter, 'Cracow's Wine Trade', 543–51.

12 See Beatrice Bourély, *Vignes et vins de l'Abbaye de Cîteaux en Bourgogne* (Nuits-St-Georges: Editions du Tastevin, 1998).

13 Constance Hoffman Berman, *Medieval Agriculture, the Southern French Countryside, and the Early Cistercians: A Study of Forty-Three Monasteries* (Philadelphia: American Philosophical Society, 1986), 93.

14 Bourély, *Abbaye de Cîteaux*, 101–2.

15 *New Cambridge Economic History of Europe*, I, 170.

16 Rosalind Kent Berlow, 'The "Disloyal" Grape: The Agrarian Crisis of Late Fourteenth-Century Burgundy', *Agricultural History* 56 (1982), 426–38.

17 Duby, *Rural Economy*, 139.

18 Mack P. Holt, 'Wine, Community and Reformation in Sixteenth-Century Burgundy', *Past and Present* 138 (1993), 73.

19 Roger Dion, *Histoire de la vigne et du vin en France des origines au XIXe siècle* (Paris, 1955, repr. Paris: Flammarion, 1977), 328–9.

20 Emmanuel Le Roy Ladurie, *Montaillou: Cathars and Catholics in a French Village, 1234–1324* (London: Penguin Books, 1980), 9, 15.

21 Martine Maguin, *La vigne et le vin en Lorraine, XIV–XVe siècle* (Nancy: Presses Universitaires de Nancy, 1982), 199–215.

22 Hammond, *Food and Feast*, 13–14.

23 Patricia Labahn, 'Feasting the Fourteenth and Fifteenth Centuries: A Comparison of Manuscript Illumination to Contemporary Written Sources' (Ph.D. Dissertation, St Louis University, 1975), 60.

24 Hammond, *Food and Feast*, 72.

25 Duby, *Rural Economy*, 65.

26 Hammond, *Food and Feast*, 54.

27 Singleton, 'An Enologist's Commentary on Ancient Wine', 75.

28 Hammond, *Food and Feast*, 14.

29 Lamberto Paronetto, *Chianti: The Story of Florence and its Wines* (London: Wine and Spirit Publications, 1970), 22.

30 Quoted in Sereni, *Italian Agricultural Landscape*, 98.

31 Lachiver, *Vins, vignes et vignerons*, 102–5.

32 Lachiver, *Vins, vignes et vignerons*, 104.

33 Holt, 'Wine, Community and Reformation'.

34 Anne Crawford, *A History of the Vintners' Company* (London: Constable, 1977), 23.

35 Crawford, *Vintners' Company*, 27.

36 James, *Medieval Wine Trade*, 35.

37 *Oxford Dictionary of Byzantium* (Oxford: Oxford University Press, 1991) III, 2199–2200.

38 Jan Craeybeckx, *Un grand commerce d'importation: les vins de France aux anciens Pays-Bas* (Paris: SEVPEN, 1958), 8.

39 Geoffrey Chaucer, *The Canterbury Tales* (trans. Nevill Coghill, Harmondsworth: Penguin, 1951), 271.

40 Hammond, *Food and Feast*, 83.

41 Hammond, *Food and Feast*, 74.

42 Hammond, *Food and Feast*, 83.

43 James du Quesnay Adams, *Patterns of Medieval Society* (Englewood Cliffs, NJ: Prentice Hall, 1969), 285–6.

44 Hammond, *Food and Feast*, 57.

45 Urban Tigner Holmes, Jr., *Daily Living in the Twelfth Century* (Madison: University of Wisconsin Press, 1973), 80.

46 Chaucer, *Canterbury Tales*, 269–71.

47 Adams, *Patterns of Medieval Society*, 111.

48 Robin Livio, *Tavernes, estaminets, guinguettes et cafés d'antan et de naguère* (Paris: Pont-Royal, 1961), 23.

49 Stanley Rubin, *Medieval English Medicine* (Newton Abbot: David and Charles, 1974), 121.

50 Marie-Christine Pouchelle-Peter, 'Une parole médicale prise dans l'imaginaire: alimentation et digestion chez un maître chirurgien du XIVe siècle', in J.-C. Margolin and R. Sauzet (eds.), *Pratiques et discours alimentaires à la Renaissance*, (Paris: G.-P. Maisonneuve et Larose, 1982), 184–8.

51 Rubin, *Medieval English Medicine*, 197.

FIVE NEW WINES, NEW SKILLS

1 Unwin, *Wine and the Vine*, 223–4.

2 Julian Jeffs, *Sherry* (3rd edn, London: Faber and Faber, 1982), 51.

3 Shakespeare, *Henry IV Part II*, IV.iii.

4 David E. Vassberg, *Land and Society in Golden Age Castile* (Cambridge: Cambridge University Press, 1984), 163–4.

5 Jean Calvin, *Institutes of the Christian Religion* (ed. J. T. McNeill, London: SCM Press, 1961), II, 1425.

6 Kay and Maclean, *Knee Deep in Claret*, 31.

7 Holt, 'Wine, Community and Reformation', 78.

8 John 15:1, 5.

9 Holt, 'Wine, Community and Reformation'.

10 Calvin, *Institutes of the Christian Religion*, II, 1264.

11 Jean Calvin, *Theological Treatises* (ed. J. K. S. Reid, London: SCM Press, 1954), 81.

12 Schilling, 1991: 47, 57.

13 Robert Sauzet, 'Discours cléricaux sur la nourriture', in Margolin and Sauzet (eds.), *Pratiques et discours alimentaires*, 247–56.

14 Fernand Braudel, *The Structures of Everyday Life: Civilization and Capitalism, 15th–18th Centuries* (New York: Harper and Row, 1981), I, 233–4.

15 Henri Enjalbert, 'Comment naissent les grands crus: bordeaux, porto, cognac. Première partie', *Annales: Economies Sociétés Civilisations* 8 (1953), 322 n. 1.

16 Lachiver, *Vins, vignes et vignerons*, 291.

17 A. D. Francis, *The Wine Trade* (London: A&C Black, 1972), 74.

18 Lachiver, *Vins, vignes et vignerons*, 295.

19 Francis, *The Wine Trade*, 92.

20 Marie-Noële Denis, 'Vignoble et société en Alsace depuis la Guerre de Trente Ans', in *Les Boissons: production et consommation aux XIXe et XXe siècles* (Paris: CTHS, 1984), 11–12.

21 G. F. Steckley, 'The Wine Economy of Tenerife in the Seventeenth Century: Anglo-Spanish Partnership in a Luxury Trade', *Economic History Review* 2nd series 33 (1980), 344.

22 Braudel, *Structures of Everyday Life*, 236.

23 Daniel Rivière, 'Le thème alimentaire dans le discours proverbial de la Renaissance française', in Margolin and Sauzet (eds.), *Pratiques et discours alimentaires*, 201–18.

24 Lachiver, *Vins, vignes et vignerons*, 310–11.

25 This information from Professor Carman Bickerton of Carleton University.

26 This section on the Arsenal is from Robert C. Davis, 'Venetian Shipbuilders and the Fountain of Wine', *Past and Present* 156 (1997), 55–86.

27 Davis, 'Venetian Shipbuilders', 71.

28 Davis, 'Venetian Shipbuilders', 75.

29 Stephanie Pain, 'How to rule the waves', *New Scientist* No. 2191, 19 June 1999, 55.

30 Jancis Robinson (ed.), *The Oxford Companion to Wine* (Oxford: Oxford University Press, 1994, rev. edn. 1997), 137–9.

31 Eleanor S. Godfrey, *The Development of English Glassmaking, 1560–1640* (Oxford: Clarendon Press, 1975), 229–32.

32 For a standard account see Seward, *Monks and Wine*, 139–43.

33 Chloe Chard, 'The Intensification of Italy: Food, Wine and the Foreign in Seventeenth-Century Travel Writing', in Gerald Mars and Valerie Mars (eds.), *Food, Culture and History I* (London: London Food Seminar, 1993), 96.

34 *The Diary of John Evelyn* (ed. E. S. de Beer, 6 vols., Oxford: Oxford University Press, 1955), epecially Vol. II.

35 The section on Pepys draws mainly on Oscar A. Mendelsohn, *Drinking with Pepys* (London, Macmillan, 1963).

36 Mendelsohn, *Drinking with Pepys*, 51.

37 Mendelsohn, *Drinking with Pepys*, 75.

38 Mendelsohn, *Drinking with Pepys*, 46.

39 Mendelsohn, *Drinking with Pepys*, 47.

40 Mendelsohn, *Drinking with Pepys*, 94.

41 Godfrey, *English Glassmaking*, 218–21.

42 Flandrin, 'Médicine et habitudes alimentaires anciennes', in Margolin and Sauzet (eds.), *Pratiques et discours alimentaires*, 86.

43 Flandrin, 'Médicine et habitudes alimentaires', 87.

44 Piero Camporesi, *The Anatomy of the Senses: National Symbols in Medieval and Early Modern Italy* (Cambridge: Polity Press, 1994), 80.

45 Camporesi, *Anatomy of the Senses*, 80.

46 Jonathan Edwards, *Letters and Personal Writings* (ed. George S. Claghorn, New Haven: Yale University Press, 1998), 577–8.

47 Flandrin, 'Médicine et habitudes alimentaires', 85.

48 Flandrin, 'Médicine et habitudes alimentaires', 85.

49 Rivière, 'Discours proverbial', 203.

50 Jean Dupebe, 'La diététique et l'alimentation des pauvres selon Sylvius',

in Margolin and Sauzet (eds.), *Pratiques et discours alimentaires*, 41–56.

51 Henri de Buttet, 'Le vin des Invalides au temps de Louis XIV', in *Les Boissons*, 39–51.

52 Michel Reulos, 'Le premier traité sur le cidre: Julien le Paulmier, De Vino et Pomace, traduit par Jacques de Cahaignes (1589)', in Margolin and Sauzet (eds.), *Pratiques et discours alimentaires*, 97–103.

SIX WINE IN NEW WORLDS

1 Steckley, 'Wine Economy of Tenerife', 342.

2 Harm Jan de Blij, *Wine Regions of the Southern Hemisphere* (Totowa, NJ: Rowman and Allanheld, 1985), 16.

3 Unwin, *Wine and the Vine*, 216.

4 J. H. Parry and Robert Keith (eds.), *New Iberian World* (New York: Times Books, 1993), IV, 375.

5 *Ottawa Citizen*, 3 October 1998, J6.

6 Prudence M. Rice, 'Peru's Colonial Wine Industry and its European Background', *Antiquity* 70 (1996), 790–94.

7 Unwin, *Wine and the Vine*, 36–7.

8 *Travels of Pedro de Cieza de Leon, AD 1532–50, Containing the First Part of his Chronicles of Peru* (London: Hakluyt Society, 1864), 235.

9 Steve Stern, *Peru's Indian Peoples and the Challenge of Spanish Conquest* (Madison: University of Wisconsin Press, 1993), 98.

10 Prudence M. Rice, 'Wine and Brandy Production in Colonial Peru: A Historical and Archaeological Investigation', *Journal of Interdisciplinary History* 27 (1977), 455–79.

11 Mark A. Burkholder and Lyman L. Johnson, *Colonial Latin America* (New York: Oxford University Press, 1998), 222–3.

12 Robert C. Fuller, *Religion and Wine: A Cultural History of Wine Drinking in the United States* (Knoxville, TN: University of Tennessee Press, 1996), 24–5.

13 Harm Jan de Blij, *Wine: A Geographic Appreciation* (Totowa, NJ: Rowman and Allanheld, 1983), 59.

14 Pinney, *Wine in America*, 8, 11.

15 Pinney, *Wine in America*, 11.

16 Unwin, *Wine and the Vine*, 218.

17 Pinney, *Wine in America*, 17.

18 Pinney, *Wine in America*, 19.

19 Fuller, *Religion and Wine*, 10.

20 Fuller, *Religion and Wine*, 12.

21 Pinney, *Wine in America*, 35.

22 Pinney, *Wine in America*, 36.

23 David W. Conroy, 'Puritans in Taverns: Law and Popular Culture in Colonial Massachusetts, 1630–1720', in Susanna Barrows and Robin Room (eds.), *Drinking: Behavior and Belief in Modern History* (Berkeley: University of California Press, 1991), 29–60.

24 Fuller, *Religion and Wine*, 76.

25 Pinney, *Wine in America*, 46.

26 Pinney, *Wine in America*, 80–81.

27 Pinney, *Wine in America*, 91–2.

28 Fuller, *Religion and Wine*, 75.

29 Mark Edward Lender and James Kirby Martin, *Drinking in America: A History* (New York: Free Press, 1987), 14, 205–6.

30 Fuller, *Religion and Wine*, 17.

31 Fuller, *Religion and Wine*, 18.

32 Pinney, *Wine in America*, 110.

33 Johnson, *Story of Wine*, 354.

34 C. J. Orffer, 'To the Southern Point of Africa', in D. J. Opperman (ed.), *Spirit of the Vine: Republic of South Africa* (Cape Town: Human and Rousseau, 1968), 83.

35 Orffer, 'To the Southern Point of Africa', 87.

36 Robinson, *Oxford Companion to Wine*, 275.

37 Orffer, 'To the Southern Point of Africa', 100.

38 John Beeston, *A Concise History of Australian Wine* (2nd edn, Sydney: Allen and Unwin, 1995), 1.

SEVEN WINE, ENLIGHTENMENT AND REVOLUTION

1 Francis, *The Wine Trade*, 124–5.

2 *The Diary of John Hervey, First Earl of Bristol. With Extracts from his Book of Expenses, 1688 to 1742* (Wells: Ernest Jackson, 1894), 170–71.

3 Lachiver, *Vins, vignes et vignerons*, 332.

4 Lachiver, *Vins, vignes et vignerons*, 333.

5 Robert Forster, 'The Noble Wine Producers of the Bordelais in the Eighteenth Century', *Economic History Review* 2nd series, 14 (1961), 22.

6 Forster, 'Noble Wine Producers', 22.

7 Denis, 'Vignoble et société en Alsace', 12–13.

8 Maurice Gresset, 'Un document sur le rendement des vignes bisontines dans la seconde moitié du XVIIIe siècle', in *Les Boissons*, 29.

9 Christiane Constant-le Stum (ed.), *Journal d'un bourgeois de Begoux: Michel Celarie, 1776–1836* (Paris: Publisud, 1992), 106.

10 Gresset, 'Rendement des vignes bisontines', 30.

11 Gresset, 'Rendement des vignes bisontines', 32.

12 Lachiver, *Vins, vignes et vignerons*, 385.

13 Jordan Goodman, 'Excitantia, or, How Enlightenment Europe took to Soft Drugs', in Jordan Goodman, Paul E. Lovejoy and Andrew Sherratt (eds.), *Consuming Habits: Drugs in History and Anthropology* (London: Routledge, 1995), 126.

14 Woodruff D. Smith, 'From Coffeehouse to Parlour: The Consumption of Coffee, Tea and Sugar in North-Western Europe in the Seventeenth and Eighteenth Centuries', in Goodman, Lovejoy and Sherratt (eds.), *Consuming Habits*, 148–64.

15 Fynes Moryson, *An Itinerary* (London, 1617), Book III, 152.

16 Goodman, 'Excitantia', 126.

17 Francis, *The Wine Trade*, 320.

18 Enjalbert, 'Grands crus. Deuxieme partie', 467.

19 Roy Porter, *English Society in the Eighteenth Century* (London: Penguin, 1982), 33–4.

20 *Oxford Today* 11:2 (Hilary Term, 1999), 63.

21 Enjalbert, 'Grands crus. Première partie', 327

22 Jean Richard, 'L'Académie de Dijon et le commerce du vin au XVIIIe siècle à propos d'un memoire présenté aux Etats de Bourgogne', *Annales de Bourgogne* 47 (1975), 222.

1975, 222.

23 Enjalbert, 'Grands crus. Première partie', 327.

24 Enjalbert, 'Grands crus. Première partie', 329.

25 Enjalbert, 'Grands crus. Deuxième partie', 469.

26 Robert Forster, *The Nobility of Toulouse in the Eighteenth Century* (Baltimore: Johns Hopkins University Press, 1960), 99.

27 *Encyclopédie, ou Dictionnaire raisonné des sciences, des arts et des métiers* (Paris, 1751–65), 'Vin'.

28 J. B. Gough, 'Winecraft and Chemistry in Eighteenth-Century France: Chaptal and the Invention of Chaptalization', *Technology and Culture* 39 (1998), 81.

29 Johnson, *Story of Wine*, 290.

30 Gough, 'Winecraft and Chemistry', 83–4.

31 Gough, 'Winecraft and Chemistry', 96–7.

32 Harry H. Paul, *The Science of Vine and Wine in France, 1750–1990* (New York: Cambridge University Press, 1996), 123–30.

33 Gough, 'Winecraft and Chemistry', 102–3.

34 Pierre de Saint-Jacob, 'Une source de l'histoire du commerce des vins: lettres de voiture', *Annales de Bourgogne* 28 (1956), 124–6.

35 Enjalbert, 'Grands crus. Deuxième partie', 471.

36 Richard, L'Académie de Dijon et le commerce du vin', 222.

37 Porter, *English Society in the Eighteenth Century*, 34.

38 John Watney, *Mother's Ruin: A History of Gin* (London: Peter Owen, 1976), 16–25.

39 Barbara Ketchum Wheaton, *Savoring the Past: The French Kitchen and Table from 1300 to 1789* (Philadelphia: University of Philadelphia Press, 1983), 159.

40 Robert Forster, *House of Saulx-Tavanes* (Baltimore: Johns Hopkins University Press, 1971), 121–2.

41 Pierre Ponsot, 'Les bouteilles du Président: les boissons d'un parlementaire bressan-bourguignon au XVIIIe siècle', in Gilbert Garrier (ed.), *Le Vin des historiens* (Suze-la-Rousse: Université du Vin, 1990), 153–60.

42 Forster, *Nobility of Toulouse*, 99.

43 Wheaton, *Savoring the Past*, 215.

44 Hans Ottokar Reichard, *Guide de la Russie et de Constantinople* (n.p., 1793), N2r, P1r.

45 Thomas Brennan, *Public Drinking and Popular Culture in Eighteenth-Century Paris* (Princeton: Princeton University Press, 1988), 279–83.

46 Quoted in Lachiver, *Vins, vignes et vignerons*, 331.

47 Louis Trenard, 'Cabarets et estaminets lillois (1715–1815)', in *Les Boissons*, 53–72.

48 David Garrioch, *Neighbourhood and Community in Paris, 1740–1790* (Cambridge: Cambridge University Press, 1986), 22–6.

49 Trenard, 'Cabarets et estaminets', 67.

50 Brennan, *Public Drinking*, 146–51; also Daniel Roche, *The People of Paris*, (Berkeley: University of California Press, 1987), 254–63.

51 Lachiver, *Vins, vignes, et vignerons*, 352–3.

52 *Encyclopédie*, 'Vin'.

53 Trenard, 'Cabarets et estaminets', 63.

54 Roderick Phillips, *Family Breakdown in Late Eighteenth-Century France: Divorces in Rouen, 1792–1803* (Oxford: Clarendon Press, 1980), 116–18.

55 Gresset, 'Le rendement des vignes bisontines', 26.

56 *Cahiers de doléances, région centre: Loire-et-Cher* (ed. Denis Jeanson, 2 vols., Tours: Denis Jeanson, 1989), I, 507–8.

57 *Cahiers de doléances*, II, 480.

58 Jean Nicolas, 'Vin et liberté', in Garrier (ed.), *Le Vin des historiens*, 163–4.

59 T. J. A. Le Goff and D. M. G. Sutherland, 'The Revolution and the Rural Economy', in Alan Forrest and Peter Jones (eds.), *Reshaping France: Town, Country and Region during the French Revolution* (Manchester: Manchester University Press, 1991), 62–3.

60 Peter McPhee, *Revolution and Environment in Southern France, 1780–1830* (Oxford: Oxford University Press, 1999), 177–8.

61 Archives Départementales de la Côte-d'Or (hereafter referred to as ADCO), M13 IX a/1, Viticulture.

62 Nicolas, 'Vin et liberté', 162–3.

63 Francis, *The Wine Trade*, 266–7.

64 ADCO, L1401, Maximum.

65 ADCO, L486, Police des cabarets.

66 Kolleen Guy of the University of Texas at San Antonio brought this print to my attention.

67 Circular from the Commission des Subsistances et Approvisionnements de la République (19 Germinal Year II/8 April 1794), ADCO L544.

68 For example, M. Maupin, *Art de la vigne, de l'art des vins, et de la seule richesse du peuple* (Paris, 1790).

69 ADCO, L1401, Maximum.

70 Circular 'Prix nationaux d'agriculture' (Rouen, Year III/1794–5), ADCO, L574, Agriculture.

71 ADCO, L465, Fête d'Agriculture.

72 ADCO, Q213, Biens nationaux.

73 Richard Olney, *Romanée-Conti: The World's Most Fabled Wine* (New York: Rizzoli, 1995), 31.

EIGHT TOWARDS AN AGE OF PROMISE

1 Francis, *The Wine Trade*, 323.

2 Norman R. Bonnett, 'The Vignerons of the Douro and the Peninsular War', *Journal of European Economic History* 21:1 (Spring 1992), 9–10.

3 Leo Loubère, *The Red and the White: The History of Wine in France and Italy in the Nineteenth Century* (Albany: State University of New York Press, 1978), 50.

4 Lachiver, *Vins, vignes et vignerons*, 394.

5 Jose Carlos Curto, 'Alcohol and Slaves: The Luzo-Brazilian Alcohol Commerce at Mpinda, Luanda, and Benguela during the Atlantic Slave Trade *c.* 1480–1830 and its Impact on the Societies of West Central Africa', (Ph.D. Dissertation, University of California at Los Angeles, 1996).

6 Norman R. Bonnett, 'Port Wine Merchants: Sandeman in Porto, 1813–1831', *Journal of European Economic History* 24:2 (Fall 1995), 246–7.

7 Adrian Shubert, *A Social History of Modern Spain* (London: Routledge, 1992), 13–14.

8 Roger Price, *The Economic Modernization of France, 1730–1880* (London: Croom Helm, 1975), 75–6.

9 Peter McPhee, *A Social History of France, 1780–1880* (London: Routledge, 1992), 154–5.

10 Gilbert Garrier, *Histoire sociale et culturelle du vin* (Paris: Larousse, 1998), 210.

11 Loubère, *Red and the White*, 302.

12 Price, *Economic Modernization of France*, 76.

13 Robert Druitt, *Report on the Cheap Wines from France, Germany, Italy, Austria, Greece, Hungary, and Australia: Their Use in Diet and Medicine* (London: Henry Renshaw, 1873).

14 Loubère, *Red and the White*, 49–50. Much of the following section on Italy draws on Loubère's comprehensive work.

15 Giuliana Biagioli, 'Le Baron Bettino Ricasoli et la naissance du chianti classico', in Garrier, *Vin des historiens*, 174.

16 Biagioli, 'Baron Bettino Ricasoli', 177.

17 Alfred Langenbach, *The Wines of Germany* (London: Harper, 1951).

18 Loubère, *Red and the White*, 275.

19 Lavoisier, *Elements of Chemistry* (Paris, 1789), I, 150–51.

20 Patricia E. Prestwich, *Drink and the Politics of Social Reform: Antialcoholism in France Since 1870* (Palo Alto, CA: The Society for the Promotion of Science and Scholarship, 1988), 20.

21 Honoré de Balzac, *Les Illusions Perdues* (Paris: Garnier, 1961), 126.

22 Edward Barry, *Observations, Historical, Critical, and Medical, on the Wines of the Ancients and the Analogy between them and Modern Wines* (London, 1775).

23 André Jullien, *Topographie de Tous les Vignobles Connus ... Suivie d'une Classification Général des Vins* (Paris, 1816).

24 Cyrus Redding, *A History and Description of Modern Wines* (London: Whittaker, Teacher and Arnott, 1833).

25 Cyrus Redding, *A History and Description of Modern Wines* (3rd edn, London: Henry G. Bohn, 1850), 349–50.

26 Robert Joseph, *The Art of the Wine Label* (London: B. Mitchell, 1988), 15.

27 Redding, *Modern Wines* (1850), 377.

28 *Wine and Spirit Merchant: A Familiar Treatise on the Art of Making Wine* (London: W. R. Loftus, n.d. [1864]), 139.

29 Nicholas Faith, *Château Margaux* (London: Mitchell Beazley, 1991), 47.

30 Asa Briggs, *Haut-Brion: An Illustrious Lineage* (London: Faber and Faber, 1994), 161.

31 Beeston, *History of Australian Wine*, 57.

32 Eveline Schumpeter, 'Le charme énivrant de Château-Margaux', *Connaissance des Arts* (November 1973), 101–5, quoted by Pierre Bourdieu, *Distinction: A Social Critique of the Judgement of Taste* (Cambridge: Harvard University Press, 1984), 53.

33 An excellent survey of drinking cultures of Paris is W. Scott Haine, *The World of the Paris Café: Sociability among the French Working Class, 1789–1914* (Baltimore: Johns Hopkins University Press, 1996).

34 Frédéric Le Play, *Les Ouvriers européens* (6 vols., Tours: Alfred Mame et Fils, 1878) V, 393.

35 Le Play, *Ouvriers européens*, V, 449–50.

36 Le Play, *Ouvriers européens*, VI, 473.

37 Le Play, *Ouvriers européens*, VI, 427.

38 Le Play, *Ouvriers européens*, V, 129.

39 Le Play, *Ouvriers européens*, VI, 136.

40 Le Play, *Ouvriers européens*, VI, 21.

41 Haine, *World of the Paris Café*, 91.

42 Haine, *World of the Paris Café*, 93.

43 Serena Sutcliffe, *Champagne: The History and Character of the World's Most Celebrated Wine* (New York: Simon and Schuster, 1988), 24.

44 Kolleen Guy, '"Oiling the Wheels of Social Life": Myths and Marketing in Champagne during the Belle Epoque', *French Historical Studies* 22:2 (Spring 1999), 216, 230–34.

45 Guy, 'Myths and Marketing in Champagne', 233–4.

46 Sutcliffe, *Champagne*, 121 (illustration).

47 Pinney, *Wine in America*, 135–9. The following pages draw heavily on Pinney's excellent book which is the standard history of wine in the United States up to the early twentieth century.

48 Pinney, *Wine in America*, 117–25.

49 Pinney, *Wine in America*, 229.

50 Pinney, *Wine in America*, 140.

51 Pinney, *Wine in America*, 164, illustration 41.

52 *Official Descriptive and Illustrated Catalogue of the Great Exhibition of the Works of All Nations* (London: Spicer Brothers, 1851), Part V, 1433.

53 Tony Aspler, *Vintage Canada: A Tasteful Companion to Canadian Wines* (Toronto: McGraw-Hill Ryerson, 1993), 11.

54 Aspler, *Vintage Canada*, 14–15.

55 Pinney, *Wine in America*, 236–7.

56 Pinney, *Wine in America*, 246–8.

57 Pinney, *Wine in America*, 251.

58 Pinney, *Wine in America*, 257.

59 Pinney, *Wine in America*, 269–84.

60 Pinney, *Wine in America*, 321–4.

61 Pinney, *Wine in America*, 354.

62 Michelle Stacey, *Consumed: Why Americans Love, Hate, and Fear Food* (New York: Simon and Schuster, 1994), 51.

63 John Dickenson, 'Viticulture in Pre-Independence Brazil', in John Dickenson and Tim Unwin, *Viticulture in Colonial Latin America: Essays on Alcohol, the Vine and Wine in Spanish America and Brazil* (Liverpool: University of Liverpool Institute of Latin American Studies, Working Paper 13, 1992), 53.

64 Cyrus Redding, *Modern Wines*, 319–20.

65 *Wine and Spirit Merchant*, 122–3.

66 Beeston, *History of Australian Wine*, 8. Much of the history of Australian wine that follows draws on Beeston's book, the standard history of wine in Australia.

67 Beeston, *History of Australian Wine*, 13–14.

68 James Busby, *Journal of a Tour through Some of the Vineyards of Spain and France* (Sydney: Stephens and Stokes, 1833), 2.

69 Beeston, *History of Australian Wine*, 40–41.

70 *Catalogue of the Great Exhibition*, Part IV, 988–90.

71 Beeston, *History of Australian Wine*. 67–8.

72 David Dunstan, *Better than Pommard! A History of Wine in Victoria* (Melbourne: Australian Scholarly Publishing/Museum of Victoria, 1994), xvi.

73 Beeston, *History of Australian Wine*, 110.

74 Beeston, *History of Australian Wine*, 64.

75 Beeston, *History of Australian Wine*, 111–12.

76 Beeston, *History of Australian Wine*, 23.

77 Jason Mabbett, 'The Dalmatian Influence on the New Zealand Wine Industry, 1895–1946', *Journal of Wine Research* 9:1 (April 1998), 15–25.

78 *Wine and Spirit Merchant*, 18–19.

79 Redding, *Modern Wines*, 317.

80 Opperman, *Spirit of the Vine*, 116.

NINE A TIME OF TROUBLES

1 William Reid (comp.), *The Temperance Cyclopedia* (Glasgow: Scottish Temperance League, n.d.), 140–41.

2 Benjamin Rush, *The Drunkard's Emblem or An Enquiry into the Effect of Ardent Spirits upon the Human Body and Mind* (New Market, VA: Ambrose Henkel, n.d. [*c.* 1810]).

3 C. C. Pearson and J. Edwin Hendricks, *Liquor and Anti-Liquor in Virginia, 1619–1919* (Durham, NC: Duke University Press, 1967), 86.

4 Pinney, *Wine in America*, 429.

5 Beeston, *History of Australian Wine*, 33, 42.

6 James Samuelson, *The History of Drink* (London: Trubner and Company, 1878), 231.

7 Lilian Lewis Shiman, *Crusade against Drink in Victorian England* (London: Macmillan, 1988), 68–73.

8 Jack S. Blocker Jr, *American Temperance Movements: Cycles of Reform* (Boston: Twayne, 1989), 24–5.

9 Prestwich, *Drink and the Politics of Social Reform*, 10–13. I have drawn extensively on this excellent book for the following passages on France.

10 Prestwich, *Drink and the Politics of Social Reform*, 37.

11 Prestwich, *Drink and the Politics of Social Reform*. 128–31. See also Barnaby Conrad III, *Absinthe: History in a Bottle* (San Francisco: Chronicle Books, 1988).

12 Haine, *World of the Paris Café*, 95–6.

13 Prestwich, *Drink and the Politics of Social Reform*, 62.

14 Salvatore Pablo Lucia, *A History of Wine as Therapy* (Philadelphia: Lippincott, 1963), 163–7.

15 Lucia, *History of Wine as Therapy*, 156.

16 Prestwich, *Drink and the Politics of Social Reform*, 54.

17 Prestwich, *Drink and the Politics of Social Reform*, 56.

18 Lucia, *History of Wine as Therapy*, 171.

19 Prestwich, *Drink and the Politics of Social Reform*, 24.

20 Pinney, *Wine in America*, 126.

21 James S. Roberts, *Drink, Temperance and the Working Class in Nineteenth-Century Germany* (Boston: George Allen and Unwin, 1984), 27.

22 For a general work on phylloxera, see George Ordish, *The Great Wine Blight* (London: Dent, 1972).

23 Harry H. Paul, *The Science of Vine and Wine in France, 1750–1990* (New York: Cambridge University Press, 1996), 10.

24 The best discussion of 'foxiness' is in Pinney, *Wine in America*, 443–7.

25 Michael Barke, "'Lo Que ha de Ser no Puede Faltar" ("What has to be cannot be avoided"): Phylloxera and the Demise of the Malaga Wine Industry', *Journal of Wine Research* 8:3 (1997), 139–58.

26 Ordish, *Great Wine Blight*, 172–5.

27 Pinney, *Wine in America*, 345.

28 Ordish, *Great Wine Blight*, 144–6.

29 Lachiver, *Vins, vignes et vignerons*, 496–7.

30 Pinney, *Wine in America*, 342.

31 Prestwich, *Drink and the Politics of Social Reform*, 9.

32 Quoted in Lachiver, *Vins, vignes et vignerons*, 466–7.

33 Information provided by Professor Geoffrey Giles, University of Florida.

34 Joan Hughes (ed.), *Australian Words and their Origins* (Melbourne: Oxford University Press, 1989), 416.

35 Garrier, *Histoire sociale et culturelle du vin*, 366.

36 Lachiver, *Vins, vignes et vignerons*, 484–5.

37 J.-J. Becker, *The Great War and the French People* (New York: Berg, 1985), 128.

38 Henry Carter, *The Control of the Drink Trade: A Contribution to National Efficiency during the Great War, 1915–1917* (London: Longman, 1919).

39 Jason Mabbett, 'The Dalmatian Influence on the New Zealand Wine Industry, 1895–1946', *Journal of Wine Research* 9 (1998), 21.

40 B. R. Mitchell, *European Historical Statistics, 1750–1975* (London: Macmillan, 1981), 298.

41 André L. Simon, *The History of Champagne* (London: Octopus Books, 1971), 123.

42 Leo Loubère, *The Wine Revolution in France: The Twentieth Century* (Princeton: Princeton University Press, 1990), 139.

43 The following references to Monthelie are based on the minutes of meetings (1912–41) of the Syndicat Agricole de la Commune de Monthelie, ADCO, 13 IX d/1, Viticulture.

44 Giacomo Acerbo, 'Agriculture under the Fascist Regime', in Tomaso Sillani, *What is Fascism and Why?* (London: Ernest Benn, 1931), 64.

45 Hermann Fahrenkrug, 'Alcohol and the State in Nazi Germany', in Barrows and Room (eds.), *Drinking*, 142.

46 Geoffrey J. Giles, 'Student Drinking in the Third Reich', in Barrows and Room (eds.), *Drinking*, 142.

47 Blocker Jr, *American Temperance Movements*, 120.

48 Aspler, *Vintage Canada*, 18–19.

49 Syndicat Agricole de la Commune de Monthelie, 12 January 1941.

50 Briggs, *Haut-Brion*, 179–80.

51 Charles K. Warner, *The Winegrowers of France and the Government since 1875* (New York: Columbia University Press, 1960), 159–62.

52 Beeston, *Concise History of Australian Wine*, 181–2.

TEN INTO THE LIGHT

1 For a general survey see Roderick Phillips, *Society, State and Nation in Twentieth-Century Europe* (Upper Saddle River, NJ: Prentice Hall, 1996).

2 Loubère, *Wine Revolution in France*, 168.

3 Garrier, *Histoire sociale et culturelle du vin*, 397 (diagrams).

4 See Scott Haine, *The World of the Paris Café*.

5 Loubère, *Wine Revolution in France*, 47.

6 Geneviève Gavignaud-Fontaine, 'L'extinction de la "viticulture pour tous" en Languedoc (1945–1984)', *Pôle Sud* 9 (1998), 63.

7 Andrew Barr, *Wine Snobbery: An Insider's Guide to the Booze Business* (London: Faber and Faber, 1988), 152–5.

8 James T. Lapsley, *Bottled Poetry: Napa Winemaking from Prohibition to the Modern Era* (Berkeley: University of California Press, 1996), 155–7.

9 Barr, *Wine Snobbery*, 152–9.

10 Lapsley, *Bottled Poetry*, 157.

11 Stephen White, *Russia Goes Dry: Alcohol, State and Society* (Cambridge: Cambridge University Press, 1996), 103, Table 4.1.

INDEX

Wines named after regions have a lower-case first letter, while the regions themselves start with a capital letter. Thus 'Bordeaux' refers to the region and 'bordeaux' refers to the wine. Individual wine regions and specific vineyards, producers, and grape varieties are indexed only when they are mentioned in a significant way.